ADDICTION BY DESIGN

ADDICTION BY DESIGN

Machine Gambling in Las Vegas

Natasha Dow Schüll

PRINCETON UNIVERSITY PRESS

PRINCETON AND OXFORD

Fourth printing, and first paperback printing, 2014

Paperback ISBN 978-0-691-16088-7

The Library of Congress has cataloged the cloth edition of this book as follows

Schüll, Natasha Dow, 1971–
Addiction by design : machine gambling in Las Vegas / Natasha Dow Schüll.
    p. cm.
Includes bibliographical references and index.
ISBN 978-0-691-12755-2 (hardcover : alk. paper) 1. Gambling—Nevada—Las Vegas.
2. Compulsive gambling—Nevada—Las Vegas. 3. Gambling—Equipment and supplies—
Nevada—Las Vegas. 4. Casinos—Nevada—Las Vegas. I. Title.
HV6721.L3S38 2012
    362.2'5—dc23   2012004339

British Library Cataloging-in-Publication Data is available

This book has been composed in Sabon LT Std
Printed on acid-free paper. ∞

Printed in the United States of America

9 10

Table of Contents

PART THREE: *Addiction*

PART FOUR: *Adjustment*

Acknowledgments

THIS BOOK HAS BEEN LONG in the making. It began nearly twenty years ago as a thesis on casino design and management in Las Vegas during the meteoric expansion of the gambling industry in the early 1990s. The thesis culminated in an examination of the gambling machines that were then beginning to dominate casino floors, devices in which the industry's design and management strategies came together and reached new levels of ingenuity and precision. As a graduate student I picked up this thread, returning to the city to conduct extended dissertation research among gambling machine addicts. Finally, these two pieces coalesced—and evolved—into the present book, which explores the relationship between the technologies of the gambling industry and the experience of gambling addiction.

My deepest thanks go to the many gamblers and former gamblers in Las Vegas who shared their experiences with me, and who inspired the trajectory of my research and analysis from start to finish. The Trimeridian problem gambling clinic offered a welcoming base during my extended fieldwork in Las Vegas, and dialogues with the pioneering psychologists of gambling addiction, Richard Rosenthal, Robert Hunter, and Julian Taber, helped to guide the course of my inquiry. I thank those in the gambling industry—among them technology designers, casino slot department managers, and marketing strategists—who took the time to explain and reflect upon their design and business practices.

An extensive constellation of mentors, colleagues, and friends sustained and enriched the project through its different iterations. My first debt is to Mike Panasitti, coauthor of the undergraduate thesis, for his collaboration in the original research and analysis; several of his insights live on in this book. Laura Nader and Paul Rabinow in the Anthropology Department at the University of California, Berkeley, provided critical mentorship and encouragement during the thesis phase. The dissertation, also completed at UC Berkeley, was supervised by a wonderful committee of anthropologists including Stefania Pandolfo, Paul Rabinow, and Lawrence Cohen; each lent inspiration, direction, and critical ethnographic and analytic tools to the project. I am especially grateful to my graduate advisor, Stefania Pandolfo, for the intellectual passion, friendship, and ongoing guidance she offered through the pleasures and challenges of fieldwork and writing. Judith Butler and Gene Rochlin have my gratitude for their thoughtful and generous engagements with the completed dissertation.

The ideas in this book took shape, and were sharpened, through exchanges with countless peers and colleagues. In addition to the valuable feedback I gleaned from audiences at the diverse conferences, workshops, and lectures where I presented pieces of the work, I had the good fortune to receive input from Bo Bernhard, Mariah Breeding, David Buuck, Lisa Davis, Jennifer Fishman, Duana Fullweily, Cristiana Giordano, Uri Grezemkovsky, Maimuna Huq, Nicholas King, Eric Klinenberg, Eduardo Kohn, Andrew Lakoff, Kahwee Lee, Joshua Linford-Steinfeld, Rebecca Lemov, Tanya Luhrmann, Thomas Malaby, Lynn Meskell, Aaron Nathan, Anand Pandian, Adriana Petryna, Tamar Posner, Elizabeth Roberts, Stephen Rosenberg, Rashmi Sadana, Sara Shostak, Peter Skafish, Miriam Tiktin, Sue Wilson, and Caitlin Zaloom. Over the years, these colleagues acted as an indispensible panel of interlocutors, readers, and writing partners.

A number of fellowships and grants made my research and writing possible. (I am often asked if the financial support allocated for "participant-observation" included funds to gamble; the answer is no!) Dissertation fieldwork was supported by a National Science Foundation Graduate Fellowship, a Berkeley Fellowship for Graduate Study, and smaller awards including the Robert H. Lowie Graduate Scholarship, the Berkeley Humanities Research Grant, and a Phi Beta Kappa Graduate Scholarship Award. Dissertation writing was supported by the Woodrow Wilson Foundation (Charlotte W. Newcombe Doctoral Dissertation Fellowship), the Alfred P. Sloan Foundation (the Berkeley Center for Working Families Doctoral Fellowship), the Doreen B. Townsend Center for the Humanities, and a National Science Foundation Training Grant in Science and Technology Studies. The School of Advanced Research in Santa Fe, New Mexico, supplied a lovely residence and generous support for the final completion of the dissertation.

I began to reconfigure the project as a book during my tenure as a Robert Wood Johnson Foundation Health and Society Scholar at Columbia University, where program directors Peter Bearman and Bruce Link, along with my fellow scholars, provided an interdisciplinary context in which the material was able to take a new form. Peter's enthusiasm, support, and guidance were particularly important. New York University's vibrant International Center for Advanced Study, headed by Tim Mitchell and Thomas Bender, was the next intellectual home for the project. Emily Martin and Rayna Rapp's Science Studies Workshop, also based at NYU, was a forum for stimulating exchanges with peers during my postdoctoral years in New York.

Mary Murrell at Princeton University Press first took on my manuscript, turning it over to her successor, Fred Appel, when she realized that she should be writing books herself. Reviewers Lucy Suchman, Emily Martin, and Vincent Crapanzano gave invaluable feedback on the first version of the manuscript. Scholars of gambling Henry Lesieur, Charles Livingstone, and Roger Horbay read the book in its draft form and offered excellent advice and suggestions. Rachel Volberg made thorough and incisive editorial comments on significant portions of the text. Mirko Ernkvist, Nigel Turner, and Kevin Harrigan read the chapters on game design and helped to clarify important details on the programming of probability, as did gambling machine specialists Mike Shackleford (a.k.a. "Wizard of Odds"), Bob Dancer, and Stacy Freidman. The Center for Gaming Research at the University of Nevada, Las Vegas, made much of the archival research possible, and its capable staff helped me track down many a wayward citation.

Final revisions to the book were conducted during my first years in the Program on Science, Technology, and Society at the Massachusetts Institute of Technology. My colleagues Mike Fischer, David Kaiser, David Jones, Vincent Lepinay, and Hanna Shell gave thoughtful feedback on the manuscript, and Sherry Turkle shepherded one portion of the work through the "passionate proofreading" of her edited volume on *The Inner History of Devices*. Stefan Helmreich and Heather Paxson in Anthropology offered a particularly robust and helpful set of comments. I also thank David Mindell, Roz Williams, and Roe Smith for their mentorship and support of my work.

Stephen Rosenberg made essential editorial interventions in the final stages of book revision, as did Peter Skafish, Mary Murrell, and David Buuck. I thank Jane Staw and Dorothy Duff for their motivational wisdom, Judy Spitzer for her astute title and cover advice, and Ayn Cavicchi for her good-humored assistance with my images, formatting, and bibliographic citations. Marie Burks brought order, balance, and pencil-sharp precision to my index, Dimitri Karetnikov and Martin Hoyem brought higher resolution to my images, and Leslie Grundfest brought the production process to closure with reassuring aplomb. My editor, Fred Appel, was admirably patient with the innumerable contingencies that arose during the book's long march from proposal to completed manuscript. Heartfelt thanks are due to Jeanne Wolff-Bernstein and Magdalena J. Fosse for so attentively bearing with me as I sifted through these contingencies in all their terrible tedium.

Friends outside my academic circle were a source of vital perspective and creative inspiration at every stage of crafting this book. Often working alongside me on their own projects in café corners and library nooks from California to New York, their companionship was an invaluable source of motivation. Thank you Nicole Alper, Matt Bird, Palo Coleman, Rodney Evans, Paul Grundl, Annie Hewitt, Marcus Johnson, Elizabeth Kolsky, Joshua Kronen, Katherine Lederer, Hillevi Loven, Gabriel Lucero, Miranda McGuire, Elise Mogensen, Anna Moschovakis, Sonia Perel, Cassandra Ritas, Bruno Schüll, Julia Svihra, Pawel Wojtasik, and Almond Zigmund. Almond, Katy, and the Lederer family deserve special mention for their kind hospitality during my residence in Las Vegas, and the G group in New York for putting wind in my sails time and again.

My parents, Walter Schüll and Diantha Dow Schüll, offered up their home for many an extended writing retreat, edited my prose whenever requested, and over the years conveyed a steady stream of relevant newspaper clippings by mail. My husband, Moreno DiMarco, accompanied me in the long final stretch of book research and completion, during which many a potential vacation was cancelled, rerouted, or otherwise compromised; it helped that he was always amenable to visiting casinos. I thank him for his patience, his reading of multiple chapter drafts, and his enduring faith in the value of the work. Our Ginger arrived on the scene at the very end, her cries and coos bringing the inevitable imperfections of book production into perspective and rejuvenating my wonder at the workings of chance.

Prior versions of some of the material presented in this book appeared in the following articles:

"The Touch-point Collective: Crowd Contouring on the Casino Floor." *Limn* 2, pp. 10-13. © 2012.

"Video Poker." In *The Inner History of Devices,* edited by Sherry Turkle. MIT Press. © 2008.

"Machines, Medication, Modulation: Circuits of Dependency and Self-Care in Las Vegas." *Culture, Medicine, and Psychiatry* 30, pp. 1–25. © 2006.

"Digital Gambling: The Coincidence of Desire and Design." *The ANNALS of the American Academy of Political and Social Science* 597, pp. 65–81. © 2005.

Note on Informant Anonymity

IN THIS BOOK I quote speakers directly from transcribed recordings, or, in the few cases where recording was not possible, from detailed field notes. In some instances I add punctuation and remove the redundancies of spoken language to enhance readability. Given the personal content of gamblers' interviews, I use pseudonyms they chose for themselves. I attempt to further conceal identities by changing certain details in their narratives.

I use the real names of gambling industry representatives when quoting from published articles in trade magazines, or from presentations delivered at trade show meetings (publicly available at libraries or for purchase online). I use their real names when quoting from my own interviews unless they spoke to me off the record or explicitly asked me not to disclose their identities, in which case I designate them by means of anonymous terms such as "a game designer" or "a gambling executive."

INTRODUCTION

Mapping the Machine Zone

ON A WEEKDAY EVENING in the fall of 1999, Mollie and I sit at the floor-length windows of a room high in the South Tower of the Main Street Station Hotel and Casino in downtown Las Vegas. Blinking brightly below us is a four-block stretch of Fremont Street, the city's former central artery of casino life. At the top of Fremont begins the long flicking perpendicular of Las Vegas Boulevard, otherwise known as the "Strip," a corridor of commercial gambling that extends for five miles in a south-westerly direction until it reaches the edge of the city and fades into gas stations, billboards, and desert. As the sky grows darker, pockets of light flare up in the relatively dim areas to either side of this infamous thoroughfare, marking off-Strip gambling establishments that cater to a burgeoning local clientele.

Mollie's frequent video poker play at these establishments has earned her a complimentary stay at Main Street Station. Her eleven-year-old son, Jimmy, lies lengthwise on the bed behind us, his gaze riveted to the television screen as his hands work the controls of the PlayStation console his mother has rented from the front desk to occupy him while we talk. "Mom, it's the Vegas game," says Jimmy from the bed. "You drive all around Vegas and try to play games." "Oh great, that's all we need," she responds.

At her first job, when she was not much older than Jimmy, Mollie dispensed change for slot machines on a US military base where her father, an air force officer, had been stationed. She now works as a hotel reservationist at the MGM Grand, the largest megaresort in Las Vegas and the second largest in the world. A gargantuan rectangle of green glass modeled after Oz, the MGM glows in the distance as we talk. "Mom, I won!" Jimmy interjects. And fifteen minutes later, with the same excitement, "Mom! I already lost 95 bucks!"

"I tell him he should be careful," says Mollie. "He might end up with a problem. But he doesn't listen. He plays video games constantly; he's just zoned into them." She pauses. "Of course, I don't set a very good example."

Mollie recounts how her play began, and how it escalated. It started soon after she moved to Las Vegas with her third husband in the 1980s, when he taught her to play video poker on a miniature, handheld machine. "I became hooked on that amazing little machine. And then I graduated to the real thing." Short stints at video poker on weekend visits to casinos turned into sessions of hours and then days. Her financial expenditure grew in step with her play, to a point where she was spending entire paychecks over two-day binges at machines. "I even cashed in my life insurance for more money to play," she tells me.

When I ask Mollie if she is hoping for a big win, she gives a short laugh and a dismissive wave of her hand. "In the beginning there was excitement about winning," she says, "but the more I gambled, the wiser I got about my chances. Wiser, but also weaker, less able to stop. Today when I win— and I do win, from time to time—I just put it back in the machines. The thing people never understand is that *I'm not playing to win*."

Why, then, does she play? "To keep playing—to stay in that machine zone where nothing else matters."

I ask Mollie to describe the machine zone. She looks out the window at the colorful movement of lights, her fingers playing on the tabletop between us. "It's like being in the eye of a storm, is how I'd describe it. Your vision is clear on the machine in front of you but the whole world is spinning around you, and you can't really hear anything. You aren't really there—you're with the machine and that's all you're with."

Turning the Tables: Machines Take the Floor

A few months after speaking with Mollie in Main Street Station's South Tower, I found myself in the midst of another conversation about the

Figure i.1. Opening day at the Global Gaming Exposition, 2005. Courtesy of Oscar Einzig Photography.

zone. This time I was standing in the back of a packed, windowless room in the labyrinthine basement of the Las Vegas Convention Center, where a panel of representatives from the gambling industry had gathered from around the country to speak on the profit-promising future of machine gambling. Echoing Mollie's wish to stay in the machine zone, they spoke of gamblers' desire for "time-on-device," or TOD. An evolving repertoire of technological capabilities was facilitating this desire. "On these newer products, they can really get into that zone," remarked a game developer from a top manufacturing company. Like Mollie, the industry panelists were invested in the zone state and its machinery.

The panel I attended was held during the World Gaming Congress and Expo, now called the Global Gaming Expo or G2E, the premier annual trade show for the gambling industry (see fig. i.1). In 2007 a record 30,000 attendees convened at G2E to take stock of the industry's latest products and applications, from video graphics to ergonomic consoles, surround-sound acoustics to marketing schemes, plastic press-buttons to player tracking systems. Equipment manufacturing industry giants like International Gaming Technology (IGT), Bally Technologies, and WMS

Gaming occupy the largest and flashiest of the 520 to 750 booths that crowd each year into G2E's 300,000 square feet of convention space. "The attention at G2E," a convention journalist wrote in 2005, "gravitates toward one essential product: the slot machine. G2E is where the evolution of slot technology has been witnessed."[1]

The one-armed bandits of yesteryear were mechanical contraptions involving coin slots, pull-handles, and spinning reels. Today's standard gambling machines are complex devices assembled on a digital platform out of 1,200 or more individual parts. "Game design is a process of integration, assemblage," as one game developer told me. This process involves up to three hundred people, including script writers, graphic artists, marketers, mathematicians, and mechanical, video, and software engineers—not to mention designers of auxiliary components like touch-screens, bill validators, and machine cabinets. "Modern slot machines are rarely the work of one company," read the blurb for a 2009 G2E panel; "they are symphonies of individual technologies that come together to create a single experience."[2]

The gambling experience has evolved in step with technological innovation. Once a relatively straightforward operation in which players bet a set amount on the outcome of a single payline, today machine gambling begins with a choice among games whose permutations of odds, stakes size, and special effects are seemingly endless.[3] Instead of inserting coins into a slot as in the past, players are more likely to insert paper money, bar-coded paper tickets, or plastic cards with credit stored on chips or magnetic stripes. To activate the game, they no longer pull a lever, but instead press a button or touch a screen. Denomination of play can vary from one cent to one hundred dollars, and players can choose to bet from one to as many as one thousand coin credits per game. On or above the play area, which typically features a video screen or three-dimensional reels behind glass, "pay tables" indicate the number of credits to be awarded in the event that certain symbols or cards appear together.[4] To the right, a digital credit meter displays the number of credits remaining in the machine. Linked via telecommunications systems to a central server, the machines also perform data-gathering and marketing functions for the casino. Critical nodes in the larger networked system of the casino rather than stand-alone units, they have "become the central nervous system of the casino," an industry representative remarked in 2007.[5]

Until the mid-1980s, green-felt table games such as blackjack and craps dominated casino floors while slot machines huddled on the sidelines, serving to occupy the female companions of "real" gamblers. Often placed along hallways or near elevators and reservation desks, rarely with stools or chairs in front of them, the devices occupied transitional spaces rather than gambling destinations.[6] By the late 1990s, however, they had moved into key positions on the casino floor and were generating twice as much revenue as all "live games" put together.[7] In the aisles and meeting rooms of the G2E, it became common to hear gambling machines referred to as the "cash cows," the "golden geese," and the "workhorses" of the industry. Frank J. Fahrenkopf Jr., president of the American Gaming Association, the commercial interest lobby that sponsors the annual expo, estimated in 2003 that over 85 percent of industry profits came from machines.[8] "It's the slot machine that drives the industry today," he declared.[9]

Several factors contributed to the dramatic reversal of slots' once lowly status in the gambling economy. Relatively unburdened by the taint of vice as a result of their association with arcade gaming, women, and the elderly, they played a key role in the spread of commercialized gambling in the 1980s and '90s, as recession-stricken states (whose federal funding had been cut by the Reagan-Bush administration) sought new ways to garner revenue without imposing taxes.[10] The low-stakes devices fit comfortably with the redefinition of gambling as "gaming" by industry spokespeople and state officials who hoped to sway public endorsement of the activity as a form of mainstream consumer entertainment rather than a form of moral failing or predatory entrapment.[11] The growing consumer familiarity with screen-based interaction that accompanied the rise of the personal computer and electronically mediated entertainment such as video games further facilitated the cultural normalization of machine gambling. Meanwhile, the ongoing incorporation of digital technology into gambling machines altered the player experience in subtle but significant ways, broadening their market appeal.[12] Gambling regulations were revised in lockstep with technological innovation, sanctioning its application to slots.

Since the early 1980s, when machine revenues surpassed table revenues for the first time, the ascendance of machines in the culture and economy of American gambling has continued unabated. The devices are now permitted in forty-one states (up from thirty-one in 2000) and are under consideration by others as this book goes to press. In 1996 there were 500,000 devices in the United States; in 2008 the count had reached nearly 870,000—not including an underground market of unauthorized machines in bars and taverns, truck stops, bowling alleys, and restaurants

Figure i.2. Machine floor at the Four Queens casino in downtown Las Vegas.
Courtesy of Quang-Tuan Luong Photography. (QT Luong/terragalleria.com)

across the country, or devices engineered to circumvent restrictions by
fitting state definitions for bingo, amusement machines, or sweepstakes
games.[13]

Bo Bernhard, native Las Vegan and sociology professor at the University of Nevada, has described the effects of machine gambling's spread as
a kind of technological "deforestation" of table games. "Right now," he
told an audience at the International Conference on Gambling and Risk-
Taking in 2000, "somewhere out there in a casino, a blackjack table is
being sawed down to make room for machines."[14] Extending the metaphor, his former mentor Robert Hunter, a well-known Las Vegas psychologist of gambling addiction, has compared the spread of gambling
machines to the insistent creep of kudzu (the ground-covering vine that
wreaked havoc on the ecosystem of the rural South when it was imported
from Japan during the Great Depression). "Survival of the fittest," remarked a casino floor manager at the Four Queens, a downtown casino
not far from the one where I spoke with Mollie, as he and I stood watching a group of uniformed men carry defunct tables out a back door and
roll in shiny new slot machines to take their places (see fig. i.2).[15] Soon
gamblers would be seated before them, and some, like Mollie, would be
playing for hours and even days at a time.

RESIDENT GAMBLING: THE RISE OF REPEAT PLAY

This book explores the significance of the meteoric expansion of modern machine gambling over the past two decades in the United States through an examination of the relationship between the changing technological configuration of gambling activities and the changing experience of gamblers. Although such an inquiry could plausibly be set in any number of jurisdictions where the activity is legal and readily available, Las Vegas offers a particularly illuminating backdrop.

In the early 1980s, cultural critic Neil Postman said that one had only to look to Las Vegas to understand America.[16] In the mid-1990s, casino tycoon Steve Wynn turned this pronouncement around, remarking that "Las Vegas exists because it is a perfect reflection of America."[17] Since then, journalists and academics alike have debated whether the rest of the country is becoming more like Las Vegas, or if, alternatively, Las Vegas is becoming more like the rest of the country. Some have called the city "the new Detroit" to signal its status as capital of the postindustrial economy, while others have pointed out that Detroit itself is now home to the popular MotorCity Casino.[18] Running alongside the debate over whether Las Vegas is a mirror or a model for America is the question of whether to view the city as a shape-shifting marvel of human inventiveness and technological sophistication or as a dystopic instantiation of consumer capitalism.[19] Whatever its relationship to the culture at large, it is clear that Las Vegas "has become a vast laboratory," as urban historians Hal Rothman and Mike Davis wrote in 2002, "where giant corporations, themselves changing amalgams of capital from different sectors, are experimenting with every possible combination of entertainment, gaming, mass media, and leisure."[20] In the Las Vegas laboratory, machine gambling figures both as a means and an end of experimentation.

A critical historical event in the rise of the machine-based gambling economy was the passage of the Corporate Gaming Act by the Nevada state legislature in 1969, allowing corporations to purchase and build casinos without subjecting every stockholder to the thorough background checks formerly required.[21] The new ease of raising capital, within the broader context of a growing service economy, encouraged Wall Street to take an active interest in the city. Las Vegas experienced an unprecedented period of growth as casinos shifted hands from organized crime to publicly traded corporations, metamorphosing into a hub for mass market vacationing and conventioneering. Throughout the 1990s, over a period that was often called the "Disneyification" of Las Vegas, one corporate-financed, corporate-run megaresort after another was constructed along the Strip.[22] Tourist visitation to the city increased fourfold between 1980 and 2008, reaching 40 million. This boom in business drew job seekers in droves, and the local population more than quadrupled over the same period—from 450,000 to 2 million.[23]

Either directly or indirectly, most residents rely on the gambling industry for their livelihood.[24] For its part, the industry relies on residents not only for its workforce but also, increasingly, for revenue. A full two-thirds of those who reside in metropolitan Las Vegas gamble. Of these, one study finds, two-thirds gamble heavily (defined as twice a week or more, for four hours or longer per session) or moderately (one to four times a month, for up to four hours per session).[25] Known in the industry as "repeat players" (as opposed to tourists or "transient players"), they typically gamble at neighborhood casinos that offer easy parking, child care facilities, and other amenities. Like Mollie, nearly 82 percent of local gamblers are members of loyalty clubs such as Station Casinos' "Boarding Pass," carrying player cards that document the volume of their play and reward them accordingly with free meals, free rooms, and other perks.[26] They also play at gas stations, supermarkets, drugstores, car washes, and other local outlets that have inspired the term "convenience gambling" (see fig. i.3).[27] "Our local players are very discriminating," observed a slot manager at one venue popular among residents; "they know what they want, and they're there five to seven days a week."

What local players want is machines, and this preference has closely tracked the evolving appeal of slot machine technology. While only 30 percent of residents identified machines as their preferred form of gambling in 1984, just ten years later the figure had sharply risen to 78 percent.[28] Generating impressive revenues for gambling establishments through the collective, steady repetition of their play, low-rolling local machine gamblers displaced high-rolling tourist table gamblers as the heavyweights of the gambling scene in Las Vegas. "This is machine city," a cocktail waitress remarked as she led me through aisle upon aisle of gambling devices at the Palace Station casino in 1999.[29]

That year at the industry's annual meeting, Las Vegas locals were frequently acknowledged as the most "mature" of domestic machine markets. Some spoke of the city as a sort of experimental barometer for the

Figure i.3. Convenience gambling.   *Top*: Video poker alcove at Lucky's Supermarket in southwest Las Vegas.   *Bottom*: AMPM gas station in north Las Vegas. Photographs by the author.

future, speculating that the rest of the nation would follow its model.[30] Seven years later, by which point the Station Casinos franchise had blossomed into thirteen properties and was capturing nearly 90 percent of its gambling revenue from machine play by local gamblers, the signs were auspicious.[31] "We're seeing more and more people coming to the Strip looking for more mature product," said one executive. "They're coming from California, the Midwest, and New York, where they're playing on a more regular basis. We're definitely seeing the trend for repeat play."[32] As states across the country push to legalize or expand existing machine gambling to cope with the financial challenges of the current economic downturn, and as gambling equipment manufacturers pursue new markets for their products, this trend is growing.[33]

GAMES AS CULTURAL CLUES

The French sociologist Roger Caillois, author of *Man, Play, and Games*, believed that games carried clues to the basic character of a culture.[34] "It is not absurd to try diagnosing a civilization in terms of the games that are especially popular there," he wrote in 1958. Caillois argued that one could make a cultural diagnosis by examining games' combination of the following four elements of play: *agon*, or competition; *alea*, or chance; *mimesis*, or simulation; and *ilinx*, or vertigo. Modern cultures, he claimed, were distinguished by games involving a tension between *agon* and *alea*—the former demanding an assertion of will, the latter demanding surrender to chance.

This tension is at the heart of the cultural diagnosis made by the American sociologist Erving Goffman in 1967 based on his ethnographic study of gambling in Las Vegas, where he worked as a blackjack dealer and was eventually promoted to pit boss. Goffman regarded gambling as the occasion for "character contests" in which players could demonstrate their courage, integrity, and composure in the face of contingency.[35] By offering individuals the opportunity for heroic engagements with fate, gambling fulfilled an existential need for "action" or consequential activity in an increasingly bureaucratic society that deprived its citizens of the opportunity to express their character in public settings of risk. For Goffman, gambling was not so much an escape from everyday life as it was a bounded arena that mimicked "the structure of real-life," thereby "immersing [players] in a demonstration of its possibilities."[36]

Along these lines, in 1973 the anthropologist Clifford Geertz famously interpreted Balinese cockfight gambling as a "tournament of prestige" that simulated the social matrix and laid bare its status dynamics. The activity, he argued, served as a medium for rehearsing the collective and existential dramas of life. Like Caillois and Goffman, Geertz emphasized the synergistic interaction of randomness and competition in the cockfight. The less predictable the outcome of a match, he observed, the more financially and personally invested participants became and the "deeper" their play, in the sense that its stakes went far beyond material gain or loss.[37] Fyodor Dostoyevsky's description of a sudden windfall at a Swiss roulette table in *The Gambler* captures Geertz's idea of deep play as a compelling mix of chance, risk, and status: "Why, I had got this at the risk of more than my life itself. But I had dared to risk it, and there I was once again, a man among men!"[38]

Caillois, Goffman, and Geertz each referred to coin-operated machine gambling in the course of their analyses, and each of them dismissed it as a degraded, asocial form of play not worthy of cultural analysis. For Caillois, it was pure *alea*—an absurd, compulsive game in which one could only lose.[39] For Goffman, it was a way for a person lacking social connections "to demonstrate to the other machines that he has socially approved qualities of character"; machines stood in for people when there were none to engage with.[40] "These naked little spasms of the self occur at the end of the world," he wrote of machine gambling in the very last line of his analysis, "but there at the end is action and character." Geertz described slot machines as "stupid mechanical cranks" operated by concessionaries at the outer circumference of the cockfight circle, offering "mindless, sheer-chance-type gambling" that could be of interest only to "women, children, adolescents ... the extremely poor, the socially despised, and the personally idiosyncratic."[41] "Cockfighting men," he continued, "will be ashamed to go anywhere near [the machines]." In other words, the devices were not a medium through which to become "a man among men," as Dostoyevsky had written of roulette; unlike the "exquisitely absorbing" *affaire d'honneur* of deep play, slot play was shallow, without depth of meaning, investment, or consequence. Incapable of illuminating the fundamental codes and concerns of a culture, machine gambling was not a properly "sociological entity," Geertz wrote.

The dramatic turn to machine gambling in American society (and beyond) since the 1980s prompts me to question such dismissals; surely, in this turn, one can find clues to the distinctive values, dispositions, and preoccupations of contemporary culture. But what kind of clues, and how to access them? Unlike Goffman's card gaming or Geertz's cockfighting, machine gambling is not a symbolically profound, richly dimensional space whose "depth" can be plumbed to reveal an enactment of larger social and existential dramas. Instead, the solitary, absorptive activity can suspend time, space, monetary value, social roles, and sometimes even one's very sense of existence. "You can erase it all at the machines—you can even erase yourself," an electronics technician named Randall told me. Contradicting the popular understanding of gambling as an expression of the desire to get "something for nothing," he claimed to be after nothingness itself. As Mollie put it earlier, the point is to stay in a zone "where nothing else matters."

In his 2003 book on gambling in America, *Something for Nothing*, the cultural historian Jackson Lears approaches gambling as a "port of entry into a broader territory," opening the book with a scene of machine gamblers who are so absorbed that they urinate into cups so as not to break the flow of their play.[42] Yet these particular gamblers are in fact quite marginal to the analysis that follows, in which Lears argues that national character is defined by a sharp tension between its "culture of chance" (epitomized by the figure of the speculative confidence man) and its "culture of control" (epitomized by the disciplined, self-made adherent of the Protestant work ethic). As machine gamblers tell it, neither control, nor chance, nor the tension between the two drives their play; their aim is not to *win* but simply to *continue*.

Sharon, trained as a doctor but working as a card dealer at the time we spoke, explained the value of continued play in terms of its capacity to keep chance at bay:

> Most people define gambling as pure chance, where you don't know the outcome. But at the machines I do know: either I'm going to *win*, or I'm going to *lose*. I don't care if it *takes* coins, or *pays* coins: the contract is that when I put a new coin in, get five new cards, and press those buttons, I am allowed to *continue*.
>
> So it isn't really a gamble at all—in fact, it's one of the few places I'm certain about anything. If I had ever believed that it was about chance, about variables that could make anything go in any given way at any time, then I would've been scared to death to gamble. *If you can't rely on the machine, then you might as well be in the human world where you have no predictability either.*

In Sharon's narrative, the gambling machine is not a conduit of risk that allows for socially meaningful deep play or heroic release from a "safe and momentless" life (to use Goffman's phrase), but rather, a reliable mechanism for securing a zone of insulation from a "human world" she experiences as capricious, discontinuous, and insecure. The continuity of machine gambling holds worldly contingencies in a kind of abeyance, granting her an otherwise elusive zone of certainty—a zone that Mollie described earlier as "the eye of a storm." "Players hang, it could be said, in a state of suspended animation," writes one machine gambling researcher.[43]

A zone in which time, space, and social identity are suspended in the mechanical rhythm of a repeating process may seem an unpromising object for cultural analysis. Yet such a zone, I argue, can offer a window onto the kinds of contingencies and anxieties that riddle contemporary American life, and the kinds of technological encounters that individuals are likely to employ in the management of these contingencies and anxieties. Over the last two decades, social theorists have focused a great deal of attention on the leading role that technology has played in the production of broad-scale insecurities—from global warming and other catastrophic environmental disasters to financial crises and unstable job markets.[44] While some have acknowledged the subjective insecurities that percolate through so-called risk society as a result of these "manufactured uncertainties" (as the sociologist Ulrich Beck has termed them), fewer have examined how individuals use technology to manufacture "certainties" of the sort that Sharon discussed above.[45] Counterintuitively, machine gambling can serve as a "port of entry," to borrow Lears's term, into this less examined but no less significant territory. Although the activity explicitly entails risk—involving money, no less, a key measure of social and economic value—it contains that risk within a dependable framework, allowing gamblers to enact a mode of self-equilibration that has become typical of everyday technological interactions.

In a historical moment when transactions between humans and machines unfold "at an ever greater level of intimacy and on an ever greater scale" (as the sociologist Bruno Latour has written), computers, video games, mobile phones, iPods, and the like have become a means through which individuals can manage their affective states and create a personal buffer zone against the uncertainties and worries of their world.[46] Although interactive consumer devices are typically associated with new choices, connections, and forms of self-expression, they can also function to narrow choices, disconnect, and gain exit from the self. More than a case study of a singular addiction, an exploration of gambling addicts' intensive involvement with gambling machines yields clues to the predicaments, tendencies, and challenges that characterize wider "zones" of life.[47]

A HUMAN-MACHINE ADDICTION

As the rise of interactional gadgetry has changed the nature of everyday life, so the rise of machine gambling has changed the face of gambling addiction. By the mid-1990s in Las Vegas, the vast majority attending local meetings of the self-help group Gamblers Anonymous (GA) played machines exclusively—a striking change from the 1980s and earlier, when the typical GA member bet at cards or on sports. "Currently in the treatment center where I work," Bo Bernhard reported on Robert Hunter's outpatient clinic in 2000, "over 90% of individuals are in treatment for video gambling."[48] He urged scholars to conduct research on how this swiftly spreading form of gambling might influence the acquisition, course, and experience of gambling addiction.

Still today, however, the preponderance of research tends to concentrate on gamblers' motivations and psychiatric profiles rather than on the gambling formats in which they engaged. This tendency was reinforced by the American Psychiatric Association's endorsement of "pathological gambling" as an official psychiatric diagnosis in 1980.[49] The diagnosis, soon to be renamed "disordered gambling," is associated with job loss, debt, bankruptcy, divorce, poor health, incarceration, and the highest rate of suicide attempts (20 percent) among all the addictions.[50] Its symptom criteria, modeled on those of other addictions, include preoccupation, tolerance, loss of control, withdrawal, escape, and denial (see fig. i.4).[51] Although previous psychiatric literature had described excessive gambling as a kind of mental illness, this literature typically emphasized the toxic and debilitating effects of gambling itself rather than focusing on gamblers' dispositions.[52] By contrast, the 1980 diagnosis presented the problem as "persistent and recurrent maladaptive gambling behavior," emphasizing gamblers' inability to resist internal impulses. If in the past all gambling had been considered potentially problematic, now there was a qualitative difference between "normal" and "problem" gambling; since problem gamblers were a discrete class of person, the rest of the population could gamble without cause for concern.[53]

PREOCCUPATION	Preoccupied with gambling (e.g. reliving past gambling experiences, handicapping or planning the next venture, thinking of ways to get money with which to gamble)
TOLERANCE	Needs to gamble with increasing amounts of money to achieve desired excitement
LOSS OF CONTROL	Made repeated unsuccessful efforts to control, cut back, or stop gambling
WITHDRAWAL	Restless or irritable when attempting to cut down or stop gambling
ESCAPE	Gambles as a way of escaping from problems or of relieving a dysphoric mood (e.g. feelings of helplessness, guilt, anxiety, depression)
CHASING	After losing money gambling, often returns another day in order to "get even"
LYING	Lies to family members, therapists, or others to conceal extent of gambling
ILLEGAL ACTS	Committed illegal acts (e.g. forgery, fraud, theft, embezzlement) to finance gambling
RISKS RELATIONSHIPS	Jeopardized or lost a significant relationship, job, or educational or career opportunity because of gambling
BAILOUT	Relies on others to provide money to relieve a desperate financial situation caused by gambling

Figure i.4. Diagnostic Criteria for Pathological Gambling, of which an individual needs five or more to qualify for the diagnosis. American Psychiatric Association, *Diagnostic and Statistical Manual of Mental Disorders IV-R*, 2000.

While the medicalization of excessive gambling helped somewhat to undermine condemnations of gamblers as weak of will or morally compromised, ultimately it did more to undermine condemnations of gambling vendors as purveyors of a socially and morally corrupting activity.[54] The gambling industry has embraced the diagnosis and its suggestion that problematic play is "confined to a small minority of constitutionally predisposed or mentally disordered problem gamblers," as one critic aptly puts it.[55] The "small minority" in question is the 1 to 2 percent of the general population who fit the requisite diagnostic criteria at any given time, along with the additional 3 to 4 percent who qualify for the less severe "problem gambling."[56] Notwithstanding the significant complications of prevalence measurement, there is broad consensus around these figures among researchers.[57] Yet many find it misleading to measure the problem within the *general* population, given that the percentage of pathological and problem gamblers among the *gambling* population is a good deal higher, and higher still among *regular* (or "repeat") gamblers— 20 percent, by some estimates.[58] By any count, problem and pathological gamblers are significantly overrepresented among those who gamble. The economic ramifications of this overrepresentation have been well established: from 30 percent to a staggering 60 percent of total gambling revenues have been found to derive from problem gamblers.[59] These numbers tell a very different story than do measures of the problem in the general population.

Going even further, some researchers point out that it is misleading to measure the problem by counting only those individuals who fit definitions for "pathological" or "problem" gambler, since *most* individuals who regularly gamble will at some point experience the hallmark features of problem gambling behavior—namely, difficulty controlling time and money spent on the activity, with negative consequences.[60] To ignore the continuum of problematic experience among gamblers is to minimize the extent of the phenomenon, they suggest. Departing from the dominant medical emphasis on the psychological, genetic, and neurophysiological factors that might predispose an isolated subset of individuals to "maladaptive gambling behavior," they seek to understand how commercial gambling activities and environments might create the conditions for—and even encourage—such behavior in consumers.

Although most screens for problem gambling do not distinguish among different types of gambling activities and environments, studies that take such distinctions into account consistently find that machine gambling is associated with the greatest harm to gamblers. "The academic literature on electronic machine gambling is, with few exceptions, faultfinding," write two scholars of gambling. "While there is unanimity about the superior revenue generating capacity of electronic gambling machines for both the state and gambling venue proprietors, there is also concurrence on the distress these machines can visit on the public."[61] An increasing number of researchers, politicians, clinicians, and gamblers themselves have begun to raise the same question of gambling machines that is often asked of consumer products like cigarettes, alcohol, firearms, automobiles, and fatty foods: *Are the problems in the product, the user, or their interaction?*[62]

In 2002 the first in a line of studies found that individuals who regularly played video gambling devices became addicted three to four times more rapidly than other gamblers (in one year, versus three and a half years), even if they had regularly engaged in other forms of gambling in the past without problems.[63] Rather than indicating pathology in the gambler, "impaired control and subsequent problem development are an understandable and 'natural' consequence of regular, high intensity [machine] play," hypothesized the authors of another study.[64] Endorsing this hypothesis, an independent federal commission in Australia concluded in 2010 that "the problems experienced by gamblers—many just ordinary consumers—are as much a consequence of the technology of the games, their accessibility and the nature and conduct of venues, as they are a consequence of the traits of the consumers themselves."[65]

Although the gambling industry has energetically dismissed this conclusion as far-fetched and scientifically unwarranted, scientists have in fact long understood addiction to be a function of the interaction between people and things.[66] "The potential for addiction," writes Howard Shaffer, a prominent academic researcher in the field of gambling addiction, "emerges when repeated interaction with a specific object or array of objects (a drug, a game of chance, a computer) reliably produces a desirable subjective shift."[67] Accordingly, he has suggested that addiction researchers should "emphasize the relationship instead of either the attributes of the person struggling with addiction or the object of their addiction."[68] When addiction is regarded as a relationship that develops through "repeated interaction" between a subject and an object, rather than a property that belongs solely to one or the other, it becomes clear that objects matter as much as subjects.

Just as certain individuals are more vulnerable to addiction than others, it is also the case that some objects, by virtue of their unique pharmacologic or structural characteristics, are more likely than others to trigger or accelerate an addiction. Their distinctive potency lies in their capacity to engender the sort of compelling subjective shift on which some individuals come to depend. "The most reliable, fast-acting and robust 'shifters' hold the greatest potential to stimulate the development of addictive disorders," Shaffer has written.[69] This fact is readily acknowledged by researchers of substance addictions, who rarely conduct their studies in the absence of some understanding of how a given drug affects its users. Yet despite growing evidence that certain repeated activities stimulate the same neurochemical pathways as drugs do, the substanceless nature of so-called behavioral addictions has led to a lopsided focus on addicts (their genetics, psychological profiles, and life circumstances) by scientists and the public alike.[70] Relatively few discussions of gambling addiction, for instance, take into account the role of modern slot machines, although "reliable, fast-acting, and robust" well describes the devices.

While all forms of gambling involve random patterning of payouts, machine gambling is distinguished by its solitary, continuous, and rapid mode of wagering. Without waiting for "horses to run, a dealer to shuffle or deal, or a roulette wheel to stop spinning," it is possible to complete a game every three to four seconds.[71] To use the terminology of behavioral psychology, the activity involves the most intensive "event frequency" of any existing gambling activity.[72] "It is *the* addiction delivery device," says Henry Lesieur, a sociologist who wrote the first book-length ethnographic account of nonelectronic gambling addictions in 1977 before becoming a counselor in the wake of machines' spread.[73] Others have called modern video gambling "the most virulent strain of gambling in the history of man," "electronic morphine," and, most famously, "the crack cocaine of gambling."[74] "As smoking crack cocaine changed the cocaine experience," Shaffer predicted in 1999, "I think electronics is going to change the way gambling is experienced."[75] Because video-based gambling machines "are faster than the mechanical form," he later elaborated, "they hold the potential to behave in the fashion of psychostimulants, like cocaine or amphetamines. They energize and de-energize the brain in more rapid cycles."[76] "I was quoted in the *Wall Street Journal* comparing video gambling machines to crack cocaine," the psychologist Hunter told me in 1995. "The industry didn't like it, but I call it an accurate quote. Cocaine addicts tell you about the last decade, but crack cocaine addicts tell you about the last *year*, and that's very similar to the video gamblers." Sensationalist metaphors aside, most researchers place different forms of gambling along a continuum of intensity that progresses from lottery, bingo, and mechanical slots to sports, dice, cards, and finally, to video slots and video poker.[77] "No other form of gambling manipulates the human mind as beautifully as these machines," the gambling addiction researcher Nancy Petry told a journalist.[78]

Forms of gambling differ not only in the intensity of play they facilitate but also in the kinds of subjective shifts they enable. Each type of gambling involves players in distinctive procedural and phenomenological routines— betting sequence and temporality, frequency and amount of payouts, degree of skill involved, and mode of action (checking books, ticking boxes, scratching tickets, choosing cards, pressing buttons), producing a unique "cycle of energy and concentration" and a corresponding cycle of affective peaks and dips.[79] The game of craps, for instance, can produce a state of high energy and suspense punctuated by euphoric wins whose thrill depends largely on social feedback. The solitary, uninterrupted process of machine play, by contrast, tends to produce a steady, trancelike state that "distracts from internal and external issues" such as anxiety, depression, and boredom.[80] Based on his clinical practice in Las Vegas, Hunter has concluded that modern video gambling "facilitates the dissociative process" more so than other gambling formats.[81] "The consistency of the experience that's described by my patients," he told me of machine gambling, "is that of numbness or escape. They don't talk about competition or excitement—they talk about climbing into the screen and getting lost."

To put the zone into words, the gamblers I spoke with supplemented an exotic, nineteenth-century terminology of hypnosis and magnetism with twentieth-century references to television watching, computer processing, and vehicle driving. "You're in a trance, you're on autopilot," said one gambler. "The zone is like a magnet, it just pulls you in and holds you there," said another.[82] The memoirist Mary Sojourner has described video gambling as "a trancelike preoccupation in which perpetuating the trance was reward enough."[83] As Mollie and Sharon told us earlier, it is not the chance of winning to which they become addicted; rather, what addicts them is the world-dissolving state of subjective suspension and affective calm they derive from machine play.

Given that this state can only exist as a function of the dynamic interaction between player and machine, it is impossible to understand contemporary machine gambling "without taking into account [the] transformation of technology and the adaptation of gamblers to the experiential possibilities the advances in technology have presented," as the sociologist of gambling Richard Woolley has written.[84] I attempt to do just that in the following pages, paying close attention to elements of gambling machine design and the kinds of affective self-management they afford gamblers. Tracking back and forth between gamblers' experience and the array of environments, objects, and software programs with which they interact, I undertake what the philosopher of technology Don Ihde has alternately called a "phenomenology of human-technology" and "materialist phenomenology."[85] Such an approach avoids the tendency of strict materialism to treat technology as an autonomous, determining force, while also avoiding the tendency of human-centered approaches to regard technology as a passive, neutral tool. Instead, at every step the focus is on the ways in which objects and subjects act together, through their encounters with each other. Action, Latour has argued, is not a preformed essence that resides within subjects or objects, but something they "coproduce."[86] "In [an] encounter," write two sociologists who apply this approach to the case of drug use, "the user is seized at those very points ... of affordance that are made possible and relevant by his/her own practices, as well as by the properties of the objects used."[87] The idea of addiction as a coproduction greater than the sum of the parts from which it emerges resonates with the scientific understandings of addiction sketched above, and is especially fitting for a study of an addiction to interactive gambling technology.[88]

In a strategic response to growing suggestions that gambling machines are to some extent implicated in gambling addiction, the American Gaming Association released a 2010 white paper called "Demystifying Slot Machines." Echoing the National Rifle Association's (NRA) famous slogan—"Guns Don't Kill People, People Kill People"—the paper asserts that "the problem is not in the products [players] abuse, but within the individuals."[89] In this one-sided account, the machine is merely "the mechanism through which pre-existing psychological disturbances are expressed," as a researcher puts it.[90] "What gaming critics fail to understand," a reporter for *Global Gaming Business* sums up, is that "machines are simply inanimate objects."[91]

As it happens, Latour has taken issue with the abovementioned NRA slogan—and with its equally one-sided counterpart, the antigun slogan "Guns Kill People"—as a way to explain why objects are never "simply inanimate": "You are different with the gun in your hand; the gun is different with you holding it. You are another subject because you hold the gun; the gun is another object because it has entered into a relationship with you."[92] In other words, neither guns nor people kill; killing is an action they can only produce together, each mediating the other. Following this mediational logic, the account of addiction to gambling machines that I present here locates addiction not discretely within gamblers or gambling machines but, rather, in the dynamic interaction between the two.

At the same time, I do not wish to suggest that the respective contributions of humans and machines to the problem are qualitatively equivalent. As anthropologists, sociologists, philosophers, and historians of technology have argued, human actors bear "particular accountabilities" when it comes to human-machine exchanges, especially those humans in a position to configure the terms of such exchanges.[93] Unlike gamblers, who could be said to act upon themselves through gambling devices with a goal of regulating their own affective states, the designers, marketers, and managers of the devices are in a position to act on others at a distance, delegating to technology the task of soliciting and sustaining specific kinds of human behavior. Latour and his colleagues have conceptualized design as a process of "inscription" whereby designers inscribe certain modes of use into the products that consumers will interact with; the resulting products carry "scripts" that inhibit or preclude certain actions while inviting or demanding others. "By setting the parameters for the users' actions," a given product—and by implication, its design team—plays a role in guiding their behavior.[94]

The gambling machine is a case in point. Undermining their own public claims that slot machines are powerless, inert things, members of the gambling industry invest a great deal of resources and creative energy into the project of guiding player behavior through technology, endeavoring to create products that can extract maximum "revenue per available customer," or REVPAC. Of this all-consuming objective they talk freely and explicitly among themselves—on conference panels, in journals, and in the aisles and meeting lounges of exposition floors. How to get people to gamble longer, faster, and more intensively? How to turn casual players into repeat players? Despite the fine line between these objectives and the solicitation of addiction behavior, most industry members manage to maintain a cognitive disconnect between the two, distancing their script for profit from its potential harmful effects on consumers. Connie Jones, IGT's designated "Director of Responsible Gambling," describes the situation well: "Our game designers don't even think about addiction—they think about beating Bally and other competitors. They're creative folks who want machines to create the most revenue."[95] Although Jones's statement is meant to defend against the charges of intentional harm that are sometimes leveled at the gambling industry, the fact that her defense rests on an open admission of the mercenary nature of game design, along with the dismissive assertion that "game designers don't even think about addiction," does more to illustrate the problem than to pardon it.

My aim in the following pages is not to single out specific designers or companies for blame, or even to blame the industry as a whole. Rather, in keeping with the relational understanding of addiction outlined above, I closely examine how addiction to gambling machines emerges out of the dynamic interaction between machine gamblers and the design intentions, values, and methods of commercial gambling environments and technologies. As the book's title is meant to underscore, the story of "problem gambling" is not just a story of problem gamblers; it is also a story of problem machines, problem environments, and problem business practices.

Mollie's Map

This book draws on research I conducted during several extended visits to Las Vegas between 1992 and 2007, including a continuous stay of eighteen months between 1998 and 2000. The research unfolded in three stages, beginning in the early 1990s as an ethnographic and archival study of the architecture, interior design, and management practices that arose during the corporate casino building boom that was then unfolding.[96] In the course of conducting my fieldwork, as the local population grew rapidly and an assortment of new neighborhood casinos opened their doors, I became more and more curious about residents' experience living and working in a city so saturated by gambling environments and technologies. As I shifted my focus away from tourist casinos along the Strip, I was struck by the ubiquity of machine gambling in the local landscape—on billboards, in grocery stores and pharmacies, in restaurants and bars, and even at car washes.

Almost everywhere I went during this second stage of research, I encountered people who claimed to intimately know someone who had "a gambling problem" with the machines. These early encounters led me to many of the gamblers I eventually interviewed, most of whom identified themselves as "gambling addicts," "machine addicts," "problem gamblers," or "compulsive gamblers"—terms that I use interchangeably in the following pages.[97] The majority I came to know by attending GA meetings as well as group therapy sessions at a clinic for problem gamblers where I became an intern.[98]

I did not limit my pool of interviews to one category of machine gambler (e.g., middle-aged, middle-income-earning men who play quarter slots); nor did I set out to construct a statistically reliable, random sample of informants, although I did make an effort to speak to as diverse a group as possible. As it turned out, the group was quite heterogeneous in terms of age, ethnicity, education, and income. Caucasian women between the ages of thirty and fifty were most heavily represented, in part reflecting the demographic characteristics of machine gamblers in Las Vegas at the time I conducted the majority of my interviews, and in part reflecting my regular attendance at women-only GA meetings.[99]

Although the social, economic, and biographical differences among the machine gamblers in my study mediated their machine play in significant ways, even more striking were the continuities of experience that the common set of machines they played seemed to bring about.[100] In the space of one day in 2002, for instance, I interviewed a young buffet waitress living in a trailer park in the northeast part of the city and an older male businessman living in a gated community in the affluent southwestern suburb of Summerlin.[101] The waitress played nickel machines, often at supermarkets, while the businessman played dollar machines at a well-appointed neighborhood casino. The waitress spent whole paychecks at a time, worrying afterward that her children would not have money for school lunches. The businessman maxed out credit cards and depleted family savings, worrying that he might not manage to shuffle his money among bank accounts in time to cover his expenditures and avoid late fees, or to intercept the mail and conceal his losses from his wife. Despite radical differences in their life circumstances, the coin denomination of their game play, and the financial consequences of their gambling, the waitress and the businessman described their interactions with machines in uncannily similar language; reading over their transcripts, I found the two narratives nearly interchangeable in this regard. Extended, intensive, and repeated encounters with the same machine interface seemed to bring gamblers from diverse walks of life into a shared zone of experience, cutting through and across the differences between them.

As my research went on, it became increasingly clear that to adequately understand the experience of these gamblers, I would need to better understand the machines they were playing. To that end I expanded the scope of my project for a third time and began to educate myself about the history and inner workings of gambling machines, as well as the design practices and marketing strategies of gambling technology suppliers. I spent long hours at the Gaming Research Center at the University of Nevada, Las Vegas, where I read through years of machine manufacturers' trade magazines, press releases, and annual reports. I also began attending gambling industry technology expositions and conference panels and interviewing executives, game developers, and marketers.

The majority of the industry members I spoke with were unguarded in their interactions with me, even when our conversations turned to the potential negative effects of the machines they built and sold. They showed me around their facilities, signed consent forms, and allowed me to record lengthy interviews in which they talked openly about their approach to technology design and marketing, the sometimes questionable effects of their innovations on gamblers, and even their own experiences playing gambling machines. Some were cavalier while others were thoughtful; some were defensive, others cynical. Although a few professed uneasiness about the possible relationship between gambling addiction and their own architectural, design, or marketing practices, most drew a strict line between the two.

The gambling addicts I met, on the contrary, were remarkably reflexive regarding their own behavior and its consequences. Belying stereotypes of addicts as blind to the futility and destructiveness of their actions, they spoke lucidly and insightfully of their predicament. Mollie reflected: "Is it about money? No. Is it about enjoyment? No. Is it about being trapped? Yes—it is about having lost the plot as to why you are there in the first place. You are involved in a series of entrapments that you can't fully appreciate from inside them." A gambler named Katrina wrote to me of the "ever-present awareness of being in a destructive process" that accompanies her involvement with machines: "Even as part of one's mind is hopelessly lost to it, lurking in the background is a part that is sharp and aware of what is going on but seems unable to do much to help."[102] Although the part of Katrina that is "sharp and aware" does not succeed at extracting her from the zone of addiction, she makes a case for its potential analytical value: "I would ask that a chance be given for the possibility that, despite close involvement, it is quite possible for someone to step outside of their situation and be 'objective' and have real 'insight' into aspects and perspectives that may be overlooked by others." This book attempts to give that chance to the gamblers I spoke with. Instead of casting them as aberrant or maladapted consumers, I include them in the following pages as experts on the very "zone" in which they are caught—a zone that resonates to some degree, I suggest, with the everyday experience of many in contemporary capitalist societies.

Toward the end of our interview, Mollie, who had always liked to draw, flipped over a page of her 12-step self-help literature, borrowed a pen, and drew a map of what it was like to live in Las Vegas (see fig. i.5). She spoke as she sketched, describing each spot on the map and its role in her daily life. She began in the upper left-hand corner of the sheet with the MGM Grand, the casino resort where she worked making room reservations. To the right she placed the 7-11 where she pumped gas on the way home and sometimes gambled, and beside it, the Palace Station, the neighborhood casino where she gambled at night and on weekends. Below she drew the supermarket where she shopped and gambled, and below that,

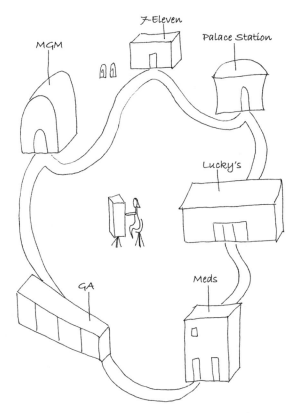

Figure i.5. Mollie's map of everyday life in Las Vegas. Drawn for the author in 1998.

the free clinic where she picked up medications to treat her anxiety disorder. Finally, in the lower left-hand corner was the strip mall where every Wednesday evening she attended the Gamblers Anonymous meeting where we first met. Mollie drew a road connecting each site to the next, such that they formed a continuous loop. She paused, contemplating the map, and then finished with a figure of herself suspended in the middle of the loop, seated in front of a slot machine.

Evoking the well-known analysis of *Learning from Las Vegas*, in which casinos' outsized signs reflect the visual priorities of an emergent automobile culture, Mollie marked each location on her route with a disproportionately large sign.[103] Yet the lesson to be learned from her map is less about the populism of commercial strip architecture and the frontier freedom of automobility than the sites of entrapment, containment, and provisional escape that spring up along the pathway of certain drives.[104] "Sometimes I'll be driving on Rancho," she told me, "and the next thing I know I'm on Paradise Road, and I won't remember getting there. I lose the time that it takes me to get to Palace Station, or get home—there are gaps. On the Interstate I'll be all the way to the exit ramp before I realize I've just done a big circle turn." The road she drew features no exits, appearing instead as a closed circuit of stations where various vices—as well as their remedies—may be pursued. Inside this circuit (or perhaps outside, it was not clear) her figure floated, anchored only to a gambling machine. "Where is that?" I asked when she had completed the sketch, pointing at the human-machine pair in the middle of the page. "That's nowhere," she responded; "that's the zone."

With Mollie's map in hand, this book sets out to explore the machine zone and the broader constellation of material, social, and political-economic circumstances out of which it emerges and from which it seeks escape. What dynamic circuit of architectural strategies, technological capacities, affective states, cultural values, life experiences, therapeutic techniques, and regulative discourses forms the context for this existential no-man's-land, in which gamblers seek to lose themselves and the gambling industry seeks to turn a profit? I take the human-machine encounter at the center of Mollie's map as my primary unit of analysis and move out from there, progressively widening the frame.[105] I have drawn my own map in four parts, each of which charts the terrain of a different position along the circuit of machine gambling.

Part one, "Design," examines how casino managers and game manufacturers script gambling environments and technologies. Chapter 1 introduces readers to the machine-oriented architecture and ambience of the modern casino and the ways they are calibrated to draw patrons to machines and keep them absorbed in play. Chapter 2 turns to the machine interface itself and the meticulous attention its designers pay to players' bodily and sensory propensities so as to facilitate longer, faster, and more intensive play. Chapter 3 ventures inside machines to consider how the shift from mechanical to digital technology has heightened the gambling industry's control over odds—and how, in turn, this shift has changed the terms of gamblers' interactions with chance.

Part two, "Feedback," takes a closer look at how the design of gambling technologies and environments at once responds to gamblers' play preferences and patterns and seeks to steer those preferences and patterns in certain directions. Chapter 4 explores the dynamic relationship between innovations in game software and the shifting inclinations of players, focusing on the widespread turn from playing-to-win to playing for "time-on-device." Chapter 5 considers the gambling industry's evolving ability to track, analyze, and adjust to individual players' predilections so as to heighten their absorption in machines. Chapter 6 addresses the counterintuitive role that choice making and a sense of control plays in gamblers' self-dissolution and entry into the "machine zone."

In part three, "Addiction," the point of analytic focus shifts from the machine and its design to the gamblers who become addicted. Chapter 7 explores what their all-consuming machine play might reveal about the larger social forces, values, and expectations operating in their lives, particularly those pertaining to social interaction, money, and time. Chapter 8 considers how the dynamics of control and loss at stake in gamblers' personal life histories play out in their encounters with slot machines, and how these seemingly aberrant dynamics express processes, tendencies, and existential concerns that go beyond their singular experiences.

Part four of the book, "Adjustment," explores the paradoxical ways in which remedies for problematic machine gambling become implicated in the very problem they are designed to "fix." Chapter 9 addresses the double bind of gambling addicts in recovery as they struggle to practice therapeutic techniques whose aims and methods are sometimes difficult to distinguish from the self-medicating practices of their machine play. Chapter 10 turns to the domain of policy, examining the diverse regulatory schemes that have crystallized around machine gambling, along with corresponding debates over whether the management of its risks is the responsibility of gamblers, the gambling industry, or the government. The book concludes by tracking the extension of machine gambling and "repeat play" to new parts of the world and into new domestic markets, and explores how members of the gambling industry and government representatives parse the ethical issues at stake in their promotion of this model for revenue generation.

PART ONE

Design

When we put 50 slot machines in, I always consider them 50 more mousetraps. You have to do something to catch a mouse. It's our duty to extract as much money as we can from customers.

—*Bob Stupak, CEO of Las Vegas Stratosphere, 1995*

THE DEFIBRILLATOR EXPERIMENT

2000. In the parking lot of a hospital complex in northwest Las Vegas, not far from a cluster of dilapidated casinos off downtown's "old Strip," a small group of paramedics stands around an ambulance drinking coffee and smoking. More often than not, they tell me, a call from a casino means that a patron has experienced a heart attack while playing a gambling machine. Given the notorious difficulty of getting in and out of casinos, such calls are met with collective dread. The head paramedic, on a break from training a new group, enumerates the obstacles surrounding entry: "The easiest access by far is the valet at the main entrance, but casinos won't let you pull in there, especially on the Strip—they think it's bad for business, they want you to feel safe." Instead, paramedics must park around the back or enter from side doors.

Once inside, they face the challenge of navigating through a confusing layout. "It all looks the same—you go up and down elevators, there are no direct routes, the carpets lead you around and around, you lose your sense of direction." When paramedics reach a victim, the challenge is no longer casino floor design but other players' reluctance to leave their machines. "The gamblers just wouldn't move to let us out," remembers a paramedic who was once forced to start an intravenous line in a narrow aisle between two rows of machines.

To reduce the time it took to reach victims, some casinos trained their surveillance personnel to watch banks of machines for heart attacks on security monitors. In 1997 they went a step further and began to train their security guards to use automatic external defibrillators, or AEDs. The paramedics suggest that I speak with Richard Hardman, the coordinator of emergency medical services in Clark County who developed the casino AED program. Hardman, a slender man in his forties, meets me at the county's Fire Department headquarters, not far from the south end of the Strip. We speak in his office, a small room with a busy desk and a television set suspended from the ceiling, hospital style.

As part of a quality assurance program in 1995, his department had noticed nearly three times as many deaths by heart attack occurring in Clark County as in other counties. A closer look revealed that two-thirds of the cardiac arrests took place in casinos, and Hardman realized that the high rate of death had to do with the delays encountered by paramedic teams negotiating their complicated interiors. Although they arrived at casino properties within four and a half to five minutes of a call, it took them an average of eleven minutes to reach victims inside. Hardman points out the life-and-death stakes: "Every minute following a cardiac arrest, your chances of survival decrease by 10 percent."

Hardman contacted a public health researcher who agreed that casinos would make an ideal laboratory for testing defibrillator use by nonphysicians, and the two designed an experimental study. Next he lobbied casino management groups to purchase AED devices and train personnel to use them—not an easy sell given their worry over legal liabilities in the event of inappropriate applications of the device. He eventually convinced casinos that AEDs only deliver shocks in the absence of breathing and pulse, when intervention cannot make things worse. "There are no judgment calls to be made," Hardman emphasized. "The AED is automatic, foolproof, it analyzes everything on its own." Casinos decided to train security officers to use the devices since they were the staff members most familiar with property layouts. As it turned out, the officers had a very short response time—only two to three minutes. "At first they resisted, but now they embrace the technology," says Hardman.

AEDs have since been used thousands of times in Las Vegas casinos, with an impressive survival rate of 55 percent (even better than that of hospitals—and far surpassing the national average rate of less than 10 percent).[1] Hardman has testified before Congress as part of the Cardiac Survival Act, and has lectured internationally. What makes his presentations so compelling are a set of real-time video recordings of AEDs in action. "Casinos," Hardman tells me, "made videos for me, unknowingly, on their surveillance cameras." Apologizing for the lack of audio in the footage, he invites me to sit behind his desk and watch the overhead TV monitor while he stands below and performs a live voice-over, a role at which he is clearly well practiced. As he indicates in advance which slight movements to look for, I sit riveted to the screen. The same drama is repeated three times—three casinos, three near deaths, and three life-saving automatic defibrillations.

The first video is black and white. A card dealer who had asked for water collapses as he leans to take a sip, falling between two tables. The cameras adjust their angles as soon as surveillance is alerted and record the defibrillations that follow. The second video is in color and begins with an overhead shot of a man in his early sixties, seated at a machine. Casino personnel had brought him oxygen when he complained of chest pains, and after the oxygen he feels better. He puts his cowboy hat on, says he doesn't need any help, and begins his long journey out of the casino. Seven different cameras track his movement as he exits the property: down the escalator, through an elevated walkway, across the casino floor, and out the door. "The cameras followed him to make sure he was okay, but there were probably some legal reasons too," comments Hardman. As he narrates, he seems to revere the casino surveillance infrastructure as much as the AEDs; it is not always clear which technologies take the starring role in the videos. A camera on the casino roof tracks the man's progress through the outside parking lot, zooming in on him as he walks between rows of cars. He collapses in the parking lot. Bystanders approach, and casino security guards quickly arrive with the defibrillator. They prep the device, apply it, and shock the man back to consciousness. Paramedics show up seven and a half minutes later. "He would have had a 75 percent chance of dying," Hardman says, "and that's the parking lot—it would have taken longer to get inside."

The third video is the most unsettling. By chance, the surveillance camera had been trained directly on the victim, who is playing at the tables. He rubs his temples, leans back, and tries to clear his head—then collapses suddenly onto the person next to him, who doesn't react at all. The man slips to the floor in the throes of a seizure and two passersby stretch him out, one of them an off-duty ER nurse. Few gamblers in the immediate vicinity move from their seats. The camera shifts down to the floor and zooms in. In less than one minute, a security officer appears on the scene bearing a defibrillator; he applies the pads, clears, and shocks the man twice. When at nine minutes the paramedics arrive, the man is conscious, then confused, then alert and talking. Cameras track him leaving the casino.

Hardman pauses from his voice-over to note that the most interesting thing about this video sequence is the reaction, or nonreaction, of the public. I had been focusing on the man himself, and until Hardman pointed out the surrounding context, I had not identified what exactly was so disturbing about the footage. More disconcerting than the fact of the attack itself is the disjuncture between the stopping of the man's heart and the play that continues unabated all around him; it is almost as if two different videos are superimposed. Despite the unconscious man lying quite literally at their feet, touching the bottoms of their chairs, the other gamblers keep playing.

1

INTERIOR DESIGN FOR INTERIOR STATES

Architecture, Ambience, and Affect

IT WAS NOT UNCOMMON, in my interviews with casino slot floor managers, to hear of machine gamblers so absorbed in play that they were oblivious to rising flood waters at their feet or smoke and fire alarms that blared at deafening levels. As the casino surveillance tapes showed, the activity can keep a group of gamblers unaware of their immediate surroundings, each other, and even a dying man at their feet. Mollie witnessed this extreme of unawareness one night as she searched the aisles of a casino for a machine to play and came upon a small crowd gathered around a man lying on the floor between a row of machines. "He'd had a heart attack and the paramedics were getting him with those shocker things," she recalled. "Everyone walking by was looking at him, but I was watching the woman on the dollar slot machine. She was staring right at the screen and never missed a beat. She played right through it, she never stopped." As the medical technicians applied the defibrillator to start a stopped heart beating, the gambler played the slot machine to keep a different kind of beat going, one that held her in a zone removed from the sights, sounds, and events transpiring around her. "You aren't really there," Mollie told us earlier of the zone, "you're with the machine and that's all you're with."

Daniel, a retired telecommunications engineer, drew a direct link between the removal he feels from his environment while in the zone and design features of that very environment:

It starts while I'm on my way to the casino. I'm in the car driving, but in my mind I'm already inside, walking around to find my machine. In the parking lot, the feeling gets even stronger. By the time I get inside, I'm halfway into that zone. It has everything to do with the sounds, the lights, the atmosphere, walking through the aisles. Then when I'm finally sitting in front of the machine playing, it's like I'm not even really there anymore—everything fades away.

In Daniel's experience, the zone he enters is in some way a function of the same architectural and ambient world that "fades away" within it. Taking his insight as a point of departure, this chapter explores the relationship between the interior design of the casino and the interior state of the zone.

Relearning from Las Vegas

In their 1972 book *Learning from Las Vegas*, architects Robert Venturi, Denise Scott Brown, and Steven Izenour made a case for the cultural significance of Las Vegas and its built environment, arguing that the city was a laboratory for experimentation with refreshingly populist architectural forms.[1] Rejecting the elitist notion that architecture's role was to instill social values and behavioral ideals, the authors embraced the city's roadside structures as spontaneous monuments to popular vernacular and frontier automobile freedom. These structures, they proposed in their landmark work, departed from the utopian, totalizing pretensions of modernist architecture and expressed a democratically inclusive response to "common values" and "existing conditions."

While modernist buildings sought to facilitate *communitas* through high ceilings, wide open space, bountiful lighting and windows, and a minimalist, uncluttered aesthetic, casinos' low, immersive interiors, blurry spatial boundaries, and mazes of alcoves accommodated "crowds of anonymous individuals without explicit connection with each other."[2] Like other popular communal spaces, casinos catered to the desires of everyday Americans to be "together and yet separate." Venturi and his colleagues elaborated: "The combination of darkness and enclosure of the gambling room and its subspaces makes for privacy, protection, concentration and control. The intricate maze under the low ceiling never connects with the outside light or outside space. This disorients the occupant in space and time. One loses track of where one is and when it is."[3] Such spaces did not pretend to remedy the social ills of the "lonely crowd," as sociologist David Riesman had despairingly designated the public at large, but instead responded to the escapist sensibilities of the American populace by satisfying them, without judgment.[4]

The publication of *Learning from Las Vegas* coincided with Nevada's passage of the Corporate Gaming Act and the new wave of casino development that it ushered in. This wave gathered momentum in the 1990s, set off by the staggering success of the Mirage, a rainforest-themed resort financed with junk bonds in 1989 by an ambitious young casino tycoon named Steve Wynn. His winning venture inspired other companies to build competing properties on the Strip, turning the idiosyncratic structures that Venturi and his colleagues had lauded into gargantuan corporate megaresorts—"total environments" whose meticulous architectural calculations left little to chance. Behind whatever fanciful thematic facades these new casinos bore—Polynesian rainforest, ancient Egypt, Italian lakeside—their interior design followed a standard blueprint for revenue maximization, offering a different kind of "learning from Las Vegas."[5] As Frederic Jameson suggested in his 1991 critique of *Learning from Las Vegas*, its authors' eagerness to dismiss modernism had blinded them to the "cultural logic of late capitalism" nascent in the architectural forms they encountered.[6] Although the aspirations of these forms were not modernist in that they were neither moral nor civic, they were nonetheless unabashedly instrumental; in place of self-mastery and social harmony, they promoted self-abandon and corporate profit.

Now, as then, casinos' "commercial vernacular style" responds to popular needs or desires for escapism as part of a larger effort to *guide* those needs and desires. "The one thing you need to know about casino planning is that the whole point of a casino is to get people walking from the registration to the main body of the casino," responded a top designer when asked by a scholar how the concept of "human engineering" influenced casino design. He went on to explain what his firm meant by "experience-based" architecture: "We try to influence movement and the circulation pattern and therefore direct people's experience."[7] Although Wynn has downplayed the role of such strategy in the design of his own casinos, stating that the winning formula behind the Mirage was the result of "confusion, not cunning," in fact each of his properties has been a fastidiously planned affair from conception to finish, from wall treatments to ambient soundtrack.[8] For instance, after he drew up floor plans for the

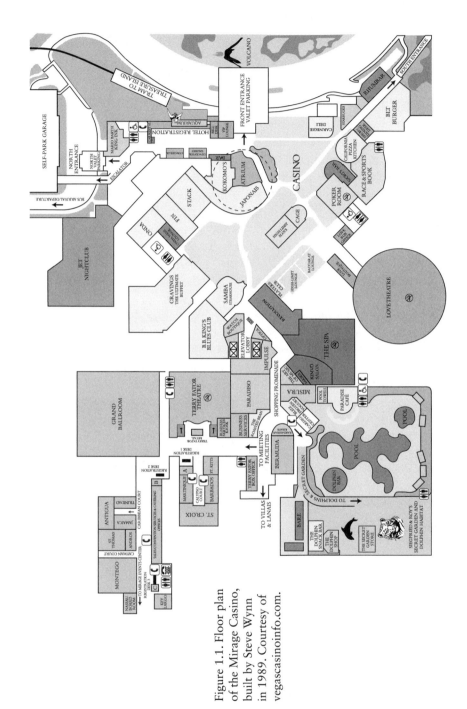

Figure 1.1. Floor plan of the Mirage Casino, built by Steve Wynn in 1989. Courtesy of vegascasinoinfo.com.

Mirage (see fig 1.1) he delayed construction so as to entertain suggestions for alterations by the design consultant and former casino manager Bill Friedman, whose pragmatic philosophy of casino design we will examine in the following pages.

Friedman, the gambling industry's maverick guru of casino design, established himself as such in 1974 when he wrote the definitive book on casino management.[9] Over the next twenty-five years, he conducted research for another book, the epic 630-page tome boldly titled *Designing Casinos to Dominate the Competition*, published in 2000. There he calls casinos mazes and makes sure his clients know what he means by this: "The term maze is appropriate because my trusty *American Heritage Dictionary* says it comes from the words *to confuse* or *to confound* and defines it as '*an intricate, usually confusing network of interconnecting pathways, as in garden; a labyrinth*.'"[10] Unlike Wynn, Friedman invokes confusion not to diminish the cunning of his own design but rather to characterize it. The architectural vision of confusion that he elaborates strongly resembles the "intricate maze" described in *Learning from Las Vegas* yet shares less with postmodern populism than with applied behaviorism.[11] "Just as the Pied Piper of Hamelin lured all the rats and the children to follow him," he writes, "a properly designed maze entices adult players."[12]

Although Friedman's maze is not the only casino design template influential in the gambling industry today,[13] the pride of place it accords machines makes it a fitting starting point for an analysis of the relationship between interior design and machine gamblers' interior states. The maze and its enticement strategies expressly seek to precipitate and modulate the otherworldly "zone" of machine gambling.

DESIGNING THE MAZE

In his writings, Friedman reproaches "casino owners and operators, architects, interior designers, and decorators" for tending to rely on subjective preferences and lofty design concepts rather than on a pragmatic understanding of what encourages or deters gambling. "Their concepts and proposals," he writes, "fail to recognize the unique objectives and behavior of gamblers."[14] His own expertise at recognizing such objectives and behavior rests not only on the exhaustive empirical field studies he conducted in eighty casinos over a period of twenty years (supplemented by a historical analysis from 1931 to the present) but also on his experience as a onetime slot machine addict. He thus establishes himself as an authority in the book's introduction: "I understand the motives and experiences of players because I was a degenerate gambler until I swore off it twenty-five years ago."[15]

Drawing on his intimate familiarity with the zone of machine gambling, Friedman goes on to describe the play that gamblers seek as an "inward focus into their own private domain [that] makes them oblivious to everything around them." He insists that "the designer, marketer, and operator who best caters to this personal, introspective experience will attract and hold the most business." Friedman's insistence that casino design cater to the escapist sensibilities of his clientele resonates with that of Venturi and his colleagues, yet his aim is neither to decry modernist pretension nor simply to accommodate the inclinations of his clients; instead, his goal is to shape an environment that can steer their behavior in accordance with the extractive aims of the larger operation.

In line with the economic priorities of his industry, Friedman pays nearly exclusive attention to machine gamblers. While many interior designers treat slot machines as mere props with which to lure people into casinos, he conceives of the entire built environment of the casino as a means for luring people to machines. "If the only commonality among casinos is that they feature gambling equipment," he writes, "then it is an eloquent statement by players that this is all that is important to them."[16] Acknowledging that his approach violates the sensibilities of professional decorators, he insists that monotonous surroundings are best: "Machines should not be hidden or camouflaged by attention grabbing décor, which should be eliminated to the greatest extent possible so as to allow the equipment to announce itself."[17] As a like-minded casino operator put it bluntly in the course of a 2009 panel on casino design, "I don't want anyone to come in and look at the ceiling—I don't make any money on the ceiling."[18] Instead of turning attention away from machines, every aspect of the environment should work to turn attention toward machines, and keep it focused there. From ceiling height to carpet pattern, lighting intensity to aisle width, acoustics to temperature regulation—all such elements, Freidman argues, should be engineered to facilitate the interior state of the machine zone. To this end he presents a comprehensive design strategy involving thirteen trademarked laws called the Friedman Casino Design Principles.

Shrinking Space: Construction, Segmentation, Shelter

The chief task of casino design, according to Friedman, is to arrange "the spatial relationships of surrounding areas, the shape and feel of the structural box that encloses the setting" in such a way as to encourage machine gamblers' entry into "secluded, private playing worlds."[19] "While players prefer gambling in bustling casinos," he notes, "they want to be isolated in their own private, intimate world from the surrounding hubbub that attracted them in the first place."[20] In response to this wish for isolation, he applies The Law of Space Elimination to architectural layout.

Echoing the antimodernism of *Learning from Las Vegas*, Friedman accuses mainstream designers of too readily assuming that a sense of space is something to foster in patrons. "As an abstraction, spaciousness sounds great. The term conjures up a sense of privacy and protection of one's territory from infringement by others. It seems to offer freedom, even independence, to move about at will, and it has a quality of affluence."[21] Yet his empirical research—in which he tracked properties' "foot traffic flow patterns" and "equipment occupancy rates" and timed the duration of prospective patrons' stays—has consistently found that the best performing slots are those located within "insulated enclaves," tucked or hidden in "small alcoves, recesses, and corners," "sheltered in the nooks and crannies."[22] Gamblers themselves confirm Friedman's insights. "I'd gravitate toward the corners," Mollie remembered, "where it felt safe, and I could get into my zone." Sharon would put her legs up on either side of her machine, using her own body to delimit the boundaries of her personal escape pod. "I don't like having my back exposed," said Daniel; "I want to be in my own little cave."

"The element [players] most avoid when gambling," Friedman concludes, "is expanse."[23] Expanse comes in the form of "excess horizontal space, excessive visible depth, and excess vertical space."[24] An empty void overhead, for example, "dissipates energy" and leaves individuals feeling exposed and anxious.[25] Friedman describes one property that failed to eliminate space as "a completely open, free-spanned, high-ceilinged airplane hangar."[26] Another failed design presents patrons with "an enormous sea of emptiness floating over endless rows of machines."[27] To illustrate the pitfalls of casinos' failure to eliminate space, he draws a representation of the slot floor at Steve Wynn's Treasure Island, labeling it "the state's most extensive uninterrupted ocean of slots" (see fig. 1.2, top). In the drawing, a woman hesitates at the edge of the slot floor, clutching her

Figure 1.2.   *Top*: Architectural rendering of Treasure Island, Nevada's "most extensive uninterrupted ocean of slots," drawn to illustrate the problem of excess space in casino floor design. From *Designing Casinos to Dominate the Competition*, by Bill Friedman, 2000, page 259.   *Bottom*: Example of successful "space elimination" through equipment congestion, truncated lines of sight, and a convoluted maze layout. Anonymous photograph available for download at flickr.com.

purse and looking apprehensively over her shoulder into the receding depths of the casino, her body angled as if to retreat from the phalanx of machines that seem "to extend, like the surface of the sea, into infinity."[28] This existentially unsettling spatial set-up, Friedman argues, neither invites entry into the physical playing area nor into the experiential playing zone that gamblers seek.

The Law of Space Elimination dictates that designers "constrict" space to create protected sanctuaries for play.[29] (Play itself Friedman describes as "open," "undifferentiated," "boundless," "extensive," and "never-ending"—precisely the phenomenological characteristics he strives to minimize within the gambling environment.[30]) One way to do this is by "segmenting" the casino floor into compact areas isolated from the rest of the casino and not visible to one another.[31] Architectural elements such as canopies, coffers, hoods, and soffits can be used to break up otherwise cavernous space and provide a sense of enclosure and "perceptual shelter." "Each cluster," writes Friedman, "perceptually surrounds the gambling equipment beneath it. It has the quality of dropping imaginary lines to connect with the equipment below. This psychologically separates the area from the rest of the casino."[32] As Venturi and his colleagues noted earlier of casino interiors, "subspaces makes for privacy, protection, concentration and control." Following this logic, the designers of the Mirage built low-hanging tiki-hut covers throughout the casino floor as a way to differentiate gaming areas and "create a feeling of intimacy in a 95,000 square foot space."[33] As one of the chief architects explained to me in 1993: "The hanging huts give a smaller scale to the space, and people cluster under low-scale things. From any one point in the casino you never feel how big it is. What we really set out to do is control your perspective"[34] (see fig. 1.2, bottom).

Focusing Attention: Convolution, Cues, Curvature

Additional methods for constricting space and controlling perspective, Friedman advises, include "equipment immediacy," whereby "gambling activity is thrust upon visitors as they enter," and "equipment congestion," whereby machines are "crammed tightly together" so that players feel contained amid their crush. Emphasizing that gamblers "prefer a jammed and convoluted layout," he recommends that "passageways and aisles be as narrow as comfort and safety considerations will allow."[35]

Patrons' orientation to the space and its technologies must be contained within the narrowest bandwidth—or zone—possible.

This is a delicate operation in which the balance of containment may be tipped too far, as Friedman acknowledges: "When all excess emptiness has been eliminated from the architectural design and layout, it can be difficult for visitors to determine where they are and where they want to go." In this disoriented state, they are liable to "wander aimlessly and gaze blankly."[36] To counteract the disorientation effect, "congestion must be effectively organized." The key is to cultivate "structured chaos" rather than "inhospitable commotion."[37] "The maze," Friedman promises, "is the antidote."[38]

He explains: "A maze layout rivets visitors' attention on the equipment immediately ahead. The slot faces at the ends of the short, narrow aisles are thrust right at them. The convoluted, dead-ended pathways force walkers to focus on the machines as they approach to avoid bumping into them. *If a visitor has a propensity to gamble, the maze layout will evoke it*."[39] Although the convolution of mazes is associated with disorientation, in fact Friedman's maze shrinks and structures space in such a way as to *orient* patrons along a certain course, "riveting" their attention to strategically placed guideposts and steering their movement toward a destination that seems to mirror—and can thus "evoke"—their underlying "propensity" to stop, sit, and play.

Just as gambling machines propel players by riveting their attention to the next hand or spin, the architectural maze pulls patrons forward by truncating their line of sight. "Walkers can only see a short distance ahead to the items directly in front of them ... [they] cannot see very far in any direction—ahead, sideways, or overhead." By "partially obstruct[ing] what lies beyond," the layout "induces [walkers] to continue farther and deeper into the gambling equipment."[40] Friedman advises designers to offer *hints* at what lies beyond, but cautions them never to overclarify or allow glimpses into the far reaches of the casino, for this might discourage patrons from moving into its interior.[41] Walkways that are too large, too open, or incongruent in their coloring, for instance, are liable to induce players to move straight through a property without stepping off into its gaming areas—a phenomenon Friedman refers to as the "yellow brick road effect." (Ironically, MGM's Oz-themed casino features a yellow brick road that exemplifies the very problem he denotes with this phrase.)

Although a casino's maze layout should not overclarify what lies ahead, it should clarify its pathways enough to prevent stalling and keep movement flowing toward machines. "Strong guidance is needed from design cues," Friedman underscores. A writer for a gambling industry trade journal describes how a problematic tunnel leading to the front entrance of Caesars Palace—an "ill-defined and disorienting space" in which traffic often jammed—was remedied by the application of spatial cues: "A band of lights was installed just above a marble baseboard. The lights flashed in a slow, sequential pattern, subliminally creating the same effect that is obvious to pilots approaching airport runways as they key on rapidly firing chase lights. The lights gave customers a focal point that led them to the casino entrance ... cues to lead them through the corridor."[42] As another interior designer has remarked, "you try to establish focal points throughout the casino in order to draw people further into the 'mousetrap.'"[43]

Corridors draw people in not only by way of cues but also by way of *curves*. Casino patrons "resist perpendicular turning," Friedman notes, for "commitment is required to slow down and turn 90 degrees into a slot aisle."[44] As a fellow industry member recalls, the reduction of "sharp lines" and the introduction of "very frequent curvature lines" became a strategic part of the casino's design repertoire in the mid-1980s.[45] "The role of the uninterrupted, curvilinear pathway couldn't be more important," commented an architect during a panel at the 2009 Global Gaming Expo.[46]

Friedman advises that curving should begin outside a casino property. "The entry to the property should beckon and invite, and should curve gently off the street or sidewalk. Driving from the street into the property entrance should be effortless."[47] Like the road that glides directly through the sites on Mollie's map, there should be no right angles, and no stop signs. As sections of the Las Vegas Strip have become more pedestrian, outdoor walkways and long moving conveyor belts have extended the principle of the curve to a walking scale, rolling out onto sidewalks and carrying players into the property from the street.[48] When Friedman slightly curved the right angle of an entrance corridor to one property, he was "amazed at the magnitude of change in the pedestrians' behavior" (the percentage who entered increased from one-third to nearly two-thirds).[49]

Inside casinos, "passageways should keep twisting and turning through gradual, gentle curves and angles that smooth out the shifts in direction."[50] Aisles leading into gambling areas "should narrow gradually, so walkers do not notice the approaching transition until they suddenly find themselves immersed in the intimate worlds of gambling action."[51] Curves that are gradual and gentle function to minimize walkers' awareness of the spatial guidance at work in the floor layout, by "smoothing out" any edges or angles that might cause them to pause, shift, or reflect on their movement. The ideal scenario is one in which players "do not analyze the various things they observe as they meander along the passageways" but instead "just glance around without apparent purpose, hoping that something will trigger their emotional passion to gamble."[52] The job of casino layout is to suspend walking patrons in a suggestible, affectively permeable state that renders them susceptible to environmental triggers, which are then supplied.

Modulating Affect: Sensory Atmospherics

Once patrons are actually seated before gambling machines, the devices themselves take over from the casino environment as the dominant force of guidance, as we will see in the next chapter. Yet even then, the environment continues to play a role—now less through architecture than through *ambience*. It is no longer the curves, cues, and congestion of the floor plan that are deployed to influence customers, but "casino atmospherics," a term that two industry consultants from the University of Nevada's College of Hotel Administration in Las Vegas coined to describe the "controllable items connected with the internal and external environment of a service facility"—temperature, light, color, sound, and aroma—that "elicit an emotional or physiological reaction from customers."[53] These items, they contend, powerfully modulate patrons' "experiential affect," helping not only to usher them to machines but also to immerse them in the zone—and keep them there.

Calling to mind a Deleuzian conception of affect as dynamic states of sensing, energy, and attention outside of conscious awareness yet critical to action, atmospherics are understood to be most effective when they operate at a level that is not consciously detectible.[54] Like casino designers' spatial strategies, their ambient strategies treat affect not as something passive or static, but as an active and dynamic capacity that can be harnessed and guided in lucrative directions.[55] A study titled "Effects of Ambient Odors on Slot-Machine Usage in a Las Vegas Casino" found that slot revenue rose by a full 45 percent in a gambling area where ma-

FOOT CANDLES		DECIBELS	
1	Dark	66-68	Very Quiet
2	Dim	69-73	Quiet
3	Subdued	74-77	Moderate
4-5	Moderate	78-81	Loud
6-7	Bright	82-83	Very Loud
8	Very Bright	84-87	Extremely Loud
9-10	Extremely Bright	88-95	Blaring
11-15	Exceptionally Bright		
16-20	Extraordinarily Bright		

Figure 1.3. Bill Friedman's guidelines for optimal light and sound levels in casino environments, measured in foot candles and decibels. From *Designing Casinos to Dominate the Competition*, by Bill Friedman, 2000, page 625.

chines had been subtly treated with a certain pleasing odor while remaining static in another area that had been treated with a different but equally pleasing odor.[56] The author speculated that certain aromas produce an "affective congruence with the situational context," encouraging longer play; an odor, "when matched to a certain environment," can "precipitate actions."[57] "From conditioned-reflex experiments with animals not known to possess conscious processes," he noted, "it seems clear that consciousness is not required for a conditioned response."[58]

Following the same logic, Friedman advises that it is best to communicate with players at a subliminal level, so that they may "simply respond to how they feel."[59] Atmospheric elements should be adjusted such that none is so salient as to distract or stress the energies of patrons. "Just a few degrees too high or too low will drive people out of an area," he writes of temperature.[60] Likewise, "intense décor reduces playing time," and "bright or vivid colors, or incompatible color schemes, can tax the senses."[61] Friedman claims to be uniquely capable of identifying the "noxious excesses" that must be eradicated: "I am extremely sensitive to my environment. I have a low tolerance for excessive brightness and loudness, emptiness and spaciousness, and inappropriate or conflicting design cues."[62] When it comes to lighting, he explains that human "perceptual systems" must expend extra energy to process the imbalance of intensity that occurs when ceiling and wall lighting sources are markedly brighter than ambient levels (see fig. 1.3, left column). "The extra effort eventually makes players feel physically tired, and *while players may not be consciously aware of why*, they often leave earlier than they intended and are much less likely to return."[63] To prevent this hidden tax on perceptual energy, lighting must be steady and even. Degree of intensity is not the only aspect of lighting that matters, for degree of angle is also critical. Consumer research in casinos has shown that light drains gamblers' energy fastest when it hits their foreheads.

Like light, sound must be neither too heavy an assault on the senses, nor too soft; above all, it must not be deflected (see fig. 1.3, right column). As Friedman explains, "sound usually bothers players only when it is bounced back at them from interior surfaces [since] it is impossible to identify the source of reverberated sounds."[64] Just as the spatial configuration and visual presentation of the casino floor should not disorient, sound should not be "flat, directionless, and jumbled together into noise that seems to come from everywhere at once." Friedman found that he could detect the negative affect produced by such sound in the facial expressions of gamblers: "If you come upon a situation where there is loud, offensive noise deflecting from all surfaces, observe the players' faces. They will show facial fatigue, tension, and distress. I have never encountered these expressions in casinos that have natural, nondeflected sound."[65]

Another acoustic element that must be carefully regulated to encourage play is music. A company called Digigram provides background music that can be scheduled by time of day, depending on the shifting demographics of a property's clientele. Casino managers, Digigram suggests, might play "something slow or mild in the middle of the day for one group of customers and then maybe build up the tempo throughout the day when there's a high occupancy of customers. *You have control of the ambience*."[66] The company cites studies showing that consumers' walking speed, time spent, and money spent in retail spaces are all highly influenced by sound.[67] The vice president for DMX music, another sound supplier for casinos, told a reporter: "Our objective is to assist [casinos] in *stimulating their customers to respond to their environments*."[68]

Like other atmospheric elements, music works best as a behavioral modulator when it remains in the background. Well-known tunes and slow passages that do not vary in volume and rhythm work well to orchestrate consumer action while remaining below the threshold of consciousness—"functional music" as Digigram calls it.[69] This acoustic analogue to curving corners and balanced lighting sources facilitates the flowing suspension of the zone state by supplying patrons' perceptual systems with a subtle, even-keeled stream of sensory input. Music that is too varied in these respects can disrupt gambling activity, for it "restores … your cognitive state to where you can make rational decisions," one analyst of casino design notes.[70]

The less aware gamblers are of architectural and atmospheric space, the more likely they are to become absorbed in play.[71] By the same token, as their absorption increases over a session of play, the more impervious it becomes to potential distraction from disequilibrated or otherwise disruptive ambient elements. "The surrounding space of the periphery is obliterated," writes sociologist Gerda Reith of gambling; space "shrinks into a single point and loses its extensity."[72] That "single point," in the case of machine gambling, is the device's screen—and it is less a point of spatial reference than it is a point of exit from space. "I go into a tunnel vision where I actually do not hear or see anything around me," said Rocky, a retired nuclear geologist. "If you really evaluate that moment, the only thing that exists is the screen." As Friedman writes, machine gamblers at play enter "a different plane in which they lose their sense of reality, existing only for the moment, for the next bet." On this "different plane," embodied existence in the material world is exchanged for a timeless flow of repeating moments. Yet the worldly elements of architecture and atmosphere, this chapter has argued, play a key role in bringing about and maintaining this otherworldly zone.

The affective appeals of casino design come palpably to the fore when they conflict with the conscious intentions of patrons—as in the case of gambling addicts attempting to resist the pull of machine play. At a Gamblers Anonymous meeting I attended in 2002, a young man named Todd recounted how a simple walk through a casino to lunch with friends earlier that day had become a harrowing ordeal of environmental temptation. As soon as he crossed the threshold of the casino floor, its architectural and atmospheric features, working in concert with its gambling equipment, triggered in him a powerful psychological and physiological reaction:

> I started shivering and shaking right there at the entrance of the gambling floor. When I started to walk across, the noise just hit my nervous system—it was just driving my nerves. I told myself to look straight ahead and just walk, but I didn't know where I was going. I stopped to ask someone—it was a change lady and she was paying somebody off at a slot machine, and I told myself *Don't look at the machine, don't look at the machine.* I walked

a little further and I was still lost, so I stopped to ask another one, and she's paying somebody off too and I'm saying to myself *Don't look, don't look.* Finally I got over to the buffet, but my friends weren't there yet, so I just sat on the bench and kept my eyes on the floor, tried not to hear all the machines around me. On the way out, afterward, my eyes found all the machines I liked to play—I knew exactly where they were, and I've never even been in that casino. I was hyperventilating; I had to practically run out the door.

In stark contrast with Daniel's experience at the start of this chapter, in which his desire and intention to gamble were matched and reinforced by the affective appeals of the casino's physical environment, Todd experienced an "affective *in*congruence with the situational context," to paraphrase the aforementioned aroma study. As the pied piper of the casino maze played an alluring song at odds with Todd's commitment to abstain from play, his "nervous system" (to use his term) was thrown for a loop.

Learning from Las Vegas, we saw earlier, called for an architecture that could respond to the escapist sensibilities of its patrons. So-called experience-based casino design attempts to do just this, yet the forms it takes are not exactly populist. One could even say that the particular instrumentality of contemporary casino design shares elements of disciplinary institutions, as is made apparent in the matter-of-fact revelation by the president of the casino design firm DiLeonardo International that he was influenced, while attending Harvard's graduate design school, by fellow students who "were experimenting with the application of environmental psychology to architectural design in prisons and other public facilities."[73]

Yet the gently curving passageways, ensconcing nooks, and softly lit machine mazes of casinos are not of a piece with the regimented and discomfiting forms of modernist disciplinary architecture the philosopher Michel Foucault described as "an architecture that would operate to transform individuals: to act on those it shelters, to provide a hold on their conduct."[74] While the structural, decorative, and ambient environment of the casino is certainly geared to influence patrons' conduct, its modus operandi is to coax rather than restrain, reward rather than punish, steer rather than transform. Instead of adjusting patrons to an architecture or atmosphere, Bill Friedman and other experience-attentive casino designers advocate "a constant adjustment of the building," as one put it, resulting in the production of "ergonomic labyrinths" that facilitate "happy imprisonment."[75] Although the sedentary, button-pressing players of casino machinery may resemble the docile bodies of factory workers, soldiers, prisoners, or students, they are not the self-conscious, self-censoring, vigilant subjects of disciplinary spaces; instead, they are uninhibited, self-abandoning, and immersed in "tiny, private playing worlds," to use Friedman's phrasing.

How, then, to characterize the particular instrumentality of casino environments? Gilles Deleuze proposed in the 1990s that discipline, formerly the dominant mode of power in Western societies, had been modified and to some degree overtaken by a logic of "control" that worked not by confinement or restriction of movement, but by the regulation of continuous, mobile flows—of capital, information, bodies, and affects.[76] Unlike the punitive subjection of discipline, control does not require a subject as such; nor does it seek to produce or manage one. As we have seen, casino design follows what one leading firm calls the "immersion paradigm," holding players in a desubjectified state of uninterrupted motion so as to galvanize, channel, and profit from what the academic consultants quoted earlier called "experiential affect." If, as philosophers and anthropologists of affect contend, contemporary capitalism is distinguished by strategic attempts to mobilize and derive value from consumers' affective capacities, then commercial casino design would appear to be a case in point. As the next chapter will show, the immersion paradigm and its logic of affect modulation carry over from the gambling environment to the gambling technology itself.

2

ENGINEERING EXPERIENCE

The Productive Economy of Player-Centric Design

WHILE SOPHISTICATED ARCHITECTURAL and ambient qualities of casino environments work to draw patrons to gambling devices, the devices themselves work to keep patrons playing, and to keep the zone state going. Instead of moving people though space, the aim is to anchor them in one spot and manage their play through time. Machines "harness technology for *continuous gaming productivity*," as casino management consultant Leslie Cummings puts it. She explains:

> While the term productivity often refers to measures such as output per worker ... *gaming productivity* refers to wagering action (play) per patron per interval. *Expediting* refers to advancing and facilitating gaming action so that players can be more productive because their play is faster, extends for a longer interval, and/or involves more dollars placed at risk (wagered) per period than otherwise would be expected.[1]

The task of expediting "continuous gaming productivity," as Cummings breaks it down, involves three interlinked operations, each of which this chapter will examine in turn: *accelerating* play, *extending* its duration, and *increasing* the total amount spent.

The idea that gambling could be a "productive," mainstream enterprise arose in the twentieth century with the growth of mass leisure and the rising importance of consumption to capitalist economies. As gambling shed its industrial-era associations with nonproductivity and wasteful-ness, it became an industry in its own right.[2] As the passage above attests, the gambling industry has since employed time and energy management techniques reminiscent of those developed for manufacturing labor in the nineteenth and twentieth centuries.[3] These management techniques, however, have been subtly modified as they have been adapted to a com-mercial domain in which the productive activity at stake (i.e., "wagering action") is an experience that consumers choose to purchase rather than labor for which they are remunerated.

In accordance with the affect-based orientation of contemporary capi-talism whose spatial applications we considered in the previous chapter, designers of gambling machines have paid increasingly close attention to gamblers' physical, sensory, and cognitive propensities. Following a model of value production in which the objective is to profit from voluntary acts of play—a model that epitomizes what the journalist and game scholar Julian Dibbell calls "ludocapitalism"—they have sought to attune their industry's machinery of production to consumer predilections.[4]

What Players Want: Neatly encapsulating what has come to be known as the "player-centric" approach to machine design, the three-word slogan for WMS Gaming's 2006 marketing campaign was broadcast from soar-ing pillars and billboard-sized video panels at the Global Gaming Expo that year, repeating itself up and down the aisles of technology on dis-play. "[This] isn't just a motto," read an oversized poster hanging near the registration area, "it's the result of an entirely unique and continuous approach to game development." Despite this claim for uniqueness, player-centric machine design follows a wider trend in user-centrism wherein product designers seek to extract value from enhanced consumer experiences, or to "mine a new phenomenological substrate," as the soci-ologist Nigel Thrift writes.[5] "Economies in general are moving from cre-ating goods and delivering services to creating experiences," observed a representative for WMS at G2E 2009, citing a business-oriented best-seller called *The Experience Economy*.[6] "That's what we should be doing—*engineering experiences*," he urged his colleagues.

The language of experience has become prevalent in the gambling in-dustry. "*We keep player experience in mind at every step*," I heard a slot machine manufacturer say in 2007. "We do a brilliant job of creating that *in-the-zone* experience," said a casino operator in 2008.[7] Before turning in the next chapters to the inner mechanisms, digital algorithms, and game software that drive play itself, we will examine the player-centric design of the interactive components that gamblers encounter at the point of play: buttons and bill acceptors, sound and video engineering, ergonomic consoles and seating components, and financial handling and access technologies. As one industry member advised his colleagues, "don't look at auxiliary products as auxiliary, but as integral to experience."[8] In their attempt to incite faster, longer, and more intensive play, designers of the gambling machine interface pay careful attention to the phenomenological requirements of the zone experience.

Accelerating Play

Speed is a critical element of the zone experience. "I play really fast," a middle-aged tax accountant named Shelly told me. "I don't like to wait, I want to know what's gonna come out. If a machine is slow, I move to a faster one." "I usually play just with one hand," said a college student named Julie; "you probably couldn't even see the cards, that's how fast I go" (her eyes widened and glazed over in front of an imaginary screen, index finger punching rapidly). Gambling addicts speak of speed as a kind of skill, even when it leads them to miss hands they might have won.[9] "Sometimes I'd get into such a rhythm on the [video poker] machine that I'd mistakenly discard winning hands," recalled Sharon, whom we met in the introduction. "It was more about keeping the pace than making the right decisions."

"Keeping the pace" is critical to the zone experience, as gamblers articulate. "The speed is relaxing," said Lola, a buffet waitress and mother of four. "It's not exactly excitement; it's calm, like a tranquilizer. It gets me into the zone." Randall, an electronics technician in his late forties, has a long-standing penchant for vehicles that enable him to escape with speed—motorcycles, racing dragsters, and video poker. "In a very paradoxical way," he reflected, "the speed of it slows me down. Both the fact that I'm in motion and the risk of it are calming, and kind of mechanical." As he recognizes, a mechanically mediated tempo functions as a form of predictability that structures and regulates his play, transforming risk into rhythm. As long as gamblers hold their speed steady, it suspends them in the holding pattern of the zone.

The technological conditions of suspension-by-speed are multiple and have changed over time. A key development was the replacement of gear-driven pull-handles with electronic push-buttons (see fig. 2.1). "You can rest your hand on the button," said the president of WMS Gaming of this

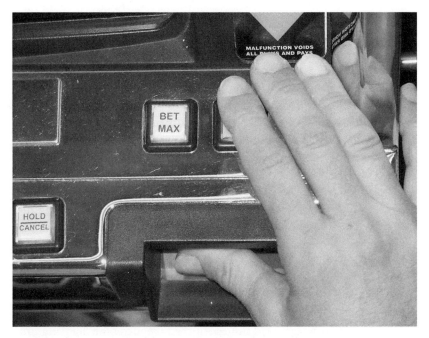

Figure 2.1. A gambler's hand resting on the console of a video poker termi-nal, his thumb positioned in the bill acceptor slot and his fingers poised to press the "Deal," "Draw," and "Bet Max" buttons. Photograph by the author.

development in 1992. "You don't ever have to move your hand."[10] "The effective difference in expediting play is dramatic," Cummings noted. "Averaging play at a rate of five games per minute pulling a handle would result in 300 games an hour. If instead the player uses the push-button, the number of games can double this rate of play, from 300 to 600 games each hour."[11] The introduction of video technology to gambling machines further accelerated play, removing the need to wait for mechanical reels to spin. Experienced video poker gamblers can play a hand every three to four seconds, completing an astonishing 900 to 1,200 hands an hour.[12] On "video slots" whose virtual reels "spin" rapidly, the rate is similar.[13] Some of these machines carry no buttons at all, instead featuring touch-screens so sensitive that they can detect the proximity of a finger before it has made direct contact. "A gaming machine is a very fast, money-eating device," said a Bally representative. "The play should take no longer than three and a half seconds per game."[14]

Innovations to the "money-eating" components of slot machines have been as important to speeding up play as push-buttons and touchscreens. Before the incorporation of bank hoppers to slot machines in the 1960s and '70s, a gambler who won more than twenty coins had to stop playing and wait until a slot attendant verified his win and paid him off before he could continue. "This didn't just slow down the play," remembered slot machine pioneer Warren Nelson in 1994, "it kind of suggested a closure, an end to the game ... it tempted the customer to cease the play and walk out the door with his winnings."[15] Since hoppers could dispense up to two hundred coins into the machine's payout tray, they increased "the probability that those coins would be played back into the machine" and at the same time ensured that gamblers could gather the wagering momentum critical to the flow of their play experience.

The introduction of bill acceptors to gambling machines further sped up play, allowing players to insert bills of large denomination and draw from credits displayed on a digital meter rather than stop to feed coins in one at a time (see fig. 2.1). Dematerializing money into an immediately available credit form not only disguised its actual cash value and thus encouraged wagering, it also mitigated the revenue-compromising limitations of human motor capacities by removing unwieldy coins from the gambling exchange. "Some players don't have very good motor skills," observed a representative from one game design company.[16] "If you have a machine that takes five or six nickels, that's time a player is spending to put in the coins and make sure they register," a casino marketer concurred. "Sometimes they put them in too fast or drop them, and that relates to dollars for the casino."[17] On coinless slots, players could "just start playing," as a trade magazine journalist happily put it in 1985.[18] They could also "just *keep* playing," since it was now easier to recycle their winnings back into the machine than to cash them out. Embedded bill acceptors became the industry standard in the 1990s, reducing the time it took to play by 15 percent and generating a 30 percent increase in the amount of money played.[19] Later on, we will see how the turn to so-called cashless gambling—in which gamblers play with tickets and magnetic-stripe cards rather than coins or cash—has further helped to overcome impediments to play associated with money insertion.

As suggested at the start of this chapter, the painstaking efforts of the gambling industry to organize the kinesthetic and temporal elements of machine play into a streamlined economy of production emulate techniques of behavioral management associated with nineteenth-century factories and related modern disciplinary environments (schools, armies, prisons). "To each movement," Michel Foucault has written of such techniques, "are assigned a direction, an aptitude, a duration; their order of succession is prescribed ... it is a question of extracting, from time, ever more available moments and, from each moment, ever more useful forces."[20] To extract economic value from individual bodies, their actions had to be precisely guided and fit into a quantifiable temporal frame. "Moments," a factory floor manager famously reported to Karl Marx in 1860, "are the element of profit."[21] Echoing the profit logic of temporal discipline, gambling consultant Cummings writes of "pruning dead time or unproductive motions from various phases of play [to get] more play into each time interval."[22] Like the management of machine workers' actions, the management of machine gamblers' actions aims to compress the greatest number of physical gestures into the smallest unit of time.

In 1939 the philosopher and cultural critic Walter Benjamin drew an extended analogy between gambling and the repetitive, serial, speeded-up process of industrial machine labor. "Gambling," he wrote, "even contains the workman's gesture that is produced by the automatic operation, for there can be no game without the quick movement of the hand by which the stake is put down or a card is picked up. The jolt in the movement of a machine is like the so-called coup in a game of chance."[23] Like workers caught up in the relentless movement of an assembly line (a scenario brilliantly satirized by Charlie Chaplin in *Modern Times*), gamblers were caught up in the relentless movement of betting, he suggested. Yet machine gamblers seated before player-centric consoles are caught in a somewhat different game; instead of struggling to coordinate "their own movements with the uniformly constant movements of an automaton," as Benjamin paraphrased Marx, they set their own pace of play. (In this respect, their experience also departs from the early forms of video gaming about which Sherry Turkle wrote in the 1980s: "The pace is never yours. The rhythm of the game belongs to the machine, the program decides."[24])

Silicon Gaming's "dynamic play rate" feature, devised in the late 1990s, is one example of a game innovation that enabled users to control the pace of play. The feature was incorporated into the Phantom Belle, a video poker machine that displayed the animated, disembodied hands of a card dealer on a supplementary video screen above the main play screen.[25] The hands dealt at the pace that gamblers played—slowly tossing cards to slower players, moving quickly for faster players, and disappearing altogether for the fastest of players. Game engineer Stacy Friedman demonstrated the dynamic play rate as we stood in the booth of the 2000 Gaming Expo. "If you play slow, it deals slow," he explained. "When you go fast, the game detects it and *adapts*." The patent for the dynamic play rate explicitly acknowledged the design rationale behind this "adaptive control method," noting that when "a player desires to play at a rate faster than the normal play rate, but his accelerated physical interaction (in inputting his money and making his selection or pulling a lever) has no effect on the play rate of the game, a degree of frustration sets in that interferes with his enjoyment of the game." When, however, the game can "adapt itself to player input, an enhanced sense of interaction between player and machine is created."[26] The dynamic play rate feature was designed to reset after pauses in play, readying itself to conform to the next player's speed.

Just as responsive, experience-based casino design entails "a constant adjustment of the building" to patrons' spatial movements, player-centric gambling machinery adjusts to the idiosyncratic range and rate of their wagering movements. Although the ultimate objective of this machinery (that is, to "increase the rate at which revenue can be generated for the proprietor of the machine," as stated in the dynamic play rate patent) remains the same as that of manufacturing machinery, designers' approach to this objective changes in the transition from the factory floor to the casino floor. In the latter context, there is a strong concern with the subjective state of the machine operator—his desires, his frustrations, his enjoyment, his sense of interaction.[27]

EXTENDING TIME-ON-DEVICE

As much as repeat machine gamblers want speed, they want to play for as long as possible. Their desire for "time-on-device," as the gambling industry terms it, moves in tandem with the industry's desire for continuous productivity. "The key is duration of play," a consultant told me. "I want to keep you there *as long as humanly possible*—that's the whole trick, that's what makes you lose."[28] "It's basically a matter of getting them into the seat and keeping them there," echoed a machine designer. "I'm trying to make the customer feel comfortable. Feel in that cocoon."[29]

To create this comfortable, ensconcing cocoon, designers outfit machines to accommodate any want or need that might arise for players. The various black boxes, panel inserts, and extra buttons that have appeared over the years on the surfaces of gambling devices embody the effort to anticipate players' every desire. "You want a situation where the customer can get anything they want when they sit down at your machine," said the owner of a Las Vegas tavern featuring slots.[30] Some individual machines are programmed with a "convergence of gaming opportunities" such that players can "explore, browse, and experiment with selections from a library of game variations in the same box, while never leaving their seats."[31] Others feature bingo ticket printers so that patrons playing them between bingo games do not waste time getting up to buy tickets. Still others carry tiny, embedded television monitors. "These emerging systems," Cummings explained in 1997, "permit players to view television shows or to enjoy closed circuit special events and personal messaging while they continue their gaming activities on the same machine. Players then do not need to exit the play area."[32] While the effectiveness of such features is debatable—for they risk distracting players from the task of "continuous gaming productivity"—their invention attests to the industry's anxiety over the possibility that gamblers will leave their seats. "In the industry's view," one designer of gambling machines told me, "the only valid reason for terminating play and leaving the machine is needing to go to the bathroom, a show starting, or your bankroll ends."[33]

To prevent termination of play for lesser reasons, computerized menus were developed for gambling machines in the 1990s. These allowed players to key requests into a pad of coded choices, directly and immediately communicating specific desires—for change, beverages, or mechanical assistance—to employees in the proximity wearing "vibrating call devices." In this way, wrote Cummings, "players can initiate service requests directly by transmitting a signal through the gaming system on which they are playing."[34] Newer versions take the form of an onscreen "service window" or "host" through which players enter their orders into a centralized system that dispatches live attendants. Equipping machines with channels along which players can signal their pressing wants and needs to the establishment and its greater technological resources preempts cessation of play by turning potential interruptions into opportunities for further engagement.

Complementing efforts to extend time-on-device by anticipating players' conscious desires, another set of design strategies operate at an unconscious level, much like the affective appeals of architecture and ambience. These strategies, which have gained increasing attention at trade shows and in industry publications, treat the machine unit as its own phenomenologically compelling mini-environment. Echoing interior designers' language of "private playing worlds" and players' language of the "zone," Bally's trademarked Privacy Zone cabinet, for instance, is constructed such that the play screen sits recessed inside a boxed frame, insulating players from the exterior world and creating a personal theater that "eliminates distractions and immerses players in their own private gaming environment." "[Machines] have become an environment in themselves, complete with lighting, signage and sound systems," read the description for a 2007 G2E panel called "Boosting Machine Productivity: Creating an Environment."

Like interior designers, machine designers strive to balance ambient intensities as a way to hold players in the balanced affective state of the zone. "We have five elements to work with—color, light, animation, sound, and space—and each can act as an attraction or an irritant," wrote an industry expert. "If the chase lights on the slot signs are running too fast, they make people nervous; if they run too slow, they put them to sleep. If the machine sound is too loud, it hurts the player's ears; if it's not loud enough, the energy level of the room suffers."[35] "You can definitely overstimulate a patron," confirmed a speaker for the 2006 G2E panel "Sensory Overload: Light, Sound and Motion on Slot Machines."

To prevent visual overstimulation, shrewd designers avoid signage that is too showy or bright, or that rises too high above machines, potentially drawing patrons' attention up and away from them. Likewise, they avoid signage bulbs that flicker too frenetically, too erratically, or too slowly. They take care to softly pixelate video monitors and to reduce their glare. Graphic engineers, whose color palette increased from 256 to millions of distinct colors over a relatively short period, strive for pleasing tones, imagery, and animation—nothing that might jar or unsettle a patron at play. WMS has recently introduced banks of machines with "emotive lighting" choreographed according to game outcomes, to reinforce play. Visuals should be "consistent with what players want," the company indicated in the G2E magazine advertisement that accompanied its 2006 What Players Want campaign.

The ad campaign addressed three of the human senses: sight, hearing, and touch, represented respectively by page-sized close-ups of a woman's eye, ear, and hand resting on the naked skin of her back (see fig. 2.2). These same body parts, at a more impressive scale, appeared in a promotional video that looped over and over on the large video panel that hung over WMS's exposition booth that year—as if to communicate their pride

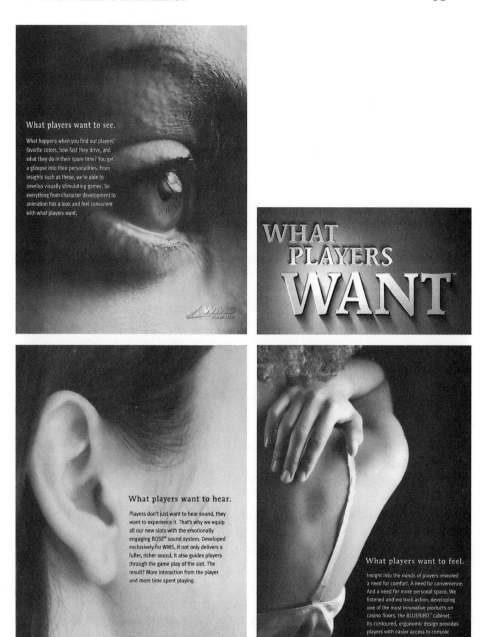

Figure 2.2. "What Players Want." Ad campaign by WMS Gaming, Inc. Printed in the Global Gaming Expo show magazine, 2005.

of place in the design process. Below, in the booth itself, the video was projected continuously from five-foot plasma screens attached to the ends of each carousel of machines on display. The point of the campaign was clear: in order to immerse gamblers in the experience of play and thereby increase their productivity, it was essential to augment slot machines' "affective grip" (to use Nigel Thrift's expression) by establishing a congruence between machine functions and the human sensorium.[36] WMS's latest iteration of this approach, called Experience Design, features "a suite of sensory innovations that heighten player experience."

Technological advances have spurred the trend in sensorially attentive design. Just as graphic designers' color palette and pixel count have increased exponentially, in the span of a single decade sound engineers have gone from using as few as fifteen sounds per game to an average of four hundred unique "sound events," each calibrated to encourage play while remaining in the background.[37] Sound, when properly configured, "can actually energize the player, keep him there longer," writes David Kranes, a consultant to the gambling industry.[38] "I can go longer if the machine sounds are right," a longtime machine gambler observed of her play. "Last weekend, the sounds were turned off on a machine I was playing, and even though it wasn't playing bad, I switched because I couldn't handle playing a silent machine—it didn't have the same flow to it."

In the days of coin play, when the industry's acoustic methodologies were cruder, sound served mainly to announce the gambling machinery and its promise to deliver rewards. Slot managers equipped their machines with stainless steel trays, for instance, so that falling money would create winning noises and thus stimulate patrons to gamble.[39] In the present era of noncoin gambling, audio engineers create digitized soundtracks to simulate cascading coins. One team "mixed several recordings of quarters falling on a metal tray and then fattened up the sound with the sound of falling dollars."[40] It is not only their digital form that distinguishes contemporary sound technologies from those of the past but also their function, which is not simply to amplify or "fatten" sound, but to *control* sound such that it provides an ongoing stream of action-inducing cues to gamblers. A case in point is Incredible Technologies' ContinuPlay— "sound technology that rewards steady play." As the WMS advertisement for sound tells us, "Players don't just want to *hear* sound, they want to *experience* it. That's why we equip all our new slots with the emotionally engaging BOSE sound system. It not only delivers a fuller, richer sound, it also *guides players through the game play of the slot.*" Such guidance prompts "more interaction from the player and more time spent playing" (see fig. 2.2).

Astute audio engineers have learned that the art of facilitating time-on-device involves paying as much attention to softening and equilibrating sound as to intensifying it. In the late 1990s, for example, the prescient audio director at the new company Silicon Gaming programmed its video slots to play every one of their different sounds in the universally pleasant key of C. To make sure the custom sound would blend smoothly with existing casino acoustics he sampled the noise of various slot floors, his aim being "to add a new and better track to the traditional sound, but not to clash with it."[41] Along similar lines, others have attempted to limit potentially disturbing elements of sound through the application of anti-noise technology. Positioning speakers to create a sound cone directly in front of players, Kranes tells us, is one way to "limit aural intrusion" and reduce fatigue.[42]

Following in the same path as sight and sound technologies, emerging tactile technologies seek to modulate and guide the gambling experience. Making the case that "connecting with users' sense of touch attracts them in a way sight and sound alone cannot," the Immersion Corporation uses haptic feedback technology to "integrate touch sensations into the human machine interface," creating "touchscreens that touch back" (see fig. 2.3). Through touch, players activate electromagnetic actuators behind the screens, each of which carries a specific vibro-tactile profile or "effect" of unique frequency, waveform, magnitude, and duration. The screen graphics seem to depress and release as if they are active buttons, responding to players with a reflex-rate snap, pulse, vibration, or push back. These effects give players a "definitive transactional confirmation" for every action they take, creating "a more intuitive, natural, and multisensory experience" that keeps them playing longer.[43] The Capacitive Touchscreen System (as Immersion's system has been renamed) affirms play gestures as a way to "capacitate" continued gambling.

Visual consistency, acoustic harmony, tactile confirmation: designers seek to extend time-on-device by creating an intimate reverberation between technical elements and the human senses. Ergonomic features are another means for lengthening gambling sessions, and work by creating a close fit between the player's body and the body of the machine. WMS's

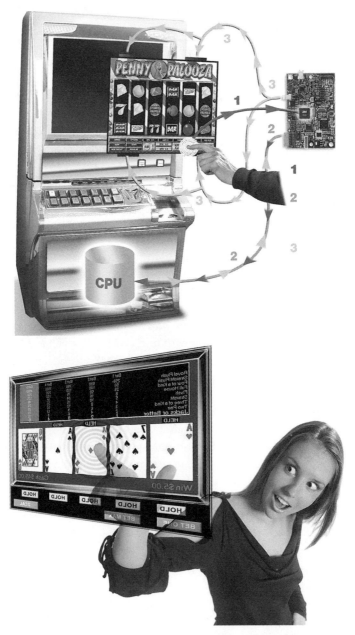

Figure 2.3. *Top*: Microtouch Capacitive Touchsense Technology by 3M. Available for download at 3m.com. *Bottom*: Touchscreens that touch back, by Immersion, Inc. Reproduced by permission of Immersion Corporation. Copyright © 2009 Immersion Corporation. All rights reserved.

advertisement on "what players want to feel," for instance, addressed not just the point of contact between finger and screen but the player's whole physical being. The ad text, appearing alongside the naked back of a woman, read: "contoured, ergonomic design provides players with easier access to console controls and more legroom for a better overall gaming experience" (see fig. 2.2).

To this same end, some years earlier a company called VLC had devised cabinets with screens that slanted at precisely 38 degrees. One of their advertisements, titled "Don't let Player Fatigue Cut Your Profits," explained the design rationale:

> Why should we force players to lean in? It's just not comfortable. We moved the players *closer to the screen*—just enough to keep their backs *snug against the backs of their chairs* (which was easy because our "no buttons" touchscreen *doesn't put a barrier* between the player and the screen). Now, because they can't slouch in their seats, they don't get tired as easily.

Instead of "forcing" an upright posture, VLC's supportive design prevented slouching by accommodating players' bodily inclinations; longer play was achieved by removing "barriers" between machine and person and fitting them "snugly" together, as a unit. IGT developed a similar slant-top machine cabinet in 2003, "realizing that their engineering-centric design culture had resulted in machines that were not always the most comfortable or intuitive for their players to use," as the creative director for the product indicates on his website (see fig. 2.4). Following this "small (r)evolutionary accomplishment," he recalls, designers across the industry were more likely to *"get a curve into a machine"* as a way to accommodate the natural curves of human bodies.[44]

The industry's increasing amenability to curves was evident during a G2E 2005 panel titled "Building a Better Mousetrap: The Science of Ergonomics," when a representative from Atronic Gaming described the development of her company's "e-motion" machine. A review of focus group data from around the world had revealed that players were complaining of arm pain from reaching to play without support, and that machines' sharp corners and hard metal were uncomfortable to lean into. "If you look at it from a player comfort point of view," she told the audience, *"everything would be smooth and rounded."* To enhance the smoothness of player experience, the prototype for the e-motion featured urethane wrist rests, left- and right-handed buttons, and an adjustable screen that moved up and down with a tiltable play field, positioning

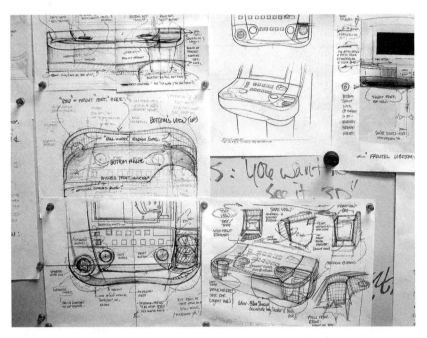

Figure 2.4. Magnetic whiteboard showing successive rounds of prototype refinement for IGT's ergonomically sleek slant top machine cabinet, the 2003 AVP. "IGT was taking a hard look at their traditional machine offering and realizing that their engineering-centric design culture had resulted in machines that were not always the most comfortable or intuitive for their players to use," recalls the creative director for the project on his website. The design objective: "Reconsider all component location and placement based upon ergonomic player preference and not manufacturing convenience." Courtesy of Nicholas Koenig, Creative Director of NKADesign.

players "within easy reach of all game controls." Insertion slots for players' reward cards were lowered so the bungee cords they often attach to them (so as not to lose the cards) would not dangle by their arms and obstruct play. Bill acceptors were lowered as well. "You want the person to be able to slide bills right in there as easy as possible, *without raising their arms at all.*" In test runs, e-motion machines were demonstrating impressive "occupancy rates" and time-on-device counts. "Ergonomics makes the slot player more productive," reported an industry journalist.[45]

Attention to consumer comfort—which Bally has gone so far as to trademark with its 2009 Comfort Zone consoles—has not always been linked to profit by the gambling industry. In 1987, the CEO of Gasser Chairs noted that only recently had casino operators begun to voice a concern that "the customer *be very comfortable* the entire time he is here."[46] The industry's then-emerging attempts to adapt its technologies and environments to the human form reflected changing priorities in the field of ergonomics in the 1980s, where efforts to fit people to machines were giving way to efforts to fit machines to people as personal computers became increasingly important to service-sector labor and the consumer economy.[47]

As in the workplace, in casinos a key initial focus of ergonomic design was on seating units. In the days when slot machines were marginal revenue earners they were built for transitory, standing play and were not typically outfitted with seats. Although stools and chairs became the standard by the 1980s, they were constructed primarily for sturdiness and longevity rather than comfort.[48] This changed in the mid-1980s when the Gasser Chair company began importing the new ergonomic codes of office chairs into the casino context, paying "meticulous attention to the height of seats in relation to slot machine handles" and designing the seats themselves to "eliminate hard, sharp edges coming in contact with the main arteries of the legs, which causes circulation to be cut and the legs to fall asleep."[49] "When somebody has poor circulation, that gets worse," commented Gasser himself in 1987, noting that his company's chairs would especially benefit elderly patrons "who typically spend hours seated at slot machines." His comment quite literally linked gamblers' blood flow to the flow of their time and money into the casinos' machines: ergonomics was economics. "Ergonomic design increases time-on-device," agreed his competitor Gary Platt in an advertisement for the X-tended Play seating line.

Like ergonomic machine design, the ergonomics of casino seating has evolved over time. "We have incredible slot stools," boasted the slot manager at Red Rock Casino in 2006. "They're state of the art and they all have rollers on the bottom, making it easy to move in and out.... [They're] height adjustable so you can adjust them to your comfort level, and they self-straighten and self-level when you get up from them."[50] IGT, incorporating the capacitive logic of haptics into the seating components on some of its newest games, has created chairs that subtly vibrate and pulse in accordance with certain game events, confirming players' experience of these events at the bodily level. The vibrating chairs, which integrate slot chair functions with slot machine functions, are part of IGT's newly trademarked development and design process, Human-Machine Interface (HMI). "Every aspect," the company writes of one product resulting from this comprehensive process, "was reviewed by well-respected industrial design experts to ensure the ultimate in player comfort, convenience, and playability … from the seat height and button surface to keyboard tilt and screen size, our engineers have created machines that will dramatically improve the player's experience."

Improving experience is a way to "monetize experience," as one industry member has phrased it, or to turn it into profit for the company.[51] IGT explains the rationale for HMI in precisely these terms: "Patrons who are physically and psychologically comfortable will occupy their seats for longer periods of time. This fact directly translates into increased revenue for the operation."[52]

Intensifying Financial Flow

While interior designers guide players to slot machines by eliminating obstructions in architectural space, machine designers expedite "continuous gaming productivity" by eliminating obstructions in the physical and temporal flow of the wagering activity. So far, we have examined how buttons, touchscreens, and ergonomics serve this function. Cash handling and access systems, the final auxiliary technologies we will consider in this chapter, do so by streamlining gamblers' access to money. More precisely, they shrink the time that transpires between a player's impulse to continue gambling and the means to continue gambling, thus minimizing the possibility for reflection and self-stopping that might arise in that pause. "If the objective is to attract customers to a slot machine in a manner that convinces them to insert currency and begin play, and to continue play once they have lost that money," asks an industry consultant of his readers in *Casino Enterprise Management*, "would it not make sense to make the component that accepts currency function flawlessly?"[53] When it comes to the state of suspended animation that gamblers call the zone and the industry calls continuous gaming productivity, an uninterrupted flow of play funds is as important as the speed and duration of the play activity itself. Technologies of financial flow have advanced rapidly over the past twenty-five years.

As recently as the mid-1980s, machine gamblers who wished to continue play when they ran out of money were required to leave their machines, make their way to an automatic teller machine (ATM) on the casino floor to acquire cash, and, finally, purchase rolls of coins from cashier cages or change attendants roving the floor with coin carts before returning to play. At that point, they had to break open the roll of coins and insert them, one by one. Although bill acceptors and digital credit counters removed cumbersome coins from the gambling exchange, they did not solve the problem of coins when it came to *payouts*. A slot-floor manager told me how important it was to keep machines' hoppers full in the days of coin play, in case patrons hit jackpots: "people didn't want to wait to be paid off, because even if it just took three minutes, to them it felt like twenty minutes; they want their machine going. So we had to do everything we could to get that machine filled as quick as possible."

Player loyalty programs solved the problem of time-consuming payouts for those who signed up, because wins could be transferred directly onto their player cards. The cards also made it easier for gamblers to replenish their play funds. In Cash Systems' Cashclub program, gamblers register for an account that ties their credit card, debit card, and checking account information directly to their player cards; when they run out of money, they can visit casino ATMs and transfer funds from these sources to their cards, then return to their machines to download the funds in the form of player credit. The similar PersonalBanker system lets players deposit funds into an account that they can directly draw upon from slot machines.

Ticket-in/ticket-out (TITO) technology, which debuted in 1999 and now runs in most casinos, made coin payouts obsolete even for gamblers without player loyalty cards by paying out credits in the form of bar-coded slips of paper printed instantly at the machine, redeemable at self-service kiosks or immediately reusable at another machine.[54] TITO quickly proved its revenue-generating power by reducing "downtime" on machines (i.e., the time wasted acquiring and handling coins or waiting for payoffs) and increasing the overall speed and magnitude of play by an impressive 20 percent.[55] Upon its introduction, this fully "cashless" system was promoted to gamblers as one of "unprecedented player convenience—they no longer need to wait for change or hand-paid jackpots, nor lug around heavy plastic cups and dirty their hands by handling coins."[56] For casinos the system did more than increase gambling revenue; it increased cost efficiencies as well, by eliminating the need for staff to fix coin jams, supply coins to players, or transport coins across the casino floor and feed them through coin-counting machines. TITO also freed up space for more gambling machines by replacing bulky cashier cages with compact kiosks.[57]

These kiosks have since become "one-stop" multipurpose ATMs, combining an array of cash-acquisition modalities in one unit. As early as 1997, casinos featured ATMs that incorporated debit and cash advance functions, allowing patrons to bypass daily withdrawal limits and "get as much cash as they want." "When the customers reach their ATM limit," explained a representative for Bank of America, "our system will allow them to access their credit card without a PIN to receive additional cash."[58] A later version of the system by Global Cash Access involved the first credit card designed specifically for use in casinos. The Arriva card treated cash advances made in casinos as "entertainment purchases" and did not penalize customers with high fees or immediate interest as on typical credit cards; on the contrary, card advances earned consumers reward points.[59] The card was offered on demand, supplying patrons with credit lines of up to $10,000 within minutes. Global Cash Access described the care they took to streamline the cash-acquisition process at their kiosks:

> Rather than just declining [players], our message will say that they have exceeded their daily limit but we will ask them if they would like to attempt a point of sale debit transaction. *So more money is allowed.* If for some reason they have exceeded that limit as well, we further ask if they would like the credit card cash advance. And our limits are much higher. *We give them every opportunity to access cash* on their debit card, on their point of sell debit card or on their credit card.[60]

Programmed to circumvent any obstacle to cash access that might arise, the system ensured that gamblers could *continue* the transaction, even if they were initially declined.[61]

As gamblers attest, drawing on bank accounts and credit sources tends to accelerate the exhaustion of their play funds, even as it allows them longer sessions in the zone. Nancy, a nurse at a local hospital, linked the intensification of her machine play—which eventually led to her bankruptcy—to the introduction of ATM machines in casinos. "I used to bring cash with me," she told me on a Sunday morning at her home in 1995, "and when it was gone I'd have no choice: I'd have to leave. That all changed with the ATMs." From a stack of mail she withdrew a thick bank statement and unfolded it on the kitchen table between us. Shuffling through its pages, she found an example. "Here's what happened on a Thursday night last month," she told me, spinning the statement 180 degrees so I could read it. Down the left column, the statement indicated a succession of ATM withdrawals that took place over a period of five and a half hours, starting at 9 p.m. The initial withdrawal was for $100, the next for $60, then 40, 40, 40, and 20—by which point she had reached her $300 limit. When her limit was renewed after midnight, the withdrawals continued until she once again reached her daily limit. When she left at 2:30 a.m., the total remaining in her account was $109. Including withdrawal fees for her eleven visits to the ATM, she had lost a total of $627.50.

The bank statement was not only a financial and chronological index of Nancy's cash withdrawals but also an index of her subjective withdrawals into the zone: between its lines, one could read the affective ebb and flow of her play sessions—the spikes of urgency that drove her trips to the ATM, and the periods of suspension in between. Her access to the zone was a function of her access to cash; the gambling machine mediated the first, and the automatic teller machine mediated the second. Together, the two machines facilitated her affective regulation as well as the transfer of her funds to the casino. "When you interact with these machines," a gambler named Katrina observed of video slots and ATMs in a letter she wrote me, "it induces a kind of disconnection from reality and real money can subtly morph into play money. I see these new systems like TITO pushing this tendency even further, because the disconnection happens more smoothly." Much as interior design calibrates the presentation of sound and light in a way that guides player experience without intruding too jarringly upon it, TITO and its fellow financial tools make money available to gamblers in a way that obscures its everyday value and helps to convert it into the currency of the zone.

In the eyes of the gambling industry, the ultimate financial access system is one that enables gamblers to replenish their play funds while *remaining at their machines* instead of pausing to execute a withdrawal, transfer, deposit, or advance. By 1997 it had become possible for players to directly access their checking accounts from the machines, transferring up to $1,000 per day in the form of play credits.[62] Nevada deferred approval for this technology in 2003, for it came too close to violating a state law that bans the merging of ATM functions into slot machines (on the reasoning that this might facilitate "impulse play" and exacerbate problematic gambling behavior).[63] But given the numerous jurisdictions without this legal obstacle, gambling technology companies have continued to develop systems that allow direct access to finances from machines.

In partnership with Bally, for instance, Cash Systems introduced Powercash, in which players can draw funds from various sources (checking accounts, credit cards, or debit cards) directly into their player club card while remaining at their gambling machines: "Powercash transactions are completed right at the gaming device, allowing your player to spend more time playing."[64] Global Cash Access, in partnership with IGT, designed a version of this financial access system to work with TITO, called the Ticket-Out Debit Device (TODD). TODD presents a small terminal mounted on the slot machine through which patrons access funds by swiping their bank debit card and entering the requested amount, which is then credited directly to the machine (unlike typical ATMs, there is no limit as long as funds are available).[65]

In jurisdictions where slot machines are not permitted to perform ATM functions, a stand-alone edition of the technology called EDITH (or the Electronic Debit Interactive Terminal Housing) may be positioned at the end of each slot machine aisle.[66] EDITH manages to bring funding sources closer to gambling machines without quite merging them into the game unit. Bringing funds even closer to gamblers are mobile ATMs such as Cash Systems' wireless handheld device: "The casino patron is simply presented the Stay-n-Play device and they swipe their ID, credit or debit card, and sign the receipt."[67] Although Nevada has rejected such portable units, they are in use elsewhere and the industry expects that they will eventually be integrated into casinos everywhere.[68] Allowing consumers to use their *own* handheld devices (smartphones, iPads, and the like) to wirelessly transfer funds to slot machines, a practice common in Europe, is another innovation the industry expects to reach the United States as regulators "catch up to the technology." "Regulations are the only element in the way of even more cash-access convenience in the casino," write the authors of a 2010 IGT white paper.[69]

In the meantime, a company called Automated Currency Instruments has attempted to bridge the separation of bank machine and gambling machine in a different way—by devising an ATM that "becomes part of the entertainment experience in the casino." In this convergence of banking and play, "entertaining displays on the [ATM] unit keep the patron interested and entertained while he or she is waiting for the transaction to complete."[70] Instead of endowing gambling machines with ATM functionality, this system endows ATMs with ludic functionality, the very act of financial withdrawal becomes an act of play.

Asymmetric Collusion

Departing from Marxian accounts of industrial production in which factory laborers become alienated from themselves in the process of operating machinery, Foucault characterized the relationship between humans and disciplinary machinery as one of connection rather than estrangement, in which "a coercive link with the apparatus of production" joined a given body to the object it handled.[71] Although linkage is certainly a more pertinent descriptor than alienation for the contemporary gambler-machine relationship, the material in this chapter suggests that the link in question is forged not through coercion, but through a kind of *collusion* between the structures and functions of the machine and the cognitive, affective, and bodily capacities of the gambler.

The turn from coercion to collusion fits with Deleuze's characterization of contemporary society as a "mutation of capitalism" in which a logic of discipline and restriction has given way to a logic of control whose protocol is the regulation of continuous and flowing movement of bodies, affects, and capital.[72] Although machine gamblers act within the enclosed space of the casino, seated before the consoles of stationary devices and repeating the same routines, they tap into a flow of credit that can bring them into the flowing nonspace of the zone and allow them to be "continuously productive" for the casino as long as that credit lasts. "Textbook capitalist exploitation thrives in peaceful and productive coexistence with the play-drive of the exploited," Dibbell observes of the phenomenon he calls ludocapitalism.[73] The affective economy of machine gambling is one among other expressions of present-day value production that are "simultaneously voluntarily given and unwaged, enjoyed and exploited," writes Thrift.[74] Design strategies for rendering continuous productivity match gamblers' desire for the insulating continuity of the zone and vice versa; gamblers become collaborators in the optimization of industry profits.

Scholars of the so-called experience economy have picked up on this tendency toward collaboration in which corporate concerns "lie ever closer to the concerns of the consumer" and products are understood to emerge through a dynamic process of "co-creation."[75] The sociologist Michel

Callon and his colleagues, for instance, have described consumer product design as an iterative process of successive adjustment in which "what is sought after is *a very close relationship between what the consumer wants and expects*, on the one hand, *and what is offered*, on the other."[76] They construe this relationship as a symmetrical "collaboration between supply and demand" wherein corporations and consumers meet on even ground, holding roughly equal hands, in order to mutually satisfy their respective desires. Echoing the corporate language of user-centrism, they write of a "mutual adaptation between what a firm proposes and what consumers want."[77]

This chapter offers a somewhat more skeptical reading of the rhetoric of symmetry espoused by corporate designers. The player-centric design of gambling technology and its adaptive attunement to consumers' desires, affects, and bodies is neither traditionally exploitative—for its instrumental use of others is collusive rather than coercive, and does not engender alienation—*nor* symmetrical. The respective contributions that gamblers and machines bring to the collusion are not equal; on the contrary, an apparent alignment between "what players want" and the methods of productivity and efficiency at work in the gambling industry obscures radically different ends.

For extreme machine gamblers, the experience of play is an end in itself—an "autotelic" zone beyond value as such, in that "no other reward than continuing the experience is required to keep it going."[78] Conversely, for the gambling industry the zone is a means to an end; although it carries no value in and of itself, it is possible to derive value from it. This is achieved by "expediting" its speed, continuity, and intensity, as Cummings indicated above in her uncanny echo of Martin Heidegger's discussion of that word in his well-known essay on technology: "expediting is always itself directed from the beginning toward furthering something else, i.e. toward driving on the maximum yield at minimum expense."[79]

In effect, gamblers' drive to remain indefinitely suspended in the zone is rerouted, via the technological detours of the gambling industry, toward a destination of complete depletion. "The more you manage to tweak and customize your machines to fit the player," Sylvie Linard of Cyberview advised her colleagues of player-centrism, "the more they play to extinction; it translates into a dramatic increase in revenue."[80] The point of "extinction" to which she referred is the point at which player funds run out. At that point, the machine ceases to respond to the player and the asymmetry of their collusive encounter comes to the fore; the gambler not only *can't* win, but *isn't playing to win*, while the gambling industry is playing to win all along (its objective, Cummings told us, is "the constant cycling of player action toward large numbers of wagers in order to place the gaming operation at the greatest win advantage relative to players"[81]). The relationship that exists between players and the industry is not so much a clash between two systems of value as it is an asymmetric interdependency between a system of value extraction that plays by the economic rules of the market, and a fleeting zone of nonvalue in which those rules are, for the player, suspended. "Man is no longer man enclosed," Deleuze writes, "but man in debt."[82]

3

PROGRAMMING CHANCE

The Calculation of Enchantment

I decided to go to school to learn slot machines—how to take them apart, and how to build them: the components, the wires, all the little parts. I became a slot machine mechanic. I was really good at the electronics, the math. I learned so much. I could take those things apart and put them back together in my sleep. I had the highest graduating score that school ever had.

I thought that learning how the machines worked would demystify them and that they wouldn't hold such intrigue for me anymore, because I would understand how their guts worked—really understand. But the truth is, even after taking them apart and putting them back together again, you still don't know how they work. The one thing I never built was the chips. There's that one little mystery chip in there that nobody explains to you, and it's what spins the reels and shuffles the cards.

My playing never eased up at all. At the school they used to have a couple of machines set up and I'd play those on coffee breaks. I got a night job with a company that built slot machines. I would assemble parts for the machines, then I'd go up the street and gamble all during lunch hour, on the same machines I was building.

—Rose

INTERIOR DESIGN may guide casino patrons to gambling machines and an optimally configured interface may increase their spending and lengthen their stay, but the hidden processes by which the machines deliver wins and losses are what set continued play in motion. Rose became a slot machine mechanic with the hope that an education in the machines' inner workings might release their hold on her. Above, she attributed the failure of this project to that "one little mystery chip" that nobody had explained to her. The chip in question contains the game's script for chance—the interlocking set of calculative operations that "operationalize chance," as one designer phrased it, so as to determine game outcomes. This calculative script serves two quite different functions: at the point of programming it lends a measure of predictability to chance, informing casino operators of the cumulative returns they can expect *over time*; at the point of play, which always occurs *in time*, it renders chance ever-more inscrutable and enchanting.[1]

In the early twentieth century, the sociologist Max Weber proposed that "man has chased [the gods] away and has rationalized and made calculable and predictable what in an earlier age had seemed governed by chance."[2] Forces of calculability and predictability, he anticipated, would increasingly "disenchant" the world such that "there are no mysterious, incalculable forces that come into play."[3] Gambling machines at once exemplify Weberian disenchantment and give it a twist. They are vehicles of disenchantment in the sense that they are "complex calculative devices that operate to redistribute gamblers' stakes in a very precise, calibrated, and 'scientific' way," allowing their owners to leverage chance for profit and accurately calculate likely long-term gains.[4] Yet in the moment of the gambling encounter the machines operate as vehicles of enchantment, galvanizing what Zygmunt Bauman has described as "human spontaneity, drives, impulses, and inclinations resistant to prediction and rational justification," or in Weber's words, "irrational and emotional elements that escape calculation."[5] They are by no means divested of "mysterious, incalculable forces" but rather abundantly invested with them.

The enchanting aspects of the modern gambling machine do not imply a failure of its disenchanted design process, for they are a direct product of that process—a kind of "manufactured incalculability," to use the sociologist of risk Ulrich Beck's phrase,[6] or "contrived contingency," to borrow a concept from the anthropologist and game scholar Thomas Malaby.[7] Writing of the British National Lottery, a Weberian scholar has observed that "rational logics and processes can themselves be (re)enchanted from within, or become the vehicles of (re)enchantment. (Re)enchantment can be a thoroughly rationally organized business."[8] "One need no longer have recourse to magical means in order to implore the spirits," Weber himself noted. "Technical means and calculations perform the service."[9]

As we will see, the sense of magic and wonder that gambling machines provoke in their users has a great deal to do with the hiddenness and opacity of the "means and calculations" by which they mediate chance. Unlike card games played around tables, the rules and odds of which are transparent, the inner mechanisms and odds of gambling devices have always been concealed in a box.[10] "There is only one game in Nevada where the player doesn't know what his odds are," a gaming regulator for the State of Nevada has remarked, referring to the slot machine. "There isn't an establishment that would agree with posting those odds on that slot machine because you are going to take away the mystery, the excitement and entertainment and risk of playing."[11] Purposive obfuscation, his comment suggests, is key to the seductive appeal of gambling machines.

Following in Rose's footsteps, this chapter ventures beneath the exteriors of these "beautiful vaults," as IGT's vice president of engineering and design has called them, in an attempt to reverse-engineer the calculative logic by which they convert chance into enchantment—and by extension, into profit.[12] The story that emerges is one of increasing control over odds (on the part of the gambling industry) by way of sequential technological disconnects between the game that gamblers see before them and with which they interact, and the actual mechanisms that determine its outcomes. When it comes to the contrivance of randomness in games, Malaby notes, there has been a turn from "explicit" means such as dice rolling or deck shuffling to the "implicit" means of computer programming.[13] This is certainly the case for gambling machines, whose mechanical components have been superseded by a digital infrastructure. "The commodity of the bet, already ephemeral, is further dematerialized with the move to computerization," writes the sociologist Richard Woolley.[14] Tracing the move from mechanical to digital reveals how the asymmetric relationship between industry and gambler plays out at the miniature scale of the microchip and its programming.

MECHANICAL TO DIGITAL: ENGINEERING THE "REALLY NEW GOD"

Contemporary gambling machines are close relatives of the coin-operated vending and amusement devices that appeared during the American

Figure 3.1. *Top*: Slot machine assembly line at International Gaming Technology's production facilities in Reno, Nevada. Available for download from media bin at IGT.com. *Bottom*: Inside view of a three-reel slot machine. 2009. Photograph by Rose Petal; image from bigstock.com.

Industrial Revolution in the last quarter of the nineteenth century, doling out food, gasoline, candy, and occasionally less material goods—magic tricks, fortunes, love tests, or advice.[15] Gambling machines distinguished themselves from their coin-operated kin by making money itself the object of reward and by adding an element of chance to the transaction: consumers could not be certain ahead of time how much, if anything, the machine might return. This formula proved immensely successful for gambling purveyors. "No other machine was ever invented from which the profits derived were so fabulous on so small an investment, and with so little effort," observed a social scientist in 1950.[16]

The forerunner of the modern gambling machine was invented in Brooklyn in the early 1880s, based on draw poker. The countertop contraption contained five drums with fifty card faces, five of which flipped up into a viewing window after a player set the drums in motion by pulling a side handle. Versions of this model, some with the cards affixed to five reels, became popular in cigar stands and bars across the country, and were known as "nickel-in-the-slots." Since the devices lacked the capacity to read and dispense proportionate rewards for the wide range of possible winning combinations, establishments paid wins in drinks, cigars, or cash.[17]

In 1898 a mechanically gifted Bavarian immigrant named Charles August Fey made automatic payouts feasible by mounting cards on just three reels, thereby reducing the range of winning combinations to a manageable number for a payout mechanism. A year later, he replaced the card faces with symbols, introducing his famous Liberty Bell, the prototype for the modern reel-spinning slot machine. The game featured three spring-loaded reels, each carrying five symbols—horseshoes, bells, hearts, spades, and diamonds.[18] When three bells matched up across the central payline, a prize of ten nickels was rendered. The reels rotated around a supporting metal shaft connected to a handle mechanism and a braking system, and a timing bar stopped the reels one at a time from left to right to create suspense. In the mid-1900s, Herbert Stephen Mills, otherwise known as the "Henry Ford of slots," increased the number of symbols or "stops" on each reel from ten to twenty, thereby decreasing players' odds of winning a jackpot and allowing machines to offer larger prizes and still remain profitable.[19] He also expanded the viewing window on the reels so that players could see rows of symbols above and below the payline, increasing the likelihood that they would experience a "near miss"—the sensation of nearly having won produced by the sight of winning symbols adjacent to the payline.

Almost as quickly as slot machines became popular, they became objects of the temperance movement's crusade against vice. Starting in the 1900s, sledgehammer-wielding reformists frequently demolished Liberty Bells and their successors, and a number of cities and states banned them. Yet antigambling laws were largely ignored or circumvented, and the technology continued to evolve. In jurisdictions where they were illegal, gambling devices were often disguised as gum vending machines, featuring fruit symbols (cherries, lemons, oranges, and so forth) on their reels and offering prizes that could be redeemed for cash. Allowing slots to flourish despite prohibition, ingenious subterfuge of this sort peaked during the Depression of the 1930s when slot income became a means of survival for gas stations, drug stores, and other small businesses.[20] The slot industry thrived in the postwar years until the Johnson Act of 1951, which effectively abolished black market slots in states where they were illegal. By the 1960s slot machines were outlawed everywhere but in Nevada and on military bases.

Slot machines underwent a significant transformation in 1963 with the incorporation of electromechanical technology that enabled manufacturers to control the motion of reels with electrical motors and a circuit board of switches rather than mechanical springs and gears.[21] Removing the motion mechanisms from the reels protected slot machines from tilting, shaking, and other physical abuse that could affect outcomes.[22] Once they became reliable, notes a historian, "the attention of designers shifted to maximizing the devices' potential to attract and retain gamblers."[23] While casino managers appreciated the tamper resistance of electromechanical machines, players liked the fact that their motor-driven hoppers could render unprecedented automatic payouts of up to five hundred coins, which meant larger and more frequent payouts.

Digital microprocessors (computer chips with memory) came on the scene of machine gambling in 1978, endowing the devices with further security and appeal. Just as motors and switches had replaced gears and springs, now digital pulses of electricity drove the motion of slot reels. The inventor of this technology articulated its rationale in his patent application: "It is desirable to provide an amusement apparatus which is *operable in much the same manner as mechanical slot machines,* insofar as the user is concerned, but which … cannot be disturbed."[24] Although players continued to interact with reels, the outcomes of their spins were now determined by a digital entity whose workings were thoroughly opaque to them.

The "mystery chip," as Rose called it earlier, is programmed with mathematical algorithms that execute a game's particular scoring scheme and predetermined hold percentage (or "house edge"), working in concert with a random number generator (RNG) to generate its outcomes. Even as a gambling device sits idle, its RNG cycles through possible combinations of reel symbols or cards at approximately one thousand per second.[25] The device is in perpetual motion, indifferent to the presence or absence of players. When a player initiates a game by pulling a handle or pressing a SPIN button, its program "polls" the RNG, whereupon it generates whichever numbers it happens to be cycling through at that exact moment—one for each of the reels displayed. These generated numbers, which typically fall between one and four billion, are fed through an algorithm that translates them—by a process known in computer programming as "indirection" or "indirect reference"—into stops on the microprocessor's "virtual reels."[26] The selected virtual reel positions are then communicated to the correlating positions on the actual, physical reels. All this is decided instantaneously, before a game's reels stop spinning. "Operating the machine requires that you pull the handle," a journalist explained in 1980, "but by then, you're no longer gambling—you're simply activating the readout."[27]

A year after electromechanical technology had been incorporated into slot machines, the French philosopher and sociologist Jacques Ellul argued that technology was becoming increasingly autonomous, diminishing the role of the humans who made and operated it. "Man is reduced to the level of a catalyst," he wrote in 1964. "He resembles a slug [fake token] inserted into a slot machine: he starts the operation without participating in it."[28] Ellul would likely have seen further evidence of increasing technological autonomy in computerized slot machine gambling, in which players quite literally become mere catalysts for autonomous machine processes.

Yet gambling companies have taken care to preserve the illusion of a mechanically actuated reel mechanism so as to perpetuate players' sense of being involved with a game that reacts to them in a kinetically lively and direct manner. Some companies, for instance, initially rigged the handles of their new machines "with springs and weights to simulate the feel of the original item."[29] "Next time you play a Bally slot," the company's president instructed players in 1981, "pull the handle very slowly and notice how you feel the way the reels back up.... We've strived to retain that feeling. We've kept the mechanical connection to our reel assembly."[30] The display of spinning reels and the carefully cultivated "feel" of the handle evoked a mechanical causality that had become obsolete on digital slot machines. Although few slots today have handles (when they do, they are called "legacy levers"), the presentation and spinning of their reels continues to suggest that a mechanism is being actuated in direct response to their actions.

The illusion is harder to preserve on video slots, whose fully digitized reels "spin" by means of computer animation. Yet game manufacturers have found ways to make these, too, appear three dimensional. WMS's Transmissive Reels "marry" mechanical to video reels by placing blank three-dimensional reels behind a semi-transparent video screen that projects graphically rich video symbols onto them as they spin. "We wanted to be sure that we wouldn't alienate video or mechanical players," said a representative of the hybrid technology.[31] Bally's Transparent Reels (now called Interactive Reels) likewise "blur the lines between video and mechanical-reel slots," superimposing a screen over actual, electromechanical reels so as to generate "animated effects which appear to float in front of the reels" during bonus rounds.[32] IGT's patented REELdepth technology works somewhat differently, producing the visual effect of "true depth" by way of "an ingenious layering of two or more Liquid Crystal Displays"—the same method used to make "multi-layer maps of war zones," the company notes. REELdepth "creates the illusion that players are playing spinning reel machines, as they mimic the look and vibration of their mechanical counterparts."[33] Paradoxically, advances in digital technology enable gambling machines to better pose as analog devices, communicating a physical functionality and degree of user control that no longer exist.

To accentuate the illusion of control, some slot machines are designed so that players can manually terminate the spinning of one or all reels rather than wait until they run their full course—either by pressing a STOP button, by pressing the SPIN button a second time, or by touching one or more reels on the video screen.[34] Although game outcomes are determined at the precise instant that the SPIN button is initially touched, gamblers using such "stop" features seem to feel they have an effect on outcomes and are known to persist at play for significantly longer periods than they otherwise would.[35]

Seeking to engender this same compelling sense of efficacy, secondary "bonus games" on video slots invite gamblers to perform actions over which they seem to have control (but do not). Anchor Gaming's 2000 game Strike It Rich, for instance, presented players with a bonus game in which the object was to guide the trajectory of a bowling ball on a screen using a tracking device. Although the device enabled players to lift the bowling ball on the video screen, aim it, and roll it toward the virtual pins, the RNG determined where the ball would land long before its simulated roll came to an end. IGT's race-car-themed bonus game similarly let players move a race car with a joystick, lending them a false sense of influence over the car's movement. The point of such games is to give players "the feeling that they control the outcome of the event," as a company product profile indicated in 2000.[36] Although one might assume that such a feeling would be disenchanting rather than enchanting, in fact it gives gamblers a sense that they are able to "animate" the gambling machine and thereby exert a sort of magical efficacy over its determinations of chance—which, at the same time, remain obscure and mysterious to them.

The opaque internal operations by which gambling machines arrive at and deliver their verdicts are a source of great wonderment and conjecture among gamblers, as is evident in the countless discussions that gamblers initiate on Internet forums. "Knowing it's computerized doesn't really explain anything," Rose commented. "That just makes it *more* of a mystery." "One of the great questions in philosophy," begins an article in the gambling magazine *Casino Player*, "is how the body of man, which is mechanical and concrete, can contain the element of mind, which is ephemeral. This has come down to the simple statement that we have a 'ghost' or 'god' in the machine. So too with today's slots."[37] Evoking the ephemeral, ghostlike will of the random number generator, some in the industry call this component the Really New God.[38] "The RNG runs on a computer chip, but people act like it's casting a spell," a designer told me.

Scholars of technology have noted that people tend to attribute agency to computerized devices (much as they attributed agency to mechanical automata earlier in history). Lucy Suchman links this tendency to the fact that computers are "internally opaque and liable to unanticipated behavior."[39] As Sherry Turkle has observed, children often personify electronic toys that fail to act in a predictable, consistent manner and thus seem to cheat: "If you cheat, you're alive," they told her.[40] The degree of fascination that a given machine holds for its users, she argues, is directly related to the degree of unpredictability and aliveness that it conveys. The joining of computerized technology to the slot machine—a device whose very purpose is to convey chance to users—is a particularly enchanting union. At once programmed and capricious, the digital gambling machine commands as much if not more fascination than its fully mechanical predecessors.[41]

The intrigue around slot machines' delivery of outcomes—and the workings of RNGs in particular—has spawned a robust trade in print and online educational material. In popular gambling magazines, alongside articles with catchy titles like "Mystery of the Machine," "Spooky Stuff," and "ESP" (in which gamblers share their "outer limit experiences" with machines), columns such as "Slot Statistics 101," "Myths and Misconceptions about Slot Machines," and "Knowledge is Power" focus on dispelling gamblers' conviction that machines somehow act deliberately. "The RNG is not alive," writes the author of a column called Beginner's Corner in *Strictly Slots*. "It's merely crunching numbers according to prearranged rules. It doesn't know whether you are winning or losing. It doesn't know when somebody new sits down to play. Nor does it care."[42]

The uneducated gambler, experts often recount, may walk away from a machine at which he has had no luck, only to become upset when he witnesses another patron win on the very next spin—feeling that the newcomer has "stolen" what rightfully belonged to him. In fact, they explain, even if an individual had continued at the machine, it is virtually impossible that he would have pressed the button at the same exact millisecond as the subsequent winning gambler, thereby triggering the RNG to generate the identical winning outcome. "You'll have people who swear they know exactly when to hit a button to make something happen, but it's just not the case," a designer has commented.[43] The author of a popular book for gamblers, himself a former game designer, points out that even if a gambler knew the pattern of an RNG's "cycle," as some do, it would still be impossible to "catch" a particular moment in that cycle: "The average person has a 50 to 350 millisecond reaction time, and mechanical and electrical delays in the machine can vary from 16 to 50 milliseconds between plays."[44] There is a mismatch, he suggests, between human capacities to process and respond to information, and those of the digital technology. This mismatch, one could further suggest, reflects the larger asymmetry between designers and players, technologies of disenchantment and states of enchantment.

LENGTHENING THE ODDS: VIRTUAL REEL MAPPING

Even for those who grasp the workings of the RNG, it is what happens next—the conversion of a number that has been randomly generated from a pool of nearly four billion into a physical reel stop that is part of a radically more limited pool of outcomes—that tends to stymie understanding. The concealed nature of the operation, along with machine events and displays that seem to represent its process when in fact they do not (the time delay of spinning reels, for example), compounds gamblers' confusion, obfuscating cause and effect in the experience of play. What exactly goes on in the conversion of random values to reel stops? "Instead of accessing some resource directly," writes gaming guru John Robison of machine programming, "you go through an intermediate step. You can do all sorts of wonderful things in that intermediate step."[45]

One of these "wonderful things" is called virtual reel mapping, a technique patented in 1982 for controlling game odds independently of a machine's actual reels. The invention was meant to overcome the continuing limitations posed by the structure of physical reels. Although digital microprocessing had turned physical reels into a mere display of the computer-determined outcome, there remained a one-to-one correlation between the number of stops they contained—which by 1970 had become 22—and those on its ghostly analog or "virtual" reels. Since the maximum number of combinations possible on such machines was 22 × 22 × 22, or 10,648, the odds of hitting a jackpot on a machine with one jackpot symbol per reel were 1 in 10,648. Thus a $1 machine could not offer a jackpot larger than $10,648 or it would risk losing money; the jackpot would have to be *under* $10,648 to ensure the house a profit.

How could game manufacturers get around this constraint, or "lengthen the odds," to use gambling parlance? They tried making machines with larger reels to accommodate more symbols, as well as machines with extra reels, but players avoided such models. When interacting with the larger-reeled, extra-reeled devices, they intuitively grasped that their chances had been diminished by the addition of symbols. Another way to lengthen the odds was to replace physical reels with a video display of simulated reels that could accommodate an infinite number of blanks and symbols. This became possible in the 1970s with the advent of video games, yet consumers were not yet familiar with screen-based technology and tended to distrust it. Although this distrust was to dissolve by the mid-1990s (as we will see in the next chapter), the mathematician and inventor Inge Telnaes provided a striking interim solution in the form of virtual reel mapping, also called "disproportionate reels" or "weighted reels."[46]

Machines using this technology continue to display 22 stops per reel—11 blanks and 11 winning symbols—yet their virtual reels can be configured to accommodate as many stops as designers like, sometimes hundreds. As on all computerized slot machines, when gamblers press the SPIN or BET button, the value generated by the RNG at that instant is translated into one of the virtual reel stops, each of which has an equal chance of being selected. However, because there are more virtual than actual reel stops, a secondary "mapping" program must be written to translate the virtual stops selected by the RNG into actual stops. The "wonderful thing" that can be done in this intermediate step is to "map" far more virtual stops to low-paying or nonpaying blank positions on the actual, physical reel than to winning positions (see fig. 3.2).[47]

The disparity between actual and virtual reels gave game manufacturers a considerably more precise way to control game outcomes, making it possible for them to promise huge jackpots on the outcomes with the slimmest mathematical odds.[48] On a machine whose virtual reels have 64 stops each with only one stop mapped to a jackpot symbol, the chances of hitting that symbol on all three reels to win the jackpot are 1 in 64^3, or 262,144. The machine could therefore offer a jackpot of up to $262,144 without losing money. On a machine with 512 virtual stops, the odds of a jackpot would be as rare as 1 in 137 million—giving the house a safe enough edge to offer $20 or $30 million prizes and still ensure long-term profit.[49] This unprecedented mathematical flexibility endowed gambling machines with a hitherto elusive "volatility" (or potential for dramatic wins), redoubling their market appeal. Virtual reel mapping "revolutionized the slot machine industry just as much as Charles Fey did when he invented the slot machine in the first place," said an employee of IGT, the company that eventually bought the rights to the patent.[50] As industry expert Frank Legato has written, the invention "was the primary impetus for the meteoric rise of popularity in slot machines."[51]

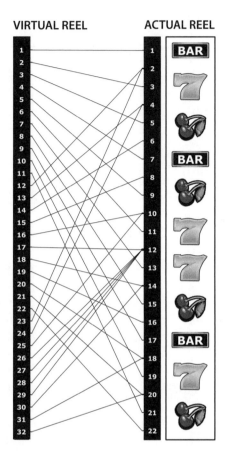

Figure 3.2*a*: Educational illustration of virtual reel mapping for a machine containing 32 virtual stops and 22 actual stops. The first 11 positions on the 32-stop virtual reel are mapped to the 11 symbols on the actual reel, but the rest are mapped to blanks, such that the odds of hitting a winning symbol are less than they appear to be. In addition, via a technique called "clustering," a disproportionate number of virtual stops are mapped to blank spaces just above or below the jackpot symbols. This ensures that they will appear more often above or below the payline than they would by chance alone, enhancing the "near miss" sensation among players. Courtesy of Game Planit, Inc.

If an understanding of the RNG reveals that the *spinning* of reels has no bearing on game outcomes, an understanding of Telnaes's mapping technique reveals that the reels themselves have no bearing on game outcomes. He stated as much in the application he filed with the US Patent and Trademark Office: "In this invention the physical reels are only used as a display of the random number generated results and are not the game itself as in standard slot machines."[52] *Not the game itself*: Virtual reel mapping enacts yet another remove between the game with which players interact and the mechanisms that determine its outcomes. Even more than the RNG, this technology shifted game developers' creative focus from the structure of the machine—the feel of its handle, the circumference of its reels—to its mathematical programming. For the first time it

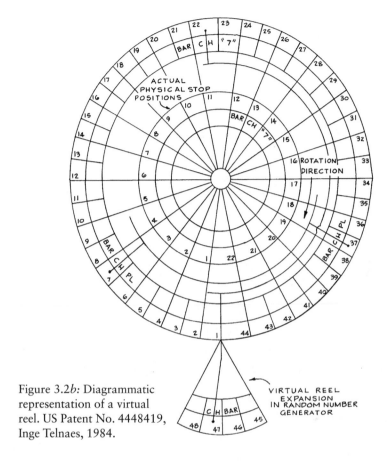

Figure 3.2*b*: Diagrammatic representation of a virtual reel. US Patent No. 4448419, Inge Telnaes, 1984.

became possible to alter a game's probabilities not by reconfiguring its hardware but by reconfiguring its software.[53]

At the same time that developers dispense with their own dependence on physical reel stops, they take care to preserve—and to profit from—players' continued dependence on the reel displays they interact with. Divested of their former mechanical function, the reels take on the new function of enchanting visual distortion. "Reels" that exist only inside the machine's chip and that are weighted heavily against gamblers are compressed onto the actual reels that spin in front of them, which appear far more weighted in their favor than they are (often carrying four jackpot symbols, as in figure 3.2a). Although each symbol that players see seems to have an equal chance of hitting, in fact each does not; the actual reel merely communicates the mapping decisions of its much-expanded virtual counterpart. Telnaes wrote candidly of his intent to distort player perception: "It is important to make a machine that is *perceived to present greater chances of payoff than it actually has.*"[54]

Kevin Harrigan, a specialist in computer software algorithms, figured out a way to calculate exactly how much greater. When he analyzed the programming on one 64-stop virtual reel, he found that if it were to pay off according to how its 22-stop actual reels presented themselves, players would win 297 percent of the time.[55] He argued that machines' misrepresentation of odds—or "physical reel distortion factor" (PRDF)—worked to hoodwink the human perceptual system and encourage player persistence.

The perceptual machinations and transformative distortions of chance involved in virtual reel mapping have led some to characterize it as a high-tech form of cheating; instead of "loading the dice" by drilling in quicksilver or "weighting the deck" by adding cards, the method of deceit is digital programming.[56] Following Nevada gaming law, "to cheat" is "to alter the elements of chance, methods of selection or criteria" that determine game results, and includes "the use of [a] device for calculating probabilities."[57] Whether or not virtual reel mapping fits this definition, at the very least it would appear to violate the Gaming Commission's stipulation that machines "must display an accurate representation of the game outcome," a variation of consumer protection laws that forbid potentially misleading graphics.[58] Telnaes's patent, as quoted above, foregrounds the invention's power to mislead, or to "present greater chances of payoff than it actually has."

As it happens, when a slot machine based on the patent was introduced for consideration at a set of hearings held by the Nevada Gaming Control Board, prominent figures in the gambling industry objected that aspects of its functioning were visually deceptive and unethical. Representatives from the two largest manufacturers at the time, IGT and Bally, voiced concerns that the technology misrepresented the outcome to the player. "From a visual standpoint," testified Bally's president, "it is misleading to the slot machine player." He explained:

> One of the reasons reel spinning slot machines have been so successful throughout their history is that players can visually see during the course of several handle pulls, all of the symbols on all of the reels as they spin and can psychologically perceive that there are actual combinations that

> should eventually show up over the course of time. It would appear to us
> that if a mechanical reel on a slot machine possesses four sevens and it is
> electronically playing as if there were one seven, *the player is being visu-*
> *ally misled.*[59]

The legal counsel for IGT agreed that "there is a deception problem involved with this kind of machine."[60]

Despite the wariness of industry insiders (which doubtless had less to
do with their concern about deception than with their concern about competition), the request to sanction virtual reel mapping was deemed "an
acceptable deviation from the criteria," as the lead lawyer for the Nevada
Gaming Control Board later put it.[61] One presiding commissioner emphasized at the hearings that players *expect* deception from machines, con-
cluding: "I feel good about this machine. I am going to vote in favor of it.
I think the concept is an exciting one."[62]

The board's endorsement of virtual reel mapping, which allowed slot
machines to offer bigger jackpots, was critical to the ascent of machines
in the American gambling market. Over one hundred devices were installed at Four Queens Casino in Las Vegas and promptly generated double the profit of corresponding nonvirtual reel machines.[63] Following
Nevada's regulatory "gold standard," other states that wished to cash in
on the taxes that would come from such earnings soon permitted the
software, with the assistance of private third-party testing and certification laboratories such as Gaming Laboratory International (GLI), "best
known by nearly everyone in the gaming industry simply as 'the lab.'"[64]
When IGT acquired exclusive rights to the Telnaes patent in 1989, the
company propelled itself to industry dominance by using the technology
in creative ways, and by suing other slot manufacturers for patent infringement.[65] After their patent ran out in 2002, the software became
standard across the entire industry. By 1997, more than 80 percent of
spinning reel slot machines (which today make up 35 to 40 percent of the
machine mix on an average casino slot floor) used the algorithm.[66]

When the dubious perceptual distortions of virtual reel mapping are
raised today, the defense is circular: Presiding judges find that the practice
is not fraud, because every regulatory laboratory approves it; regulatory
laboratories like GLI claim that their job is not to scrutinize and upold
consumer protection laws, but only to test the features of machines that
casino operators ask them to; manufacturers and casino operators claim
that regulation is not up to them.[67]

RECONFIGURING LOSS: NEAR MISSES

Virtual reel mapping has been used not only to distort players' perception of games' *odds* but also to distort their perception of *losses*, by creating "near miss" effects. Through a technique known as "clustering," game designers map a disproportionate number of virtual reel stops to blanks directly adjacent to winning symbols on the physical reels so that when these blanks show up on the central payline, winning symbols appear above and below them far more often than by chance alone (see fig. 3.2a).[68] Harrigan has calculated that if gamblers were to observe the symbols appearing just above and below the payline after each spin on the 64-stop virtual reel machine he analyzed, they would be led to assume that the game had a payback percentage or likely "return to player" in the range of 192 to 486 percent (in 1988 an industry analyst calculated the even higher figure of 250 to 1,000 percent for IGT's machines).[69] He calls this perceptual distortion of odds the "payline window distortion factor above/below" (PWDFa and PWDFb).

The legal counsel for IGT had raised the problem of clustering and near misses during the 1984 hearings, cautioning that "a picture of a jackpot appearing four times as often as it actually is seen by the computer, either above or below ... may account for the success of the play perhaps of these machines. To the extent that the inducement is a phantom symbol, *I think it is false advertising.*"[70] He noted for the record, however, that if virtual reel technology were approved, "certainly we would like to be able to do that because I think that is a competitive advantage." (And they did go on to do it, with great success.)

By recasting losses as potential wins, near misses (which, some have pointed out, are more accurately conceived as "near wins") prompt further play.[71] "It makes you want to press the button and continue," remarked a participant in one study. "You live in hope because you got close and you want to keep trying. You get to learn the pattern and just need to get it right."[72] Behavioral-psychological explanations for why near misses are so compelling include the "frustration theory of persistence," in which near misses "have an invigorating or potentiating effect on any behavior that immediately follows it," and the related theory of "cognitive regret," in which players circumvent regret at having almost won by immediately playing again.[73] "Almost hitting the jackpot," noted the behaviorist psychologist B. F. Skinner in 1953, "increases the probability that the individual will play the machine, although this reinforcer costs the owner of the device nothing."[74]

The gambling industry claims that near misses never occur in its North American machines, yet the claim rests on a remarkably arbitrary and narrow definition of the near miss. That definition emerged from a set of legal hearings in 1988, when a Japanese company called Universal was brought before the Nevada Gaming Control Board at the behest of its American industry competitors.[75] Universal had built a highly successful line of reel-spinning machines that produced near-miss effects in a novel way: before displaying the outcomes of a spin to players, they checked to see if a player had won or lost; in the event of loss, the devices initiated a secondary operation to display the losing outcome to the player as a near win directly on the main payline (e.g., 7, 7, and the third 7 just below the payline).[76]

Universal pointed out that its competitors created near-miss effects too, through the clustering technique described above, in which "programmers simply load more near-miss scenarios into the virtual reel, so that they come up more often."[77] Legal counsel for IGT freely admitted to this: "Yes, we have subliminal inducements above and below the payline and people see things peripherally."[78] Yet such near misses were "naturally occurring," one Gaming Board representative testified, given that their source lay in the configuration of a machine's reels prior to a spin rather than secondary software applied after a spin. Universal protested that the effect on players was the same whether near misses were programmed "naturally" and displayed "peripherally," or programmed through secondary software and displayed in the main payline. The only difference, the company argued, was one of technique—their own being the more advanced. As part of its case, Universal offered to sponsor a professorship in computerized technology at the University of Nevada; the appointee, they suggested, could act as an educational consultant to the board, whose existing regulations and expertise were based on the operation of traditional, mechanical slot machines.[79]

The board ruled against Universal, revising its regulation to state that the outcome of each reel on a gambling machine must be separately determined by a random number generator, and the results of those determinations must be the ones displayed: "After selection of the game outcome, the gaming device must not make a variable secondary decision which affects the result shown to the player." Although virtual reel mapping is a computational process that gets applied *after* the RNG has selected a virtual reel stop and therefore could be said to function as a kind of "secondary biasing system," the board chose to regard this built-in method for creating near misses as one that did not tamper with the purity of chance. I. Nelson Rose, the country's leading authority on gambling law, has commented of the decision: "Nevada drew the line at the computerized near-miss on the pay line; anything else goes."[80]

Over time, the ruling came to be characterized as the "outlawing" of near misses. Ellen Whittemore, the head lawyer for the board at the time, today lists the "banning" of near misses as one of her major accomplishments. But in fact, what the board did at the close of its hearings in 1989 was to make near misses legally permissible as long as they were accomplished via virtual reels and clustering techniques—which had by then become well entrenched in the industry. A cynical view of the ruling is that the commissioners found a way to simultaneously legitimize and legislate against—or *appear* to legislate against—a set of misleading industry design tactics that had flourished under their watch, and that had contributed substantially to the larger economic flourishing of the industry. Even more cynically, one might view the outcome of the legal proceedings as a way to protect American gaming companies against foreign competition. A less cynical view is that a long-standing mechanical design paradigm had left the commissioners unequipped to adequately grasp the workings of the digital technology they were asked to regulate. Whatever the case, the board's decision to focus on the mechanism of random generation as the site of its regulatory intervention (while ignoring new methods for shaping the *delivery* of randomness and players' perceptions of it) set the terms of permissibility for such methods.[81]

To produce near-miss effects on early video slots, which had no need for a mapping function (because they had no physical reels; all reels were virtual), game developers simply added extra video reels—"puffing" those toward the left with winning symbols while gradually "starving" those to the right, so that players were likely to experience a feeling of having "just missed" as they watched them stop sequentially from left to right.[82] In other words, while virtual reel mapping creates near-miss effects vertically on each reel, multireel video slots do so horizontally, across the reels. Known as "unbalanced" or "asymmetric" reels (as opposed to "disproportionate" or "weighted" reels), the technique is permitted by law because it adheres to the requirement that the outcome of each reel be determined through independent random processes. The technique has waned as video slots feature more and more "reels" whose many combinations naturally generate near misses. Contemporary video slot designers also rely on so-called teaser strips to communicate greater odds of winning to players than actually exist. Weighted with high-paying symbols, teaser strips appear when video reels "spin" and are replaced by strips with lower-paying symbols when the reels stop.[83]

From virtual reel mapping and its disproportionate reels to video slots' asymmetric reels; from the illusory player control conveyed by stop buttons and joysticks to the illusory odds conveyed by teaser strips: These methods, supported by a whole corporate, legal, and regulatory apparatus, gave machine designers greater control over the odds and presentation of chance while fostering enchanting "illusions of control," distorted perception of odds, and near-miss effects among gamblers. In what amounts to a kind of enchantment by design, finely tuned, chance-mediating technologies function as "really new gods," captivating their audience.

From Disenchantment to Enchantment

"Does [rationalization] mean that we, today," Weber asked in 1922, "have a greater knowledge of the conditions of life under which we exist than has an American Indian?"[84] On the contrary, he argued that rationalization had been accompanied by an increasing ignorance of how technologies were designed and built, and how they functioned. "Unless he is a physicist," he pointed out, "one who rides on the streetcar has no idea how the car happened to get into motion. And he does not need to know. He is satisfied that he may 'count' on the behavior of the streetcar, and he orients his conduct according to this expectation; but he knows nothing about what it takes to produce such a car so that it can move." As we saw at the start of this chapter, Rose reached a point where she no longer felt that she could "'count' on the behavior" of the gambling machine, and sought to know what it took to produce its movements. What becomes of her hope that opening up slot machines and taking apart their interiors might release their hold on her? If she had learned to understand microprocessing chips—the one component of machines about which slot mechanic school had not taught her—would this knowledge have finally disenchanted her play and extinguished its persistence?

In the late 1990s Roger Horbay, a former addiction counselor in Ontario, began to design software to educate players and policy makers about gambling machines. His motivation, he told me, was the frustration he felt in his role as addiction counselor and trainer of other counselors. No matter how he explained what was going on inside the devices, few could grasp how they worked—especially not how they configured probability and randomness, or "contrived contingency," to use Malaby's aforementioned phrase. "*How can be it be random and also weighted? How can there be a fixed house edge if it's chance?* People couldn't get their heads around it," Horbay recalled. When he met computer-scientist Harrigan, the two decided to develop their own slot machine simulator. "The idea was, let's develop our own game, make it transparent for users, let them really see how a typical slot machine works."

Designing the educational software proved neither straightforward nor simple. On the grounds of intellectual property rights, technology companies denied their requests for the "paytable and reel strip sheets" or "PAR sheets" (sometimes also called "probability accounting reports") that showed how games' odds were configured and how their virtual reels were mapped.[85] "The secrecy is intense," said Horbay. "Casinos can't even get PAR sheets from a manufacturer when they own the machines. They're in vaults." He and his colleague went on reconnaissance missions to industry trade shows, acquiring as much knowledge as they could from the information available at companies' booths. Eventually they went to the US patent office, where many slot machines are publicly patented.[86] They took the patents to their own labs and hired forensic scientists to reverse-engineer the math. The resulting educational software, Safe@Play, lets users explore the insides of reel machines to see how their mechanisms actually work. One can "unroll the reels," "pull out the microprocessor," and watch how the random number generator works; the program "reveals concealed game features."[87]

As an experienced addiction counselor, Horbay acknowledges the limits—and even the absurdity—of his own disenchantment enterprise. "Even if we demystify the machines through education, [compulsive gamblers] will still play them." I asked him to explain. "Because once you're hooked in, something else kicks in to keep you there; all trains of thought are evacuated and only one dominates." The "something else" to which Horbay referred—the hold of the zone—overrides any hope for beating chance that may have initially inspired machine play, and that a machine's programming may have reinforced through its enchanting perceptual distortions. As Mollie told us in the introduction, an initial seduction by the prospect of winning was what prompted her repeated engagement with gambling machines, yet through that engagement she discovered the machines' capacity to bring her into the zone—a state of ongoing, undiminished possibility that came to trump the finite reward of a win. Horbay regards gambling machines' seductive inscrutability not as the *hold* on players but rather the *hook*—the "early entrapping mechanisms," as he phrased it, or the "drive-in to the zone." These entrapping mechanisms, he believes, exploit the cognitive expectations of new gamblers such that they persevere at the interaction to a point where the self-maximizing aim of winning turns into the self-liquidating aim of the zone. He promotes his software chiefly as a form of prevention, a way "to block the on-ramp to addiction." Once players become caught in the loop of repeat play, he told me, "no rational action is possible."

Gambling addicts are well aware that they are beyond reason in the zone, and that knowledge of the machines' inner functions will do little to curb their drive. "I don't wonder or worry about the mechanism," commented Lola, the buffet waitress. "I know the machines are computerized, that they've got a chip, but it really doesn't matter—in fact, I don't think about it at all when I play. I couldn't care less, I just want to see the next cards." Shelly, the tax accountant, said the same: "Although I've had discussions with people as to how the machines work, sometimes even with people who build and program them, while I'm playing I never really think about the insides of the machine." Randall, the electronics technician we met earlier, had inspected machine interiors and understood how their memory chips worked. "I'm a reasonably intelligent person, I'm rational. But when it comes to gambling, reason just skippity-hops out the door." Rose eventually realized the futility of her demystification plan: "After getting my degree I knew everything that was going on in that machine. It was a conscious knowledge when I'd start to play—I'd picture what was happening inside the computer. But then I would turn that knowledge off."

Designers themselves often describe a "turning-off" of knowledge while playing the very machines they have designed. When designing, they operate within the domain of calculative rationality—they pick a machine's colors and sounds, formulate its sophisticated mathematical algorithms, calculate its payout rates and risk probabilities, and scrutinize its performance. (In the terms of a Weberian analysis, they attempt to make "calculable and predictable what in an earlier age had seemed governed by chance.") When playing, however, calculative rationality falls away. "Even though I know my chances statistically," Anchor Gaming's John Vallejo told me, "I'm guilty of doing risky, superstitious things when I play.... I feel a sense of anticipation that I know doesn't make sense, and I take risks that I know aren't feasible." "I designed the math on these games but it doesn't matter; I do risky, irrational things when I play," echoed a Bally designer. "Knowing the odds doesn't interfere with my playing. *Somehow that knowledge becomes irrelevant when I sit down at the machine.*" As Suchman has suggested in her writing on human-machine relations, "even for those who possess [knowledge of its internal workings], there is an 'irreducibility' to the computer as an object that is unique among human artifacts."[88] The computerized gambling machine takes on a life of its own even for its designers, becoming an enchanted agent of sorts rather than an assemblage of discrete components. Gardner Grout of Silicon Gaming has described how a sense of the machine's agency enhanced his play experience: "I'll often block out what I know about the machines because if I admit to myself that it's a completely random event that has nothing to do with my actions, then I'm just not going to have the experience that I want to have. So I sort of shut that side of my mind off. It's like I *delude* myself."

Multiple lines of delusion are at work in the encounter with gambling machines. Industry designers actively marshal technology to delude gamblers—at times worrying about their delusionary tactics (as in the Gaming Board testimonials presented above), and at other times defending these tactics by insisting that they give gamblers "what they want." Gamblers, for their part, collude in the delusion, "turning off" any knowledge they may have about the inner mechanisms of the machines so as to enter the compelling state they seek. The same sort of "asymmetric collusion" that happens around the sensory, affective dimensions of play described in the last chapter happens here—but in this case the asymmetry lies in the encounter between two distinct practical, cognitive, and temporal orientations to the enchanting force of chance.

While designers' orientation is calculative, rational, and focused on a distant statistical horizon in which profit is guaranteed, gamblers' orientation is experiential, affective, and focused on the unpredictable outcomes of the very next spin; as their involvement in play deepens, they are likely to become less invested in winning than in continuing to play. It is not that repeat gamblers act "illogically" while playing machines, two gambling researchers clarify, for "their strategies are complex, intuitive and adaptive"; yet these strategies, as we will see in coming chapters, "are not avaricious and do not rely on 'rational' calculation of odds."[89] Although "one might 'know' that the odds are poor and that one inevitably loses over time," writes another researcher, a different "type of knowing … may take over in the process of gambling, especially if machines are designed with this effect."[90] In the gap between calculation and intuition, rationality and affect, the gambling industry seeks revenue while players seek the zone.

PART TWO

Feedback

Types of machines are easily matched with each type of society—not because machines are determining, but because they express those social forms capable of generating them and using them.

—*Gilles Deleuze*

THE RAT PEOPLE

A gambler named Darlene posted the following activity log to
an internet recovery site for gambling addicts:

3 a.m., was nearly alone, had to go to the bathroom, didn't
want to leave the machine

5 a.m., still there, choking on smoke, starving, cramping
from bladder pain, butt hurting from sitting

6 a.m., finally got up, put my coat on but still couldn't leave.
Got attendant to watch machine while I peed. Almost cried
with relief. Looked at myself in bathroom mirror, was shocked
at what I saw. I do not ever want to look on the face of that
woman again—the desperate one, the smoky, hungry one who
doesn't have the sense to go to the bathroom or go home. Continued playing—standing up, coat on

8 a.m., breakfast eaters arriving and I became terrified that
someone I knew would see me. Finally left ...

How did I get to this point? 15 hours? I've never done anything in my life for 15 hours straight, except take care of my
babies. I'm well past that point in my life, could be a grandmother. And what kind of Grandma would that be? Some idiot
with no self-control, who becomes paralyzed, hypnotized—by
what? A machine? The music? The lights? WHAT IS IT??

I've lived a somewhat charmed life—never alcohol, never
drugs, never running or being run on. Good and accomplished
kids. Opportunities. Life has been sweet, wonderful and very
blessed. I don't understand this.

Responses to Darlene's post of machine-induced abjection contained sympathy and words of encouragement, but her urgent query—*What is it?*—went unanswered. She restated the question:

> You all say you've "been there." Is that true? Have others experienced the same inability to move? Why does that happen? Can anyone explain the paralysis? The hypnotic effect it has on you? This is not my imagination; for me it was very real—I could not get up off my seat. Do you understand how powerful that is? I didn't even have the strength to go to the bathroom!

Responses, once again, affirmed Darlene's experience of seeming paralysis but did not answer her question. "I can relate to how you feel, I used to spend full days sitting in front of a video poker machine," wrote one gambler. "I never could leave my seat at the machine either," wrote another; "I was glued. I've sat for 10 hours straight, then barely could make it to the bathroom without an accident—and sometimes I didn't make it." And another: "I know the feeling. I used to sit in that damn chair in the casino and COULDN'T PHYSICALLY MOVE. Only when my money was gone could I leave, SICK TO MY STOMACH."

Darlene, not satisfied with the empathy conveyed in these posts, pressed on:

> I am still interested in the whole "hypnotic" phenomenon. Does anyone have any insights into how that works? Why do some of us get caught into a kind of paralysis that blots out time, responsibility, logic, even movement? It's not normal to ignore the urge to pee, yet that is what happened to me and apparently to some of the rest of us.

One woman responded in a more diagnostic register, cataloging symptoms and their correlating physiological explanations:

> The symptoms you describe—lightheadedness, nausea—after being at the casino for prolonged period of times are related to a combination of one or more of the following: no food, no sleep, too much caffeine, improper elimination, sitting too long,

overstimulation (bells, lights) and the emotional upheaval of winning/losing. Interestingly, female compulsive gamblers often suffer from repeated bladder infections and yeast or bacterial infections (too much sitting, too little water, not urinating).

Yet these clinical speculations, like the preceding responses, failed to address the heart of Darlene's query. She persisted:

> I want to dwell a little more on the other thing, the hypnotic effect of the video machine. I refuse to believe that anything could be so strong, and yet something tells me that this whole package is designed to hook us and hook us good. These machines and the accompanying casino atmosphere must be calculated to throw us into some kind of trance.

Finally, a different kind of answer posted to the site:

> Darlene dear Darlene,
>
> Slot machines are just "Skinner boxes" for people! Why they keep you transfixed is really not a big mystery. The machine is designed to do just that. It operates on the principles of operant conditioning. The original studies on conditioning were done by B. F. Skinner and involved rats. I'm sure you remember this from grade school: The rats are in a box without outside stimulus (like a casino!). There is a lever (or pedal) in the box. When the rat hits the lever a pellet (food) comes out (like a slot machine and quarters). The rat learns that by pressing the lever he gets a treat (positive reinforcement).
>
> Now comes the sneaky part. If every time the rat hit the lever he got a treat, that would be the end of it—he would just hit the lever when he was hungry. But that's not how conditioning works. Enter the concept of intermittent reinforcement. Simply put, it means that the rewards (pellets) are dispensed on a random schedule—sometimes the rat gets none, sometimes a few, sometimes a lot of pellets (sounding familiar yet?). He never knows when he's going to get a pellet so he keeps pushing that lever, over and over and over and over, even if none come out. The rat becomes obsessed—addicted, if you will. THIS, then, is the psychological principle that slot machines operate on, and how it operates on you.

Darlene wrote back:

> !!! My God, what a response! I feel as if I've taken a refresher course in behavioral psych! Even not understanding how the conditioning and response dialog worked, I still knew that something sinister was at work here, enticing "normal" people into a snare.... You put into words what I knew to be the facts!
>
> Perhaps we should form a splinter group, calling ourselves "The Rat People," since we all know that when the pellets drop, they could just as well be cyanide as chocolate. In my mind's eye, I see a 61-year-old Rat Woman, tired, miserable, hungry, thirsty, bladder full, hair disheveled, skin dried out and caked with nicotine residue, clothes wrinkled and baggy, hunched over some damn slot machine, pushing the endless lever, hoping for another pellet ...

The post on intermittent reinforcement not only satisfied Darlene but went on to spark a cascade of behaviorist-inflected sentiments that had not previously found expression in the forum. Over the next weeks, rats repeatedly reared their heads. "When I gamble I feel like a rat in a trap," commented a gambler. "Yes, I feel like a Rat Person, coming out of my dark hole to surface when the money is all gone," said another. Rats—along with carrier pigeons, rhesus monkeys, and Pavlov's salivating dogs—made continued guest appearances in gamblers' posts. "I'm sure to be the first one in line to hit the lever to see what my prize is," one man wrote.

4

MATCHING THE MARKET

Innovation, Intensification, Habituation

As Mollie and I sat at the window of her complimentary room at the Main Street Station in 1998, she reviewed the progression of her gambling. It had started in the mid-1980s, when her husband showed her how to play video poker on a handheld machine. "I honed my skills on that amazing little machine, skills like knowing which formulas to use to make decisions, like whether it's better to keep the king or the queen if you've got two fours. I became hooked, really hooked." From there she graduated to actual video poker machines, then to a version called Deuces Wild, then Double Bonus, and most recently, to Triple Play—a version that allows her to play out the same hand on three separate rows, simultaneously. She explained to me: "Three rows, three possible outcomes— it's a kind of tolerance, like with drinking. I keep needing more intensity, and the machines keep matching me."

The next time I heard the word "tolerance" used in association with gambling machines was at the annual industry meeting in 1999, where a panel of industry experts had gathered from around the country to speculate on "The Video Future." "Technology is extending to every area of society," said one panelist. "People are attuned to what's around them, and it's becoming the norm for them to use these sorts of devices—in fact, they're coming to expect it. *There's a growing tolerance for technology.*"[1] In contrast with Mollie's use of the word to signal her dependency in the face of increasing technological intensity, here it was meant to signal the market's adaptive strengthening in response to technological innovations that led to games of greater complexity. "People are adapting to more complex types of games," the panel moderator observed.[2]

Whether framed as an addictive or an adaptive phenomenon, the tolerance to which Mollie and the panelists referred is shaped most powerfully by a game's "payout schedule," or the mathematical script that determines the frequency by which it delivers (or does not deliver) wins.[3] As behavioral psychologists found in their mid-twentieth-century experiments with carrier pigeons and lab rats—and as gambling researchers find today—the capacity of a given "reward schedule" to reinforce behavior depends less on the net gain or loss that subjects experience than on the frequency and pattern by which rewards are dispensed or withheld.[4] When I asked a longtime IGT executive why certain games were more compelling than others he pointed me to a textbook on psychologist B. F. Skinner's theory of behavioral reinforcement, or "operant conditioning."[5] As it happens, in 1953 Skinner had pointed in the other direction, using the slot machine to exemplify the most potent of reinforcement schedules—in which subjects never know when they will be rewarded, or how much.[6]

Invoked earlier by the self-designated "rat people" posting to the online forum for gambling addicts, this type of schedule dispenses rewards frequently enough to keep gamblers playing, yet not so frequently that a device will lose money. "A gambling enterprise," wrote Skinner, "pays on a kind of schedule which sustains betting even though, in the long run, the amount paid [out] is less than the amount wagered."[7] He described how reinforcement schedules can be "stretched" to prolong duration of play such that gamblers continue to play even when they start losing: "The stretching may be accidental (an early run of good luck which grows subtly worse may create a dedicated gambler), or *the ratio may be deliberately stretched by someone who controls the odds*."[8] The invention of virtual reel mapping examined in the last chapter freed game developers from their dependence on the structural dimensions of mechanical reels and in so doing gave them an extraordinary degree of control over odds and the ability to experiment with innovative payout schedules. As this chapter will show, the application of video technology freed them from physical reels altogether and allowed them to push their experimentation even further, producing games whose reinforcement schedules could more effectively "stretch" the rate and duration of gamblers' play.

FROM HOOK TO HOLD

"Math is the sharp end of my spear," game designer Nicholas Koenig told us earlier, implying that slot machines' hidden mathematical programming was critical to the task of "hooking" players' attention. Yet as much as math functions as an enchanting hook or "spear" (in the form of near misses and other visual distortions of odds), it functions as a reinforcing *hold*, as Koenig went on to explain: "Once you've hooked 'em in, you want to keep pulling money out of them until you have it all; the barb is in and you're yanking the hook." Shifting to a less aggressive metaphor, he spoke of math's hold as a matter of gentle persuasion. "It's like the player is reclining on a math model and you need to get them comfortable; they're investing a lot of money into an invisible structure and they need to be made to feel that they can trust it. *The machine needs to communicate that trust through its delivery of rewards.*" The point is to get players to "like the feel of the math," echoed the chief technology officer for IGT.[9] "Math is what will make them stay," said Marcus Prater, a top Bally executive at the time of our interview.[10]

To strengthen the holding power of games' math, machine manufacturing companies staff departments of advanced mathematicians who run so-called math farms to simulate the efficacy of different payout schedules. These simulations inform the delicate demographic operation of "matching math with markets, player types with schedule types," as Prater characterized the task. "Two machines can look similar on the outside," he told me, "but in fact they operate according to very different formulae of chance." Switching registers, he said the same of human beings: "Different types of humans manifest themselves through different machines, different math—it's a whole ecology." By adjusting the mathematical configuration of their games, designers seek to address an ever-wider range of human preferences within the human-machine environment of the gambling arena. "We understand humans and are creating math for them," Prater said (see fig. 4.1).

As far as player types go, "basically there are two polar opposites and several gradations in between," explained John Vallejo, then at Anchor Gaming. *Action players*, otherwise known as *jackpot players* or *play-to-win players*, are willing to lose big in order to win big and so prefer "high volatility, low hit frequency" games that reward risk and perseverance with large payoffs, but may entail long dry spells without wins of any

Figure 4.1. "Inside the Mind of the Slot Player," feature story in casino trade magazine. Courtesy of *Casino Journal*.

kind.[11] "They don't care about small-end stuff," said Vallejo, "they're willing to invest a couple hundred dollars because they're going for the jackpot." *Escape players*, on the other hand, otherwise known as *time-on-device players* or *play-to-win-to-play players*, are willing to forgo large jackpots for regular wins and extended play time, and so prefer "low volatility, high hit frequency" games programmed to dispense constant little payouts (or reinforcements, in Skinnerian lingo).[12] Known as "drip-feed," "grind," or "dribble-pay" games, they nibble slowly at a budget until it is gone. "Some people," Vallejo remarked, "want to be bled slowly."

Prater showed me the payout graphs for two games under design at Bally, each corresponding to "a distinct audience of risk takers," as he put it. One had a series of dramatic spikes and reached zero relatively quickly, indicating large, infrequent jackpots and shorter time-on-device; the other had a longer-lasting, gradual slope with more frequent but smaller spikes, conforming to the preferences of a more risk-averse player for steady wins over a longer duration of play. "On both machines you end up in the same place, which is zero," he explained. "It just takes longer to get there on the second one; it erodes your bankroll more slowly" (see fig. 4.2, top, for a hand-drawn version of the graph by Koenig). Over the long haul of cumulative play, both game types are profitable for gambling establishments; their task is to figure out the particular mix of offerings that will best conform to market preferences. "This is a balancing act," writes a game designer and consultant, "that requires careful attention to exactly how the game plays and how it feels to the player."[13]

This chapter argues that game developers' mathematical adjustments, more than simply detecting and conforming to existing market preferences, have transformative effects on those preferences. In a tight feedback loop, games' reinforcement schedules take shape around the inclinations of players at the same time that these inclinations take shape through repeated, extended exposure to the particular "formulae of chance" programmed into games. "Players, markets, and game features are dynamic entities with their own fads and trends," reads an instructional booklet that IGT provides to its prospective technicians. "New games are continuously being introduced, and markets change in dynamics. Technology changes and so do the players."[14]

The following pages trace one particular line of change that has emerged through mutually responsive shifts in the configuration of gambling technology and the market's style of play. Since the 1980s, with the spread of legalized gambling and "repeat play," game developers and players have gravitated toward games with a high hit frequency mathematical structure. As developers have learned that such games yield greater revenue, machine gamblers have learned that they yield greater time-on-device—or *seem* to, by "eroding their bankroll" in small increments rather than large spikes (see fig. 4.2, bottom).[15] Although much of this learning was accidental—an effect of mathematical tinkering and player response to that tinkering—the industry has since attempted to strategically steer players (or "migrate" them, as they often describe the process) toward the cherry-dribbling, slow-bleeding pole of play, a profit-from-volume formula that one industry member has referred to as the "Costco model of gambling."[16] The myriad matching maneuvers that game developers have devised to "deliver a good math experience," as Prater put it, at once adapt to players and intensify their play. "The industry is maturing, players are maturing, and there is a requirement for more and

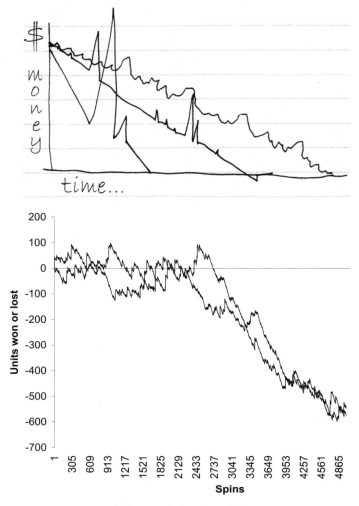

Figure 4.2. *Top*: Projected play trends for three different games, assuming the same initial bankroll. The shortest line represents a game with "high volatility" and "low hit frequency"; the longest shows "low volatility" and "high hit frequency"; the middle line shows moderate volatility and frequency. Drawn for the author by game designer Nicholas Koenig. *Bottom*: Play outcomes for two simulated gamblers on the same gambling machine, set at a hold percentage of only 5 percent. The graph follows the two gamblers from their first bet through 5,000 spins, representing four to eight hours of play (depending on the speed of the machine and the speed of play). The downward slope illustrates the "churn" by which play funds are gradually eroded over time. Although both gamblers experience wins, the house edge gradually consumes the winnings as they are reinvested in play. Assuming that each bets $3.00 per spin, their averaged loss at the end of the play period is $900.00. Graph built by gambling analyst Nigel Turner.

more," said a marketing manager for Aristocrat, referring to the increasing complexity of his company's games.[17] As players are enrolled in this "maturation" process, they become tolerant of the new levels of play intensity they encounter in games, spurring designers to redouble their efforts in turn.

PLAYING FOR TIME: VIDEO POKER

On a Wednesday afternoon in 1998, Lola and I made our way through the aisles of gambling machines on the casino floor of Sam's Town, heading toward the buffet where she would begin her shift in a few minutes. *Play and Eat!* read a sign above one row of machines; *It's Steak Night!* read another. Since it opened in 1979 on a patch of desert at a quiet intersection in southeast Las Vegas, Sam's Town has been one of the most popular of locals-oriented casinos in the city. Like other establishments with strong local patronage, the venue attracts customers by offering free meal coupons and player loyalty programs with perks for those who gamble in large volume. That afternoon, the casino was neither full nor empty. Machine gamblers dotted the space, seated one or two per machine bank. "Nobody really talks to each other when they're playing," said Lola as we passed them, "so just about anywhere you sit you're isolated."

The floor plan at Sam's Town is straightforward: long narrow rows, good visibility, and direct pathways. The layout principles at work in locals' casinos, which began appearing in the late 1970s to accommodate the swelling population, depart in key respects from those of tourist establishments. Although vacationing tourists are likely to feel exhilarated by the spatial disorientation and sense of mystery created by a sinuous, labyrinthine floor design that winds them through a property, locals have no patience for such interiors. As a member of one design team explained to me in 1993: "Locals want things clearly marked, with easy circulation. They want to park, get in there, and gamble—they want to be lined up like cattle." He recalled that a popular local casino had tried out a looping floor design like those of the fantasy-themed resorts then being built on the Las Vegas Strip, but lost so much revenue that it was forced to change back to the former grid format. "Locals just won't tolerate it. *They want the quickest route.*"[18] Perhaps from overexposure to the staged disorientation of tourist casinos' interiors, or perhaps because they know already where they want to go, regulars prefer direct and easy access to machines. Locals-market casinos are not designed for enchantment; they are designed for convenience and habit.[19]

Video poker is the predominant machine on offer at neighborhood venues, reflecting locals' strong preference for the game. IGT chose Sam's Town for the debut of its poker machines in 1979, the same year the property opened.[20] Twelve devices were placed near the front door as an experiment, and to everyone's surprise they became an overnight success. "People were playing that bank of machines around the clock, standing in line," a designer recalled. What drew players was precisely what most in the industry believed would keep them away: the introduction of *skill* to machine play—"an entirely new performance attribute," as an industry historian has written.[21]

Standard video poker consoles feature five card backs in a line across the screen. To initiate the game, players press a DEAL button, whereupon the random number generator "deals" them five cards from a virtual deck of fifty-two (or more, if one or more wild cards are used). Each card face appears on the screen with its own HOLD button beneath (see fig. 4.4, top left). Players choose which cards they wish to hold or discard to make winning hands, and then touch the DRAW button to replace the unheld cards. The machine polls its random number generator again (this time selecting from the remaining forty-seven cards in the virtual deck) and renders new cards to replace the discarded ones, revealing the outcome. Players win different amounts for different combinations, such as three-of-a-kind (8-8-Q-8-3) or a flush (e.g., five diamond-suited cards).[22]

By opening the market to gamblers who had no interest in the pure luck formula of classical reel spinners, "video poker inverted the whole equation of gambling machines," as one game developer put it. "On slots you just pulled the handle and waited for the reels to stop—it didn't draw me in," remembers one longtime Las Vegas resident who had played live poker for years before switching to video poker soon after the devices were introduced. Although the elements of choice making and skill might seem at odds with the dissociative flow of the zone, in fact they heighten players' absorption by turning the passive expectancy of the traditional slot experience into a compelling, interactive involvement (a paradox to be explored at greater length in chapter 6).

Bob Dancer, who has won millions by "exploiting the tiny loopholes left open by the industry" and runs popular workshops for Las Vegas locals who aspire to do the same, distinguishes video poker players from slot players: "The slot player wants to be chauffeured, while the video poker player wants to drive." These "different animals," as he calls them, map neatly onto the tourist-local divide—a divide, that is, between infrequent, novice players and experienced repeat players. "Tourists want newness, surprise, entertainment," said Vallejo; "they like games with no skill involved, where you push the button and see the results. The tourist market is not very sophisticated." As the founder of Aristocrat told a reporter, "you've got a totally different situation in the vacation markets, where people have to accept what they are given, and the locals markets, where they're not going to just accept what they're given."[23] In the eyes of the gambling industry, a preference for video poker has become the mark of "mature" repeat machine gamblers who are no longer compelled by the bells, whistles, and pure-luck spin of classic three reel stepper slots—just as they are no longer compelled by the twisting pathways and exotic gimmicks of interior design in tourist venues. "Video poker is locals' game of choice," Prater told me in 1999.

Locals are drawn not only to the choice-making process of video poker but also to the liberal odds it offers savvy players.[24] "The better you are, the higher the payback [percentage], until it reaches the designer's [payback] percentage," explained Gardner Grout of Silicon Gaming. With a tone of admiration, he admitted that his own customers beat him at the very games he had designed: "I can't believe the high scores some people get. These are programmed games and I should be the best person there is, but people just blow me away at these things. I can't even see the cards they go so fast—and they're making the right choices!" Those proficient enough to approach optimal play strategy earn themselves longer time-on-device; their payoff for skill is not to walk away with a jackpot, but to extend the play session.

Game developers at IGT, a company that launched itself into a competitive industry position after acquiring the patent for video poker in 1978 (when the company was still called SIRCOMA), recognized that players valued time-on-device and saw a way to glean their own sort of value from it. "If you were to take $100 and play slots, you'd get about an hour of play, but video-poker was designed to give you two hours of play for that same $100," explained Si Redd, one of the game's developers.[25] The game's provision of doubled time-on-device lay in the design of its payout schedule (or the delivery pattern of its rewards). Unlike its mechanical, reel-spinning cousins—which might deliver big jackpots but were liable to drive players out of action quickly with no wins at all—video poker offered players a varied range of jackpots, many of them small or moderate. While traditional slots had an average reward frequency of only 3 percent, the new video poker machines typically rewarded players on 45 percent of plays—just the kind of schedule that prolongs the persistence of a behavior, as Skinner had noted.[26] Although video poker machines took in half as much money as three-reel slots per unit of time, they brought in twice as much revenue because gamblers played at them four times as long. The time-on-device formula proved lucrative for the industry when it came to local repeat players who typically had "more time than money."[27]

Ten years after video poker was introduced at Sam's Town, the game was generating well over half the total machine revenue at locals' casinos in Las Vegas.[28] Beyond casinos, it became a substantial source of income at local "convenience" venues throughout the city—restaurant lobbies, bar counters, gas stations, Laundromats, drugstores, and supermarkets. Such venues had never been able to profit from traditional reel-spinning slot machines, which had little local appeal and required frequent servicing. Video poker attracted and retained regular and local gamblers like no other game could and carried minimal service requirements. The city's rapid population growth supplied a large local market for the devices.[29] "The machines proved so popular," IGT's website recollects, "that the original upright model was adapted to a bar-top model, which created a powerful new revenue stream for local taverns."[30] In 1983 a local operator told a reporter: "We have over 500 machines in Las Vegas bars and only two of those are [reel-spinning] slot machines. Though I never thought I'd see it happen, I think the days of the traditional slot machine, certainly among experienced players like the locals in bars around here, are numbered."[31]

In 1984, only five years after its introduction, 32 percent of Las Vegas residents who gambled cited video poker as their preferred game; by 1998, that share had increased to 54 percent (compared to only 11 percent of tourists).[32] The preferences of the local market for interactive, time-on-device play had taken definite shape, and along the way a new logic of game design had proven itself.

If "players, markets, and game features are dynamic entities," as IGT's educational booklet told aspiring slot technicians above, then how exactly did the design of video poker evolve in concert with its players' emerging preferences? Since gambling laws required that the virtual deck of cards from which the RNG "draws" must contain exactly fifty-two cards, video poker was closed to the sort of creative mathematical reconfiguration of odds that we have seen at work in mechanical and video slots, whose reels can be expanded to include hundreds of symbols.[33] "With a game like video poker," Vallejo explained, "there's a finite mathematical universe and only so many elaborations you can squeeze out of it—it's not so flexible statistically." What video poker designers *could* do was change the payout values assigned to different winning combinations, and variations on the original game format quickly began to appear. In the Deuces Wild variation that Mollie referred to earlier, 2s become wild cards (such that the odds of winning hands go up while payouts drop to compensate); in a variation called Double Bonus, hands with four-of-a-kind are especially valued, as they are in Double Double Bonus. Conferring additional value to small and moderate wins increased video poker's hit frequency and at the same time increased the occasion for reinforcement. ("Frequent small payoffs appear to reinforce customers more" noted the casino interior designer Bill Friedman whom we met in chapter 1.[34])

In close step with the evolution of video poker's payout schedule, gamblers appeared to collectively change their play strategies, shifting their goal from jackpots to moderate wins. "If you play enough, you start to get a sense of how the machine pays," said Dom Tiberio, a senior mathematician at Bally who gambles in his free time. "We locals learned that you could win more often by playing 4-of-a-kind than you could on the original video poker machines. *You get to play longer that way.*" Instead of royal flush jackpots, locals reoriented their play toward lesser but more likely wins, known in the industry as "attainable jackpots." (A longtime supermarket slot attendant I spoke with noted one consequence of players' turn away from royal flushes: "In the past, more of my customers would get angry at the machines—hit them, break their glass, curse them—but that has really tapered off.... I think it's because they aren't playing for the big jackpot so much anymore, so they get less angry if they miss a [winning] hand.") As gamblers adjusted their play in this manner, Tiberio explained to me in 2000, "manufacturers started focusing on what we call the 'upper-middle region of the pay schedule,' and now you'll see a lot of that." That year, a casino billboard appeared along a lengthy thoroughfare that cuts diagonally through a number of residential neighborhoods, prompting drivers: "*Why Be Loyal to the Royal ...*" Farther along the road, a second billboard continued the query: "*When You Can Score the Four?*"

"It's almost as if the gambling public has developed a tolerance for [royal flush] jackpots," commented Hunter in 1999. He went on:

> When video poker was first introduced, the prototypical player would talk about the number of Royals they had hit, or how many in one day. Nowadays, not so much. The video poker machines that are most popular now, that are in fact crowding out the other machines, are not programmed to attract people to hit Royals, but to hit four-of-a-kinds, double bonuses, and triple play deals. *You get a less powerful reinforcer than a Royal, but you get more frequent reinforcement.*

"This kind of reinforcement is perfect for escape gamblers," he continued, "because they don't care about making money—they care about staying there as long as possible. I think the casinos have picked up on this."

What Hunter described was a process of responsive adjustment in which the gambling industry "picked up" on their most dedicated customers' desire for extended play time and recalibrated their machines accordingly, while those customers simultaneously "learned" (as Tiberio put it) how to recalibrate their interactions with the newer machines.[35] As the devices more precisely adapted to market inclinations, market inclinations shifted in turn; the dynamic was one of subtle modification through feedback. Increasing games' hit frequency increased the rate at which play was reinforced, and players' changed expectations were then accounted for in subsequent design innovations, further ratcheting up the rate of reinforcement.

The subtle, coshaping dynamics unfolding between market preferences and game design have registered saliently in the changing composition of the gambling addiction population in Las Vegas. By the early 1990s, approximately 97 percent of the women and 80 percent of the men in treatment at Hunter's clinic played only video poker, and the figure was rising as more men began to play machines.[36] While in the past the typical gambling addict had been an older male who bet on sports or cards for ten years before seeking help, now it was a thirty-five-year-old female with two children who had played video poker for less than two years before seeking help.[37] With the introduction and development of a game whose mode of reinforcement—and thus profit—relied on minor but continuous rewards rather than on significant but sporadic rewards, a new gambler profile was taking center stage in the experience of gambling addiction. This profile embodied, in extreme form, the broader market's gravitation from action to escape play, volatility to time-on-device—a trend that would grow in the next decade.

A Smoother Ride: Video Slots

Although video poker came to dominate the preferences of repeat machine gamblers in Las Vegas during the 1980s, gamblers in general remained wary of computerized, screen-based games, holding fast to their preference for mechanical reel spinners. Given virtual reel technology these devices were able to offer large jackpots, but they lacked the frequency of payout that could sustain regular, extended play. To understand the widespread turn to time-on-device play among American gamblers, it is necessary to take a detour through a different gambling market, where a different form of video gambling was pioneered before it was eventually disseminated throughout the United States. This new form—the "multiline" video slot—found a novel way to intensify hit frequency, time-on-device, and rate of reinforcement.

In 1951 in the United States, the passage of the Johnson Act restricted casino gambling to the state of Nevada, causing the collapse of most major domestic slot machine manufacturers. The act happened to coincide with the legalization of casinos in New South Wales in Australia, which soon became the second-largest slot machine market in the world. A company named Aristocrat (today second only to IGT in the global market) quickly established itself as the leading domestic manufacturer of gambling machines, and over the following years developed an international reputation as a technological innovator. In the 1990s, as Australian gambling corporations partnered with cash-strapped state governments to revitalize the country's economy, machine gambling was deregulated. Almost overnight, slot machines filled community centers and clubs across the country, creating a thriving locals market.[38] When Aristocrat reached its manufacturing capacity, the company bought new laser metal cutters to speed up production and meet the continuing demand for its machines.[39] By 1998 over 80 percent of Australians gambled and 40 percent did so on a regular basis.[40] "Down there, you're more likely to get run over by a slot machine than by a car," remarked an American game developer while browsing Aristocrat's well-appointed display booth at the 1999 Global Gaming Expo, a year in which Australia had one-fifth of all the gambling machines in the world and five times the US per-capita ratio.[41] Australia currently has the highest machine-to-person ratio of any major gambling jurisdiction, with approximately one machine for every eighty Australian adults.[42]

In Australia video poker is virtually nonexistent, as are mechanical reel spinners. Instead, nearly all gambling devices are video slots, known until recently in the United States as Australian-format or Australian-style slots, and known colloquially in Australia as "pokies" (invoking the first mechanical gambling devices, which were based on poker).[43] Video slots are built on the "multiplier" formula that Bally popularized in the late 1960s on its mechanical slots, permitting gamblers to wager multiple coins per turn (typically three, sometimes five), each coin multiplying their payback on a winning outcome.[44] In 1968 Bally introduced a multiple-*payline* (or multiline) machine, allowing gamblers to wager on multiple rows of symbols appearing in the display window—the top three symbols, middle three symbols, and bottom three symbols.[45] Betting one coin activated the first play line, two coins activated the first and second play lines, and three coins activated all three lines of play. A five-line variation was soon fashioned by adding two additional lines of play diagonally, connecting each corner of the three-by-three symbol matrix in the game window. The game offered over 50 percent chance of winning on at least one line per spin, which meant that a player's budget—and thus time-on-device—could be greatly extended; it also meant that the machines were five times more reinforcing than single-line games.

By the early 1970s, multiline multipliers were common in the United States. Yet the physical parameters of mechanical reels imposed limits on further expansion of the formula, and American players and manufacturers shied away from the video formats that could have overcome those limits. Meanwhile, something different happened in Australia. Recognizing that video arcade machines were quickly growing to rival mechanical pinball machines, Aristocrat decided to develop its gambling technology in a video direction.[46] In 1987 the company introduced a video slot machine designed to look and feel like its two most popular mechanical spinning reel games; the device was immediately and extraordinarily successful. Encouraged by this success, Aristocrat experimented further with video technology to create pay schedules that could dispense smaller rewards more frequently, appealing to the low-rolling, repeat players who constituted the overwhelming majority of Australia's gambling market after deregulation in the 1990s.

In 1993 Aristocrat put out the first nine-line video slot. Instead of betting three coins on just one line, now players could bet as many as five coins on each of the nine lines, for a maximum bet of forty-five coins per spin. The appeal of such a game was clearly not that it required far more coins to attain optimal odds, but that it hit winning combinations far more often, allowing longer play. In subsequent iterations of the video slot formula, paylines continued to rise—not just straight across the screen but also zigzag. A video format made it easy to add (or rather, simulate) more reels, to display longer portions of the reels, and to highlight winning paylines that might not otherwise be apparent to players with pulsing colored lines.[47] The 2006 game shown in figure 4.3 features five reels, four rows of symbols, and *fifty* different lines on which to wager.

With each line added to video slots, their hit frequency and reinforcement quotient has increased—along with their popularity. Although the games tend to give players slimmer odds at winning big jackpots, they also tend to carry less risk of sudden losing streaks and the quick depletion of play funds. Even when depletion does occur rapidly (which can happen if the credits wagered and the speed of play are high enough), it is nevertheless *gradual*, occurring over many increments and thus preserving the flow of play—or giving gamblers what various designers I spoke with called "a smoother ride" (see fig. 4.2, top graph). As an Aristocrat representative commented of multiliners in 1999, the games can "give the impression of value for their money, but still extract money from people quickly."[48]

Whether they actually give longer time-on-device or just the impression of it, the trick to multiline slots is this: while mechanical slots either pay *nothing* on a given spin or significantly *more* than the amount of the initial bet, multiliners pay *something* frequently—*but usually for less than the amount of the initial bet*.[49] "By creating wins where players receive less than their wager," writes a game designer and consultant, "we give them a sense of winning but also continue to accrue [their] credits."[50] This "sense of winning" is communicated by presenting gamblers with the same audiovisual feedback—colorful blinking lines, sounds, a musical score—that occurs during actual winning. "The perception," said Randy Adams of Anchor Gaming, "is that you're winning all the time, when you're really not—you're putting 25 nickels in and winning 15 back, 45 in and winning 30 back, over and over."

As with virtual reel mapping and near misses, "perception" is at stake— yet in this case, the perception imparted is not merely of machines' *promise* to reward, for they actually deliver on that promise, in a manner of

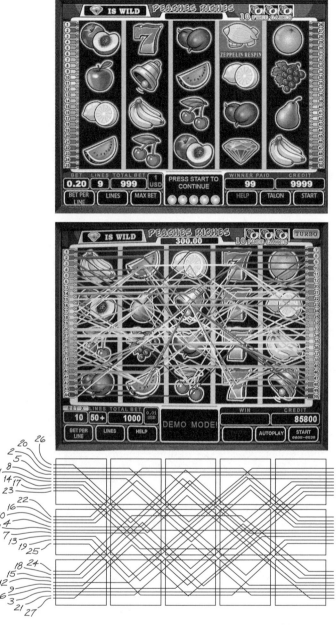

Figure 4.3. *Top Images*: A 2006 fifty-line video slot machine, at rest and after spin. Photographs by the author. *Bottom*: Diagrammatic illustration of a twenty-seven-line pay arrangement for a machine with a 3 × 5 display format. US Patent No. 5580053, Philip Crouch, 1996.

speaking. That is, they mask the actual fact of losing by rendering a new kind of quasi-winning (different from the near miss) that one team of researchers has called "losses disguised as wins," or LDWs.[51] Multiline video slots' subtle yet radical innovation is precisely their capacity to make losses appear to gamblers as wins, such that players experience the reinforcement of winning even as they steadily lose. "Positive reinforcement hides loss," a designer at Silicon Gaming explained to me. Compounding this reinforcement are the ambient and sensory cues that accompany "winning," such as lights, music, and visual graphics. The steady, partial "winning" that gamblers experience on video slots does not disrupt or inhibit play as large jackpots have been shown to do, but, rather, accommodates a "play-to-win-to-play" mode of gambling in which time-on-device is the aim.[52]

What we might call the "reinforcement potential" of multiline video slots is further compounded by the fact that they allow players a measure of modulatory control, presenting a complex array of buttons with which they can vary the number of lines and coins on which they bet, giving them a taste of the interactive decision making that proved so compelling on video poker machines yet without requiring their actual skill.[53] To borrow from the language of the gamblers' online forum that opened this chapter, they give the "rat people" a hand in the design of their own Skinner boxes. "By purchasing more lines to play on a slot machine," an Australian researcher points out, "a player can increase the frequency of reinforcement and reduce the amount of un-reinforced trials."[54] Betting on all lines not only ensures a more consistent rate of reward; it also "insures against" the regret players might feel if wins appear on lines they have not played.[55] "In a way," observes a longtime slots player from Australia named Katrina, "each game becomes like a mini raffle. Effectively, by playing all these lines you buy into the mad logic of buying every ticket in the raffle. You feel obliged to purchase all the lines 'just in case.'"

Initially, there was concern within the US gambling industry that the convoluted options and unclear outcomes of video slots might not sit well with their market, which was still largely made up of tourists in the mid-1990s. "The Australian market is more sophisticated than we are," one skeptical game developer told me in 1997, "they understand all of the unbelievably complicated winning combinations on those new format machines." "I'm in the business and I don't even understand them," confessed a representative for Bally as we stood before a bank of video slot machines in Aristocrat's booth that year at the industry meetings. Down the aisle at IGT's booth, a company representative attributed the sophistication of the Australian market to frequency of play. "They play all the time down there, four to five times a week. I think it's a learning curve." Vallejo of Anchor Gaming ventured a cultural explanation. "The typical American player is not familiar with complex gaming because Americans don't want to think or strategize, they want everything up front. But we're moving toward the Australian model as people become more comfortable with complexity." Bally's Prater agreed: "The Australian market is kind of like the video poker market here in Vegas, where players go to casinos three times a week and understand the pay schedules. Maybe that's where the States are headed, as these machines spread."

"Will we repeat the Australian experience here in North America?" queried the moderator for a panel called "The Video Future" at the 1999 industry meetings.[56] "Video gambling is gradually making inroads in a number of US gaming jurisdictions," answered Aristocrat's marketing director, "but each one is at a different evolutionary stage of acceptance."[57] The first US jurisdictions to adopt Aristocrat's multiline machines were Indian reservations and the Midwest. The vice president of slot operations from Mohegan Sun, a tribal operation in Connecticut, had doubted that the games would appeal to "less technologically oriented customers," but to his surprise their appeal cut across age, sex, and class.[58] Casino managers in Las Vegas experienced the same surprise after the Nevada Gaming Control Board approved multiliners in 1996.[59] "Our older clientele has embraced them," said the vice president of slot operations at the Palace Station in 1999, reporting that seventy-five-year-old bingo players were gambling on the Australian-format machines. "We have a lot of locals with limited bankroll who visit three to four times a week, and they're coming for the time-on-device," she said. "The video reels have been a major transition."[60] To accelerate the market's adoption of new machines, a conference attendee in 2004 suggested incorporating video-slot game structures and mathematical models into traditional three- and five-reel mechanical (nonvideo) machines; this could create a kind of "gateway product" to familiarize patrons with a video format and ease their transition. "It's a good way to migrate players," said the panelist, "it helps the adaptation along."[61]

As the adaptive migration to video slots has gathered momentum, paylines have multiplied extravagantly. At the 2005 Global Gaming Expo, Aristocrat introduced a fifty-line video slot to commemorate its fiftieth year in existence, and in 2007, a one-hundred-line slot (that helpfully "incorporate[d] a new patented line indicator to further ease player use and understanding," a company press release noted). Packing even more so-called multiplier potential into its video slots, the company's ReelPower technology features "payreels" whose digitized symbols change position in relation to each other on each spin, such that players can bet both horizontally and vertically, "on reels, lines and combinations of the two," for a chance to win in 243 different ways.[62] "The vast majority of players purchase all five ReelPower reels," Aristocrat's website tells visitors. Increasing multiplier potential still further, games with a "scatter" mode do not require that symbols line up in any direction. Super ReelPower, which adapts the scatter mode to the ReelPower formula, gives gamblers a staggering 3,125 ways to win.

Some machine manufacturers have taken their innovations in other directions, quite literally. Incredible Technologies' "sidewinder" machines, for instance, spin horizontally, while its "angle pay" machines begin from any position along the top row of symbols, slanting down to the right. WMS added three dimensions of play to its machines with Wrap Around Pays, in which "paylines can begin on any of the five reels and wrap around, creating winning combinations that were never possible before."[63] IGT, for its part, introduced MultiPlay video slots with play screens split into four quadrants, each featuring a mini-multiliner with its own "exceptionally high base-game hit frequencies."[64] Each matrix spins independently, rendering four different outcomes. Released in 2009, the machines are performing "off-the-charts"; one fabulously popular model offers players two hundred lines on which to bet. "The lines have escalated far beyond the point where you can keep tabs on what you are winning or losing," Katrina observes. "Before you have time to examine the screen too closely, you push the button for the next spin."

As paylines have multiplied to new heights and gamblers have been given options to bet more and more credits—up to one thousand per spin on one model—the denomination of play has plummeted. Before the rise of video slots, most in the gambling industry had anticipated a move from quarters to dollars as the standard denomination of play; they regarded nickels and pennies as coins of the past, to be found only in grind joints catering to the poor, elderly, and risk-averse. To their surprise, not only have higher-denomination players shifted game allegiance to nickel and even penny machines, but, when playing those lower-denomination machines, they are losing more than ever as a result of the multicoin betting options. In 1999 the moderator for "The Video Future" panel reported that an anxious casino manager had hired him to track down dollar slot players, who had rather suddenly gone missing from their usual machines. He found that they had downshifted to newer-generation quarter machines, but were gambling so many credits per spin and playing for so much longer that they were losing up to $400 a day on average.[65]

By 2000 nickels began to overtake quarters as the most popular denomination of play. Like the dollar players who were spending more time and money on multiline quarter machines, quarter players were doing the same on nickel machines. "These machines aren't really creating nickel players," remarked one game developer, "they're just giving quarter or dollar players more value" (by which he meant more revenue to gambling purveyors). "A nickel game isn't a nickel game when you're betting ninety nickels at a time," another pointed out.[66] The rise of pennies came quickly on the heels of nickels. Machines of two-cent denomination or less make up 90 percent of the machines in some Australian markets. In Nevada in 2008, only 18 percent of machines were of the penny denomination—yet this figure represents a substantial jump from 6.3 percent in 2004, and merely 0.2 percent in 2000.[67] If digital microprocessing and virtual reel technology had granted game developers the control over odds that they needed to promise large jackpots and popularize slots, multiline video slots allowed them to partition the wager itself into ever-tinier increments and thereby simultaneously lengthen gamblers' play sessions and increase industry profits. "The frequency is so high and players get so much more time-on-device, they love them," said an IGT game developer. "They can literally play all day."[68]

Encouraging gamblers to "play all day" on mechanical reel spinners of low denomination would have been considered a terrible marketing plan in the past, but when it came to video slots the gambling industry saw that profits were not about the size of gamblers' stakes but about the volume of their play. "If you provide them with the right amount of time-on-device, they will stay and play," said a representative of AC Coin. "If you take it too quickly and they lose, they're going to leave."[69] Koenig,

who earlier in the chapter emphasized the importance of creating customer trust through machine math, explained the profit logic of time-
on-device by way of a vignette involving his mother: "Once my mom put
$20 in one of my games and it took her money right away. She was pissed
and I pretty much lost her as a customer. The best way for me to get all
of her money is not to take her first $20 quickly like that; instead, I need
to keep giving her back most of what she bets, so she'll keep playing until
it's all gone." For gamblers and the industry alike, the value of play has
shifted from the axis of singular monetary wins to the axis of temporal
duration, or from volatility to volume (see fig. 4.2, top).[70] "Over fifty
percent of our games on the G2E floor will be in the one-cent denomination, a direct reflection of the industry's move to penny slots as a way to
increase time-on-device," Aristocrat's marketing manager told a reporter
in 2003.[71]

The renaissance of penny play depended not only on video technology
but also on the invention of new money-handling technologies. The physical slimness of the penny had always made it a difficult object for machine hoppers to handle, causing jams and payout errors. Although bill
acceptors and tokenization systems helped to ease penny play, something
more was needed to cope with emerging game designs involving as many
as five hundred pennies a spin. To derive value from the penny, the gambling industry had to find a way to make the penny itself disappear. In
2000, ticket-in, ticket-out technology (TITO) such as IGT's E-Z Play inadvertently facilitated the dematerialization of the penny by rendering the
insertion of coins (and bills) obsolete. Although players did not immediately embrace TITO, they warmed to the technology as they learned that
it could facilitate play on the low-denomination multiline games with
which they were then becoming familiar. This gave Aristocrat—which
just that year had earned its license to enter the Nevada market—a strong
a new foothold in the US market.

The company took a unique approach in Las Vegas. "We're sticking to
our strategy of targeting the repeat player rather than the transient player,"
Young told a reporter. "Everyone says you have to be on the Strip, but we
didn't take that position. We said, let's *surround* the Strip and get the
product to places where people play often. Let the Strip add them later."[72]
While most in the gambling industry continued to associate the local Nevada market with a preference for the game of video poker and the play
denomination of 25 cents, Aristocrat was confident that it could sway
some of that market over to its low-denomination Australian-format video

slots.[73] Indicating success in this regard, over 30 percent of the slots at Station Casinos were penny machines by 2005. "Nowhere is the penny craze more evident than in the local casinos of Las Vegas," reported an industry journalist that year.[74] By 2008 the Las Vegas Convention and Visitors Authority had added the response option of "penny" to its Residents Survey question on preferred denomination. While 43 percent of locals still played quarters that year, a respectable 23 percent preferred pennies and 22 percent, nickels; two years later, the number of quarter players dropped to 38 percent while penny players rose to 29 percent. In accordance with the downward denominational turn, by 2008 locals were betting an average of 15.5 coins per spin, significantly up from 4.5 coins ten years earlier; by 2010, they were betting 25 coins per spin.[75] Mirroring video poker trends, the betting habits of local video slots players appeared to be shifting in line with changing technology, following what Hunter described earlier as a sort of "tolerance" formation. As the Australian sociologist Richard Woolley has observed, "gambling behavior [is] incrementally reformatted over time by the new betting options and game features presented."[76]

In Australia, where the vast majority of gamblers are repeat players, and where virtually all gambling machines are video slots, the effects of this behavioral "reformatting" are evident within the community of gambling addiction. Public health studies have consistently shown that problem gamblers prefer higher lines of play and lower-denomination credits, following the betting formula known as mini-maxi (in which they bet minimum or moderate credits on the maximum number of lines, thus increasing the steadiness of rewards while decreasing their size).[77] One study found that they spent nearly 90 percent of their playtime on games of one-cent credit denomination, and that two-thirds of their losses occurred during such low-denominational play.[78] As the journalist Marc Cooper remarked in 2005, "the new generation of gambling machines has, predictably, produced a new generation of gambling addicts: not players who thrive on the adrenaline rush of a high-wager roll of the dice or turn of a card but, rather, zoned-out 'escape' players who yearn for the smooth numbness produced by the endlessly spinning reels."[79]

Upping the Ante: Tolerance for Technology

While low-denomination, multiline video slots have gradually gained ground within the microecology of local gambling in Las Vegas, innovations in video poker—some of them overtly mimicking the multiplier formula—have maintained the game's leading position among residents who play most regularly and for the longest sessions.[80] IGT alone, still the "undisputed king of video poker," today offers fifty different versions of the game.[81]

The most popular are "multihand" games that incorporate the divide-and-multiply strategy of video slots.[82] The first of these was Triple Play Draw Poker in 1998, allowing players three games at once and three times as many coins to bet.[83] "The idea sprang up and hit me right between the eyes," recounted the inventor, Ernie Moody. "What if players could play one hand and draw from three different decks? When you get dealt a really good hand, it's really good, and if you're dealt a bad hand, you'll have lots of chances to improve it."[84] *Players will never have to play two machines [at the same time] again!* notes IGT's website, alluding to regular gamblers' tendency to play two adjacent machines simultaneously so as to intensify their experience. By condensing three hands into one round, the game at once accelerates play and increases hit frequency. As on video slots, this formula strengthens the game's reinforcement schedule—in this case, not by multiplying lines or reels or bonus functions but by adding decks of cards.

Echoing Mollie's account earlier in this chapter, Randall, the electronics technician, described how the trajectory of his play followed the evolution of the video poker format, culminating with Triple Play Poker: "When I first played all they had was Jacks-or-Better. Then they came out with Deuces Wild. Then Bonus Poker, then Double Bonus, then Triple Play, where you play three hands at one time." "Once people played multi-handed video poker," Moody recalled, "it was hard for them to go back to single-handed play."[85] For Mollie, this difficulty expressed itself in a dream: "I was wandering through a casino looking for the right slot machine. They were all single-play video poker. I saw a Triple Play machine but somebody sat down in front of me. I tried some others but none of them was right for some reason—they were either too slow or I was losing too quickly, or they just weren't my machine." Randall professed a similar need for the Triple Play machine:

> That Triple Play machine is like the greatest thing ever invented. I can no longer play Jacks-or-Better, I can't play Deuces, I can't play Bonus—I can only play Double Bonus or Triple Play. The other stuff doesn't do it for me anymore. I'm wondering what the future is—in five years are you going to be able to play 10 hands??

Since we spoke, Triple Play has indeed evolved—into Five Play, Ten Play, Fifty Play, and even Hundred Play Poker (see fig. 4.4). As in Triple Play, the initial hand in these variants is identical across all decks; after a player chooses which cards to hold, the replacement cards are dealt from multiple different decks. IGT's website describes Hundred Play Poker as follows: *It's poker to the max. 100 different hands on the same screen. Ten credits per hand.* Fifty Play poker is thirty to forty times faster (and more likely to render a win) than a game of single-hand poker; instead of seeing a royal flush once every eighty hours, a player sees one every two to three hours—along with many smaller wins.[86] Rather than overstimulating players, the intensified speed and reward frequency of such a game enhances the flow of play. "You get a smoother ride," video poker expert Bob Dancer told me, repeating what is often said of multiline video slots. "It's a bumpier ride with just one hand."[87] "When I hit a jackpot nowadays," said Randall of his multihand video poker play, "I don't even blink, I don't miss a beat." In the language of behaviorism, he has habituated to a higher magnitude of "event frequencies," achieving a kind of tolerance (or decreased responsiveness) to the spikes of chance that happen during play.

Perhaps the crowning glory of the multiplicative trend we have been examining is the byzantine game of Spin Poker. Merging the multiple payline attributes of Australian-format video slots with the multiple choices of video poker, the game displays a matrix of poker hands that spin like reels; when the reels stop, wins are calculated across nine lines, including diagonals and zigzags (see fig. 4.4, bottom right). Triple Spin Poker offers gamblers three games of spin poker on one screen, taking this hybrid of choice making and high-hit frequency to yet another level. IGT's pitch for the game explicitly references the trend toward increasing paylines and decreasing denomination, noting that "Triple Spin Poker is a natural part of that evolution."

As designers continue to promote that evolution—ramping up machines' mix of lines, reels, decks and coins; decreasing denomination of play; and scattering wins into reward formulae ever-more precisely configured to maximize gamblers' investment of money over time—gamblers continue to adapt, reaching new levels of tolerance to such conditions and prompting designers to respond in turn, upping the ante with further innovation. Designers, we have seen, understand this feedback loop to be driven primarily by the "maturation" of player preferences ("faster and faster, change your games faster—players get used to them and also

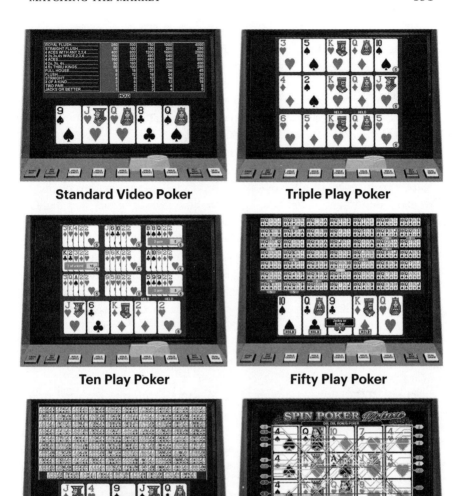

Figure 4.4. From left to right: progressively more complex versions of video poker. Courtesy of Action Gaming / VideoPoker.com.

fed up with them faster," said Sylvie Linard of Cyberview[88]). Yet gambling addicts insist that machines themselves are a crucial driver of the process. "I keep needing more intensity, *and the machines keep matching me*," Mollie told us earlier. As she sees it, her addiction emerges from an ongoing process of human-machine adaptation in which her own changing needs (i.e., what she requires to enter the zone) are spurred on by the continual "matching" of those needs by design.[89]

Gamblers are precise in their accounts of how their tolerance is continually built up via technological advances. The Australian gambler Katrina, for instance, recalls how apparently small and innocuous changes to game design ended up pushing her habituation to higher and higher levels. "I have been associated with electronic gaming machines for about 20 years," reads a letter she sent to me in 2008.[90] "I can think back to when I was satisfied with playing 1 line and then fast forward to the time when I was happy playing 9 lines, but now I play 20 lines. I have become accustomed to it and it is hard not to be dissatisfied by going back to older models." Katrina recognizes that there are certain intensities of machine events with which she cannot cope; intensities that are too low or too high produce intolerable states of under- or overstimulation in which she cannot "lose herself" in the zone of play, an experience typical of repeat machine players.

At the 2006 Global Gaming Expo, a panel of players reported to a room full of industry representatives on their respective tolerance thresholds with respect to the latest machine designs. "One thing I like about penny slots," the moderator explained, "is the wonderful freedom to shift how many lines I play. But I'm not ready to play 100 lines of anything yet." An older woman told the audience: "Me, I'm comfortable up to 25 lines. I will play 40, but I really, really try to avoid 100 line games … the money just flows through too quickly. I play twice a week or more for 6 to 8 hours and it would just drain me." Both women identified the numerical limit of lines-per-game at which their own personal comfort zones were exceeded; the second woman described how too many lines would disrupt the money-to-time ratio to which she was accustomed. At the same time, both acknowledged that their comfort zones would shift over time as they adjusted to new intensities of contingency and reinforcement ("I'm not ready to play 100 lines of anything *yet*," said the moderator).

In her letter to me, Katrina elaborates on the process by which the repeated experience of particular machine events prompts successive readjustments in her behavior, propelling her play to new levels. She notes that it is when patterns "begin to emerge"—or when she feels they do—that she becomes caught:

> People who play machines infrequently or on a very superficial level can remain relatively unaffected by the machines' repetitious processes. But if you play quite frequently *you have all these things constantly working on you and you develop a familiarity with the many different scenarios that play out amidst the "randomness" of it all.* Each time you sit down at a machine you have a history of memories of what has happened hundreds or even thousands of times before (if you have played for many years).... Rough patterns of how it all works begin to emerge, and *you find yourself expecting certain things.*

Katrina characterizes her addiction as an ongoing cognitive and affective adaptation to upticks in the intensity of machine reinforcement. What finally gives the industry the upper hand in this process is not simply the fact of her habituation or "machine tolerance," as we might call it, but the way in which technological innovation destabilizes that tolerance wherever it develops—introducing new and unexpected increments of intensity and elements of surprise into the exchange, thus provoking further responsive adjustments in her internal expectations.

To illustrate the process, Katrina relates how one common feature of video slots, called "bonus rounds" or "free spins," has affected her play. This type of feature randomly presents gamblers with an animated bonus game offering them a prize, a chance at a prize, or free spins on the machine—all of which grant more time-on-device.[91] The "game-within-a-game" works in dynamic concert with the payout schedule of the base game, serving as a second layer of reinforcement. "At first," she remembers, "free spins were just a novelty, just another innovation to contend with. I was not to know how they would change the dynamics of my play. But soon, I would dismiss outright any machine that did not have this feature." The novelty began to eclipse other aspects of her play, "to the point where normal game play lost some of its appeal. Although still important, to a degree it became a means to an end, a sort of biding of time until the free spin feature occurred." Normal game play, to which she had habituated, became a mere "biding of time," driven by the anticipation of the free spin and its contingent arrival.

Katrina describes how the stakes of this contingency rise as her credits diminish:

As your credits start declining, the anticipation and focus on free spin symbols starts to rise. Since they reward so much more than regular play, they become a sort of a savior. When the free spin feature is activated, then there is a kind of relief. Assuming the outcome [of the spin] is fairly good, you can then be satisfied for a while and your focus on free spin symbols diminishes to a degree.

Katrina's susceptibility to the contingency of the free spin rises and diminishes, waxes and wanes; in moments of its waxing, her pursuit of the free spin (and the "relief" it affords when it arrives) dwarfs the more familiar routines of her slot play.

Drawing on her years of experience, she carefully distinguishes among the various "scenarios" that can unfold with regard to free spins during a session of gambling:

Due to the unpredictable nature of the free spin feature you can sometimes feed hundreds of dollars into the machine without getting it. Or you can be "spoiled" and get it quite regularly. On other occasions you get them intermittently. Depending on how long the session is with a particular machine, all three of the above scenarios can occur in a cyclic but disordered fashion in the one sitting.

As much as these different scenarios guide Katrina's external actions, they intimately affect her internal state, as she tells us in a discerning phenomenological account of her own play:

Sometimes there is a frequent appearance of free spin symbols but no forthcoming free spins. In that case, you become highly focused on the *symbols* representing free spins. What subtly intensifies your focus on free spin symbols are *certain sounds* attached to these symbols when they appear in the window. Your emotions rise and fall with the appearance of free spin symbols, and *with the music*. If the buildup of anticipation and focusing is chronically frustrated in this way, then there is a great tendency to plow through your credits. At the same time, there is often an internal dialogue going on as to whether to push the "collect" button. However, it is a difficult situation because while you are contemplating this you are still pushing the button and also hoping something will happen, like the free spins showing up ...

Once you reach the point of no return you usually don't care about collecting [your credit] anymore. Sometimes when the credits are almost down to nothing *the free spins will suddenly appear*, but if they don't and the credits expire, you will do various things. Sometimes you leave, but more often you will put more money in, and the free spins may come soon after and start the ball rolling all over again. It all moves quite quickly. The free spins just exacerbate the downward spiral you are on.

Machine sounds, music, the chance appearance of free spins: each of these contingent game events conditions Katrina's experience, expectations, and actions.[92] The movement of her play—which invariably reveals its trajectory to be that of a downward spiral—unfolds in a continuous, rapid, responsive interaction with the machine, precluding pauses or spaces in which she might reflect or stop.

The final free-spin scenario that Katrina describes explicitly invokes the "zone"—the elusive point of absorption, beyond contingency, that machine gamblers perpetually seek. For Katrina to reach the zone and to remain there for a spell, a particular set of circumstances must arise:

> The best scenario is when the free spins have been coming around regularly and perhaps normal game play has been good as well, and consequently the credits are up pretty high—this is what you have come to feel is the ideal situation. *This is where it particularly feeds into that zone where you can play for quite some time without the credits diminishing very much*—they may seesaw, but they maintain a relatively high level. *You can just relax and 'lose' yourself at what is ironically a very precarious but 'safe' level of play and you really don't want it to end.* Of course, at some stage it inevitably starts to take a nosedive.

Katrina understands the zone as at once "safe" and "precarious"—a gentle seesaw of play credit that is mirrored in a gentle seesaw of player affect, both of which might at any instant lose momentum and come to a standstill. The zone state is attainable only at the threshold where rhythm holds sway over risk, comfort over perturbation, habituation over surprise.[93]

As we have seen, this threshold constantly shifts as a function of dynamic interaction between players' habits and the industry's technological innovations. The interaction deviates markedly from an economic formulation of the relationship between supply and demand, in which market demand (understood as the static preferences of rational consumers) steers supply such that the two meet in equilibrium.[94] Instead, repeat machine gambling can be characterized as an asymmetric interplay between two different modes of feedback: while individual gamblers follow a logic of "negative feedback" in which they continuously adjust their actions so as to attain the zone's homeostatic balance, the industry and its designers follow a logic of "positive feedback" in which they incrementally ratchet up the intensity of play required of gamblers to achieve the zone.[95] Out of the asymmetry between these two modes of feedback emerge the industry's innovations and the players' machine tolerance.

5

LIVE DATA

Tracking Players, Guiding Play

One night while I was playing at the Crystal Palace, a man sat down next to me and said, *You know, I invented this machine.* I asked him, *How did you come up with the machine?* And he said, *Well, I interview people like you and ask them what they think the machine should do, or not do.* He said, *I'm always talking to everyone, wherever I go, getting input.* It was his creation and he wanted feedback. He got excitement hearing how I felt about playing it. I said, *It's a wonderful product, it's sleek, attractive, every ten minutes it gives you a little something, and you don't have to put in coins—I hate dirty hands.* I helped him, by giving him input.

         —Lola

RANDY ADAMS'S NAME kept popping up. "He's the man, he's Mr. Inventor," said Marcus Prater at Bally. "He's the idea guy," said his colleague at Anchor Gaming.[1] "Randy Adams really knows how to get in the head of a fifty-year-old woman and figure out what she wants," commented a panelist admiringly during a presentation at the 1999 World Gaming Expo. I contacted Adams's secretary after watching a rerun of Geraldo Rivera's *Las Vegas, the American Fantasy.* In the program, after interviewing local psychologist Robert Hunter, Rivera launched into a baritone description of the gaming industry and its henchmen, who had "the art of gambling down to a science." He introduced Adams: "Innovative game designer Randy Adams is a master of manipulation, updating the technology of the games to ensnare today's video generation. Adams is the slot king."

Anchor Gaming's company headquarters was based in a corporate office complex on Pilot Road near the Las Vegas airport, not far from Bally Technologies and a number of other companies. In the lobby showroom, a nasal, female voice, presumably the soundtrack for a bonus feature, periodically intoned from one of the machines on display: *Don't even go there! Don't even go there!* Adams arrived late and in a whirl, looking not unlike Gene Wilder's Willy Wonka—a clean-shaven man in his late forties with a small frame and a large puff of hair somewhere between blond and gray. He led me down a hallway to his office, a many-windowed room whose large desk was covered with casino floor plans and game brochures.

As he swung into his oversized leather chair, a tall man in his seventies strolled into the room, thin with a protruding belly. Adams pointed to him and told me, "Right there is the guy who developed the first poker machine." Stan Fulton, chairman of Anchor Gaming, had been involved in developing video poker when IGT was founded.[2] Fulton pointed back at Adams. "And that's the Michelangelo of slot machines. Right over there." He continued, with the dramatic pauses of a Baptist preacher: "His life, is devoted, to finding out, what the customer wants, and then providing them, with what they want."

"Very well put," said Adams.

"To him"—Fulton resumed, still pointing—"a great evening is grabbing a bite somewhere and being on the casino floor, talking with the people: *Why do you like that machine?*" Fulton swiveled his head and fixed me with an intense gaze: "*Why do you like that machine?*" He turned slowly and exited the office.

As we saw in the last chapter, the gambling industry's quest to "match the market" entails a constant adjustment and readjustment of its products to players' changing preferences. This chapter shifts focus from the *products* of player-centric design to the *process* of player-centric design, concentrating on the industry's diverse methods for gathering knowledge

about players—particularly repeat players. Like machine design, these
methods have significantly evolved over the past two decades. The text of
an IGT advertisement from 1988, appearing beneath a row of gamblers
standing beside their favorite machines (see fig. 5.1), emphasized the importance of knowledge gathering to the player-centric approach that was
then emerging:

> They and thousands of other players like them are the ones who teach us
> the most about making successful casino games. That's why casino slot
> managers spend so much time watching and listening to players. We've
> discovered what players like and what they don't. The excellent companies
> tend to be more driven by close-to-the-customer attributes than by either
> technology or cost. Put another way, the closer we are to [players], the
> longer we'll all stay on top of the game.[3]

Although complex forms of consumer tracking and marketing enabled by
information and communication technologies have replaced the simple
techniques of "watching and listening" presented in the IGT advertisement, the basic goal of staying "close to the customer" has only strength-
ened. "We must not become disconnected from our players and find ourselves in an engineering vacuum," an IGT designer reiterated in 2004.
"We need ongoing connectivity with our players."[4]

Demonstrating just how entrenched this need for connectivity had become by the twenty-first century, the 2006 Global Gaming Expo featured
a panel called "And Now ... A Word from Players." The first of its kind,
it took the form of a public focus group in which regular gamblers (a
college student, a husband and wife in their fifties, and a single woman
in her forties) would provide insight into "the player experience itself—
what's happening at the machine." The panel description read: *"This
conference is full of industry experts ready to share their opinions about
games and marketing, but what is the end user thinking? This panel of
experienced slot players will expose slot directors, marketing experts and
others to their feelings and opinions about what makes a successful gaming experience. Learn from the real 'experts.'"* If the 1988 IGT advertisement cast players in the role of passive teachers, here they figured as veri-
table "experts" who would "expose" the industry to their insights. Their
expertise lay in their intimate experience with gambling technologies, and
their public revelation of this expertise promised to inform the better
engineering of their future experiences. At once agents and objects of the
industry's campaign to extract value from so-called consumer intelligence,

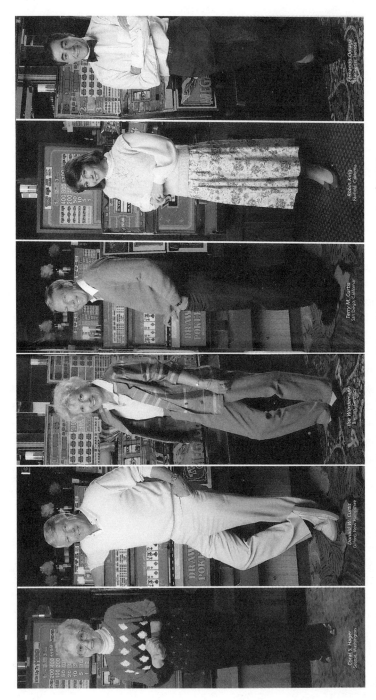

Figure 5.1. Advertisement by International Gaming Technology. Printed in *Casino Gaming*, April 1988.

repeat players are drawn further into the feedback loop of design and experience.

From Intuition to Analysis

Although the public format of the aforementioned G2E panel was unique, focus groups have long been a part of the strategic repertoire of game developers. Participants interact with new games and then rate their features, sometimes using "perception analyzer dials" similar to those used to gauge public opinion in political races. Gardner Grout of Silicon Gaming told me of one focus group his company held when a game called Banana-Rama was under development in 1998. "We weren't expecting it at all, but the players got paranoid about the animated monkeys on the bonus screen." The monkeys sat looking out of trees, their heads turning to watch the reels spin and swiveling back toward players when the reels stopped. They laughed and danced when players won, but otherwise stared at them, unblinking and expressionless; some of the test players found this "creepy" and complained. "Not everyone got paranoid and it would have cost too much to redo the graphics and animation," he remembered, "so we added some stuff where you could tickle the monkeys on the interactive screen and they'd giggle, or you could drop a coconut on one of their heads."

Over the years, many in the industry have lost faith in the value of focus groups to the game design process. "People tell you what they want and you produce it and it doesn't work. Absolute failure. They don't really know what they want."[5] Today, focus groups are more often used to "confirm hunches" than to guide game development. A top executive at IGT who held a master's degree in psychology suggested to me that methods of cross-cultural anthropology, such as participant observation, were better suited to the task of game design. Randy Adams agreed. "You could do it up on a PowerPoint type presentation and sit down with a little laptop in front of these people and tell 'em to use the key and play the game," he told me, "but you're not gonna learn anything that way. The only true test is the [casino] floor." In 2000 John Vallejo described the field trips he and his colleagues at Anchor Gaming routinely took:

> The casino floor is like our own extended focus group. We sit and play, participate, ask players what they think about our machines, and about other machines. The whole team does this—it's as important for the sound

engineers to know the customer as anyone else; even the math guy spends some hours observing, asking questions. *You have to experience it to understand what people really want.*

Evoking the scene that Lola recounted at the start of this chapter, Adams told me of his own style in the field. "I go out there and sit down at a machine. I turn to the person next to me and say *I design these things, that's why I've been sitting here playing this machine next to you for twenty minutes, because this is what I do. Let me show you the storyboard for a new game—I want to know what you think.* They'll tell you everything."

In 1999, a veteran game designer spoke of such tactics with a mixture of pride and defensiveness. "The guys in the trenches—out there in casinos, on the floor—can run circles around the MBA guys who are starting to come in. The MBAs have been cubby-holed by their business training. I kick the hell out of 'em, and I don't do it with metrics or pie charts." Adams echoed this cowboy bravado:

> Other sorts of corporations come in and look at us guys with straws in our teeth and think they can take over, but the truth is, they can't run this business using the typical MBA-type philosophy of business administration. A compartmentalized design process with focus groups and committees for each game feature, endless meetings over every color and sound, take a very, very long time to get the product to the field—it's just too bureaucratic.

Although slot machine manufacturers in the 1980s and 1990s conducted standard business research from time to time, it was supplementary rather than central to their design process. In addition to arranging the occasional focus groups, sometimes they filmed and analyzed gamblers' play, recorded their reactions to game storyboards, or compiled databases of gamblers' preferences to help inform design choices. After the machines had been developed and placed on the casino floor, there were "live data" to collect in the marketplace and real-time assessments to cull from machines' internal self-monitors. Yet this research was neither gathered nor applied in a systematic, scientific manner. "We absorb the information that's available," said Adams with a shrug. "I wish I could tell you that it's all scientific, but Stan is right to call me Michelangelo—I'm more like an artist than a scientist."

To illustrate the artistic, accidental nature of game design, a graphic artist at Silicon Gaming described one game whose fish icon changed color several times and ended up holding a saxophone. "There was no real reason or logic to it; it's like anything in advertising and marketing—everybody's got an opinion, and nobody's right and nobody's wrong. It's subjective." Once, Prater recalled, a Bally design team spent a full month perfecting a "ding" sound for a game, "to make it comforting instead of annoying. But we didn't rely on any rules or tests, we just listened to it until we liked it. We don't know why certain sounds work, we just know they do." He reflected on this approach: "There are gaming guys who have been in the business ten, twenty, thirty years—long enough to know what works; it's more intuitive than scientific, it's a matter of instinct."

Over the last decade, however, the place of instinct in the gambling industry has been steadily on the wane. The "days of guesswork and instinct may be over," one industry analyst wrote in 2008.[6] The waning of instinct is apparent not only in game development but in casino operation as well, where, another industry analyst has written, "modern management techniques are replacing 'judgmental and intuitive' operational styles with the emergence of a 'new breed' of gaming executive."[7] Bruce Rowe, a Harvard-educated MBA at Bally who considers himself "an analytical type," typifies this new breed. "Quite candidly," he told me at G2E 2007, "most technology people in this industry are not analytical." A third of them, he estimated, had only completed high school; another third only college; and just a handful had earned MBAs. This was problematic, he ventured, given the mind-bogglingly complex "combinatorics" of the contemporary gambling scene and the staggering array of decisions they entail: how to dynamically mingle the right number of games, how many of each, their price, their placement, their hold percentage, their denomination, and more.[8] (As we learned in the last chapter, denomination alone entails a phenomenal number of choices; while in the past the range of a maximum bet was narrow—75 cents to $1.50—options now range from one cent to $10, and in the case of multicoin video slots, options are variable within the same game.) To make these decisions, Rowe asserted, "an analytical approach is necessary." By "analytical," it soon became apparent, he meant an approach that made use of software to analyze consumer data. "It's getting impossible to make these choices without technological assistance," he told me. "It would be an analyst's folly to think his intuitions and assumptions were not arbitrary and irrational." Technology's role was to "lend a rational analysis of what's going on in this complicated matrix of choice."

As the task of staying "close to the customer" is increasingly delegated to analytic technologies, the artistry and tacit know-how of traditional game development are losing their central role. The remainder of this chapter will examine the information-gathering and analytic technologies that have been developed and applied within the gambling industry in recent years. These encompass player tracking systems, data visualization and behavioral intelligence software, and the capacity to detect and respond to player preferences in real time via downloadable game configurations running on a telecommunications network. Each of these tools allows the industry to "match" its machine market with greater precision. "This is a whole new world that we couldn't get our hands around before," comments Gary Loveman, who holds a degree from the MIT School of Management and was a professor at the Harvard Business School before becoming CEO of Harrah's Casinos. "This is the replacement of intuition and hunch with science."[9]

THE RISE OF PLAYER TRACKING

Player tracking systems played a critical role in the turn from intuition to science. The first such system was formed in 1985 at Harrah's casino in Atlantic City, inspired by the airline and credit card reward programs that were then gaining popularity.[10] Players in the club carried punch cards that attendants notched for each jackpot hit; with enough notches, they could redeem the cards for meals and other rewards. The gambling industry quickly realized that such clubs were not only a way to gather a wealth of data about customers (as other businesses had already used them) but were also a way to incentivize their continued patronage by allocating reward points.[11] They computerized the system, giving gamblers plastic cards with personalized magnetic stripes to insert into slot machines each time they played. Typically worn around the neck or attached to the wrist by colorful bungee cords, so-called loyalty cards connected gamblers to a central database that recorded the value of each bet they made, their wins and losses, the rate at which they pushed slot machine play buttons, when they took breaks, and what drinks and meals they purchased. Instead of earning points for the amount they wagered in one sitting, players now earned points for the amount they wagered over time. In effect, tracking technology brought low stakes "repeat players" into the scopes of casino managers, where formerly only high rollers had appeared.

By tracking gamblers' machine play, managers were able to collect "vital information" about their customers, as one trade journalist phrased it in 1990.[12] Gambling machines, he noted, were transformed from stand-alone game boxes into networked "electronic surveillance devices." While the terminals continued to function as objects of attention and absorption for players, they were now also "capable of monitoring, recording, and cross-referencing attentive behavior for purposes of productivity," as the art historian Jonathan Crary observes of contemporary video entertainment more generally. "Attentive behavior in front of all sorts of screens," he goes on, "is increasingly part of a continuous process of feedback and adjustment within what Foucault calls a 'network of permanent observation.'"[13]

Yet the surveillance of player tracking works differently than the panoptic mode of surveillance about which Foucault wrote, and for which casinos and their hidden security cameras are so well known. The latter subjects gamblers (and casino employees) to a relentless gaze that threatens to expose and punish any who might risk foul play; in this disciplinary setup, the awareness of being watched is meant to function as a kind of internalized camera, keeping behavior in check.[14] In contrast, tracking technologies unobtrusively record gamblers' unfettered play, at once dispensing rewards and collecting clues to how the technology might better coax continued play; in this case, it is best that gamblers remain *unaware* of their surveillance.

Tracked gamblers are treated less as individual subjects than as "dividuals" in the Deleuzian sense—bundles of traits and habits (associated with pin numbers, codes, passwords, and personal algorithms) that can be systematically compared with those of others, allowing casinos to more precisely identify and market to distinct customer niches[15] Casinos can also triangulate any given gambler's player data with her demographic data, piecing together a profile that can be used to customize game offerings and marketing appeals specifically for her; although she has been broken down into discrete data points in the process of tracking, in the moment of marketing she is reassembled as a distinct individual who can be examined from every angle. Using player tracking, it has become possible to glean "a massive 360 degree view of the guest," remarked one G2E presenter in 2007.[16] "I am watching everything. I see it all," said

Richard Mirman, senior vice president of business development at
Harrah's.[17]

Initially engineered to track consumers inside just one casino, player
tracking systems soon acquired the ability to follow them across diverse
consumer spaces by linking machines in taverns, supermarkets, pharmacies, and convenience stores. In 1997 the managers at Foxwoods, a
sprawling Native American casino in Connecticut, envisioned a "cashless environment wherein patrons use the WC [Wampum Card] as an
all-purpose transaction debit card for all expenditures in both the resort
and in the local community."[18] This vision of the entire "local community" as a site for the collection of live data extends the reach of player
tracking beyond the physical boundaries of the casino.[19] Similarly, Harrah's Total Rewards plan tracks play from coast to coast by pooling information from its national chain of properties into a single centralized
database.[20]

A game developer I spoke with in 2000 speculated that newer tracking
cards would not require insertion in machines for recognition to take place;
instead, machines would detect card-carrying players as they passed,
making it possible to seamlessly track their migration through a given
landscape. "Think of the data—it would be fascinating, the stream of
people and their flows." Six years later, during an industry meeting at Station's Red Rock Casino, Radiofrequency Identification (RFID)—originally
devised to monitor the peripatetic movements of criminal offenders and
soon thereafter employed by retail operations to trace the purchase of consumer products—was given a trial run among conference participants.[21]
Applied in casinos, RFID uses tracking tags embedded in player cards to
follow patrons as they move through a space, in real time.[22] By integrating transactional data and flow of movement, casinos can "analyze their
customers' every move."[23]

Yet how, exactly, to make that analysis? How to leverage "the stream of
people and their flows" so as to inform strategic modifications to casino
games, layout, or marketing campaigns? In the past, so-called operational
adjustments were based either on trial and error or on projective modeling techniques such as "stochastic migration," in which theoretical individuals created from samplings of actual behavior (typically recorded by
note-taking observers) were followed through virtual simulations of an
environment before and after a proposed design change—moving a bank
of machines a few feet left, for instance, or widening the entryway to a
gaming area.[24] While the challenge for such techniques was how to gather

enough of the right information on existing consumer behavior to forecast the effects of a particular design change, the challenge for tracking techniques is different: How to extract meaningful insight from a continuous stream of so-called live data overwhelming in its volume and detail? How to render legible the ever-growing "silos" of raw informational rainfall?

The metaphor of deluge is salient in the phrasing of this query by one company specializing in casino data analysis: "Does the tidal wave of customer and transaction data your business generates power it to new levels of insight and profitability, or are your executives swamped by the rising tide?"[25] At the 2007 G2E meetings, a data analysis specialist impressed upon his peers the magnitude of the informational flow: "You've got 20,000 [behavioral] models per second, streaming off the floor."[26] A fellow specialist echoed him in 2008: "We have too much data, all these different systems are collecting data.... How to integrate it and turn it into insight?"[27] Individual analysts, even when working in groups, are unable to gather, much less analyze, this scale of information. Within the data lie behavioral patterns imperceptible to the human eye, eluding intuition and logic alike; only massive data crunching can reveal those patterns and suggest ways to leverage them for profit. Technology needs more technology.

Behavioral Analytics: Actionable Intelligence

An increasing number of behavioral analytic software suites have been developed to help members of the gambling industry navigate the deep informational seas that have formed in the wake of tracking technology. A data visualization system by Mariposa (now partnered with IGT) promises that its users can overcome their "piecemeal, bubble gum and duct tape approach" to marketing and "fully understand and predict player behavior patterns."[28] "Imagine being able to change your floor mix based on a predictive model for optimized use," prompts the company brochure. "Data visualization allows you to literally see who your customers are, where they're from, what games they like to play ... all in real time."[29]

The system represents gamblers as graphical icons in the shape of chess pawns, arrayed on maps of the casino floor (see fig. 5.2). Clicking an icon or "player locater" opens a detailed profile of that player, showing how many trips he or she made to the casino over a specified period, on what

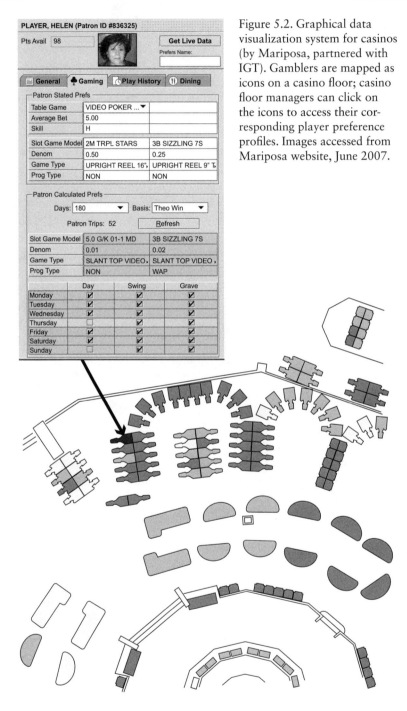

Figure 5.2. Graphical data visualization system for casinos (by Mariposa, partnered with IGT). Gamblers are mapped as icons on a casino floor; casino floor managers can click on the icons to access their corresponding player preference profiles. Images accessed from Mariposa website, June 2007.

days of the week, at what time of day, and, where applicable, the gambling preferences of a spouse. Gamblers' "stated preferences" are listed above their "calculated preferences." The profile for "Helen player," for example, indicates that her stated preference for upright reel games played at 50 cents a spin does not match her calculated preference for slant top video poker and denominations of one and two cents. Highlighting the significance of such insights, the software's website suggests that casino managers can "know more about players than they know about themselves." At the top right of the screen, casino floor managers may click "get live data" to view Helen's play at any given moment.

A company called Compudigm, now partnered with Bally, created a business intelligence tool called seePOWER that specializes in analyzing data from multiple gamblers to reveal group "tendencies and preferences," as one press release put it. The technology works by transforming massive amounts of player tracking information into colorful heat maps that represent the collective behavior of patrons in and over time (see fig. 5.3). The visualizations are created by downloading tracked information nightly to a data warehouse, where it is "scrubbed" through whatever parameters a particular casino specifies, a process that primes it to answer certain kinds of questions: *What days of week and times of day do women in their thirties with children tend to play? Which machines do retired men prefer?* When rendered in visual form, the information becomes what technicians call "actionable intelligence," organized to facilitate insight into the financial implications of slot floor reconfigurations or new marketing promotions.

Because it "taps the ability of the human brain to interpret pictures and animation much faster than numbers," seePOWER makes otherwise invisible patterns and anomalies quickly intelligible to casino managers.[30] A company representative gave me a demonstration of the software on her laptop computer during the Global Gaming Expo in 2007. She pulled up a heat-map titled "Time Played—Females," picturing data for women players on one casino slot floor over a twenty-four-hour period. Dark red clots of color appeared around the machines that had been played the longest, encircled by bands of progressively "cooler" shades for those played less—lighter red for sixteen hours, pink for twelve hours, orange for eight, and so on (see fig. 5.3). In a time-lapse animation, these shaded contours undulated as activity waxed and waned at different machines. An animation of the same area over five consecutive days revealed a curious pattern: every evening at approximately the same time, female pa-

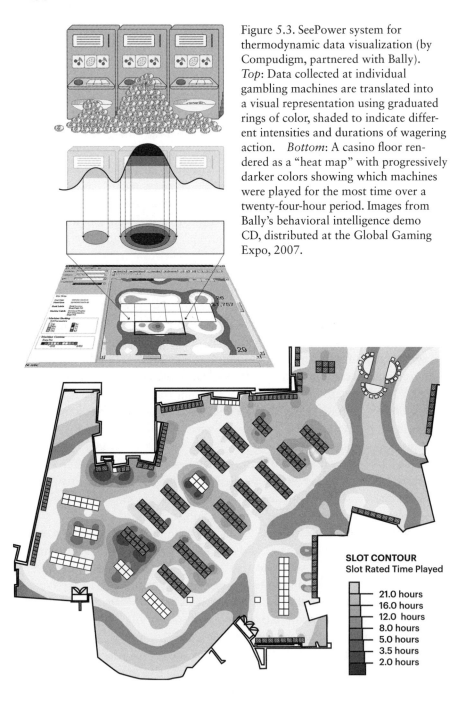

Figure 5.3. SeePower system for thermodynamic data visualization (by Compudigm, partnered with Bally). *Top*: Data collected at individual gambling machines are translated into a visual representation using graduated rings of color, shaded to indicate different intensities and durations of wagering action. *Bottom*: A casino floor rendered as a "heat map" with progressively darker colors showing which machines were played for the most time over a twenty-four-hour period. Images from Bally's behavioral intelligence demo CD, distributed at the Global Gaming Expo, 2007.

SLOT CONTOUR
Slot Rated Time Played

21.0 hours
16.0 hours
12.0 hours
8.0 hours
5.0 hours
3.5 hours
2.0 hours

trons under thirty years of age were moving from one side of a popular bank of slot machines to the other (or leaving altogether), while men over fifty were taking their original seats. Upon further investigation it was discovered that the men were exiting a nearby showroom near the machines at the close of a revue performance and pestering the young women. "They never would have seen it without Compudigm," the representative told me. Casino managers responded by creating "a whole new protective area for those women" containing the machines they liked to play, and sending out a direct mailing to promote the new slot shelter. Profit levels not only returned but increased.

To inform targeted marketing campaigns, seePOWER's data visualizations extend beyond the physical confines of the casino, generating "outside maps" that complement the "inside maps" by further illuminating the behavior of targeted groups. "Let's say we want to see the profitability of females fifty-five and older. *Who are these ladies? Where do they live? How can we target them better?*" The representative showed an animated map of an unidentified city, titled "ground floor, little old ladies, carded play time." As the clock in the upper left-hand corner spun, the city flared and pulsed with color, registering the home addresses of older women gamblers as they began and ended sessions of machine play on the ground floor of one casino over the course of a day. In the wee hours, small ponds of color dotted the landscape, with red centers indicating the neighborhoods most heavily populated by current onsite players. Starting at 8 a.m., the center of the map blossomed dramatically outward into a bright red flower, reaching maximum size at 11 a.m. and shrinking back in the evening; across the city, discrete geographic pockets of "little old ladies" continued to gamble throughout the night. Armed with this information, the casino was in a position to tailor its offerings to the play schedules of this particular player segment.

Most casinos, Compudigm boasts, experience nearly 20 percent additional revenue within eight months of using its software; those that install a data warehouse directly on their premises are "armed with up-to-the-minute information," able thus to cope with "atomic level data across the enterprise in real time."[31] The cover of a brochure for the system features two giant hands spread open over a casino floor, holding a large bubble in which a man playing a slot machine appears, crystal-ball-like. As Mark Andrejevic observes in his study of business surveillance and data-capture systems, consumers have "become increasingly transparent to marketers even as the algorithms used to sort, target, and

exclude them have become increasingly complex and opaque."[32] As we
will see next, it is not only the tendencies and preferences of player niches
that such algorithms serve to identify and analyze, but also those of individual players.

Touch Points: Relationship Management

From early versions of player card systems to cutting-edge data management software suites, tracking technologies are more than tools of market
reconnaissance, also functioning as tools for "relationship management."
As in other service industries, "relationship" is essentially a euphemism
for a strategic exchange in which customers relinquish personal data that
corporations then use to better market to them and thus gain their "loyalty." The knowledge produced by Mariposa, for example, makes it "the
perfect 'bonding' tool"—a way to "close the loop on ensuring your program performance is at its best." Customer tracking technologies enable
"bonding" not just by gleaning the information needed to customize appeals to gamblers, but also by directly communicating those appeals to
gamblers at play. "Technology is allowing all these new touch points,"
said a representative from Konami Gaming.[33]

Because the ability to analyze and "touch" players depends on their
voluntary participation in loyalty programs, the industry makes a concerted effort to ensure maximal enrollment. A full 70 percent of gamblers
use loyalty club cards, and the figure is steadily growing (among Las
Vegas locals, the figure is over 80 percent). If a gambler plays without a
card, systems like Mariposa and seePOWER identify that individual so
that slot managers can dispatch a casino representative to persuade him
or her to sign up for one. "The anonymous player costs you money," a
proponent of tracking technology told a G2E audience in 2005, "whereas
the carded player—you know what motivates him, what he likes to play,
you can pick up that rifle and shoot right at him for what he wants from
a targeted marketing approach. Otherwise, you're busy waving a shotgun
around the room thinking, *How am I going to get this guy?*"[34]

To convince patrons that it is better to be known than anonymous,
casinos present player tracking as a convenient service and a means for
acquiring the rewards to which they are entitled. "Loyalty programs are
about giving your customers a reason to give you data, so that data can
be used to earn you money," said an industry member in 2008, laying

bare the profit motives behind the language of "relationship."[35] "Interactivity," notes Andrejevic, "is not necessarily a two-way street; more often than not, it amounts to the offer of convenience in exchange for willing or unwitting submission to increasingly detailed forms of information gathering."[36]

A striking example of "unwitting submission" is found in Bally's method for tracking players regardless of their participation in a loyalty club. The system incorporates biometric recognition into gambling machines via miniaturized cameras linked to a central database; when a player activates the machine without using a player card, the camera "captures the player's image and stores it along with their game play," creating a "John Doe" file. Although the casino does not know the patron's actual name, it can track his behavior over time "for a total view of the customer's worth."[37] "Invisible to the user," the system ensures that the opportunity to cultivate a relationship with the uncarded patron will not be lost.

To most profitably manage player relationships, the industry must determine the specific *value* of those relationships. "What is the relationship of a particular customer to you, and you to them? Is that customer profitable or not?" asked a Harrah's executive at G2E in 2008.[38] "What is the order of value of that player to me?" echoed Bally's Rowe.[39] Using statistical modeling, casinos "tier" players based on different parameters, assigning each a "customer value" or "theoretical player value"—a value, that is, based on the theoretical revenue they are likely to generate. On a panel called "Patron Rating: The New Definition of Customer Value," one specialist shared his system for gauging patron worth, recommending that casinos give each customer a "recency score" (how recently he has visited), a "frequency score" (how often he visits), and a "monetary score" (how much he spends), and then create a personalized marketing algorithm out of these variables.[40] "We want to maximize every relationship," Harrah's Richard Mirman told a journalist.[41]

Harrah's statistical models for determining player value, similar to those used for predicting stocks' future worth, are the most advanced in the industry. The casino franchise, which maintains ninety different demographic segments for its customers, has determined that player value is most strongly associated with frequency of play, type of game played, and the number of coins played per spin or hand. Gamblers exhibiting a high play "velocity" (i.e., those who hit machines' buttons very fast) are easily convinced to gamble more and thus are especially valuable to the company.[42] Player value algorithms set calendars and budgets to predict when and how much a player can be expected to gamble, generating "behavior modification reports" that suggest what kinds of solicitations he or she might respond to. A gambler "overdue" for a visit gets a mailer, followed by a telephone call. "We get him motivated, back in an observed frequency pattern," CEO Gary Loveman told a journalist.[43]

Harrah's has even developed a way to calculate a player's "predicted lifetime value," or how much he or she is likely to lose to the franchise over his or her lifetime. Customers deemed most profitable receive special treatment, including quicker responses from telephone systems that are programmed to bounce incoming phone numbers off a customer database and place callers in the queue according to their value tier. In this way, "every player is accounted for and gets something depending on their value to the property they're playing at." Similarly, Bally uses the customer data it gathers as the basis for "player-centric bonusing." Unlike game-centric bonusing, in which machines randomly reward whoever is sitting at them, the player-centric system categorizes individuals by their unique spending profiles and rewards them with bonuses accordingly. "Maximize your marketing dollars by building deeper, more profitable relationships with them," reads an advertisement for the system.

In 2005 Harrah's came up with a way to measure, act upon, and optimize player value within the span of an individual play session. Enacting a Pavlovian system of real-time relationship management, software feeds a player's data through an algorithm that calculates how much that player can lose and still feel satisfied, thereby establishing personalized "pain points." When the software senses that a player is approaching the threshold of her pain point, it dispatches a live "Luck Ambassador" to dispense rewards such as meal coupons, tickets to shows, or gambling vouchers.[44] A representative explains: "When you get close to that pain point, the Ambassador comes out and says, *I see you're having a rough day. I know you like our steakhouse. Here, I'd like you to take your husband to dinner on us right now.* So it's no longer pain. It becomes a good experience."[45] The voucher is intended to function as a little "win" to keep gamblers on course with continued play.

Much like secondary bonus games, Luck Ambassadors attempt to enhance primary games' holding power by supplementing their reinforcement schedules. Unlike secondary bonus games—which are preprogrammed and happen randomly—they do so in a dynamically responsive, customized manner. Some have raised the question of whether it is ethical to reward players who are losing to keep them playing longer, pointing out that it is illegal to adjust a game's mathematical odds over the course of a play session.[46] Yet because the system is technically considered a form of marketing, it does not fall under the jurisdiction of regulators. However classified, it gives casinos a way to monitor player affect by integrating historical data with live data, and to optimize that affect for continued play through strategically calculated and timed interventions.

A Stanford professor has devised a more fully technologized version of Harrah's Luck Ambassadors in the form of a handheld device called Micro seePOWER that keeps casino staff apprised of how players' experience is unfolding at machines. Integrated with Compudigm's system, the device's screen displays a small yellow face whose different expressions signal key information about the current value of a given player (see fig. 5.4). Eyes far apart on the face, for instance, mean that a player is very profitable, while eyes close together mean not profitable. A pointed-down face indicates a downward trend to play and signals that the player might need a little boost (in the form of a bonus reward) to keep him or her playing. "The staff doesn't have to make any calculation," a Bally representative told me, "the machine does it for them." Like casino-wide data visualizations, the technology makes gamblers visible to casino floor managers by turning a stream of potentially befuddling behavioral information into immediately actionable knowledge.[47] No longer required to rely on intuition as they observe gamblers at play in front of game screens, managers themselves consult screens—on which gamblers appear as emoticons of legible expression. "Visual analytics enables you to remove the emotion and guesswork from your business analysis and forecasting," an industry analyst notes.[48]

Meanwhile, gamblers remain in the intuitive domain of "emotion and guesswork." Katrina, we saw at the close of the last chapter, is not removed enough from the unfolding events of her own live data to gain a strategic handle on its patterns; rather than seeking to forecast future earnings she operates in the perpetual present tense of the play zone, a zone characterized by affective adaptation rather than analytic leverage. Mirroring the asymmetry between gamblers' and casinos' respective abilities to know the odds of machine play, and to perform the kind of statistical calculations that can predict the value (affective or financial) they should expect to derive from it over time, is the profound imbalance that

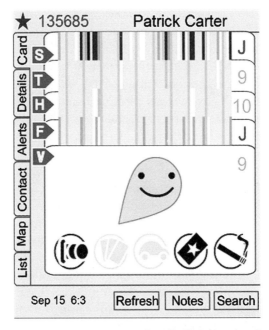

Figure 5.4. Micro SeePOWER, a handheld device that displays real-time "player value" data on its screen. Image from Bally's behavioral intelligence demo CD, distributed at the Global Gaming Expo, 2007.

has come to exist between their respective abilities to "know" each other and to perform the kinds of intensive analysis and real-time modulation of play circumstances that might allow them to derive value from that knowledge.

DIAL-UP GAMBLING: FLEXIBLE CONTROL

Downloadable gaming, which is rolling out as this book goes to press, "brings the power of the Internet to the casino floor" and in so doing gives the gambling industry a new way to make live data actionable in real time.[49] In casinos outfitted with this technology, also called nework- or server-based gaming, games will no longer be stored in machine cabinets but rather will be downloaded from an online server or "jukebox." A journalist explains: "In the past, changing out a slot machine was a complicated operation that entailed opening it, replacing the computer chip inside, then changing the glass display that markets the game's theme. The alteration ... could cost thousands of dollars, from ordering parts to modifying the machine."[50] Using systems such as Cyberview's "point, click, convert," in as few as twenty seconds casinos will be able to adjust game elements (e.g., denomination, house edge, font size), to match player preferences as they emerge and shift.[51] "I'll be able to automatically tune my games to [my customers]," said IGT's Andy Ingram.[52] The casino floor's game content will cease to be static, becoming "dynamically responsive" to patrons' affective and behavioral contingencies.

The responsive dynamism of network-based gaming stems from the fact that it was "designed not only as a game delivery system, but as a tool for [casino] operators in analyzing the performance of the slot floor."[53] An IGT representative described the ongoing feedback by which analysis informs game delivery: "games are deployed on the floor, then there is analysis of the deployment, then decisions can be made on adjustments and alterations to the floor; all the time we are responding to player input through this mechanism." It is a question of "how to adapt, adjust, redesign, redeploy."[54] Executives for Cyberview (acquired by IGT in 2008), the first company to receive regulatory certification for downloadable game technology, emphasize the "flexible control" it grants casino managers, allowing them to detect, understand, and react to the contingencies of their markets in real time. The idea of flexible control resonates with the definition of "adaptive control" in mechanical engineering (and more generally, cybernetics): a form of control able to adapt itself to changing conditions, without relying on prior knowledge about those conditions. More specifically, it resonates with the rise of "flexible specialization" or the turn from Fordist mass production of standardized goods to a mode of production able to adapt its output to customers' fluctuating demands and whims of taste.[55]

Instead of having to speculate on the preferences of future clientele when choosing which games to install, casino managers whose slot floors are equipped to receive game content from an online server will have the capacity to switch out games to match the market's gambling behavior as it unfolds.[56] "Throughout the day there are more locals, so we might have more video poker. At night, we might have more slots," said a slot executive at Treasure Island, where the technology was tested in 2006.[57] The ability to detect and respond to behavioral and traffic patterns as they happen, ramping up game odds at busy times and lowering them at off-peak times or switching out under-performing games altogether, will

allow casinos to keep their floors fuller around the clock. "It will eliminate peaks and valleys in revenue, even out the jaggedness," comments a
Cyberview representative. The incoming stream of live data, together
with live-streaming games, "will make the revenue stream smoother."[58]
(Like players themselves, the industry seeks a smoother, less volatile ride.)

Revenue will gain a further boost by virtue of the material fact that
machine cabinets will become thinner when their content is downloadable, reducing "machine footprint" on the casino floor and thus also reducing operating costs, since management "will not have to staff the
eliminated machine area, nor pay for the heat/light/power to maintain the
reduced space."[59] Moreover, since every cabinet in the casino will be able
to offer the same multitude of games, casinos will need far fewer of them
to serve a far greater number of gamblers. "Casinos need not be massive
halls with a sea of slots," write the authors of an industry technology
review called "Floor of the Future," invoking Bill Friedman's spatial terminology from chapter 1. "Rather, they can be tiered vertically in raised
or lowered areas and/or carved up along a horizontal plane into mini-
areas."[60] These areas could be designed to fit the spatial, ambient, and
cultural preferences of specific demographic and ethnic groups, from
temperature and lighting levels to decoration and ceiling height. Areas for
the elderly, for instance, could be laid out to accommodate "those with
canes, walkers, wheel chairs, and motorized 'scooters,'" while "mini-
environments could also be developed to cater to different cultures via
the design of the gaming device cabinets, signage, employee uniforms,
carpet, wall coverings and ceilings."[61] Machines could be virtually "re-
skinned" for special events like Cinco de Mayo or Chinese New Year, and
in this way, a diversity of "people-dynamics and preferences [could] be
accommodated."[62]

As much as downloadable game technology can help casinos accommodate group preferences, it can help them accommodate individual preferences by transmitting personalized content to machine consoles. Some envision a future in which sensors on machines will be able to initiate a
particular patron's favorite game as he passes by a machine, prompting
him by name to continue the play. Others worry that customers might become uneasy if the new "flexible control" were to become known or visible
to them. "Won't people feel that they are being controlled by the technology, behind their backs?" asked an audience member at the G2E 2006
meetings. "People have always thought we had a big button in the office to
change up games," a slot director pointed out at the 2007 meetings, "and

with network-based gaming it's actually accurate—now we *do* have the big button capability."[63] In 2008 an IGT representative echoed the concern: "Players already believe there's a big dial in the basement ... what'll happen when they find out we're actually *building* that dial?"[64] Given machine gamblers' preexisting "fear that someone is behind the curtain adjusting game configuration," how to ensure their acceptance of the new technology?[65] Cyberview's Todd Elsasser ventured one solution:

> You can't do it behind his back—switch things up while he turns around to get a drink. What should be happening instead is that the player himself is *voluntarily* asking for changes to the game. Switching a percentage in the back room is not that difficult technologically—but having the player himself *ask* for it is the fundamental change that downloadable technology brings. Maybe he wants lots of cash back and game flow instead of a big jackpot. By setting up options and making them extremely visible to a player—giving him *choice*—"just tell us what you want and *you* can select it"—you make it the player's full conscious decision. The player can now better tell *you* how to market to him. *He has complete control.*[66]

Inviting the player to voluntarily configure his own game and thereby giving him "complete control" would neutralize his fear of *being* controlled, Elsasser suggested. Instead of risking that the "rat people" become aware of the box, this logic goes, let the rats design their own Skinner box.

Sylvie Linard, chief operating officer of Cyberview, reiterated the strategy: "Players are very intelligent, so why not be open and transparent and let them play *with* the [casino] operators, and add to the game with us? Some like free spins, some like interactive bonus rounds—so why not put players into the equation and ask them to build their own games, on demand? It's a question of treating them as adults and getting them on board."[67] The authors of "Floor of the Future" speculate along the same lines: "as players became more knowledgeable, they would be able to choose the PAR [paytable and reel strips], hit frequency and volatility specific to their preference at any point in time. It is not too far-fetched to envision a situation where, through a simple game generator, *the player could develop his own game to play.*"[68]

In its current form, network-based gambling allows players to choose games from an online library, yet the attributes of the games available for download (their denomination, reinforcement schedule, volatility) have been preformulated based on aggregate market preferences rather than live data generated by individuals at play. In other words, while downloadable game offerings can respond to the mathematical and aesthetic preference profiles of *groups* (constructed from the weighted averages of its members), they cannot yet respond to the preferences of specific players, in real time. "Right now, the slot machine makes [game] decisions completely by itself without knowledge of the person who is there, and we know that players want something more than that," said IGT's Rich Schneider. Involving players in the configuration of game elements would bring the adaptability or "flexible control" of network-based gambling to a whole new level, moving the industry beyond crude techniques of "wide broadcast" toward more refined consumer customization.[69] As the authors of "Floor of the Future" comment:

> The player could designate "his game" within the system and the system could then download that game to wherever the player wanted to play. The player could conceivably start, stop, move, leave and return during a day, over a multiple-day trip, or even between trips or casinos in a given chain.... It is conceivable that a player could play a game indefinitely.[70]

"Imagine knowing what each player likes and giving it to them," said Schneider. "Wow! To give them what they want, when they want it, or *when I want to give it to them*."[71]

Game developers emphasize the new learning and knowledge to be gained by allowing players to configure their own games. "You will be able to listen more to players," Linard noted, "because when they decide they want machines to do some funny thing, you can learn from that— *you learn from what the people want*."[72] Once again, "what people want" is a critical element in the ever-closing feedback loop of game design. From watching and listening to player tracking, behavioral intelligence software to downloadable game technology—there is a move toward putting players "into the equation," as Linard phrased it earlier. Giving players the option to assemble their own games defines the cutting edge of player-centrism; such a capacity would enable the industry to accommodate individual idiosyncrasies of desire that fall outside of statistical norms, turning gambling machines into personalized reward devices.

Not all in the industry are convinced by Linard's and Elsasser's celebratory visions of machine gambling as an extensive buffet of options and players as designers of their own games. If the industry's growing "flexible control" leads some game developers to worry that players might feel manipulated, others worry that giving players control over game design might leave them feeling lost in a sea of choices. They might, for instance, encounter difficulty when asked to select games from a long list—not only technical difficulty, but difficulty with the very act of choosing. "They won't find the one they want—there will be too many choices," worried longtime slot operations manager Butch Witcher in 2004.[73] "Does the player really want more choice?" asked industry pioneer Mick Roemer in 2007. "Sometimes when you give players too much choice they get confused, and it kind of takes them out of the zone."[74]

An Australian game developer, well familiar with his own market's capacity to adapt to complexity, was not concerned about patrons' ability to contend with multiple choices. "They'll come in and choose from a catalog of games and say *I want this particular game in this particular denomination with a green background*; it won't be a problem."[75] But what should that catalog look like? Bruce Rowe at Bally was wary of presenting too massive a list of options. "How much choice can we give players, without decision-paralysis setting in?"[76] He went on to cite a popular book by the psychologist Barry Schwartz titled *The Paradox of Choice: Why More Is Less*. Al Thomas of WMS made reference to the same book: "It's an idea called the tyranny of choice—the more choices you give a person, the less likely they are to pick the one that satisfies them, so you have to really help them make those decisions." The holy grail of consumer choice, he insisted, will not be a jukebox of infinite configuration options. Like others in his industry, he pointed to the Internet bookseller Amazon.com and Apple's iTunes online music store as exemplary choice-guiding models. "They don't just show you all their songs or books—they help you *navigate* the choices, they make suggestions, they help determine what the experience should be for you."[77] The key is to modulate choice, to guide it, to "help determine" it.

Incredible Technologies introduced a non-networked system of guided choice for slot machines in 2009, called Versatile Volatility. It "takes the mystery out of math" by simply asking the player, *How do you like to win?* and then providing him with three options: *Often* (for low volatility, high time-on-device), *Steady* (for medium volatility), or *Big* (for high volatility). The system, which runs on aptly named Flexible Math software, "gives casino operators and players what they covet most—control," writes one reviewer before going on to contradictorily note that "Versatile Volatility also was created to educate players and empower them with a sense of control."[78] As the company's website insists, the feature "proves that empowering video slot players is indeed possible and most importantly, profitable." The aim is to let players "see under the hood just a little bit," said one of the developers. "Not to the point where they're confused or intimidated—just enough that they can say *OK, I'm not a high roller, I'm more of a low roller kind of person, and so I can choose that play experience.*"[79] A company called Talo Nevada, headed by the man often credited with inventing player tracking systems for slot machines, has also developed a way for slot machines to match gamblers' desired pace of play—but instead of empowering the gambler to choose his own volatility, the machines use player tracking to "gauge what pace a player likes and gear that game toward his desire."[80] It remains to be seen just how expansive or limited game choices will be on network-based systems of the future, and just how empowered or guided players will be in making those choices.

Whether or not players will be able to directly communicate their preferences to the network-based system, the system will be able to directly communicate with *them*—not only through personalized game offerings but also through personalized marketing appeals. In effect, downloadable gambling will turn the game interface into a portal for live marketing and other forms of relationship management. "We've essentially bastardized the gambling machine to become a core part of our customer relations management systems," noted one industry representative. Unlike promotional mailings or more general casino promotions such as those enabled by behavioral analytical tools like Mariposa and seePOWER, marketing that streams directly into game play is "a real-time method of communicating with your players when they're playing," said a speaker on a G2E panel called "New Innovations, New Experiences, New Efficiencies."

"Now we can provide [casino] operators with a tool set allowing them to talk to and market to a consumer while he's actually consuming the product," elaborated Schneider of IGT, a company whose in-game marketing system, Experience Management, captures the gambling industry's attempt to link technological innovation, consumer experience, and profit efficiency.[81] The system is designed to "give [casino] operators the ability to optimize the player experience at every touch point"—and thereby to optimize casino revenue. Functioning like a fully digital version of the Luck Ambassadors system described earlier, the software allows casinos to "have a conversation with the customer right at the point of decision," said an industry executive, "and really start to influence their behaviors at the game."[82] Casinos could instantly credit players with rewards when they reach their personal "pain points," for instance. "I can generate an offer and display it on the screen at that exact moment," said Mark Pace of WMS. "*I can engineer his experience in real time.*"[83] Like casino interiors, machine hardware, and game software, tracking and marketing systems are designed to respond to player experience as a way to *shape* that experience.

At the same time that the gambling industry focuses its efforts on retooling casino floors for network-based gambling and its new experiential possibilities, the complementary phenomenon of wireless or "mobile" gambling is emerging.[84] While downloadable game technology gives casinos the power to bring games to players in any area, wireless game technology lets players bring games with them as they move from area to area—to play poolside, perhaps, or while waiting in line for the buffet. In certain casinos in Las Vegas, a gambler in the middle of a game at a physical terminal who wants or needs to be somewhere else in the establishment can transfer the game onto a special handheld device and bring it with him. Taking player-centrism to a new level, these portable devices function as a kind of wearable game technology, accompanying players through physical space. Casinos look forward to the day when regulations will permit them to integrate patrons' mobile phones into the system via their internal GPS capabilities, or via "dongles" (small necklaces to be distributed by casino management) that would grant them those capabilities.[85] By enabling games to circulate in physical space, wireless gambling could turn "every square foot into an incremental revenue driver for the property"; in other words, it could make the continuous productivity of the gambler mobile.

The act of gathering live data—and marketing based on that data—would also become mobile. As a G2E panelist from Microsoft commented in 2007, "It's an interactive experience, and it's also CRM [customer relationship management] *gold*—you interact and at the same time I collect amazing data, I garner and grab as much of that information as possible to then personalize your experience as you continue to stay with me."[86] Knowing the exact position of customers in a property would allow for "location sensitive mobile marketing" in which those heading toward a certain gambling area could be prompted with coupons encouraging them to bet there.[87]

Industry forecasts for the mobile gambling future, and for refinements to its existing player tracking, behavioral intelligence, and downloadable gambling systems, predict ever-more-flexible forms of control over patrons, technologies, and environments. The networked infrastructure of contemporary casinos typifies the kind of power that animates "control societies" as Deleuze described them in 1990, writing just as digital information and communication technologies—on which the consumer tracking and marketing techniques described in this chapter are based—were coming onto the scene of everyday life. That same year, an industry commentator remarked on the promise of the player tracking systems then emerging: "The power a player has within a casino can be *reduced and redistributed* to give a manager more control in steering the player's gaming habits."[88] This "control in steering" has evolved into a networked system of real-time monitoring and modulation. "You get a full response history," a game developer told an audience at G2E 2004, "and you can answer the question: *Have we induced them to do what we wanted them to?*" The system has become adaptively flexible, managing at once to place players at the wheel and to steer their movement; to put control "completely" in their hands—at their fingertips, as it were—and at the same time to guide the movement of those hands by turning a digital dial in the back room of the casino. As in control societies, an invisible web of communicating information technologies works not to "discipline and punish" but to incite and reward. "The man of control is undulatory, in orbit, in a continuous network," Deleuze wrote; *in the zone*, might be another way to phrase it.[89]

The technical systems of the gambling industry not only typify but also pioneer the forms of tracking on which such control depends. "Knowledge is power and perhaps nowhere is this more evident than in the gaming industry," asserted an industry magazine in 1999, before Internet corporations like Google, Amazon, and Facebook had become famous for their innovations in consumer monitoring.[90] Many surveillance and marketing innovations first used in casinos were only later adapted to other domains—including airports, financial trading floors, consumer shopping malls, insurance agencies, banks, and government programs like Homeland Security.[91] A member of the gambling industry suggests one explanation for why casinos so often prove to be sites of innovation and testing for these new forms of tracking and control: "The unique advantage of our industry is that we have hundreds of touch points a week or month, thousands per year, so you've got a profuseness of data that you don't have in other areas."[92] As this chapter has shown, the industry's relentless quest to acquire and mobilize this "profuseness of data" becomes yet another register on which the asymmetric collusion between the gambling industry and gamblers plays out. In an ever-more refined recursive loop, tracked players contribute to the making of machines, spaces, and services that fit them better, through their own "player-instigated action," to use a common industry term.[93] The gambler's affect and behavior at once condition and are conditioned by the system.

6

PERFECT CONTINGENCY

From Control to Compulsion

THE PSYCHOLOGIST Mihaly Csikszentmihalyi popularized the term "flow" to describe states of absorption in which attention is so narrowly focused on an activity that a sense of time fades, along with the troubles and concerns of day-to-day life. "Flow provides an escape from the chaos of the quotidian," he wrote.[1] Csikszentmihalyi identified four "preconditions" of flow: first, each moment of the activity must have a little goal; second, the rules for attaining that goal must be clear; third, the activity must give immediate feedback so that one has certainty, from moment to moment, on where one stands; fourth, the tasks of the activity must be matched with operational skills, bestowing a sense of simultaneous control and challenge.[2] Machine gambling, as we have seen, possesses each of these properties: every hand or spin presents players with a small goal; rules are limited and well-defined; bets are made and decided in a matter of seconds, giving players immediate feedback on their actions; reel-stopping features, responsive touchscreens, and multiline, multicoin betting options lend players a sense of potential control over contingency that invests them in the game, and video poker reinforces this effect by introducing an element of actual skill.[3]

Unsurprisingly, the "zone" of intensive machine gambling is characterized by the hallmark psychophysiological shifts and desubjectifying effects of flow. Gamblers "forget themselves" and feel carried forward by a choreography not of their own making; much like mountain climbers who describe merging with the rocks they climb, or dancers who report feeling "danced" by music, they feel "played by the machine."[4] Yet their experience differs in a crucial respect from that of the artists, athletes, and scientists who appear in Csikszentmihalyi's writings. For these professionals, flow is life affirming, restorative, and enriching—a state of "optimal human experience" that enhances autonomy in day-to-day life. Repeat machine gamblers, by contrast, experience a flow that is depleting, entrapping, and associated with a loss of autonomy.[5] What accounts for this critical difference?

Csikszentmihalyi has acknowledged that any flow activity is "potentially addictive," inviting dependency on its power to suspend negative affective states such as boredom, anxiety, and confusion, or what he calls "psychic entropy."[6] Nonetheless, in keeping with the existentialist bent of his work, he regards such dependency as something that derives from individuals' propensities rather than from any specific properties of a given flow activity. While individuals inclined toward self-actualization engage in a positive, nonaddicting sort of flow he terms "escape forward," transcending the constraints of their reality by creating new realities, those inclined to shrink from the world engage in a negative sort of flow or "escape backward," dulling their experience of reality through the repetition of behaviors that seldom lead to empowering affective states or open new possibilities.[7] Addiction to flow, he claims, stems from the motivation behind it rather than the medium facilitating it; whether escape turns forward or backward has to do with its subjects rather than its objects.

To characterize addiction as a condition of subjective impasse is apt, but incomplete. As suggested at the outset of this book, addiction is a condition that develops out of sustained interaction between a subject and an object; both sides of the interaction matter, each in their own way. Previous chapters have paid close attention to how the material and computational design features of machine gambling format and modulate its flow so as to facilitate "continuous gaming productivity." Although Csikszentmihalyi allows that certain activities "may provide a reward structure" more likely to produce flow, and that "an understanding of flow is relevant to the design of leisure products and services," he neither elaborates on the profit motives behind the design of user flow nor reflects on how these motives might lead to products and services whose configuration risks drawing users' escape motivations in a "backward" direction, such that they lose themselves without self-actualizing gain.[8]

This chapter—the sixth stop on the circuit of this book and the last before we turn to the person who sits in front of the machine—builds on the foregoing analysis by focusing in on one particular aspect of flow and its role in the addictive experience of machine gambling: the element of player control. How is it that "capacitive" features—those that gambling industry expert Leslie Cummings defines as promoting "a sense of autonomy" whereby "players can interact with and control some game aspects"—become the point of entry to the zone that gambling addicts describe?[9] What are the technological conditions by which interaction turns into immersion, autonomy into automaticity, control into compulsion?

BEYOND ENTERTAINMENT

Despite their persistent talk of "what players want," when game developers try to explain what exactly that might be, a considerable degree of contradiction arises between what they *say* and the aspects of their design to which players appear most drawn. If asked directly, developers invariably claim that players want "entertainment" or "fun," defining this as stimulating engagement that derives from risk, choice, and a sense of participation. "Entertainment is the common denominator," Randy Adams told me. "People want entertainment." Gardner Grout confidently stated the same at the start of his interview: "Entertainment is what people want." Yet toward the end of our exchange he said precisely the opposite. "What we didn't get at the beginning is that people don't really want to be entertained. *Our best customers are not interested in entertainment*—they want to be totally absorbed, they want to get into a rhythm."

The gambling industry's occasional failure to grasp its best customers' desire for rhythmic absorption comes to the fore when those customers reject its innovations. "We spent a lot of time designing bonus features with animations that come up when you win a prize," Marcus Prater told me in 2000, "but some people don't want to sit through that—they just want to keep playing." The former CEO of Aristocrat similarly observed: "There's an initial excitement to secondary bonus games, but then people get annoyed—they experience it as ten to twenty seconds of machine downtime."[10] This intolerance for downtime is especially true of "the really serious, hardcore video poker players," as Prater calls them. "They don't want to be bothered. They want to lock into their monitor and their choices and the reward schedule." When the fastest of these players became impatient with Silicon Gaming's dynamic play rate—whose animated hands, although designed to "adapt" to different speeds of play, could not deal cards fast enough to keep up with their lightning-fast pace—designers were forced to reconfigure the feature. "Now, if a player goes fast enough," designer Stacy Friedman told me as we stood in his company's G2E booth in 1999, imitating their frenetic pace by rapidly pressing on the buttons of the machine in front of us, "we disable the feature and the cards pop up without any animation."

"Injecting Hollywood or the Silicon Valley mentality into our field," reflected Mick Roemer in 2005, "hasn't proven to keep the players going; in fact, it's gotten them bored ... *People like to get into that particular zone.*"[11] "Gambling is not a movie," echoed a casino operator in the course of a G2E panel, "it's about *continuing to play.*" Players who find innovative digital contrivances bothersome or interruptive challenge engineers and their philosophies of entertainment. Casino mangers "get more requests of *Can you turn that off?* than *Can you turn that on?*" an IGT representative remarked with some disappointment.[12] More often than not, the features and effects intended to "entertain" are precisely the ones players wish would fade into the background as their sessions intensify. "We come up with really impressive things that aren't so great for revenue, because often they have nothing to do with what's good for game play," said a speaker for a panel on "Sensory Overload." "Unless you give people a 'play through' button, you get real problems."[13]

The Luck Ambassadors program described in the last chapter is a case in point. A consultant who had been hired by Harrah's to research and evaluate the system explained to me why it was not as appealing to gamblers as its designers hoped it would be:

After the system identified players who were losing, the Ambassadors would approach them—*Hi! Are you feeling lucky today?*—and offer them $5. Usually, the players would look at them like they were crazy, because to get the five bucks they had to fill out a form and go through a whole process. One woman got so frustrated that she put her own five dollars in the machine, to get them to go away and let her play. Some players got pissed off and just left.[14]

The Luck Ambassadors software failed not only by interrupting individual play sessions, but also by repeatedly shutting down the entire casino computer system at the properties where it was being tested, during which no play could be tracked—a disastrous scenario for a business that runs on player reward cards and whose customers expect their play to be accurately recorded and rewarded. Corporate managers focused on this tendency to crash, rather than on reports that players were not responding positively to the live Luck Ambassadors who approached them; they persisted in believing that if the system could be made to stop crashing, it would work. "But it was clear to me," the evaluation researcher said, "that they just didn't understand what their players were after." The blind spot of Harrah's innovative program for incentivizing play was the manner in which it interrupted that very play.

Similar issues come up in industry discussions around network-based gambling and the direct forms of communication and marketing it enables. Kathleen McLaughlin, an executive who has worked for WMS, Harrah's, and IGT, expressed her wariness of direct marketing at the G2E 2008 meetings. "It's terrific that we're going to be able to speak to people while they're playing, but we have to be careful that we don't distract them at the point of play."[15] In the past, she recalled, some casinos placed small television monitors on machines, thinking players would stay longer if they could watch soap operas and sporting events. Instead, "people got distracted from their play and channel surfed, and revenue per square foot went down." Presenting gamblers with intrusive pop-up advertisements or access to their Facebook accounts would replicate this negative effect, she warned.

Bally's Bruce Rowe likewise countered the palpable enthusiasm for technological novelty among his fellow marketing innovators. "Innovation should not stifle the main purpose of our business, which is machine revenue. We can drive down revenue by putting features in front of players that divert them from their primary goal—which is to play the machine. *We're not in the entertainment business; this is still gambling.*"[16] His colleague Rameesh Srinivasan made the point in a more reverential tone: "At all costs, the sanctity—the sacred nature of the game—must be protected."[17] McLaughlin elaborated on the importance of respecting gamblers' desire for the "zone":

> Gambling, as I see it, is an irrational behavior that is impulsive. Unfortunately, the degenerate player does not want to be interrupted from an audio perspective and a visual perspective. *What they really what to do, from all the research I've ever seen, is to play and forget and lose themselves.* So the

> more I bombard them with auditory and visual cues that interrupt what they're focused on, the more I can have a negative impact on the impulse or desire to—as players say—*get in the zone*.[18]

As her statement plainly demonstrates, for all their emphasis on the primacy of "entertainment" as a consumer goal, among themselves a good number of industry insiders recognize that many of their most dedicated customers are after a different experience—one characterized not by stimulation, participation, and the gratification of agency, but by uninterrupted flow, immersion, and self-erasure.

PERFECT CONTINGENCY

Gamblers most readily enter the zone at the point where their own actions become indistinguishable from the functioning of the machine. They explain this point as a kind of coincidence between their intentions and the machine's responses. "My eyes feel like they're lining up the bars on the screen—I see them turning, and then stop, *like they're under my influence*," said Lola of machines' reels. "It's like you go around in them and *you decide where to stop*." Mollie spoke of her video poker play in terms of a communicative vibration: "Sometimes I feel this vibration between what I *want* and what *happens*." It is "as if the player 'shadows' the machine events," a psychologist of gambling has written, "playing in tune with the machine."[19] Randall used the same wording, likening his gambling to the playing of music, an activity in which person and instrument are harmonically synchronized to a common beat. Although the decisive act of a gambler starts the reels spinning or the cards flipping, the immediacy of the machine's response joins human and machine in a hermetically closed circuit of action such that the locus of control—and thus, of agency—becomes indiscernible. What begins as an autonomous act thus "becomes part of the automatic actions and reaction of the doer," as the game scholar Gordon Calleja writes in his study of online digital games, resulting in "a loss of the sense of self."[20]

In her research on children's game software, Mitzuko Ito explores the counterintuitive association that arises between the exercise of intentionality through control-lending features and a sense of losing oneself in the game. Noting a trend toward the design of games with "interactional and auditory special effects [that] serve to give the experience of *being able to control and manipulate the production of the effect,*" she observes that although such effects would seem to invite active rather than passive participation, in fact they tend to bring about states of absorptive automaticity rather than reflective decision making, blurring boundaries between players and the game.[21] They do this, Ito argues, by way of their "unique responsiveness," which "amplifies and embellishes the actions of the user in so compelling a way that it disconnects him from others and obliterates a sense of difference from the machine."[22] As Sherry Turkle writes in her landmark study of early video games, "the experience of a game that makes an instantaneous and exact response to your touch, or of a computer that is itself always consistent in its response, can take over."[23]

Immediacy, exactness, consistency of response: the near perfect matching of player stimulus and game response in machine gambling might be understood as an instance of "perfect contingency," a concept developed in the literature on child development to describe a situation of complete alignment between a given action and the external response to that action, in which distinctions between the two collapse. The psychoanalyst D. W. Winnicott wrote of early infancy as a state of seeming merger with the mother's body (and by extension, with the wider environment) that derives from the seamless adaptation of the mother's responses to her infant's needs, wants, and gestures. Over time, as a mother gradually lessens the immediacy of her response—in other words, as the perfection of its synchrony diminishes—the infant gradually accepts that he does not have magical control over the world and learns to tolerate suspense, unpredictability, and frustration, a critical step toward effectively relating to others.[24] Child researchers have long observed that children older than three months come to *prefer* "imperfect contingency," in which environmental responses are closely yet not perfectly aligned with their own vocal or gestural actions in intensity, affect, or tempo. Autistic children are an exception; they remain distressed when an exogenous entity does something that demonstrates vitality of its own, and they are especially intolerant of social contingency, or the unpredictability of another's perspective or intentions. Preferring sameness, repetition, rhythm, and routine, they retreat into circular, self-generated perfect contingencies such as rocking or swinging, or object-based interactions that allow close-to-perfect stimulus-response contingencies such as bouncing a ball or pressing a button.[25]

Some have looked to autism for insight into phenomena of extreme absorption in video games, especially games whose "tactical and kinesthetic operations are very simple and tightly bound," consisting of a repeating loop of inputs and outputs that requires no complex cognition (the simple game of Space Invaders is one example).[26] Even online role-playing games that engage multiple participants in an evolving social narrative give occasion for narrowed interactive processes involving predictable input/output scripts, during which players have been observed to "settle into mechanistic, operational play" and become "functionally autistic," as one game scholar has put it.[27] Ito similarly notes that children's game software can promote play that becomes "somewhat antisocial, relying on a tight coupling of player and machine, often at the expense of [other people]."[28] "Conversation gives way to fusion," Turkle comments.[29] Although video games do not involve monetary wagering, their processual characteristics make them an apt point of comparison for intensive machine gambling—an activity that has more to do with the affective equilibration of the zone than with the thrill of risking or winning money (which is not to say that money is irrelevant to the encounter, as we will see in the next chapter).

The operational logic, capacitive affordances, and interactive rhythm of the modern gambling machine endow it with a "computational specificity," to borrow Turkle's phrase, that makes it a particularly expedient vehicle for retreat into the "functional autism" of perfect contingency. The clean, stripped-down circuit formed by the pulse of the random number generator, the win-or-lose binary of its determinations, the rise and decline of the credit meter that registers those determinations, the gambler's apprehension of that oscillating variation, and the rhythm of her tapping finger reduce the gambling activity to its mathematical, cognitive, and sensory rudiments. As chapter 4 showed, carefully calibrated payout schedules turn a potentially "bumpy ride" into a "smooth ride," masking disjunctive events of chance with a steady blur of small wins. At a fast enough speed, repeat players cease to register these events as discontinuous or even to distinguish them from their own inclinations. Things seem to happen automatically, or "as if by magic," Csikszentmihalyi writes of flow. "I'm almost hypnotized into *being* that machine," Lola told me. "It's like playing against yourself: *You are the machine; the machine is you.*" A sense of difference from the machine is so effectively banished that the gambler's absorption becomes, for limited stretches of time, almost total.

"The key to the magic," recognized Harrah's vice president of innovation in his comments to a 2006 G2E audience, "is figuring out how to leverage technology to act on customers' preferences [while making] it as invisible—or what I call *auto-magic*—as possible, to enable experience."[30] Designers, he elaborated in 2008, are in the business of "auto-magically making something happen by some inbound-outbound channel."[31] When the flow of play is encumbered by extraneous or excessive stimuli, gamblers become too aware of the mechanisms operating upon them and the immersive magic of the zone is broken. The most effective designs manage to minimize gamblers' awareness of the machinery that mediates their experience, dissolving what the philosopher of technology Don Ihde calls the "alterity relation," or the sense of a technological object's distinctness from oneself.[32] As we saw in chapter 3, this relation plays a key role in the initial enchantment of machine players, who are drawn to the seeming aliveness of the gambling machine and its deliveries of chance. Yet over the course of repeated play something closer to what Ihde calls the "embodied relation," in which a person feels that a technological object is an extension of his own cognitive and even motor capacities, replaces a sense of the machine's alterity. "The machine is perfected along a bodily vector, molded to the perceptions and actions of humans," Ihde writes of technologies designed to promote a sense of embodiment. "The closer to invisibility, transparency, and the extension of one's own bodily sense this technology allows, the better."[33] "I get to the point where I no longer feel my hand touching the machine," Randall told me. "I feel connected to the machine when I play, like it's an extension of me, *as if physically you couldn't separate me from the machine.*"

Departing from Ihde's and Randall's narrative of connection and bodily extension, the most extreme of machine gamblers speak in terms of bodily *exit*, suggesting that "disembodied" is a more apt descriptor for their relationship with technology than "embodied." An insurance agent named Isabella, for instance, likened her entry into the zone to the way that characters on a science fiction television program get sucked into video screens: "On TV they express it by *pulling*—the bodies actually disappear into the screen and go through the games of the computer. That's what gambling on the machines correlates to: for the time that I was there, I wasn't present—I was gone." Lola likewise spoke of exiting her body and entering the machine through a kind of pulling. "You go into the screen, it just pulls you in, like a magnet. You're over there in the machine, like you're walking around inside it, going around in the cards."

She went on: "My body was there, outside the machine, but at the same time I was inside the machine, in the king and queen turning over." Ironically, the heightened attention that player-centric design pays to gamblers' senses and bodies—ergonomic seating and consoles that mold to natural human posture, immersive audio effects, capacitive touchscreens that respond to fingers with transactional confirmation—has the effect of *diminishing* their sensory and bodily awareness, suspending them in a zone where the continuity of electronic play supersedes the physical and temporal continuity of organic being.[34]

It is not just the body of the player but also the body of the machine that withdraws into the background, even as its console, screen, and game processes continue to enable the zone state. "The machine isn't even really there," Julie explained, "it's important in the beginning because you see it, but as you play the machine becomes less and less important. It starts out the machine and then it's the cards—choosing which cards to keep—and then it's the game, *just playing the game*." The initial alterity of the machine, along with the initial agency of the card-choosing player, dissipates in the zone of play. "The physical machine and the physical player do not exist," writes Turkle; players do not act on the game, but become the game.[35] The moment when this happens is the moment when gamblers enter the zone—a state in which alterity and agency recede.

AUTOPLAY

Many gambling addicts notice that over time they require less and less interaction with the machine in order to enter the zone and achieve a sense of "becoming the game." Some reach a point where all they need to do is play through two or three hands, or simply insert a coin in the machine. "It was almost automatic," said Nancy. "After the first press I was gone."

The "autoplay" feature that Australian slot machines often carry literalizes the automaticity that Nancy described, allowing players to insert funds, wait for their credits to register, and then press a button or touch the screen to trigger the game to *play itself*. (The equivalent feature for the game of video poker, called "autohold," delegates to the machine itself the task of deciding which cards in the dealt hand to keep.[36]) In jurisdictions where the autoplay feature is not formally offered on machines, some gamblers manage to reproduce it by loading credits onto the machine and jamming the SPIN button with a toothpick so that it plays continuously. Here the elements of choice and challenge said by game developers to distinguish contemporary games slip back into the raw chance of the traditional slot machine—except that now players do not even pull the handle themselves; instead, they merely watch as the credit meter goes up and down. (We recall Jacques Ellul's comment on the increasing autonomy of technology: "Man is reduced to the level of a catalyst ... he starts the operation without participating in it.")

Thus far we have examined how participative features can draw gamblers into a flow of play that erases the self. Autoplay, which entails a forfeiture of individual agency nearly from the get-go, provides an object lesson on how machine gambling can continue to compel players even as the degree of participation shrinks to almost nil. Designers' struggles to make sense of machine gambling when there no longer seems to be an agent at the controls of the game—that is, when play becomes "autoplay"—rehearse the conflict between their rhetoric of stimulating entertainment and players' preference for the rhythmic continuity of the zone. "There's no entertainment in autoplay," Gardner Grout observes, "it's just pure chance—you might as well give the cashier your money and have her take a calculator and say, *this is what you've won, this is what you've lost.*" I ask Prater, who has just told me that the future of gaming is about fun, engagement, and player participation, how he would explain the appeal of the autoplay feature on Australian machines. "I don't know how to explain it," he replies after a long pause, and then continues:

> I think there's a little bit of the Vegas locals market in it. You've seen video poker players [*he raps repeatedly with both fingers on the table, eyes wide and staring ahead*]. Those players are not interested in entertainment, or bonuses. In fact bonuses interrupt them. They're hauling ass. Triple play poker, watch 'em play that game. They're going so damn fast [*he hits the table*]—it's automatic, its ...

As his voice trails off, I express my confusion about the comparison he has drawn: Didn't he just tell me that local video poker players sought to exercise choice and skill in their machine gambling? Is he now saying that they don't make decisions, as in the case of autoplay?

> Oh no, they're making decisions—in fact it's all about choices and decisions, but it's ... it's ... it's a little like jamming the play button with a matchstick

in that they don't seem to be ... [*long pause*] ... its hard to tell what they're playing *for*. Sometimes it seems like they're *just playing*, like a kind of autoplay. [*He raps rapidly on table with both fingers.*]

Randy Adams, in his own discussion of video poker, likewise draws a link between its automatic and agentic qualities. On the one hand, "it's a unique game because of the decision-making process it involves—what cards you select makes a difference, and that's stimulating, challenging, fun." On the other hand, "you have more potential to develop a personal rhythm and pattern, zone out." The contradiction present in designers' accounts of video poker corresponds to two opposing views of the local, repeat player: she is at once a savvy expert who chooses video poker because she demands the highest degree of challenge and autonomy in play, and a player who gambles in a manner that is driven and passive, without aim except for its own continuance. These two players end up being one and the same, and the conundrum perplexes Prater. To communicate what he cannot find the words or numbers for, he taps out a rhythm at high speed atop a table strewn with payout schedules and probability accounting reports.

He is better able to articulate the phenomenon when he speaks of his *own* gambling. Confiding his guilty glimpses into a game that seems to maximize something other than entertainment, Prater tells me of the odd behavior he is liable to engage in while conducting field research on casino floors:

> I'll feed it twenty, forty bucks, see how it plays, try to get to the bonus screen. And even I am guilty, in these new high-coin games, of ... you know [*he taps the table repeatedly from here on*]—getting a thirty coin win and using that "Play Again" feature—where you hit the play button immediately to make the credits automatically register all at once so you can keep gambling instead of waiting for them to rack up one by one. *So I don't even experience the joy of my win—in fact I cut it off, to get back into the game.*

Like Prater, once players are absorbed in the zone, the aesthetic, excitatory, and capacitive features that initially drew them stop mattering; operational flow overrules agentic gratification. "I get to where I don't even really see the plays anymore," said Randall. "I go on autopilot. One time I won a jackpot and I wasn't even sure what the cards were."

The turn to automaticity is evident not only within individual sessions of play but also in repeat players' orientation to machine play over time.

"When you become a compulsive, you don't find the game stimulating or challenging like you did at first," Adams confirms, "which is why you see so many of the late generation video poker degenerates switching to video keno, because there's really not much to that game, *it's automatic.*" As he tells it, compulsive and noncompulsive gambling fall along the same continuum: players "become" compulsive through repeat play, "switching" to games and modes of play that allow them to more perfectly and quickly enter the zone.

In the late stages of video poker addiction, Sharon devised her own form of autoplay:

> I wouldn't even look at the cards. I'd just put bills in, get my credits, and press the buttons in rapid succession: *DEAL, DRAW, BET MAX—DEAL, DRAW, BET MAX* [*"bet max" refers to the button that selects maximum credits per hand*]. I'd just watch the credit meter go up and down. If I were dealt a winner and it would go up, I'd think, *How many times can I press this before all my money gets consumed?* All that stuff that draws you in the beginning—the screen, the choice, the decisions, the skill—is stripped away.

Essentially, Sharon found a way to deskill video poker, turning it into a purely random slot machine. Bypassing the control factor that originally drew her to the game, she gave herself over to the uncontrollable, stochastic flow of chance (in Thomas Malaby's terms, she exchanged "performative contingency" for "pure contingency"[37]). Ceasing to be an agent who bets to win against the random number generator, she coincided with its digital procedure such that her play quite literally became the play of the machine.

In her 1991 essay "A Cyborg Manifesto," the theorist of technology Donna Haraway argued that humans had become so entwined with technology that they ought not to be considered as solely organic in nature, but as "cybernetic organisms" or cyborgs—beings whose "natural" side is always coupled with a technological one that feeds back upon and alters it.[38] At once dismissing the notion that human beings are most authentic when unfettered by technology and acknowledging the perils that biological, military, and information technologies might pose to us, she emphasized that our increasing enmeshment with machines should not come at the expense of developing just, symbiotic relationships with the world, with each other, and with ourselves. "Machines," she wrote with guarded optimism, "can be prosthetic devices, intimate components, or friendly selves."[39]

What of the player-centric gambling device? As we have seen, despite its intimate and friendly overtures, its script for faster, longer, and more intensive wagering sets repeat players on a path toward self-liquidation rather than the "self-actualization" that Csikszentmihalyi describes as the ideal outcome of flow. The unstopping flow or "escape backward" that characterizes addiction to machine gambling is not exclusively a function of player motivation. It also has to do with the configuration of the machine, whose programmatic interactive parameters allow gamblers little in the way of tactical or performative improvisation. Like running on the uniform rubber belt of a treadmill at the gym instead of the variable ground of an open field, the interaction with the gambling machine does not leave much room for a gambler to "play," as such. Instead, the machine anticipates, measures, and responds to every motion she makes, tightly managing game possibilities and channeling motion in one set direction. This is not the exhilarating, expansive, enabling experience of which Csikszentmihalyi wrote or the symbiotic union that Haraway imagined in her cyborg manifesto; rather, it is an entrapping and ultimately annihilating encounter.

The longer a gambler perseveres at machine play, the greater the odds are that she will emerge from the encounter drained of energy, resources, and vitality. This depletion registers in players' bank accounts and also in their physical bodies. Above, Lola spoke of her body as a corporeal remainder of sorts: "My body was there, outside the machine." Left unattended in this way, her body continued to function and express itself—abjectly so, at times. Twice she unwittingly vomited on her shirtfront during sessions of play, and once wet herself. Robert Hunter described a former patient who prepared in advance for the abandonment of bodily being that accompanied her fugues into machines: "She was a charming seventy-five-year-old woman whose average gambling time was seventy-two hours; she used to wear double-layered dark woolen pants so she could urinate a couple of times without anybody noticing." A retired firefighter with diabetes named Pete recalled a day when he felt his blood sugar level drop while at play but was unable to cash out and stop playing; he stayed three more hours until his credit was depleted, by which point he was slipping into a diabetic coma. The effects of machine play on

gamblers' bodies are sometimes more cumulative than dramatic, as Bo
Bernhard reported of the clinic where he worked alongside Hunter: "Two
[gamblers] have carpal tunnel—about 15 degrees of motion in their right
playing arm—because of excessive video poker play. We're talking about
challenging the limits of the human body here when we're talking about
video gambling addictions."[40]

These cases do more than illustrate the pathological excess of individual gamblers. When considered alongside a thorough account of the technology that mediates the gambling interaction, they give clues to the role
this technology plays in facilitating, formatting, and amplifying that excess. "The opportunity for open-ended or excessive gambling is the fundamental configuration of [gambling machine] consumption," observes
psychologist Mark Dickerson, "built into the design and structural characteristics of [gambling machine] technology."[41] To be sure, intensive absorption and an attenuation of bodily awareness is characteristic of many
activities, not all of which involve technology per se. "A chess player in a
tournament is typically unaware for hours that he or she has a splitting
headache or a full bladder," Csikszentmihalyi reports; "only when the
game is over does awareness of physical conditions return."[42] But unlike
chess, ritual trance, or the execution of a surgical operation, all of which
have natural endpoints, machine gambling is a potentially inexhaustible
activity whose only sure end is the depletion of gambler funds. The operational logic of the machine is programmed in such a way as to keep the
gambler seated until that end—the point of "extinction," as some gaming
executives call it—is reached.

At times, industry professionals inadvertently lay bare the perverse logic
underlying their design script for "continuous gambling productivity," as
well as its potentially abject consequences. In the farcical prelude to his
1998 review of coming gambling technologies, editor of the trade journal
Global Gaming Business Frank Legato went so far as to cast himself in
the role of gambler-slave in a futuristic account of the lengths to which
his industry would go to keep gamblers at play:

> Last night I dreamed I was chained to a slot machine. I was being forced to
> spin and spin and spin ... to keep feeding the bill acceptor. They brought
> my food to me at the slot ... I wasn't allowed to leave until every last penny
> was sucked from every bank account I had. Or until I died—whichever
> came first... Everything in the future casino is going to be designed to keep
> your backside parked in that slot stool, continuously donating your money

to the house. What about the "bodily function problem"? I'm sure they'll get around to that. The "Jack-Potty." Or maybe "Handle-Pull Huggies," available at the gift shop.[43]

Unwittingly invoking casinos' nascent experiments with the in-house heart defibrillators considered at the start of this book, he closed his sketch with these words: "Automated CPR comes to mind ... train the slot attendants as paramedics. Hit the 'flat line' button on your slot console if you think you're having a heart attack." Despite its humorous tone, Legato's dystopic vision of automated gambling points to the darker side of his industry's revenue seeking project—a project made no less disturbing by the player-centric attentiveness that distinguishes it from his references to "forced" play and being "chained" to the machine. As gambling machines become increasingly adept at tailoring their responsive output to the input of particular users, those users are increasingly bound to stay the course that is plotted for them, colluding in their own "extinction."

PART THREE

Addiction

The panic of the [addict] who has hit bottom is the panic of the man who thought he had control over a vehicle but suddenly finds that the vehicle can run away with him. Suddenly, pressure on what he knows is the brake seems to make the vehicle go faster. It is the panic of discovering that it (the system, self plus vehicle) is bigger than he is.... He has bankrupted the epistemology of "self-control."

—*Gregory Bateson*

CONVENIENCE GAMBLING

Lucky's Supermarket, 1 a.m.

A customer comes through the blue glass sliding doors and sits at one of the twenty video poker machines that line both sides of the corridor entranceway to the supermarket. On a stool behind a high desk in the corner of the slot department, Jan rolls open her drawer to check the jackpot log and calls out to the newcomer, "Betty, that one hit three times today, and a royal flush at four o'clock!" Betty moves to another machine.

Jan is in her forties, plump with close-cropped, curly brown hair, wearing glasses and a dental retainer. She has spent two years dispensing change on the graveyard shift, 11 p.m. to 7 a.m. "Most regulars come at night," she tells me, "and they come to play, not to shop." The majority are women, and Jan guesses that they're lonesome. I ask if they talk with one another, but it seems that aside from a few who chat a bit between 11 p.m. and 3 a.m., for the most part they keep to themselves. One elderly woman has a sick husband at home and can't sleep at night, so she gets him into bed, leaves the supermarket phone number on his night stand, and comes to gamble. Another woman shows up regularly at 3 a.m. with four young children who go into the store to buy things or sit on the bench and yell to get her attention while she plays.

Last week a newcomer played for three days straight, arriving at the start of Jan's Tuesday shift and staying until the end of her Thursday shift. "She was well dressed, a real estate broker it looked like, but she didn't change clothes or go home once. She went into the store a couple of times to buy cottage cheese and coffee and crackers." The woman maxed out three credit cards and finally left because she had to wait until the next morning for banks to open.

Jan's favorite customer is a young waitress who works at the Stratosphere casino. She had taken piano lessons as a child and plays two machines at a time, as if they formed a piano. "You could just watch her for hours," says Jan, "her fingers are so graceful, they just glide over the buttons." She stares through her glasses at the bank of machines with a slight smile, as if watching the fingers play.

Smith's Supermarket, 4:00 p.m.

Marge, a pretty, dyed blonde in her fifties wearing an oversized blue glittery sweater, bangly gold earrings, and a beret cocked to one side, has worked for ten years as a change person at Smith's. She can predict which machines her customers will choose to play and for how long. Some play for days at a time; she returns for a new shift and finds them still at their machines. Yesterday a woman bought a whole cart of groceries, lost everything she had, returned all the groceries, and put that money in the machines too. A man's two toddlers ran around the store with no shoes; employees kept bringing them back but they'd climb out of the cart and be off again. He promised repeatedly to leave, but did not. "He was oblivious to what was going on around him. The little one ran out into the parking lot and I threatened to call the police. I told him, *Go home and get a babysitter, I'll hold your machine for you.*"

Marge, who moved to Las Vegas to gamble, plays video poker on her days off. She is not permitted to play in establishments that lease machines from Anchor Gaming, the company that operates its devices at Smith's. But no matter, since she prefers a casino environment. "People talk to each other too much at grocery stores and gas stations. I don't like to recognize people or talk when I play. I prefer to be anonymous."

Savon Drugstore, 2:00 p.m.

Barney, gaunt and looking well over his stated age of seventy, floats ghostily in the bright red of his oversized change vest. He moved to Las Vegas not long ago and has worked in the slot section of the Savon Drugstore on Flamingo Road for three months now. He extends a skinny finger toward the horseshoe of video poker machines huddled near the entrance of the store, where gamblers quietly focus on blue screens. "I used to play poker, live poker, with people. I was good. I could win. But poker with machines isn't about winning." He gazes for a long while at his customers before turning his rheumy eyes to mine: "It's a more direct way to your destiny."

Diner on Maryland Parkway, 11 a.m.

O. B. sits a few stools down from me at the lunch counter, waiting patiently for a roll of quarters so that he can continue to play video poker at the machines located in the diner's small foyer. The single Bandaid on his cheek is magnified by large glasses with gold square rims. He wears a gold necklace, button-down shirt and blazer, semiflared Western pants, and cowboy boots. His legs stretch forward and bend slightly, crossing at the ankles; he holds his hands together in his lap. By way of introduction he explains the bandage: the prior afternoon he'd had a growth removed from his face. "They said there was a risk it might become cancerous, but also a risk that removing it would leave a scar." O. B. laughs and holds up his hands—one of them large and tan with light brown hair and a gold ring, the other small, hairless, and pink, only partially developed. "I know all about scars," he says, placing the small hand back into the big hand and settling both into his lap, "so I told her go ahead and take it off."

As a young bowling champion in Southern California, O. B.'s disability had earned him the nickname "Onearm Bandit," O. B. for short. The irony that his eventual slot machine addiction lent to this moniker was not lost on him. Beyond this irony, he has discerned a connection between his bowling and his machine play. "Back then when I had problems I'd go to the alley, concentrate on my game, socialize with friends.

Today when I have problems, I come here—or to the gas station, or to the casino—to play video poker. I do it to forget, to get lost." What he comes to forget is his profound loneliness, his tense relationship with his adult son, a drug addict, and the situation that awaits him at home, where he acts as sole caretaker for a bedridden friend who has succumbed to illness. "I could say that for me the machine is a lover, a friend, a date—but really it's none of those things. It's a vacuum cleaner that sucks the life out of me, and sucks me out of life."

7

GAMBLED AWAY

Liquidating Life

PATSY, A GREEN-EYED BRUNETTE in her mid-forties, began gambling soon after she moved to Las Vegas from California in the 1980s with her husband, a military officer who had been restationed at Nellis Air Force Base. Video poker machines had been introduced to the local gambling market in the late 1970s, and she discovered them on her trips to the grocery store. "My husband would give me money for food and milk but I'd get stuck at the machines on the way in and it would be gone in twenty minutes.... I would be gone too, I'd just zone into the screen and disappear."

Ten years later, Patsy's gambling had progressed to a point where she played video poker before work, at lunchtime, on all her breaks, after work, and all weekend long. "My life revolved around the machines, even the way I ate," she recalls as we talk outside the Gamblers Anonymous meeting where we had met. Patsy dined with her husband and daughter only when the three met in casinos; she would eat rapidly, then excuse herself to the bathroom so that she could gamble. Most often she gambled alone, then slept in her van in the parking lot. "I would dream of the machines, I would be punching numbers all night." Eating alone, sleeping alone, Patsy achieved a sort of libidinal autonomy. Her time, her social exchanges, her bodily functions, and even her dreams were oriented around gambling. "When I wasn't playing," she tells me, "my whole being was directed to getting back into that zone. *It was a machine life.*"

The Dutch historian Johan Huizinga wrote in the late 1930s that play involves "stepping out of 'real life' into a temporary sphere of activity with a disposition all of its own," a sphere he sometimes called the "magic circle."[1] Two decades later Erving Goffman proposed a less divided relationship between play and real life, characterizing games of chance as "world-building activities" that rehearse life "by immersing us in a demonstration of its possibilities."[2] Incorporating aspects of both approaches, Mihaly Csikszentmihalyi and a coauthor wrote in 1971 that "games of chance successfully delimit, by means of both physical implements and rules, a slice of reality with which the player can cope in a predictable way.... By being able to foresee the possibilities of the game, the player achieves a measure of control over the environment."[3] In a recent ethnographic study the anthropologist Thomas Malaby similarly argues that gambling provides "a semibounded refraction of the precarious nature of everyday experience, a kind of distillation of a chanceful life into a seemingly more apprehensible form."[4] Games in general, he elaborates, "contain the same kind of unpredictabilities and constraints that saturate our experience elsewhere, albeit combined in a contrived fashion."[5]

Despite their differences, across the board these scholars are concerned with the nature of the relationship between play and real life, and how the former might break with, rehearse, delimit, or refract the latter. Patsy, above, describes a form of play that was neither a radical break from, a rehearsal for, nor even a clarifying delimitation or refraction of her everyday experience. Instead, it was something that spilled over into that experience, coming to dictate her eating and sleeping schedule and even the content of her dreams; it was something her life *became.* "My life revolved around the machines," she remembers. As the distinction between Patsy's ordinary life and her machine gambling fell away, another mode of life emerged; neither one nor the other, it was an all-consuming "machine life" that she experienced as utterly compulsive.

While previous chapters have explored the architectural, technological, and informatic conditions of the zone, this chapter will explore what machine life can tell us about the wider context of gamblers' lives. What clues to collective predicaments and preoccupations might we find in this solitary, driven form of existence, caught between the everyday world and the otherworldly state of the zone? Intensive machine gambling, we will see, manages to suspend key elements of contemporary life—market-based exchange, monetary value, and conventional time—along with the social expectation for self-maximizing, risk-managing behavior that accompanies them. The activity achieves this suspension not by transcending or canceling out these elements and expected modes of conduct, but by isolating and intensifying them—or "distilling" them, following Malaby—to the point where they turn into something else. By following this process, it becomes possible to track how shared social conditions and normative behavioral ideals contribute to shaping gambling addicts' seemingly aberrant "machine lives," and to discern in those lives a kind of immanent critique of broader discontents.

SUSPENDING CHOICE

Since the late 1970s, in the context of diminishing governmental regulation and rising expectations for individual self-regulation and responsibility, citizens of capitalist democracies have come to regard the self "as a kind of enterprise, seeking to enhance and capitalize on existence itself through calculated acts and investments," to quote the sociologist Nikolas Rose.[6] Following the "calculating attitude" that Max Weber perceived in the methods of financial accounting and managerial productivity (an attitude he took to be characteristic of capitalist modernity), life choices are expressed and evaluated through a vocabulary of "incomes, allocations, costs, savings, even profits."[7] The calculative repertoire of the enterprising self today includes the tools of risk analysis and management, leading one scholar to characterize contemporary selfhood as a sort of "privatized actuarialism" in which individuals reflexively apply to their own lives the same techniques used to audit and otherwise ensure the financial health of corporations and government bureaucracies.[8]

As in the spheres of insurance, finance, and global politics, the application of risk-assessment techniques at the scale of individual lives is a means for controlling—and even profiting from—the particular contingencies of post-Fordist, finance-based capitalism. Specifically, the model actuarial self is expected to indemnify itself against the increased risks of unemployment that have accompanied the emergence of "flexible,"

short-term regimes of service-based labor and the eclipse of social welfare programs, while simultaneously reaping the economic rewards that
come with exercising its own flexible and sometimes risky responses to
this field of contingency. To fulfill this double expectation, individuals
must be extremely autonomous, highly rational, and ever-alert masters
of themselves and their decisions; constant contingency management is
the task.[9]

Practically speaking, this task is framed in terms of choice making.
"Everyday risks present us with the necessity of making a seemingly
never-ending set of choices," writes the sociologist Alan Hunt; as ever
more domains of life demand it, choice becomes inescapable.[10] "Modern
individuals are not merely 'free to choose,'" Rose elaborates, following
his colleague Anthony Giddens, "but *obliged to be free*, to understand
and enact their lives in terms of choice."[11] As the psychologist Barry
Schwartz points out, the pressure to sift through an "oppressive abundance" of choice can tyrannize and debilitate, increasing the potential
for disappointment, regret, and guilt, and leaving individuals "feeling
barely able to manage" their lives.[12] Others note that it is not merely the
abundance of choice that burdens, for citizens of contemporary capitalist societies must, more often than not, make those choices without the
knowledge, foresight, or resources that would enable them to be the
maximizing, actuarial virtuosi of self-enterprise they are exhorted to be.
Confronted with multiple choices and risks, they base their conduct as
much on emotion, affect, and reflex as on calculative rationality.[13] Choice
making under such conditions, Hunt points out, engenders anxiety and
insecurity.

What links can be drawn between the often perplexing circumstances
of choice, the cultural imperative for individual contingency management, and the zone of intensive machine gambling? If gambling devices
present players with a technologically contrived form of contingency, as
suggested in the first half of the book, then play itself might be understood as a form of "technologically contrived contingency management."
While at play, individuals are continually in the position of making consequential choices—choices, that is, between right and wrong decisions,
continuing a winning streak or ending a losing streak, ramping up or reducing their magnitude and speed of investment, and so forth. In this
sense, machine gambling multiplies occasions for the kinds of reflexive
risk taking and choice making that are demanded of subjects in contemporary capitalist societies. At the same time, it takes the edge off the task

of contingency management by distilling risks and choices into a digitized, programmatic game whose contingency is "perfect" (in the sense discussed in chapter 6) and whose consequence is measured in pennies—quite literally. As we have seen, gambling machines contract the scope and stakes of risky choice to increments so tiny that their volatility is "smoothed" and their erosion of player bankroll disguised. Although gambling has very real consequences in players' daily lives, within the moment-to-moment process of repeat play, inconsequentiality holds sway. In the smooth zone of machine gambling, choice making becomes a means for tuning out the worldly decisions and risks it would ordinarily concern; every choice, that is, becomes a choice to continue the zone.

Suspending Social Exchange

The tuning out of worldly choices, contingencies, and consequences in the zone of machine gambling depends on the exclusion of other people. "I don't want to have a human interface" says Julie, a psychology student at the University of Nevada. "I can't stand to have anybody within my zone." Machine gamblers go to great lengths to ensure their isolation. Some select machines in corners or at the end of a row, while others place coin cups upside-down on adjacent machines to prevent people from sitting beside them. "I resent someone breaking my trance" says Randall, who cashes out and moves to another machine if someone talks to him while he is playing. "I preferred the machines that didn't make noise when you won," Patsy remembers, "so no one would know—or try to make conversation." Sharon has learned to buy a liter of Pepsi and two packs of cigarettes before sitting at the machines so that cocktail waitresses will not interrupt her. "I put my foot up on one side and that's the final barrier: *Leave me alone.* I want to hang a DO NOT DISTURB sign on my back."

Even as the zone they seek ultimately effaces their sense of self, machine gamblers' rigorous exclusion of relationality appears, at least initially, to be an act of extreme autonomy and even selfishness. In this sense, machine gambling would seem to fit the script for the maximizing self—a being that is expected to pursue its goals without being hindered by human ties, commitments, and dependencies. "Other people break the flow and I can't stand it," says Julie of live-card gaming. "I have to get up and go to a machine, where nobody holds me back, where there's no interference to stop me, where I can have my free rein—go all the way with no obstacles." Other people figure as a form of "interference" that acts as a drag on her propensities.

Alongside machine gamblers' self-interested drive to pursue the zone unhindered by others runs an equally strong current of self-protection and distrust of social relations. This becomes readily apparent in the comparison with traditional card gambling, an intensive interpersonal engagement that Goffman described as an "eye-to-eye ecological huddle" in which each participant could "perceive the other participants' monitoring of him," and in which success came to whoever best deciphered the unintentionally disclosed signs of opponents' strategies.[14] "In live games," Julie similarly observes, "you have to take other people into account, other minds making decisions. Like when you're competing for a promotion— you're dealing with other people who decide which one is the best. You can't get into their minds, you can't push their buttons, you can't do anything about it—just sit back and hope and wait. But when you're on a machine, you don't compete against other people." In this account, "live games" are relentless character contests demanding that she "take other people into account" in order not to be displaced or passed over by them, and yet, perversely, providing no clear feedback on which she might base her calculations or hedge her bets. The immersive zone of machine play, by contrast, offers a reprieve from the nebulous and risky calculative matrix of social interaction, shielding her from the monitoring gaze of others and relieving her of the need to monitor them in return.

Lola, the buffet waitress we encountered earlier, describes this reprieve as a kind of vacation: "If you work with people every day, the last thing you want to do is talk to another person when you're free. You want to take a vacation from people. With the machine there's no person that can talk back, no human contact or involvement or communication, just a little square box, a screen." Machine gamblers like Lola frequently connect their preference for the asocial, robotic procedure of machine play to the hypersociality demanded by their jobs—in real estate, accounting, insurance, sales, and other service fields. In the 1970s, the sociologist Daniel Bell characterized the postindustrial economy as one driven by the provision of services rather than factory labor, exchanges between people rather than between people and machinery.[15] Extending Bell's insights, Arlie Hochschild argued in the 1980s that the shift from assembly-line production to service provision had been accompanied by a shift from physical labor to "emotional labor" in which "the emotional style of offering the service is part of the service itself."[16] While physical machine labor carries the risk of alienation from one's body, emotional labor carries the risk of becoming estranged from one's feelings and affects as they are processed and managed in the marketplace of social relations.

Josie, an insurance agent, experiences a similar kind of emotional exhaustion from the labor of reassurance and persuasion that she engages in with her clients. "All day long I have to help people with their finances and their scholarships, help them be responsible. I'm selling insurance, selling investments, I'm taking their money—and I've got to put myself in a position where they will believe what I'm selling is *true*. After work, I have to go to the machines." There, she finds respite from the incessant actuarial practices and interpersonal pressures that her vocation entails. Carol O'Hare, a former machine gambler who has served as executive director of the Nevada Council on Problem Gambling since 1996, found the same respite, as a reporter describes: "By day, she sold computers, explaining the merits of Random Access Memory and performance speed to moms and dads. After 5 p.m., O'Hare would park herself in front of a video poker machine, medicating herself with the rhythms of choosing and discarding poker hands."[17] "At the machines," Josie elaborates, "I was safe and away. Nobody talked to me, nobody asked me any questions, nobody wanted any bigger decision than if I wanted to keep the king or the ace." It makes a twisted kind of sense that in Las Vegas, a city that the urban historian Mike Davis has called the "Detroit of the postindustrial economy," machines are less likely to serve as a means of production from which users become alienated than as a means of relief from the alienation of social labor.[18]

Patsy recalls her work as a welfare officer at the State of Nevada's food stamp office: "All day long I'd hear sad stories of no food, unwanted pregnancy, violence. But it all slid right off me because I was so wrapped up in those machines. I was like a robot: *Next. Snap. What's your zip code?* I wasn't human." In the simplified, mechanical exchange with gambling machines, she insulates herself from the complicated and often insurmountable needs and worries of others, to a point where she herself becomes robotlike, impervious to human distress and her inability to assuage it. "The machines were like heaven," Patsy remembers, "because I didn't have to talk to them, just feed them money." The digitized process of "feeding" and response is a form of exchange emptied of the uncertainties and inscrutabilities of social relations.

O'Hare has described how machine play relieved not only the burdens of her work exchanges but also those of her family exchanges, invoking the 1980s soap commercial in which a woman sinks into a bubble bath with a blissful smile, oblivious to the ring of the phone, the shouts of her children, the barking dog: *Calgon, take me away* … Like slipping into a warm bubble bath, video poker allowed her to slip into a dissociative bubble in which the pressing demands of her life as a financially struggling single mother dissolved. Like O'Hare, other machine gamblers told me of leaving small children at home alone, gambling away their inheritances or college money, and even forgetting their names during machine play. "My son was the first thing to go out of my head when I began to play," said one father of a troubled teen.

In the 1980s, as machine gamblers began to present themselves for addiction treatment, clinicians and researchers noted that their narratives of withdrawal from the world of human relations departed from those of the competitive, status-seeking men depicted in Goffman's *Where the Action Is*, Henry Lesieur's now-classic 1977 study, *The Chase*, and other psychological and sociological literature on gambling addicts.[19] When Lesieur began to study machine addicts, most of them were women. Their accounts led him to hypothesize a gendered split between "action gambling" and what he called "escape gambling": men were action gamblers who preferred live games (cards, horse races, and commodities trading) while women were escape gamblers who preferred machines; men sought sociability, competition, and ego enhancement while women sought isolation and anonymity; men were after thrill, excitement, and sensation while women wished to dull their feelings, escape distressing problems, and relieve themselves of the burden of excessive interpersonal interaction.[20] Lesieur relaxed the gender assumption of the action-escape split when he began to encounter escape-seeking male gamblers, particularly long-haul truck drivers who played video poker at rest stops along their routes; if anything, these gamblers were burdened by loneliness rather than surplus sociality, suggesting that extreme machine play was less an escape from gendered social demands than it was an escape from the world of social ties altogether—its taxing excesses and painful absences alike.

This escape is evident in the scenes presented above from supermarkets, gas stations, and pharmacies—spaces populated as much by the socially overburdened as by the lonely and isolated. As O. B. tells us, he gambles not only to gain a reprieve from the grimness of the caretaking role in which he is caught but also to gain a reprieve from his estranged relationship with his son and from his yearning for female companionship. Rocky describes his descent into gambling as a response to isolation from his family, disillusionment with peers, and a sense of disconnection from society as a whole. Following a successful career in geoscience sparked by the energy crunch of the 1970s, he was "caught in a workforce reduction in the mid-1980s, when the Arabs eased up on their embargoes and problems began to develop in nuclear reactors." Distant geopolitical forces had opened horizons for him, and then suddenly shut them down. His wife, laid off as well, returned to live with her parents and took the children with her. "I fell apart," Rocky recalls. "I was in a shambles." He moved to Las Vegas to take a job with the Department of Energy but quickly became disillusioned by unethical practices of nuclear waste disposal at the Yucca Mountain test site and decided to retire. He found himself home alone watching the Monica Lewinsky trials on television, an experience that only accentuated his sense of being "out of sync with the moral codes of our society." He began to spend mornings, and then afternoons and evenings, playing video poker at local pubs. He told himself he went there for the companionship, but he rarely talked to anyone. At the machines he found an exit from the human world.

"The exchange wasn't messy like a human relationship," Sharon tells me of her video poker play in the course of recounting a difficult romantic breakup. "The machine got my money, and in return I got isolation and a chance to make hands. The interaction was clean cut, the parameters clearly defined—I decided which cards to keep, which to discard, case closed. All I had to do was pick YES or NO, and I knew, when I pressed those buttons, that I would get the desired response that I needed." Addicts of gambling machines invariably emphasize their desire for the uncomplicated, "clean cut" exchanges machines offer them—as opposed to relationships with other humans, which are fraught with demands, dependencies, and risks. "At the machines I felt safe," Sharon remembers, "unlike being with a person. I may win, I may lose; if I lose, that's the end of the relationship. It's understood, part of the contract. Then it starts again, fresh." Machine gamblers enter a kind of safety zone in which choices do not implicate them in webs of uncertainty and consequence; digitally formatted, choices are made without reference to others and seemingly impact no one. This mode of choice making at once distills the autonomy of the actuarial self and unravels it, for behavior is no longer self-maximizing, risk-taking, and competitive but, rather, self-dissolving, risk-buffering, and asocial.

SUSPENDING MONEY VALUE

At the same time that machine gambling alters the nature of exchange to a point where it becomes disconnected from relationships, it alters the nature of money's role in the social world. Money typically serves to facilitate exchanges with others and establish a social identity, yet in the asocial, insulated encounter with the gambling machine money becomes a currency of disconnection from others and even oneself. Contrary to Clifford Geertz's interpretation of gambling as a publicly staged conversion of money value into social status and worldly meaning, the solitary transaction of machine gambling converts money into a means for suspending collective forms of value.[21] Although money's conventional value is important initially as a means of entry into play, "once in a game, it becomes instantly devalued," observes the gambling scholar Gerda Reith.[22] "You put a twenty dollar bill in the machine and it's no longer a twenty dollar bill, it has no value in that sense," Julie tells me of bill acceptors in the mid-1990s. "It's like a token, it excludes money value completely." With credit play, says another, "money has no value, no significance, it's just this thing—just get me in the zone, that's all." "In the zone state," echoes Katrina, "there is no real money—*there are only credits to be maintained*."

Attesting to the conversion of money value into zone value, Sharon admits that she would rather "play off" a jackpot than cash it out, as this would mean halting her play to wait for the machine to drop her winnings, or, in the event that its hopper is low, for attendants to come pay her off. "It's strange," says Lola, "but winning can disappoint me, especially if I win right away."[23] As we have already seen, winning too much, too soon, or too often can interrupt the tempo of play and disturb the harmonious regularity of the zone. Julie explains: "If it's a moderate day—win, lose, win, lose—you keep the same pace. But if you win big, it can prevent you from staying in the zone." In gambling, Reith writes, money is "prized not as an end in itself but for its ability to allow continued consumption in repeated play."[24] If in the everyday economy time is spent to earn money, within the economy of the zone money is spent to buy time. "You're not playing for money," says Julie, "you're playing for credit—credit so you can sit there longer, which is the goal. It's not about winning, it's about continuing to play."

Paradoxically, in order for money to lose its value as a means of acquisition, that value must be at stake in the gambling exchange. "The transaction must involve money," Australian gambling researcher Charles Livingstone elaborates in a Marxian vein, "because money is the central signification of our age, the materialization of social relations and thus the bridge to everyone and everything that is to be had in modernity."[25] In other words, it is possible for a sense of monetary value to become suspended in machine gambling not because money is absent, but because the activity mobilizes it in such a way that it no longer works as it typically does. Money becomes the bridge *away from* everyone and everything, leading to a zone beyond value, with no social or economic significance. In the zone, instead of serving as a tool for self-determination, money becomes an instrument for "sustained indeterminacy," as Livingstone puts it.

Peter Adams clarifies the nature of this indeterminacy by arguing that machine gamblers seek through play to transcend the limits of finitude: constraints of space and time, the gaze of intersubjectivity, and the bounds of personal mortality. The zone state, he argues, arises out of a delicate tension between finitude (embodied in the fact of a limited monetary budget) and the possibility of transcendence that comes with each spin or hand. The zone "is a fine balance," Adams writes, "and [gambling machines] are the ideal instrument for achieving it." Machines facilitate the "fine balance" of the zone by allowing gamblers to constantly recalibrate the rate and magnitude of their betting such that they may continue approaching the transcendence of personal, social, and financial limitations, without ever quite arriving at that transcendence.[26] Julie breathlessly recounts the recalibrations that transpire over the course of a typical play session:

> I got four aces four times, that's 200 dollars a shot, 800 credits each time, that means I could have cashed out 800 dollars total. But each time I hit, I'd play it down to 200 credits from 800 credits and I'd say, "*Well, I'll just hit the aces again and then I'll leave*." Then I'd get four of a kind and have

like 437 credits and I'd say "*I'll just go to 400 and leave*," and then at 400
I'd just push the button again and drop below 400, and I'd say, "*Well now
I'm down past 400 I'll just get back up to 400 and then I'll cash out.*" And
then I'd find myself closer to 300 and I'd say, "*Once I get down to 300 I'll
go.*" And then when I got below that I'd say "*Well, I might as well keep
going, I've already blown what I was gonna blow—I might as well try to
get the aces again*," and it would continue ...

Whenever Julie arrives at the ending point she has set, she resets it, thus
never reaching a point of stopping and cashing out. No matter how high
her credits become, their value as tokens for "time-on-device" holds sway
over their market value—even as this value initially (and ultimately) serves
as the condition for her play. "In the long run," Livingstone notes, the
zone's "stream of indeterminacy is determined, but the [machine] gambler is concentrated in the immediate, and in the immediate moment of
pushing the button, indeterminacy, as it were, rules."[27]

It is when credits get too low that money's determinacy moves to the
fore and begins to matter once again. "I get really tense if I only have
twenty credits left," says Lola, "the tension, the anxiousness, starts building in me; all I really want at that point is enough credits to just keeping
playing." "When you start losing," Julie tells us, "the pace picks up—
you're running out of player credit, you're running out of money, you
begin to chase ..."[28] As the worldly value-charge of money intrudes upon
the zone, it introduces tension where tensionlessness is sought and relationality where dissociation is sought. "In the back of my head I know it's
going to end, I know the transition is going to come—no longer the world
according to the zone, but the real world. The things I escaped from start
crowding back into my brain."

Even as the world crowds back in, the moment that definitively frac-
tures the zone always feels sudden; before the instant of total credit expenditure, there is still a chance, however small, of continuing. In the
moment of its total loss, money returns to the scene as a tangible limit
and a medium of dependency. "Money disappears in the zone," writes
Livingstone, "yet in the moment when the money's gone, so too is 'the
zone.'"[29] The value of money reasserts itself precisely because money in
its conventional, real-world state remains the underlying means of access
to the zone.

This is not to say that money's real-world value remains unaffected by
zone value. "Gambling changed my relationship to money," notes Randall.

"I'd conserve gas so I'd have the money to gamble, and instead of going to the grocery store regularly, I'd wait to go to Walmart and do it all at one time—that way I wouldn't have to waste the gas to go more than once. I *economized*." In "machine life," acts of everyday economizing— the responsible accounting behavior of the risk-managing self—are harnessed to the nonmaximizing, self-liquidating ends of the zone. "I pinch pennies at the store, skip a meal to save money, watch for sales or bargains, yet think nothing of dropping $100 into a slot machine and watching it go away in 10 minutes," says Rocky. "Money became the means to gamble, that's all it was to me," Isabella remembers. "I'd pour out the milk so I had an excuse to go to the grocery store to gamble." Caught between the zone and the ordinary world, gamblers "economize" in a register of value that has no clear reference point. Patsy tells me of the compulsive budgeting rituals she enacted in between her play sessions:

> For me, getting the money together was part of the process. I'd go to the bank and get $1,000, $400, whatever amount. I had a weird thing where I could never just take out $20, or just spend $43—I had to spend in hundreds. And other weird things too…. Like if I won, I could spend back to $500 but I would never keep $600; it would be okay to put back $800, but I had to keep another certain amount—there were lots of strange little rules that didn't make any real sense, financially speaking.

After gambling, Patsy would sit and count her money, "over and over again, in my car, at stop lights in the dark, in my lap, hundreds of dollars— *what was the use?*" Money became fetishlike, unhinged from exchange value—a "weird thing," as she calls it above, that served no clear purpose. "I spent a lot of time thinking about money, touching money, calling the bank to keep track of my money, to know the time frame of when checks cleared, counting it and counting it … but in fact, I wasn't actually *counting* at all." The year after Patsy stopped gambling she did her back taxes and was shocked to discover that over a six-month period of gambling, during which she had not been "counting," her losses had exceeded $10,000.

"In a society such as ours," asks the cultural historian Jackson Lears in his book on gambling in America, "where responsibility and choice are exalted, where capital accumulation is a duty and cash a sacred cow, what could be more subversive than the readiness to reduce money to mere counters in a game?"[30] Because gamblers play *with* money rather than *for* it, he concludes that they pose a challenge to the maximizing ethos of American culture.[31] Yet as their "machine lives" show us, despite their seeming renunciation of money they continue to act, however perversely, *within* the mainstream monetary value system. This becomes readily apparent when one considers gamblers' extensive know-how and use of everyday finance and banking practices. In *The Chase*, Lesieur describes with remarkable ethnographic detail gamblers' expert techniques for acquiring the means to gamble—some of them thoroughly or partially illegal, yet many involving complicated arrangements with mainstream financial entities.[32] Then as today, gamblers operate inside the financial system, juggling mortgages, credit cards, bank loans, and alimony payments.

"I always had income coming in," Patsy tells me, "every week it was something—a $600 paycheck, $500 child support, my husband's retirement checks. We always had like three credit cards so if I had a bad spell I'd just put it on the cards." The resources of a conventional financial lifestyle support Patsy's compulsive gambling, and occasionally vice versa: "One time I had maxed out the three cards, but then I hit a jackpot and paid them all off." This sort of fiscal triage does not exactly subvert the logic of the actuarial self; if anything, it intensifies or "maxes out" that logic. Although it may seem contrary to calculative rationality, it shares something with the quotidian shuffling of debt among credit sources that has become typical among Americans. (It also shares something with sanctioned practices of high-finance speculation at the center of contemporary capitalism—stock and bond exchange, the trade in derivatives and other exotic financial instruments, hedge funds, and banking more generally; these practices treat money as a free-floating set of tokens that can be "played with" without regard for real-world social and economic constraints, often producing dizzying swings in fortune that distort all sense of value.[33])

Although gambling addicts' treatment of money neither neatly renounces nor neatly rehearses the workings of the everyday value system, it *alters* this system in a way that brings its discontents and contradictions to the fore. On this point, Josie's earlier words bear repeating: "All day long I have to help people with their finances and their scholarships, help them be responsible. I'm selling insurance, selling investments, I'm taking their money—and I've got to put myself in a position where they will believe what I'm selling is true. After work, I have to go to the machines." By day, she advises others on how they might best insure against future losses, yet one gets the sense that she does not quite believe in what she is selling; it

is as if her awareness that the levels of risk assigned to lives and investments by the insurance industry are always more arbitrary than stated
leads her to take greater personal financial risks. Her gambling both em-
ploys and rejects the actuarial logic of insurance and the monetary value
that undergirds it. "In my life before gambling," she tells me, "money was
almost like a god, I had to have it. But with the gambling, money had no
value, no significance, it was just this thing—just get me in the zone, that's
all…. You lose value, until there's no value at all. Except the zone—the
zone is your god."

Suspending Clock Time

The element of time is another resource of calculative selfhood that gambling addicts manage to revalue through their machine play—again, by
distilling its real-world value to the point where it assumes another value
altogether. "Time is liquidated to become an essential currency of the
problem gambler," writes Livingstone. "It may well be the most important and significant currency. But time as such is elided during the term of
the session. It ceases to exist in its socially recognizable form."[34] While
gambling addicts may remain for seventeen hours or even whole weekends at machines, the "clock time" (as they call it) by which those long
stretches are measured "stops mattering," "sits still," is "gone" or "lost."
"I would get off work in the afternoon, and I would plan to play just one
roll [of quarters]—but I would go right into a complete daze and look
down at my watch and see I had to be at work again in two hours," Randall tells me. "I would have gambled almost in a blackout for hours."

The time of the machine zone departs from the order of *chronos*—"the
time of measure that situates things and persons, develops a form, and
determines a subject," as Deleuze and Guattari describe it—to follow instead the "the indefinite time of the event," a kind of time measured by
"relative speeds and slownesses," proceeding "independently of the chronometric or chronological values that time assumes in other modes."[35]
Mihaly Csikszentmihalyi similarly observes that time in flow activities
seems to "adapt itself" to one's experience rather than the other way
around, such that "the objective, external duration we measure with reference to outside events like night and day, or the orderly progression of
clocks, is rendered irrelevant by the rhythms dictated by the activity."
Flow activities mark their own pace, achieving "freedom from the tyr-

anny of time."[36] Commenting on the signature absence of clocks from casinos, Reith writes that "clocks are markers of a shared, objective temporal consensus, imposing order on the flux of human relations and their surroundings." "In the timeless void of the casino," she goes on, "the length (or rate of play) of a game becomes gamblers' measure of time, constituting their own internal 'clock.'"[37] Like money, time in the zone becomes a kind of credit whose value shifts in line with the rhythms of machine play; gamblers speak of *spending* time, *salvaging* it, *squandering* it. Randall, noting a phenomenological kinship between his video poker play and his race car driving, comments that both activities make him feel he is "bending" time: "I go into a different time frame, like in slow motion ... it's a whole other time zone."

Just as gamblers must maintain sufficient monetary credit to keep the "sustained indeterminacy" of the zone going, they must maintain sufficient temporal credit; too little time, and the real world will impinge upon the zone—work shifts to begin, doctors appointments to be kept, children to be picked up from school. When time begins to "run out," players thus seek to extract more and more plays from it, as Julie describes in the passage below. In the same manner that she extends zone value by resetting her credit target every time it is reached, so she extends zone time by constantly resetting the endpoint of her play:

> When the time comes to leave and the things I escaped from start crowding back into my brain, I find myself rationalizing, *Well, I don't really have to go today* ... and I ask an attendant to hold my machine while I run to the payphone to call and buy myself more time, and then back to continue, and now there's three more hours. And when those three hours are up, I think, *I'll have to save money for the phone calls I'll have to make to cancel all the appointments I am going to miss....* I'm thinking of how to arrange things so that I can stay there, *how to economize.*

In the intervals of tension that threaten the continuation of her play, Julie calculates in two registers of time at once—clock time and zone time. How can she parlay the former into the latter? Or, as she asks above, *how to economize?* At the edges of the zone, Julie must remain mindful of the coins she needs to "save" to cover the cost of phone calls that might free up clock time and thus buy her more zone time. (Again, we see that the zone never entirely loses its economic market metric, for real-world money is what buys the clock time that buys zone time.)

When she can buy herself no more time and real-world demands press upon her, Julie resorts to speed, as she does when her play credits are running dangerously low. "When I absolutely have to be somewhere, then I have to play as much as I can possibly play before leaving. I start chasing, I play faster and faster—*Oh God, I only have fifteen more minutes, ten more minutes* ..." Like Randall, who feels that he can "bend time," Julie's conviction is that she can intensify her experience of gambling time by ramping up the "event frequency" of her play; less of a lag or hiatus between play events, she seems to reason, means that more can occur.[38] In the zone, she experiences time as event driven rather than clock driven.

To understand event-driven time in its broader social-historical context, it is instructive to consider Walter Benjamin's mid-twentieth-century analysis of manufacturing technologies, in the course of which he drew a comparison between the temporalities of assembly-line labor and those of gambling. Both activities involved a continuous series of repeating events, each having "no connection with the preceding operation for the very reason that it is its exact repetition."[39] "Each operation at the machine," he wrote of factory work, "is just as screened off from the preceding operation as a coup in a game of chance is from the one that preceded it.... Starting all over again is the regulative idea of the game, as it is of work for wages." This "starting over again," this constant beginning that is discontinuous with all previous beginnings, meant that each act of labor or play was experienced as a nonchronological event "out of time." Even as industrial work depended on clocks so that time could be precisely measured and segmented, that very mode of measurement and segmentation erased time by "screening off" each of its moments from the others. Likewise, Benjamin argued, the isolation of each gambling "moment" from the rest—"the ivory ball which rolls into the *next* compartment, the *next* card which lies on top"—removed gamblers from the ordinary passage of time.

While Benjamin highlighted how gambling dechronologizes time by turning it into a disconnected series of events, Goffman's later analysis focused on the temporality of gambling events themselves, in which action and outcome are compressed into a single moment: "The distinctive property of games and contests is that once the bet has been made, *outcome is determined and payoff awarded all in the same breath of experience.*"[40] Present-day machine gambling further shrinks the time span of uncertainty, immediately resolving the event of the bet with the quick press of a button. Its "rapid succession of events of anticipation and consummation," as the Australian gambling scholar Jennifer Borrell writes, has the effect of continually collapsing an uncertain future into the present.[41] Machine gamblers experience a time that has been technologically infused with a surplus of moments, allowing them to feel they can alter its course depending on how fast or slow they play.

The machine zone's elasticization of time, like its elasticization of money, distills key elements of contemporary social and economic life. Clichés like "time is money," "time is running out," and "life moves fast" capture a phenomenon of which machine gambling is only one example—namely, that capitalism operates at increasingly high speeds. E. P. Thompson wrote of the new temporal relations that accompanied the transition to industrial society, in which working habits were restructured such that time was not something that passed, but something that was spent, as a sort of currency. He was concerned with "time-sense in its technological conditioning."[42] Since he wrote, the rise of digital information, communication, and transportation technologies has sped up production, travel, consumption, and financial transactions to a degree that previous eras would have considered astonishing. Digital technology has "compressed" time by packing ever-more moments into service-based and financial-sector work, media and entertainment, and private life.[43] Under such conditions, the actuarial self must also be a time-maximizing self; she must either maintain a fast tempo or else fail to be the enterprising being she is supposed to be, falling "behind the times," so to speak. One could say that the industry of machine gambling profits by issuing a perverse version of this imperative to gamblers, some of whom respond at the cost of acquiring an addiction. Whatever else they may be, intensive machine gamblers are individuals who embody the imperative to act at a continuous high velocity. As such, they reveal both the pervasiveness and the existential perils of the wider social valorization of speed.

If real-world temporal tendencies express themselves in the zone and in gamblers' addiction to it, it is also the case that the technologically accelerated temporality of the machine zone enters into and saturates gamblers' experience of real-world time. "Time in general, not just when I'm playing," Sharon notes, "becomes very distorted. I feel like I can manipulate it very easily, salvage much more than I can from a small unit of it: go grocery shopping on the way to the casino, and while I'm there make a doctor's appointment on the cellular phone, and then on the way home get the shoelaces I need.... Everything I do is relative to gambling time."

As Lesieur wrote, "the process of getting even is all [a gambler] thinks about when he reflects on his total situation. Therefore he concentrates on each immediate situation and the next bet he will make. *The time span is shortened to the short-term chase and the specific event he is in.*"[44]

"I'd be later and later and later to work," Patsy recalls. "At break time, I'd ask my supervisor, *Do you mind if I go to the bank?*—and I'd already be out the door. My sense of time was totally out the door. I was just *wound*. I'd win a royal [flush] and I'd be ticked off because I'd have to wait for them to come pay me off. The other workers would look at the clock when I came back and I would think, *What are you looking at the clock for? Mind your own business.*" At every chance, Patsy attempts to escape clock time, such that she becomes almost like a clock herself: she is "wound"; she is "ticked off" as time ticks by during her wait for a jackpot payoff; when she returns to work, resentful co-workers look pointedly at the clock. "When I wasn't playing," she told us at the start of the chapter, "my whole being was directed to getting back into that zone. *It was a machine life.*"

MACHINE LIFE

In the comparison he drew between machine-driven assembly lines and games of chance, Benjamin captured the nascent contours of what Patsy calls *machine life*. "The mechanism to which the participants in a game of chance entrust themselves," he wrote, "seizes them body and soul, so that even in their private sphere ... they are capable only of a reflex action.... They live their lives as automatons ... who have completely liquidated their memories."[45] Benjamin's description of gambling as a "mechanism" that possesses its players and liquidates their experience resonates in the narratives of machine gamblers today. "I was like the walking dead," Patsy remembers. "I went through all the motions, but I wasn't really living, because I was always channeled, super-tunnel vision, to get back to that machine." "Awake, my whole day was structured around getting out of the house to go gamble," echoes Sharon. "At night, I would dream about the machine—I'd see it, the cards flipping, the whole screen. I'd be playing, making decisions about which cards to keep and which to throw away."

In Sharon's account, the game interface structures her waking life and dream life with its unending flow of minute "decisions." As this chapter has argued, a complicated relationship exists between the technologically mediated mini-decisions that compose machine gambling and the ever-proliferating choices, decisions, and risks that actuarial selves face in free-market society. Machine gambling narrows the bandwidth of choice, shrinking it down to a limited universe of rules, a formula.[46] Although the activity multiplies choices, it digitally reformats them as a self-dissolving flow of repetitious action that unfolds in the absence of "choosing" as such. In this sense, it is not the case that gambling addicts are beyond choice but that choice itself, as formatted by machines, becomes the medium of their compulsion.

"I was addicted to making decisions in an unmessy way," Sharon remarks, "to engaging in something where *I knew what the outcome would be*." As she told us in the introduction to this book, "Most people define gambling as pure chance, where you don't know the outcome. But I do know: either I'm going to *win*, or I'm going to *lose*.... So it isn't really a gamble at all—in fact, it's one of the few places I'm certain about anything." In his 1902 essay, "The Gambling Impulse," the psychologist Clemens France similarly observed that "a longing for the firm conviction of assurance for safety" underlies all gambling:

> The uncertain state is desired and entered upon, but ever with the denouement focal in mind. In fact, *so strong is the passion for the conviction of certainty that one is impelled again and again to enter upon the uncertain in order to put one's safety to the test.* ... Thus, paradoxical as it may sound, gambling is a struggle for the certain and sure, i.e. the feeling of certainty. It is not merely a desire for uncertainty.[47]

Gamblers' "struggle for the certain and sure"—or for the "certain rapid resolution of an uncertain outcome," as Goffman put it—is compounded by the technology of machine gambling.[48] As machine gamblers will continue to tell us in the next two chapters, what they seek is a zone of reliability, safety, and affective calm that removes them from the volatility they experience in their social, financial, and personal lives. Aspects of life central to contemporary capitalism and the service economy—competitive exchange between individuals, money as the chief symbol or form of this exchange, and the market-based temporal framework within which it is conducted and by which its value is measured—are suspended in machine gambling. The activity distills these aspects of life into their elementary forms (namely, risk-based interaction, actuarial economic thinking, and compressed, elastic time) and applies them to a course of action formatted in such a way that they cease to serve as tools for self-enterprise and instead serve as the means to continue play. The process of distillation and suspension amounts to "*a mutation that is totally immanent to late capitalism*," as Tiziana Terranova has written of a similar phenomenon; "not so much a break as an intensification, and therefore a mutation, of a widespread cultural economic logic."[49]

In this mutation, the suspension of the actuarial imperative is never entirely complete. This incompleteness is reflected in the ambivalence that gamblers express toward the "choices" they face while gambling, describing them as at once emancipatory and entrapping, annihilatory and capacitating, reassuring and demonic. Lola, the buffet waitress, speaks of "resting in the machine," then later in her narrative describes video poker's relentless stream of card choosing as commanding—the activity "hooks," "holds," and "captures" her attention. "*You have no choice* but to concentrate on the screen," remarks Julie, "you simply cannot think about anything except which cards *you are going to choose* to keep and which *you are going to choose* to discard." Even as gambling addicts in the zone strive for release from the procession of choices they face in their daily lives, they remain caught in the predicaments of the enterprising self.

8

OVERDRIVE

Chasing Loss, Playing to Extinction

I would start each morning with a handheld video poker game—that would set the pace of my day. I'd wake up and reach for it, and I'd play three games: If I won two out of three then I'd have to go play at Lucky's [supermarket]. I'd get disgusted with myself, playing that stupid little machine in the morning to determine whether I was going to go to work or go play. I tried to convince myself that it mattered, but the fact is, I always went and played anyway.

One day I threw it against a brick wall in a parking lot. I drove back later and it was still there, and the damn thing was still working. I was so determined to stop playing. I gave it away as a gift, sent it to somebody. And wouldn't you know it—somebody bought me one for my birthday.... So I gave that one away too. All those silly little things you do with yourself to try to get control, but you don't have any.
—Randall

THE PLACE OF CONTROL in gamblers' stories is often inconsistent. Lola told me that she played video poker because she wished to be "in control," and then moments later confided, without a sense of contradiction, that she wished she were a robot, free of self-directive capacities. Randall, above, claims to have played video poker machines to "determine" his day—but he was also "determined" to stop playing them, in spite of the uncanny assertiveness with which they thwarted his efforts. The paradox plays itself out over and over in the narratives of compulsive gamblers: at the same time that they seek control, they seek to be rid of it. Both drives, in a sort of dynamic tension, are present in their exchanges with gambling machines.

As we saw in the first half of this book, opportunities for control are programmed into gambling machines in the form of options, choices, and assorted "capacitive" features. The repeated, accelerated exercise of these controls, we also saw, can lead to states of absorption in which control, as such, disappears. In part, this disappearance is attributable to the machines' ability to conjure a cognitive and psychological state virtually free of the events, difficulties, and "irresolvables"—the contingencies—that life entails. Yet players collaborate in this conjuring and in the processes by which control is gambled away. This chapter considers how they come to do so, and why they do so with such persistence.

The life histories of gambling addicts, as Randall's narrative suggests above, are riddled with vicissitudes of control. By turns, they are in control, out of it, and under it; they possess it, lose it, attempt to reestablish it, and seek refuge from it. In these vicissitudes, it is possible to discern the psychological substance of gamblers' collusion in the compulsive relationship with the gambling machine: that which inclines them toward the zone and which the exterior technological apparatus we have examined fits itself into and runs alongside. The dynamics of control and loss operating in gambling addicts' lives—and in their machine play—are sometimes extreme. Yet these dynamics are not simply the expression of a susceptibility to pathology, for they evince processes and tendencies that are typical of machine gambling more generally.

ISABELLA

A few minutes before the start of the evening therapy group at the Trimeridian problem gambling clinic, a new member entered the room and took a seat. Isabella looked younger than her thirty-eight years, lean and pale in jeans and a sweatshirt, her fair hair gathered in an elastic band, wearing glasses and no makeup. She sat in a chair placed slightly farther away from the table than the others, her legs crossed and arms folded, her face set in a steady, unreadable expression.

It was Isabella's first night, and the counselor asked that she introduce herself. She addressed us with an unwavering gaze and clipped sentences, as if editing her words as she delivered them. We learned that she was a freelance insurance agent and lived with her infant son, a younger sister who was mildly retarded, her sister's small child, and a fifteen-year-old girl she had adopted five years earlier—all of whom depended on her financially. As she spoke, her voice communicated a hint of self-protective withholding at odds with the forthrightness of her words.

Isabella dropped out of the group after two weeks. Her car had been repossessed on Thanksgiving Day without warning, leaving her homebound and unable to work, forcing her to apply for welfare. I spoke with her the following month at her three-bedroom home in a residential, working-class area of northwest Las Vegas. When I asked her to tell me how she had started to gamble, she placed her infant son in a carry cradle and disappeared into her bedroom to retrieve the loose pages of an autobiography she had composed as an exercise for the Trimeridian therapy group. "Anything I tell you would just repeat what's already there," she explained, handing me five handwritten pages.[1]

Each of us four kids was born in a separate state. I spent most of my childhood in Louisiana. We were crushingly poor. My father made twenty to thirty dollars a week as a traveling insulator and we lived in poverty—dirty, bug-ridden, insincere, lazy, depression-laden, illiterate poverty. But we were expected to rise above it. It was a childhood of contradictions.

My father was the most intelligent person I've ever known, but ignorant of feelings. He was an alcoholic and stayed away from home as much as possible. He was abusive, beatings were normal. We were owned, we were property, and he could do whatever he wanted with us. I remember sitting on his lap at sixteen, him trying to French kiss me. The hardest part of the abuse after I learned to keep my father at bay was that he also went after my sister D., who couldn't defend herself. He liked weak people, and he liked making strong people weak. I'm still angry that that may be all there was. When I got old enough to understand what was going on and to have a voice about it, I alienated every human being in my life who came close to infringing on me in any way.

Failure was not an option, but I did fail at everything I initially set out to do, and with each failure I felt less worthy, thereby setting myself up for more failure. At seventeen I left for college. I did well at first, but then I started drinking and hanging out at the beach. I lost my scholarship and quit college, went to work at an insurance company. I met my husband there—he was the only man who beat me in a contest, so I decided to marry him. It took two years to convince him. I chose him because he was stable and took care of bills and had a future. He got a job offer in another state and said *You can come or stay, I don't care*. I went. In reality, we didn't love each other, it was a boring union, and we felt increasing indifference.

We moved to Vegas and he worked as a bartender. Between all those adoring women and the cocaine, he found his relief from our boredom. I found it in gambling. I also found revenge and spite. I got great painful pleasure in telling him how much I blew—it provoked the only emotion I could get out of him. He was a very bland man and never showed emotions for any reason, he just sat in front of the television with his remote control. But he lived in fear of my gambling. The losses progressed to a two- to four-thousand-dollar-a-month habit. Life was pretty destructive. He divorced me with as little emotion as I felt. It was a pitiful waste of six years for us both.

I then decided to get even. I slept with all the men I met that I perceived as abusive or as hurting a person in their past. Sex turned into something I used for control. I did not get emotionally involved, and that seemed to be the sort of woman they fell for. I was self-sufficient, angry, and smart. I manipulated all my relationships, except one, until I had that man crying. I loved it, it was power. It also depleted all my kindness and empathy and I was mean, ugly, hard, violent, lying—I was a pitiful creature. I don't even remember their names. They did drugs, drank, hit women, abused themselves and all the people they touched. They deserved to get a taste back, and I gave it to them, in spades. And during this time, even with everyone around, I was alone. I have never in my life had a trusting, reciprocal relationship with a man, not yet. I can manipulate them if I need to. I get great satisfaction from driving them down after they zero in on me like I'm their next victim.

I met Bill at a car wash. He saw me and liked the way I walked. I liked his walk too, long legs, nice ass, great car. I called him, we dated, and all the lies came back on me. I feel now maybe it was time for me to get it back, who knows. He slept with every woman he could find. He told me all the things I wanted to hear. He was smarter, more worldly, I wanted him. I never loved him; I obsessed about him. I couldn't tame that mean spirit and

I could never find a control button. Three years it went on: abuse and comfort and abuse and comfort. Finally I had a breakdown. Two days I blanked out, and when I came back I was dead—no emotion, no heart, no brain. I had allowed him to take every single iota of anything that belonged to me. I had nothing left inside of me. Once again I had some man using me and I was just depleted.

That's when I packed a gym bag and walked to Northern California, to my grandmother's place. She had been my only protector, she kept everyone away. I took Interstate 93 and 95 all the way up. It took me three days of walking, I had terrible blisters on my feet. When I arrived my grandmother and my older sister D. nursed me. My grandmother died the next year, in 1993. My father was up there too, and a month later he learned he had terminal lung cancer caused by asbestos. He moved into a travel trailer and took visitors as he saw fit. He truly used me, and I him, for the anger release. I told him he owed me and my siblings an apology. He said he had never abused anyone, and didn't understand how I needed closure. He died a year later.

When I returned to Las Vegas, I finished my college degree with a 4.0 average. I got a job sitting on a computer doing entry work, at the boss's beck and call. We were doing marketing for casinos and I tabled all the data, found out all the nasty stuff. I was fired from the company because of my attitude, and I was happy to go.

I started gambling again after I met the father of my son, killing time waiting for him to get off work. It began slow and progressed to uncontrollable in about six months—I went from spending twenty dollars a week on the machines to nine hundred dollars, entire paychecks. When I began to fall in love, he quit. I found out I was pregnant afterwards, and I never told him.

I tried to sell insurance freelance, but I had no desire to deal with people. I'd set out for work, intending to keep the appointments I'd made, but I felt so sick and heavy and exhausted that instead of working I'd go in the casinos. I'd drink soda water with a little lime, and play, and zone myself away from the nausea. I got so big I had people telling me *You're going to give birth to that baby right here*. They'd tell me I shouldn't be in a casino, and I'd yell at them just not to blow smoke in my face. It was awful, the smell, afterward.

I gambled throughout my pregnancy, up until days before I gave birth. I would sit in that chair for fifteen, sixteen, seventeen hours, people smoking all around me. My son would move around, my legs would go numb. I wouldn't feel how uncomfortable I was until later. I made an effort to eat healthily, but when I was gambling, food just didn't matter. Instead of eating, I took antacids. If I felt like I was going to pass out, I'd put a cup upside down on my machine and go get cookies from the gift shop because I didn't want to take the time to sit down and eat—I wanted to get back out to my machine.

Even after he was born I couldn't stop gambling. I'd leave him at home with my sister for hours and hours. Later, after losing everything, there would be stains all the way down to my hips from the leaking of my breasts. He'd be at home hungry, and I'd be gambling it all away. Now I'm trying to stop gambling, but I get so bothered by the machines when I get baby formula at the store. I try to close my eyes and get past them, but it doesn't always work.

My older sister D. died after my son was born. Terminal lung cancer, none of us expected it. Asbestosis, from my father's work as an insulator. He brought it home on his clothes. It's in all of our lungs, the whole family. I could get it at any time—it could flare up and in eighteen months I could be dead, at any moment. I have a right to believe that bad stuff happens, because it truly does happen, I know it does.

Isabella's past was riddled with damaging losses of control. She had learned that it was risky to depend on others, whose desires so often proved obscure and volatile. She narrated her relationships as zero-sum games in which there had to be a loser. She married a man because he beat her at a contest; when all he did was "sit in front of the television with his remote control," she provoked him with her gambling losses—her own kind of remote control. After their union dissolved, she set out to "get even." She abused men until she met one whose "control button" she could not find. She understood that relationship as a time for her to "get it back." When it ended she was emptied out, "depleted." When she fell in love with a man, he "quit." During her pregnancy with his child, she "zoned herself away" at the machines, ending up in zeros.

At the close of our conversation, Isabella spoke of her astonishment at the unconditional interdependence she felt with her son, which for her was new. It scared her, both because she was afraid it would not last, and because she associated it with the losses of previous attachments.

I'm telling you, although nursing is a wonderful feeling, it takes a while to get used to it.... My whole life I've had to deal with people who felt they had a right to my body, my thought process, my life, my everything—it was like they didn't understand that it was mine—but I fought hard to get it back. Then my son comes along and all of a sudden it's not my body anymore, it belongs to him.

Yet while her son was "at home hungry," Isabella leaked milk at the machines, "gambling it all away" (her money, her milk). She feared that she would bring previous dynamics of control into her relationship with her son, and struggled to prevent that from happening.

My son is so precious to me, but I'm scared of becoming abusive to him. I will not—but the impulse is in me, I have no choice, I am exactly like my father; it's easy for me to be abusive. Sometimes the meanness sneaks up on me and I am brutal to someone. I am always fearful of that becoming uncontrollable. I fight it with logic and empathy. I try to be overly fair about things, and I make a point never to take advantage of someone who is not fair game. It's my rule in selling insurance, and in life.

The zone of machine play was the one place where Isabella felt "safe and away," as Josie put it earlier, from the dangers and rules of life. Yet the very dynamics of risk, loss, control, and dependency from which she sought relief seemed to drive her play. As we saw in the last two chapters, machine gambling renders these dynamics safe by reducing them to something more mechanical, manageable, and predictable than life. Although gamblers like Isabella feel they have lost control over the choice of whether to gamble and when to stop, while playing the machines they remain somehow in charge; the control they experience, constricted as it may be, affords them a chance to change their relationship to loss—not by stopping or reversing it but by performing it themselves.

WILLING LOSS

A clue to the seemingly paradoxical logic of gamblers' behavior lies in the distinction they frequently draw between losses that come as unexpected events and those they play a hand in producing themselves, through their interactions with machines. While they feel at the mercy of loss events that come unbidden—geographic dislocation, illness, violence, abandonment, death—they feel in control of those that result from their own gambling; they speak of the latter as a means for converting the passive distress born of the former into something more active and masterable. "If one happened to stumble over an obstruction," Kenneth Burke wrote of the ordinary relationship to the contingencies of life, "that would not be an act, but mere motion." "However," he continued, touching on addicts' desire to take charge of loss, "one could convert ... this sheer accident into something of an act if, in the course of falling, one suddenly willed his fall."[2] Gambling addicts often spoke of their machine play as a way to convert accidental, unwilled loss into "willed" loss of the sort Burke points to, as when Lola remarked: "It's me hurting myself and not something else [hurting me]; *I'm the one controlling it.*"

Alexandra's development of a gambling problem followed the path of "willing loss." Five years before we spoke, her adult son became suddenly ill and died. She recalled the effect this had on her:

> My son's illness was something that was so out of my control, because it was something I could do nothing about. By "control," I mean if he broke his leg, I could try to reset it—I'd take him to the hospital, have it fixed, and that would be part of my controlling the situation. But I couldn't fix this; nobody could. It was the first time things were so out of order, so unfixable. That, and the gambling.

Devastated by his death, Alexandra retired from her job as a casino card dealer and found herself spending every night gambling until morning at the twenty-four-hour Albertson's supermarket down the street from her home. "I found a refuge, if you will, in those machines. Playing, I would not think about ... anything." Even as she acknowledged that gambling became, like her son's death, "out of my control," she recognized the paradoxical sort of control that it granted her: "the weird thing is that I *did* feel in control of the gambling; I mean, I knew I wasn't in control of the machine because it was a computer, but *I was in control of my own ... losses.*"

Maria, a social worker and mother of three, identified a similar kind of "loss control" at work in her own gambling. She described this by way of analogy to her repeated interactions with abusive men, calling to mind Isabella's narrative:

> Rather than take the chance of living with the fear of when they would do it to me, I would rather start from a place where I knew they were going to

do it and by God, I was going to pick *who* was going to do it and *when* it
was going to happen [*she slaps her leg rhythmically to emphasize the words*].
I would gravitate to risky people, almost like *I* was causing my own losses,
not them—I was the one controlling it, like with the gambling.

Through machine play, Maria choreographed the circumstances of her
own losses, converting them, as Burke put it, "into something of an act"
that nonetheless must end in a lost wager.

The phenomenon of dealing with a traumatic loss or its circumstances
by reenacting that loss, or by putting oneself in situations where there
is a high probability of loss occurring again, is one that Sigmund Freud
strove to understand, most famously in his theory of "repetition compulsion."[3] The theory was inspired by a game that his toddler grandson Ernst
had invented, in which he repeatedly cast an object away from himself
and pronounced it *Gone!* In a later version of the game, Ernst threw an
object attached to string and then reeled it back in, pronouncing it *Here!*
Recognizing that his grandson derived a measure of satisfaction at causing something to be "gone" (the "here" part of the game seemed of secondary importance to Ernst), Freud surmised that the game was a response
to the frequent absences of the child's mother: when Ernst declared his
spool "gone," he acquired a feeling of mastery over those absences and
the sense of abandonment they caused him.[4]

Stories like Isabella's, Alexandra's, and Maria's illustrate that gambling
addicts play a similar game of "gone" through machine play. As life contingencies tear people, situations, and certainties from them, they attempt
to "replay" their losses through the digitally mediated process of wagering and rewagering that the devices afford. Ernst's game sheds light not
only on the internal mechanics of addicts' behavior but on its external
mechanics as well, helping us to understand how gambling machines serve
to dampen, undo, or otherwise master the more absolute losses they have
experienced. As Freud's account shows, Ernst could not play his game of
loss alone; to rehearse the back and forth of his mother's presence, he
needed the material artifact of the child's spool—an object that can be
reeled out, and reeled back in. When considered alongside this simple
technology, the contemporary gambling machine appears to be a kind of
complex, digitized spool whose "capacitive" features lend gamblers a
sense of control over things they value being "gone."

As previous chapters described, gamblers can respond to the arbitrary
gains and losses of play by sequentially recalibrating the intensity of their

wagering—betting one credit at a time instead of five, for instance—and in this way come to feel they are steering the credit contingencies of the game rather than being swept along by them. Alternatively, they can modulate the pace of their wagering and thus derive a feeling of influence over the end of play. "Sitting at the machines was almost like putting myself in an exchange where I knew I would get cut off when the quarters ran out," Maria recalled. "The challenge, the compulsion, was to post-pone that—*to control when the end would strike.*" By scheduling eco-nomic loss in this way, she gained a sense of command that eluded her in other chancy situations. Julie, whom we met in the previous chapter, de-veloped her own strategy for swaying chance through machine play:

> Once you choose to throw away a card and get a new one, the machine shuffles the whole deck a thousand miles per hour and the card that comes up *depends on the second that you press the button* to make the shuffling stop. It has to do with timing; you've got to get the timing right, you've got to catch it, you've got to hurry. I think the only thing you can control is the speed. You know what's going to happen [*her voice slows to a whisper*], you just don't know *when*, but you can control how soon it happens. The rest is all chance, and speed is the only way to *control the chance.*

If chance is what surprises or catches us in time, her account suggests, then machine-accelerated speed is a way to run ahead of the surprise and catch moments of chance—a way to be in charge of chance.

Beyond Control

Perhaps the most striking and deliberate case of "willing losses" that I encountered during my research was that of Sharon, an Italian American woman in her forties whose family had moved to Las Vegas when she was in her late teens. Her story shares the concern with exerting control over loss that we have been examining, yet she arrived at compulsive machine play from quite a different direction than gamblers like Isabella. Far from having experienced a lack of agency over events in her life, Sharon seemed afflicted by an *excess* of agency; her spiral into addiction arose from a confrontation with the limits of her self-maximizing drive and ambition to control everything in her life.

"My story that I tell is not the story of what I never got," she told me, "it's the story of what I had and *squandered.*" She narrated her life as an endeavor of control, both in its accomplishments and its squanderings. "My starting plan," Sharon recalled, "was to get a couple of degrees at the university, attend a top medical school, and become a successful, widely published doctor." When she learned that the highest number of class credits a student had ever taken during summer session was nineteen, she took twenty-four, obtaining six petition overrides to do so: "It was something that had never, ever, been done, nor conceivably could be done." She rose to the challenge, all the while working full time as a casino card dealer and studying on her breaks.

Sharon's drive for mastery extended beyond education to her physical body. "In those days," she remembered, "I was consumed with the project of manipulating myself to perfection." She vigilantly monitored her bodily intake and outtake, drank only organic juices, ate only natural foods, never let her weight rise above 125, ran six miles a day, drank brewer's yeast each morning, knew how to eliminate water from her system, knew how to attain muscle mass and reduce body fat. "My control was not only external; internally, I could manipulate my macro molecules to get X production of amino acids. I wouldn't let any toxins into my body." At a certain point, however, she came face to face with the limits of her enterprise:

> When I realized that I could never maintain perfection, that I could never be stronger than nature, I gave up entirely. I knew I was losing because I had upped the ante to the point where I was going to need plastic surgery. I was going to have to go away to special health farms and such, for months at a time. It was clear that I had reached a ceiling, simply because I wouldn't have the financial means to carry out the project. *When I realized that I couldn't fully control it, I abandoned it totally.*

In Sharon's narrative of the trajectory that led to her compulsive machine play, the realization that she was playing a losing game against nature— and ultimately, against the inevitability of aging and death—marked a turning point.

This realization was reinforced during Sharon's last semester of medical school in another state, when her best friend committed suicide and her brother was murdered. Following these events, her abandoned project of self-perfection turned into one of self-annihilation. She began plotting her losses, such that losing itself became a game to win.

> My last year of medical school I made my finest effort because I knew that at the end of that, whatever I had hyperachieved was going to have to be remembered for a long time, because I was going on the mother of all gam-

bling binges. Nobody knew this except me; I had planned it for a year. I knew that this was going to be the definitive self-destructive trip, and that's what motivated me to do so well in that final year. After that, there were no more classes, no more degrees to get; I was done with my education.

When the clock struck the exact hour of midnight and my obligations and responsibilities were through, then all bets were off—I didn't shower, I didn't change, I didn't care, because now it was Part B of my agenda. I used the last 800 dollars in my checking account to rent a U-Haul truck, loaded everything up, and drove home through three States with no sleep, still wearing dirty scrubs from a sixteen-hour shift in the critical care ward. I pulled up in front of my family's house, read the contract on the U-Haul rental, and saw that if I had the truck back by a certain hour I'd get a $59 refund. So I threw open the garage door, threw open the back of the truck, and proceeded to bring all my boxes into the bedroom. I piled them all up in a double row, threw a sheet over them. I threw on a sweater, returned the truck, and I was gone, for four nights and five days.

I sat in front of those video poker machines and I spent everything that I had saved and everything that had been waiting for me when I got home. I could see, like a domino effect, that I had crossed the line and was throwing away ten years of full time education. I devastated myself emotionally, physically, financially, psychologically.

It is as if Sharon, when faced with the failure of her customary strategies for high-performance control, resorted to high-performance destruction instead, willing a "devastation" of herself so complete that it could somehow match, neutralize, or efface the pain of suddenly losing her brother and closest friend. After recounting her story, she asked, only half-joking, "Am I the best dysfunctional addict you ever interviewed? Do I get an A+ in addiction?"

In the aftermath of her binge, Sharon got a job dealing blackjack at a casino where her father had once been pit boss. She used the income she earned there to support a video poker habit that soon eclipsed all else in her life, becoming an ongoing routine for self-liquidation in which she remained stuck until shortly before we spoke. "With the machines there really is no chance," she told me, "because you know you're going to lose. That made it even safer—I felt like *I almost controlled that fact.* The task was to go to the casino, get a certain amount of money from the ATM machine, and lose it in the video poker machine. A neat transfer of funds. If I had the amount of money to continue to practice that control, I'd probably still be playing. It's just that I ran out of money to lose."

Sharon's mode of "willing loss" both resonates with and departs from the examples considered earlier. Instead of attempting to manage the rate and timing of her losses, she abandoned herself entirely to chance; more than a bid for control in the face of traumatic loss, her play was a surrender to existential odds in the context of an ongoing struggle with mortality. She moved "beyond control" in the sense that what she ultimately came to rehearse through machine gambling was the impossibility, rather than the possibility, of controlling chance.

As Sharon's story dramatically conveys, for all that the hypothesis of mastery over loss explains of gamblers' investment in machine play, it raises new questions. As we observe their play, it becomes apparent that mastery never arrives, and even appears to recede as a possibility. "The sad thing," Maria recognized, "is that the only real control you can have over the end is to make it come faster." Despite gamblers' recognition of the slim margin of control that machine play grants them, their play continues, requiring us to reevaulate what "control" in fact is for them, and what they might be trying to achieve by it.

The machine itself, we have already acknowledged, plays a significant role here—for it is not a passive medium through which gamblers act out their drives, but an interactive force that powerfully exerts its program for "player extinction" and in so doing constrains the possible outcomes of play. Yet what, besides gambling machines' script for player extinction, could explain the "turning" of control into its opposite? Or, as Alexandra posed the question:

> At first, I was in control of going and staying as long as I wanted and I could even leave with winnings. But then it got to where something else was controlling the situation. The sun would be coming up, and I'd ask myself: *I want to go—what makes me stay? Why do I sit here?* It's this THING, this IT that comes in to you, and you keep playing and playing ... this thing that possesses, addicts, keeps you there. *What is this thing that is controlling me???*

Freud was similarly puzzled: If mastery was the aim of Ernst's game of "gone," then why was he driven to repeat that loss over and over again, seemingly without resolution? What drove his seemingly futile enterprise?

The child's "mechanical" drive to relive a frustrating and painful event hinted at "a compulsion to repeat which overrides the pleasure principle,"

he answered. Freud had formulated the concept of the "plea
ciple" in his earlier work to describe the drive for gratificatio
and avoidance of pain behind most human endeavor. Accord
principle, gratification and pain avoidance were "life instincts" that motivated beings to stay in perpetual motion. Yet Ernst's behavior suggested
to Freud that the ultimate goal of this motion was to return to a state of
rest, stillness, and peace in which all needs and desires (the basis for selfhood, on his account) were cancelled out. He came to believe that the life
instincts at play in his grandson's game were ultimately in the service of
"death instincts"—a more primitive set of tendencies whose aim was to
extinguish life's excitations and restore stasis. What he called the death
drive (and sometimes, the "nirvana principle" or the "compulsion to destiny") was not a macabre longing or wish for self-destruction, he clari-
fied; rather, it expressed a being's "effort to reduce, to keep constant or to
remove internal tension."[5] The death drive went "beyond" the pleasure
principle in the sense that its aim was not to gratify or otherwise master
the desires of the self, but to neutralize and discharge them—and thus, to
dissolve the self altogether.[6] Since complete self-dissolution would entail
death, "dying" could be understood to be the paradoxical goal of life.

But a puzzle remained: If this were the case, then why was it, Freud
wondered, "that the living organism struggles most energetically against
events ... which might help it to attain its life's aim rapidly—by a sort of
short-circuit"?[7] He concluded that a being's acts of self-preservation had
to be understood as the steps required to cancel out the particular stimuli
it encountered in the world and thereby return itself to a state of rest. The
seeming "circuitous pathways" or "detours" that composed a being's life,
in other words, represented the particular route it had to travel on the
way to the "peace" of its terminus. The so-called death drive *animated*
(rather than thwarted) life and its perpetual oscillations of tension and
release.

Within this analytic framework, addictions can be understood as a
pathological intensification of the death drive, in which an individual attempts to bypass the roundabout struggles of life in order to "attain its
life's aim rapidly—by a sort of short-circuit," to use Freud's words. It is
not that the addict desires death as such (although death in a literal sense
can play a key role in gamblers' addiction, as we will see in a moment),
but that she desires release from the perturbing contingencies and uncertainties of existence. Alcohol, narcotics, and absorbing activities like
machine gambling serve as a potent means for muting these contingencies and uncertainties, extinguishing cognitive and affective tension, and

suspending a sense of self—that is, for achieving the state of desubjectifi-cation and magical "oneness" with the world that we examined in chapter 6 under the name of "perfect contingency." The game of video poker, for Sharon and others, becomes a mechanism for gaining unimpeded access to the zero state of the zone ("it's a more direct way to your destiny," the pharmacy slot attendant Barney told us earlier).[8] As the psychoanalytic scholar Rik Loose writes of gambling addicts, they "take a short cut, so short that they create a short-circuit."[9]

The drive toward self-dissolution gathers a runaway momentum (expressed in gamblers' propulsive "chase") that pushes life beyond the regulating oscillation of tension and release to the point where it becomes a "machine life," to use Patsy's phrase from the previous chapter. As gamblers develop a tolerance for the short-circuiting of life that machine gambling affords, they become increasingly intolerant of life's detours—from the discursive meanderings of social exchange that come with any interruptions of their play, to spatial detours like circuitous carpet design, to temporal detours like animated bonus features or the "clocking up" of credits. "The vast majority of people I have observed do not wait for their wins to clock up," Katrina noted, going on to echo Freud: "Instead they 'short circuit' the process by continuously pushing the button to make pays clock up instantaneously, or by using the 'take win' button, and on some machines, by inserting coins/notes while pays are clocking up." The autoplay mode we examined earlier, in which gamblers abandon all control and give themselves over fully to the process of play by simply letting the game play itself, registers the outer limit of machine players' intolerance for life's "circuitous routes," and the point at which they give themselves over fully to "machine life." Recall that Sharon eventually stopped looking at the cards she had been dealt: "You reach an extreme point where you don't even delude yourself that you're in control of anything but strapping yourself into a machine and staying there until you lose.... All that stuff that draws you in the beginning—the screen, the choice, the decisions, the skill—is stripped away, and you accept the certainty of chance: *the proof is the zero at the end*."[10]

We can now appreciate that gamblers' drive to "zero out" tension may run deeper than their drive to tame or master loss. In line with Freud's insights, their "gamble for control" appears to be underwritten by a wish to move past the need for control altogether. From this perspective, the financial losses they sustain while gambling are not merely collateral consequences of their bid for control but, instead, its more profound aim. With this recognition, one of the most counterintuitive aspects of machine gambling begins to make more sense: the intolerability of wins. Alvin, a former resident of Las Vegas who had moved to the Midwest to "escape video poker machines," stopped into a Gamblers Anonymous meeting while passing through town to visit his children. He recounted an earlier trip: seconds before his return flight home at an airport video poker machine near his departure gate, he had won a six-thousand-dollar jackpot. Although he boarded the plane and flew home, upon arrival at the midwestern airport he found he could not stand to be in possession of his winnings—they weighed on him as an intolerable excess. "I couldn't handle that I had left with that money. I wasn't through yet. I had to lose it all. Return the money. That's exactly what I did—I flew right back and returned the money to the machines." His circular movement away from and back to Las Vegas traced the detours of his drive to close the circuit that his winnings had opened.

Sharon narrated a similar end to the four-day binge that followed her return from medical school. "When I finally lost it all, I came home. I felt dead and empty and exhausted. I lay down on top of my moving boxes to sleep, but when I turned my head like this, right there in the reflection of that mirror alongside the boxes I saw three nickels. I got this incredible adrenaline rush, like ALL IS NOT YET LOST." "Was it the return of hope?" I asked her. "No, not exactly hope—it didn't feel good like hope. It was a feeling that I wasn't *done* yet—that I couldn't rest yet. It was three o'clock in the morning, but I got into my car and drove on an empty tank to the closest casino—and I lost those three nickels."

"Every now and then," Rocky told me, "I was so exhausted that I actually wanted to lose, so that I could go home. If I'd get close to losing and win again, I'd think *Oh great, now I've got to sit here until it's gone.*" "Sometimes," Alexandra elaborated, "there's even a weird satisfaction— no, not a satisfaction, a relief—when I lose. When it's all gone, and I have no choice to play anymore, and I can go home and sleep." Gambling credits are a source of excitation that keep her awake, all energies bound toward resolution; only when they are depleted can she sleep. Pete, the retired firefighter, went so far as to pray for the total depletion of his play credits—the only thing that could release him from the clutches of his drive to continue gambling:

After sitting at a machine for fourteen hours, so tired I can barely keep my eyes open, no money in my pocket, no gas in my car, and no groceries at home, I still can't leave because I have four hundred credits in the machine. So I sit there for another hour until it's all gone, praying for me to lose: *Please God take this money so I can get up and go home.* You might ask, *Why didn't you hit the cash out button?* That never occurred to me—that was not an option.

"If I still had money left to play," he explained, "it was like I was glued to the machine. The whole place could burn up and if I had had credits there would be no way I'd leave, I'd just say to myself, *Forget it—I'm not leaving unless I can take the machine with me, I'll die of smoke inhalation first.*" "You want to hit the collect button but you can't," said Randall. "If the money were sitting out in the tray like the old days it would be easier to walk away, but when it's in the machine as credits, you just can't get it out." Maria told me of the losses that brought her near to ending one gambling session, and the wins that spun her away again, stringing her play along: "I parlayed it into two hundred dollars, then got down to one dollar, and with that I hit another hundred dollars. I didn't leave until I spent the whole hundred dollars again. I couldn't leave until it was all gone."[11]

Wins, for some gamblers, carry the weight of what the philosopher Georges Bataille called the "accursed share"—a surfeit that produces an unsettling sense of excess that its possessors try, in vain, to exchange, cancel, or otherwise dispose of.[12] Gambling addicts, through their interactions with machines, attempt to do just that: to redeem their credits, settle their debt, stop circulation, and return to a zero state. In Alexandra's case, it is not difficult to identify the deeper source of intolerability that she strives to escape through gambling: much of what she gambled away was her son's $45,000 life insurance policy, an "accursed share" she hadn't known existed until she learned of it upon his death. Acknowledging that losing this bitter inheritance was part of her aim in gambling, she remembered the frustration she felt on winning a $1,100 jackpot on a quarter machine: "I moved to a dollar machine—so I could lose it faster. *I played like I was throwing it away.*"

We recall the bank statement that Nancy showed me in chapter 2, logging the sequential ATM withdrawals that led to the depletion of her entire account balance over six hours of machine play, a sort of printed record of her drive toward zero. "My car payment, my insurance payment, my rent—I lost everything. I went back and forth between the ATM and the machine about four or five times in one night; it took me about five hours to lose it all. I played myself to death, right down to the nickel slots."

Playing to Death

Although Freud meant the "death" in "death drive" more figuratively than literally, gambling addicts often invoke literal death—and their own in particular—when describing the machine zone. They do so via suggestion ("the definitive self-destructive trip"), association ("I'll die of smoke inhalation first"), metaphor ("I played myself to death"), and direct reference (as we will see in a moment). The pervasiveness of this theme in gamblers' narratives suggests the possibility of a link between their relationship to actual death and their relationship to the deathly state of the zone. The following pages focus on a selection of cases in which this link is particularly striking—not to distinguish these cases in a class of their own, but because they bring to the fore an underlying preoccupation with mortality that runs through gambling behavior more generally.[13]

"It was like I just dropped out of the world," Joanne told me of her worst stretch of machine gambling. As it happens, she was quite familiar with the experience of dropping out of the world. "The fact is," she responded when I asked her how she came to be in Las Vegas, "I'm not supposed to be here. I'm supposed to be dead. I'm a walking medical miracle. They lecture about me all over the world. No one can ever believe that I'm still here." Joanne was admitted to a hospital for a routine operation just after her thirty-eighth birthday, and woke up six months later in a hospital hundreds of miles away to learn that the doctor performing her surgery had been intoxicated, and that her operation had been followed by massive organ failure and infection throughout her body. "I burst my sutures and remained open from hip to hip," she recounted. "The medical students would visit to see my insides." Joanne remained in a coma, wasting to eighty-four pounds before she was airlifted to a catastrophic surgeon. He was amazed at her dire condition and doubted that she could be saved. Over the next few years she underwent twenty-six surgeries. Four years without solid food, two colostomies, a final surgery. Then a hernia, and an operation to install wire mesh to hold her organs in. Today, her abdomen is mostly scar.

"I think coming through all that gave me a feeling of immortality," Joanne reflected. "I feel special, almost invulnerable, like a survivor. It was as if lightning had struck me, but I lived. *How can someone be so unlucky, and so lucky?*" She went on to explicitly connect some of her current behaviors to her past brush with death: "I notice myself doing risky things, like driving home on an empty tank, and sometimes driving a little dangerously—I mean, I stop at red lights, but sometimes when I turn, I just don't look. *And gambling is sort of like that—a way of risking yourself, like playing with your own death*." "The machines," she continued, "let you take that risk, with no interference to stop you." The machines were at once a means of controlling, via replay, the trauma of nearly losing her life, *and* a means of bringing herself to a zero state beyond all trauma.

A similar relationship to death is at work in Diane's story. A tall, red-headed cocktail waitress in her forties, she understood her addiction as a kind of destiny that she carried within herself until it was externally activated by the gambling devices she encountered. "Even before I discovered the machines, I had it in me," she explained, "so it's not the machines that did it, but they are the most satisfying thing to my addiction that I've ever encountered, and *they let that thing inside me grow, and take over*." As she elaborated on what this "thing inside" might be, a narrative rife with traumatic experiences and brushes with death began to emerge. The fourth child in a family of three girls and three boys, her life had been punctuated by the deaths of her brothers: one died when he was young; another when he was thirteen, of a drug overdose; the third as an adult, in an unlikely car accident on Boulder Highway. "I wasn't surprised when he died too," she commented. And there was more: her father had committed suicide, as had his father, and some of his uncles. "It's a sick family tradition," she wryly noted of suicide. Not long before we spoke, her cousin, who had "five children and a really bad gambling problem," had jumped off Hoover Dam. ("The weird thing is," she added, "after she parked her car on the bridge and jumped off, they found 2,000 dollars in there ... maybe she knew that the only way not to spend it back was to end her life.") Finally, Diane related how she herself had narrowly escaped death at seventeen, when a stranger raped and strangled her. "It's a strange feeling," she told me, "*to know that somebody killed you and left you for dead*."

She connected this "strange feeling" to her constant worry over her teenage son. "I check on him three or four times in the night to make sure he's breathing. I feel so nervous leaving him alone." At the machines, and only at the machines, Diane learned, was she able to stop worrying about her son. "It's a kind of numb relief; there's really nothing else I can do where I can forget my son." When her money ran out and play stopped, he was the first thing to come back into her mind. "What if something happened to him and I wasn't there? That's always my first thought, and I have to go home immediately and check." Diane's sister suffered from the same sort of obsessive worry. "She thinks we're like that because we know things can happen to people. Other families think everyone grows up and has kids and is fine, but we know it isn't that way."

Taken in the context of her life experience, one might understand Diane's gambling as an attempt to gain control over and thus ward off the pain of losing half her family, and the terrifying prospect that her own son might be similarly taken from her. Yet one might also understand it as her way of bringing herself closer to the "numb relief" of being dead—a state in which there is no cause for anticipating further loss. She hinted at this possibility in the course of describing her fascination with the endings of mystery novels. "I read mysteries backward—I read the ending first, then I go back and read the rest of the book. I want to see how the author's mind worked to get it to that point." She was captivated by the temporal mechanics of emplotment, the circuitous pathways by which authors drive a story to its destination; she looked for how the end might be unfolding in every moment, so as to know how endings were arrived at. "I want to fast forward in time and then go back, and know at each step what I'm driving at. *The machines indulge that more than live games, they let me fast forward quicker to the end.*" Again, her words registered both a desire for mastery over life and a desire for life to be done with, finished, "*gone.*" Eventually, Freud noted, his grandson Ernst discovered a way to make *himself* gone—by crouching below a mirror to make his own image disappear. In a sense, this is what gamblers do through machines.

Like Diane, Sharon was tuned in to the precarious nature of existence, beset by a constant feeling that the world was an accident waiting to happen. "It's like I'm face to face with the possibility of annihilation at any moment. The gray areas, the unknown, and the anxiety and anticipation and catastrophizing that come with it, the predicting-the-possible-end scenarios that unfold in my brain.... There is no safe house in my head." Also like Diane, she learned that attending to the serial presentation of choices offered up by gambling machines kept at bay the runaway risk scenarios that spun through her head. As she told us earlier, "the interaction was clean cut, the parameters clearly defined—I decided which cards to keep, which to discard, case closed. All I had to do was pick YES or NO." Machine play reduced risk to a repetitious toggle of switches—on/off, yes/no, win/lose, open/close, here/gone; as soon as she took a risk, its outcome was revealed—*case closed*.

Sharon attempted to replicate this closure effect in other domains of her "machine life." Before she could sleep, for instance, she had to close all portals of contingency, by "zeroing out" the odometer on her car, locking every door and every window in the house, and unplugging all the phones. "I need total disconnection," she explained. "I call it 'setting my internal reality externally.'" Like Alvin and Diane, she could not tolerate remainders—credits still in the video poker machine; the flash of fifteen cents glimpsed in the mirror on the floor under her bed; pounds in excess of her 125-pound weight limit; miles counting up on the odometer, recording the movements of each day. These leftover tokens of life in its uncertainty and transience—some of them reminders of devastating events—had to be brought to zero if she was to find rest.

Sharon's compulsion to "zero out" extended all the way to herself, suggesting again an inner drive to self-cancel that propelled her rituals of control. She went so far as to fantasize, often, about her own death; it would be, she said, a complete and perfect liquidation:

> Sometimes I think the summation of my entire existence, my claim to fame, will be that when I die, it'll be really easy for people to go through my worldly possessions, because they'll be organized and categorized and cleaned and neat. That will be all that I will have accomplished, because my primary intent was to avoid pain and mess. You know how when some people die their affairs are an incredible mess to get in order? Well, to me that disorder is a kind of commentary on the degree to which they lived. When I die, whatever I've done will already have been archived, sorted, *gone*. I even have contact numbers for my life insurance policy, my burial plan. I really think it'll take somebody like two hours to settle all my affairs and erase the whole existence of Sharon. *End of story*.

Sharon's fantasy was that she and her personal effects would be completely wrapped up, bound, and cancelled out—as if her life had never happened. "Did I miss a big part of the puzzle?" she asked me. "Is the idea of living to do so in the most orderly and safe fashion? I try to see the logic and the security in living another way, but I don't."

Sharon's compulsive involvement with video poker reflects the "puzzle" of how to live life that she confronts. Machine gambling at once places her directly in the line of chance and mediates chance in a way that grants her a sense of resolution and certainty. Recalling again her words at the start of this book:

> Most people define gambling as pure chance, where you don't know the outcome. But at the machines I do know: either I'm going to *win*, or I'm going to *lose.*... I don't care if it *takes* coins, or *pays* coins: the contract is that when I put a new coin in, get five new cards, and press those buttons, I am allowed to *continue*. So it isn't really a gamble at all—in fact, it's one of the few places I'm certain about anything. If I had ever believed that it was about chance, about variables that could make anything go in a given way at any time, then I would've been scared to death to gamble. *If you can't rely on the machine, you might as well be in the human world where you have no predictability either.*

Sharon's "reliance" on the machine brings us back to the fact that the vicissitudes of control gamblers experience in machine play—their bids for it, their loss of it, and even their most extreme push toward a zone beyond it—are not simply an expression of their preexisting preoccupation with control. Rather, they are a product of the interaction between this preoccupation and the design of the game (a "co-production," to borrow Latour's term, of gambler and machine). There is something like an elective affinity between gamblers' psychodynamic processes and the processes of machine play.

Gamblers' reliance on machines becomes most clear when the devices violate their promise, or "contract," as Sharon called it above. She described the effects that such breaches of contract had on her:

> When a coin jams, or when the hopper empties, I really feel paralyzed at those moments. It's not a question of moving to the next machine, it's not a question of waiting for a mechanic, it's a question of WHY-ISN'T-THIS-MACHINE-WORKING!?!? It was worse than a broken washer or car. With the video poker machine I could not tolerate any malfunctions, because it was the ONE thing I could rely on. If the machine malfunctioned or ran out of money, I would not be comfortable to trust that machine, to feel safe, and I'd have to leave that machine and sometimes even that casino, because that basic contract had been betrayed. I was confronted with the fact: YOU ARE NOT IN CONTROL. I would get very, very overdrive into my addiction at those moments, because the behavior response I depended on wouldn't happen.

As Sharon's words convey, it is not only gamblers' own vulnerabilities and dependencies that come to the fore in moments of mechanical failure, but also those of the machines, which seem to take on humanlike aspects—fragility, unreliability, unpredictability, and a capacity for betrayal.[14]

At times this betrayal takes a different form than mechanical malfunction, manifesting instead as a seeming reluctance on the part of the machines to let gamblers play the game they have come to play—a game, that is, of perfect contingency, in which the self/machine distinction dissolves. Isabella recounted such an instance:

> I broke down crying toward the end of that binge, right there at the machine. That day the machine didn't give me what I had come for; it took my money too fast. I was praying to God, and then it just ate up my last coin. I broke down sobbing, tears coming down my face. I'm sitting there thinking, *How stupid this is, to be sitting in front of a machine crying, like the machine really cares,* and I know they've got video cameras all around me and people are laughing at me and I'm crying more and more. After that I only gambled another two weeks: I lost everything on purpose so I could start clean.

Something greater than the loss of gambling funds is at stake in this scene. Like Sharon, Isabella sought perfect contingency and self-suspension; yet on losing her last coin she found herself deposited, remainder-like, back into the world, where she had to confront the impossibility of making herself "gone" at the machine. The bitter sense of betrayal she felt was triggered in this case by mechanical success, for the machine functioned as designed, accomplishing its program to liquidate her assets; it was Isabella, instead, who "broke down," her program of self-liquidation obstructed by the very device that had allowed it to gather momentum. The cessation of her play and the rupture of her zone unmasked the asymmetry of her collusion with the gambling machine. Seeing herself through the eyes of the hidden video cameras that recorded her despair, she became acutely aware of herself as a subject in the world.

But Isabella rallied beyond this point of devastating clarity, turning even this encounter into a possibility for gaining some margin of control over loss: "After that ... I lost everything on purpose so I could start clean." In the very attempt to extricate herself, she rehearses the same drive that got her there to begin with.

Returning to Alexandra's question—*What is this thing controlling me?*—it would appear that this "thing" is neither fully within the person nor fully scripted by the machine but, rather, a hybrid force to which both contribute. In machine gambling, the industry's aim to liquidate player assets (or to bring about "player extinction") works in a kind of partnership with the player's own push toward self-liquidation (or "self-extinction"). In this sense, the efficacy of machine design lies not in its introduction of a foreign or corrupting force into the human psyche but in its ability to draw out and channel inclinations already present in gamblers. As Diane told us above: "[the machines] are the most satisfying thing to my addiction that I've ever encountered, and they let that thing inside me grow, and take over."[15] Gambling machines could be said to distill the psychic economy of the death drive as Freud described it, converting life's suspensive circuits into an unimpeded path toward the zone.

PART FOUR

Adjustment

If the human condition consists in man's being a conditioned being for whom everything, given or man-made,
immediately becomes a condition of his further existence,
then man "adjusted" himself to an environment of machines the moment he designed them.

—*Hannah Arendt*

TERRY'S MACHINES

Terry, a small woman in her early sixties with short gray hair
and deep-set blue eyes, lives in a ground floor studio unit of
the Archie Grant Projects in north Las Vegas. It's evening and
the only light in the apartment comes from the lamp between
our two chairs and the television screen in front of us. She
smokes 120s, ashing them into a large, black cigarette tray
on her lap; it seems as if every fiber of the carpeted, curtained
space has been infused with smoke. Terry's nasal oxygen in-
haler is held in place by thin plastic tubing that ropes up
around her ears and joins beneath her chin. The tubing runs
down the folds of her housedress and winds around her feet,
then off in the direction of a motorized, gurgling noise that I
assume to be a component of her oxygen equipment, hum-
ming from an area of cluttered shadows at the other end of
the apartment. A large box of medications rests atop a pyra-
mid of three television sets. The film *Terminator* is playing,
and from one of the sets, Arnold Schwarzenegger's steely face
stares at us. Terry presses a button on her remote control—
"let's terminate him"—and his face blinks off the screen.

"Addiction runs in my family," she begins. Between drags,
she catalogs the dependencies of her six children: Her youngest
boy is an alcoholic and former drug addict; her oldest daughter is a bingo fanatic and plays the lottery; another daughter
goes from man to man; two other daughters have overeating
problems; her youngest girl is multiply addicted—to crack cocaine, alcohol, abusive men, keno machines, and video poker.

"Maybe I have most of these addictions myself," she muses, "just in different degrees."

I had met Terry the week before, at a Gamblers Anonymous meeting at the Triangle Club, an addiction self-help meeting center and café off Boulder Highway near Sam's Town casino. She moved to Las Vegas from Illinois in 1983 when her doctors recommended a dry, desert climate for her chronic lung disease. She had just completed an accounting degree and speculated that Las Vegas would be a good place to use it. For a while she worked as a bookkeeper as she had planned. "Then I was terminated at my job because everything got computerized, and I had no training on computers." She began to gamble every day; ironically enough, she favored computerized video poker machines. "I never did care for the machines where you just spin the reels and hope for 7s. With the video poker it seemed like I had more control." It took her a long time to realize that despite the skill factor of the game, a digital chip nonetheless controlled the odds. "It still baffles me, how they control them the way they do, with these chips.... How foolish I was to think I had any control over that machine."

Terry's play continued steadily. "If I were to put a date to when I really got addicted, it would be April twenty-fifth in 1988, when I hit a royal flush on a quarter progressive machine for $2,495." Terry remembers the date so well not only because of the amount of money she won but also because it was her daughter's birthday and because later that same day her younger sister died. "You just don't forget something like that." A winning streak followed this tragic set of synchronicities and continued throughout the spring. Terry hit so many jackpots at the El Cortez, the downtown casino she calls her "second home," that she couldn't possibly eat all the free meals she had coming. Then, all of a sudden, her luck turned. When she picked up her last free dinner ticket the woman at the counter told her, "This is your last meal, until you hit another jackpot."

By the end of summer, Terry was forced to sell the car she had purchased with her winnings and was to be evicted from her apartment if she failed to come up with four hundred dollars. Afraid of being on the streets, she turned to her church and was able to arrange a loan. Ever since then, for the past ten years, Terry has struggled to get her gambling losses under control. This struggle has involved Gamblers Anonymous, individual counseling, and fee-for-therapy groups that she learned about on the radio—but all to little avail. "It doesn't help that the technology keeps advancing," she tells me, "and that I'm surrounded by it."

"It would probably be good for me to move away from all the triggers," she reflects, "but then I'd be without all the support I have, because Las Vegas is the boot camp of problem gambling recovery. So I'm kind of stuck here."

9

BALANCING ACTS

The Double Bind of Therapeutics

A GAMBLERS ANONYMOUS MEETING is under way on the second floor of a small commercial plaza a few miles east of the Strip. A real estate agent in a maroon pants suit and a braided gold necklace tells the group that she leaves her home every morning unsure if she will gamble or not. "In between my appointments, something might push my buttons and trigger me to play at any moment. I'm not sure what would set me off. It feels dangerous out there."

A middle-aged man in blue jeans and a sweatshirt picks up on this sense of danger. "I know the [GA] rules—don't go to casinos, don't be around [gambling] machines—but I live in Vegas, so how is that possible? I like to go to a bar to have a drink sometimes, but I can't seem to do that without there being a damn machine there staring back at me. Hell, you go to the drugstore and they have them. Every time I fill my prescriptions I run the risk of getting stuck for hours at the machines."

"The grocery store is open all night," says a petite woman in her sixties. Gripping the large shiny purse on her lap so hard that her knuckles turn white around her rings, she admits how terrified she is to go shopping by herself when her husband, a successful banker, is out of town on business. She prays in the parking lot outside of Lucky's supermarket, repeating to herself, *I have to eat, I have to eat*, then hurries past the video poker machines that flank the entranceway.

A woman in her thirties wearing a waitress uniform shares next. "The gambling is all around me—I live in it, I work in it, it's constant. It's all I ever hear about from my coworkers and the people I wait on at the diner, from the time I get there until the time I get in my car. Then I have to fight it on the way home, driving past Boulder Station, all those places. I've got to keep on a certain side of the road and just keep driving."

"You need complete vigilance, every moment of every day," says an older man who had been coming to GA for years. "You can be driving around one minute on an errand, and then without planning it you get stuck in a gas station for hours. It's like someone else is in motion and you're just along for the ride. One thing I do now is close up my hands when I walk through places with machines; I hold something or I keep my hands in my pocket." He demonstrates, holding up his arms and curling his fingers into tight fists.

Earlier, Terry called Las Vegas the "boot camp of problem gambling recovery." As her words attest, the city's extensive machine gambling infrastructure is overlaid with a robust therapeutic network for those who become compulsively caught in its devices.[1]

Tacked to the wall above a bank of video poker machines in a gas station serving a residential neighborhood that I visited in 1998, flyers advertised self-help groups, fee-based clinics, and other locally available therapies to treat gambling problems (see fig. i.3, bottom). The machines themselves bore stickers indicating the 1-800 number for Gamblers Anonymous (GA), a fellowship that held approximately one hundred meetings per week in Las Vegas and its suburbs.[2] In 1997, a for-profit group called Trimeridian Resources for Problem Gambling opened a Las Vegas clinic offering a range of individual and group counseling options.[3] As locals learned through regular radio advertisements, the Eli Lilly pharmaceutical company had commissioned Trimeridian to recruit local video poker players for a double-blind experimental trial involving the drug Zyprexa, a widely prescribed antipsychotic that researchers hoped might also reduce cravings to gamble.[4] The trial was based at Charter Hospital, which housed an in-patient treatment clinic for problem gamblers from 1986 until the national collapse of its hospital chain in 1998. After Charter closed, the clinic's former director, Robert Hunter, founded the nonprofit Problem

Gambling Center in a blighted downtown neighborhood. The center, which charges only $5 to attend a group counseling session, was established   with   financial support from Station Casinos, among other local gambling businesses.[5]

At first glance, therapeutic enterprises would appear to operate at cross-purposes with commercial gambling. While the gambling industry designs techniques and technologies to induce extended consumption, the recovery industry—comprising researchers, funding bodies, in-patient and out-patient therapy groups, and purveyors of individual counseling—designs techniques and technologies that promise to weaken the bind of this consumption. Given the pursuit of objectives that are so precisely at odds, one might expect the methods of the two industries to differ also—yet they share two crucial traits. First, both are geared around the idea that behavior can be modified through external modulation; like gambling machines, therapeutic products are designed to be "user-centric" and amenable to custom tailoring. Second, both work by bringing about in their users a state of affective balance that insulates them from internal and external perturbations.

The resonance between machine gamblers' employment of gambling technologies and their employment of therapeutic technologies evinces the blurring of the line that might otherwise cleanly separate recovery from addiction; in both, gamblers seek means of self-modulation that can produce a continuous, homeostatic state and keep risk at bay. As we will see, the attentive state of balance they characterize as "recovery" bears an uncanny resemblance to the tensionless state they call "the zone." "The kind of serenity I feel when I'm doing my [therapy] exercises comes closest to the serenity I felt at the machines," Terry told me. It is not only that gambling addicts' machine play is isomorphic with their therapeutic practices, but also that a certain complicity and even interchangeability develops between the two, merging the zones of self-loss and self-recovery. "It's tricky," a local therapist recounted, "because I've seen people use their antianxiety medications to heighten the sense of escape they feel playing machines."

Recovering gamblers in Las Vegas, simultaneously plugged into two sets of "self-medicating" technology, find themselves in a double bind: the point that appears to be the end of their addiction seems to circle back to its source. Mollie drew this circling-back into visual relief in the map presented at the start of this book, in which her clinic and the site of her

Gamblers Anonymous meeting lie on the same road that takes her to the casino and the supermarket slots (see fig. i.4). Like Terry and others who wish to stop gambling, she faces the challenge of how to navigate this no-exit road in a way that partakes of its remedies while dodging its risks. This chapter explores that challenge and its consequences.

TAKING INVENTORY, MANAGING RISK

On a Saturday morning in the windowless conference room of Trimeridian's office suite, a longtime therapist of gambling addicts named Julian Taber handed out copies of a four-page document to the participants in his group therapy session. The document was a catalog of addicting items to which he alternately referred as the Consumer Lifestyle Index and the Inventory of Appetites.[6] The items were listed in no apparent order, each followed by boxes to check for "6–12 month use" and "lifetime use" (see fig. 9.1). The ten of us in attendance proceeded together through the list and marked each weak link in our respective chains of will, adding new items along the way. A vocal young woman proposed that "Spending just for the sake of spending" and "Searching for, buying and collecting certain items" be clustered together with two new categories—"Shopping for shopping's sake" and "Buying and returning things," compulsive tendencies she considered to be of the same family but slightly different from the two already included in the index.[7] Underlining the nonproductive, circular character of addicts' conduct, Taber suggested that "Buying *for the sake of* returning" might make a more accurate phrasing of the second habit, and it was added to the list. Half the people in the room, including the author, gave themselves a check for that behavior.

Daniel, a retired telecommunications engineer whom we met earlier in the book, thought that "Carbohydrates" and "Vitamins/other health foods" should be included on the index, musing that although the first was bad for his body and the second good, he was nevertheless addicted to both. A younger man pointed out that "Video games" and "Internet use" were obvious missing items, and a soft-spoken woman volunteered the less obvious "Taking care of your child," an idea that produced a quiet pause before it was added to the list. Everyone agreed that "Self-help"—a blanket category covering tapes, literature, techniques, and self-directed as well as group programs—belonged on the handout. At that point it

- Cocaine
- Heroin
- Amphetamine or similar "pep" pills
- Morphine or related opium-like drugs
- Gambling for money
- Marijuana
- Seeking and having sex with another person
- Seeking and using pornography
- Watching television
- Talking for talking's sake
- Searching for, buying and collecting certain items
- Lying (for no good reason)
- Aspirin or other non-prescription pain medications
- Controlled (prescription only) pain medications
- Laxatives
- Nasal decongestant sprays and inhalants
- Stealing, shopping, petty theft, etc.
- Sugar-based foods (candy, baked goods, ice cream)
- Fatty, oily or greasy foods
- Salt from the shaker and/or salty foods

- Pipe, cigar, cigarette, snuff or chewing tobacco
- Alcohol, beer, wine, liquor, whiskey, etc.
- Barbiturate and similar sedative drugs
- Hallucinogenic drugs (LSD, PCP, mescaline, etc.)
- Caffeine (tea, coffee, cola beverages, etc.)
- Exercise, jogging, playing sports or working out
- Spending just for the sake of spending
- Work for the sake of being busy
- Anger, fights and arguments
- Trying to manipulate and/or control other people
- Trying to get attention for attention's sake
- Reading for reading's sake
- Trying to get others to care for me / do things for me
- Antihistamine pills or other decongestant pills
- Antacids, stomach remedies
- Fast and/or reckless driving (not including DUI)
- Valium, Librium and related "minor tranquilizers"
- Physical violence
- Cough and/or cold medications
- Religious Activity

Figure 9.1. Consumer Lifestyle Index / Appetite Inventory. Created by Julian Taber for use in the treatment of gambling addiction.

seemed there was nothing left to say, and the collective inventory-taking exercise that had begun an hour earlier came to a close. We stood to stretch, to visit the washroom, to step outside and smoke.

The lessons imparted by the exercise we had performed on ourselves reflected both the "expanding inventory of everyday risks" facing consumers (as the sociologist Alan Hunt has written) and the ever-broadening definition of addiction that had come into cultural circulation since the 1980s.[8] The first lesson, communicated by the sheer number and diversity of items on the list, was that *anything can addict*. Although no substance or activity was bad in and of itself, any consumer behavior—no matter how necessary, benevolent, or life enhancing it might be when practiced sparingly or even regularly—could become problematic when practiced in excess, or "for its own sake." "Anything that's overly done is not good for us; if you get excessive with running it's an addiction," remarked Daniel. "Religion too—there are people who just have to go to church all the time and that's an addiction." When participants unanimously voted self-help itself into the catalog of addicting items, this lesson was confirmed. The implications were dizzying: If the potential for addiction lay even in the remedies intended to treat it, then where did addiction start and end, and how could it ever be arrested or recovered from?

The second lesson was that *anyone can become addicted*. An older participant in the group commented: "Aren't we all born with addictive tendencies, to some degree? For one person it's shopping, for another person it's cleaning, or working. For me, it's gambling and cigarettes." Daniel concurred. "It seems like addiction or compulsion is in everybody; some of us do one thing and some of us do another—even normal people have addictions." Rocky, the nuclear scientist, went so far as to suggest that susceptibility to addiction was a constitutive part of normalcy. "I think we all have the potential for some behavior to become extreme— it's just that most of us have another behavior to counterbalance it. The idea [of health] I've been fiddling with—that certain behaviors balance out other behaviors in some complicated way—is an equilibrium concept."[9] Health, as he construed it, was a function of balance between behaviors that were neither inherently good nor inherently bad. The potential to become addicted was not an aberration, we learned, but a liability that all humans carry.[10] Determined neither by constitution nor environment alone, addiction resulted from the interaction between the two; accordingly, it was a mercurial and circumstantial condition, unhinged to specific objects and open to a proliferating chain of attachments and substitutions. A subcomponent of this second lesson was that individuals were likely to have more than one susceptibility, or, as Taber put it, "a variety of possible dependencies." (Participants in GA meetings frequently expand the typical self-identification of "compulsive gambler" to "compulsive person" or, even more expansively, "compulsive everything.")

These two lessons—that the world is a field of potentially addicting elements and the human being a field of potential dependencies—set the ground for the third and most important lesson, on how we should understand our own role in addiction. At the close of the session Taber summed up this lesson: "Addiction is a problem of you governing your own life—not the government doing it for you." By "govern" he did not mean that gamblers should *abstain* from all potentially addictive activities—an impossible task because that would be to abstain from life—but that they should vigilantly *monitor and manage* themselves, adjusting their behavior and applying treatments when necessary. This last lesson falls neatly in line with the more general demand of neoliberal society that individuals participate robustly in consumptive markets while assuming responsibility for their conduct—from the economic to the legal to the medico-psychological. Following the template for actuarial selfhood that we explored in chapter 7, gamblers in recovery are expected to engage "in the continual inspection of their internal states and modifications of their own behavior," as the sociologist of gambling Gerda Reith notes.[11] The following text, posted by a gambler to an Internet recovery forum, resounds with this injunction:

> At the moment, I am in remission, keeping my illness maintained, contained—just like my son does with his ADHD meds, just like my husband does with his diabetes meds, like my mother-in-law with her cancer support groups. Like someone with cancer, diabetes, or even the common cold, I MUST take care of myself, I MUST take my medicines. I take my meds every day—counseling, prayer, reading posts, e-mailing with my fellows, going to meetings, learning about myself, helping my fellows, and even taking a medication for anxiety/compulsive behavior. Now I have the "medicines" to keep me from ever being that sick again.

More than simply reiterating the familiar rule of 12-step[12] programs that individuals assume responsibility for their own recovery, the personal catechism articulated in the post specifies that responsibility means availing oneself of an array of therapeutic techniques and technologies, all of which fall under the sign of "medication." The task is to discern which of these techniques and technologies, at any given moment of behavioral risk, might enable a needed adjustment.[13]

This technologically inflected vision of addiction recovery correlates not only with neoliberal directives, but also with a broad shift in the conception of health. Health is increasingly regarded as a balancing act that requires ongoing monitoring and modulation via medico-technological interventions, rather than as a default state or as something that can be definitively accomplished or "recovered." Echoing Rocky's earlier comment that health is an always-precarious equilibrium, the anthropologist Joseph Dumit terms this formulation of health "dependent normality." The "pharmaceutical self," as he names the subject of this mode of health, experiences his symptoms "as if he is on bad drugs, too little serotonin perhaps, and in need of good drugs ... to balance the bad ones out and bring both biochemistry and symptoms to proper levels."[14] The recovering gambling addict is similarly exhorted to pursue the different techniques

NAME: _____ DATE: _____

ID NUMBER: _____

PG CRAVING SCALE
100mm Visual Analog

"0" = Not at all   "100" = Most Ever

0_____100
"I would like to gamble"

0_____100
"I intend to gamble in the near future"

0_____100
"Gambling will make me feel better"

0_____100
"Gambling would get rid of any discomfort I am feeling"

0_____100
"I feel I can control my gambling"

Figure 9.2. Daily Craving Scale for Pathological Gambling. Client self-monitoring tool used by the Las Vegas Trimeridian problem gambling clinic.

and technologies by which the balance of health—a sort of homeostatic zero state (not altogether different from the zone, as we will see)—can be maintained.[15]

The understanding of addiction recovery (and health more broadly) as a question of technological self-management owes much to the self-enterprise culture of contemporary capitalism. The daily and weekly "Craving Scales" with which the counselors at Trimeridian armed their clients, for example, explicitly borrowed from the larger set of calculative tools that consumers are encouraged to make use of in planning their futures and governing their lives (e.g., cost-benefit analysis, the financial audit, budget forecasting, and other accounting and actuarial techniques).[16] The scales asked addicts to numerically rate the duration, intensity, and frequency of their gambling urges according to a set of subjective measures, so that they could better assess the current state of their risk for addictive behavior (see fig. 9.2).[17] As on a financial balance sheet, zero was the target rating for such measures as "Gambling will make me feel better" and "Gambling would get rid of any discomfort I am feeling." Like the inventory-taking exercise recounted earlier, this self-rating technique was meant to help addicts detect the symptomatic imbalance of their addiction—not so that they could remove the underlying condition, but so that they could keep it in check.

Daniel's story of how he came to enroll in Trimeridian's recovery program exemplifies the sort of calculative self-inspection that gambling addicts are encouraged to undertake. After calculating that he could afford to spend $2,400 a year, or $200 a month, on slot machines, he consulted his carefully kept ledger of gambling sessions and saw that he had more than surpassed this limit, having played on 25 percent of the days in the year, for an average of five to seven hours per session. Upon further investigation he found that his year-end gambling expenditures fell between $15,000 and $20,000; based on a cost-benefit analysis, he concluded that it would be worth the treatment cost to enroll in Trimeridian's five-week intensive outpatient program, which charged an average of $1,000 for twelve sessions, on a sliding scale. Once enrolled, the self-audits he produced using Trimeridian's craving scales were supplemented in individual and group therapy with guided strategizing on how he might avoid or remove particular addiction "triggers" from his life, and which counteractive behaviors—exercise, medications, hobbies, prayer, activities with family and friends—he could employ to move himself back toward zero, or "out of the red and into the black," as he phrased it.

The remainder of this chapter explores how gambling addicts' therapeutic projects are complicated by the fact that "zeroing oneself out" also characterizes the zone of their machine play, as was so strikingly evident in the previous section of this book. Although the project of recovery would appear to be an instantiation of actuarial selfhood while the zone would appear to be a rejection of it, gamblers describe both as states of dynamic equilibrium that they maintain through constant acts of self-modulation; the microtechniques of the recovering subject, like those of the practicing addict, work to quell perturbations in the system and "zero out" excess affect. This likeness undermines the divide between the two and implicates each in the other. As we saw in chapter 7, intensive machine gambling is no simple escape from the modes of actuarial selfhood that burden players in their everyday lives, for it rehearses those very modes. By the same token, the "balancing act" of addiction recovery rehearses the very escape mechanisms it is meant to overcome.

Circuits of Self-Medication

Gamblers describe both their machine play and their application of therapeutic practices in terms of self-medication. In their stories, it is not always clear which instances of self-medication follow a line of self-destructive escape (what Csikszentmihalyi would call "escape backward") and which follow a line of self-attentive recovery; the kind of affective balance sought and the means to hold that balance are similar enough in each case that they seem to blur into each other. This blurring comes to the fore in a comment Mollie made. "A very common 'slip' when we read aloud from our GA handbook," she noted, "is to say that we have *sought through prayer and mediCAtion*—instead of *mediTAtion*—which is laughable but truthful, because we have all self-medicated so much."[18]

Janet described this self-medication as a constant tuning and retuning of the various technologies that modulate her inner state. A young woman who wears thick glasses and a hearing aid, she feels near-constant anxiety because she is ashamed to ask people to repeat themselves when she has not heard them clearly, fearing she will seem stupid. At the time of our interview she played video poker every day at the grocery store to gain relief from this anxiety. She had learned that she could enter the zone most efficiently when she turned her hearing aid off, or to "another frequency." When she combined video poker and this refrequencing of her hearing aid with the amphetamines her husband was dealing or the Ritalin her son was taking for his attention deficit disorder, she achieved this relief even more readily.

It is not unusual for gambling addicts to describe the effects of their machine play as pharmaceutical-like. "The machine is like a really fast-working tranquilizer," said Randall. "Playing, it takes two minutes to disappear, to forget, to not feel. It's a wonderful way to alter my reality—an immediate mood shifter." Machine play can also shift bodily sensation. Nancy, the nurse we met in previous chapters, recounted how she felt sudden cramps one day while driving down Boulder Highway and pulled into a gas station to gamble. As she began to play, she was overcome with a numbness that remained until her last quarter ran out, whereupon she felt severe pain, looked down, and saw that she was hemorrhaging. "It interferes with the pain receptors or something," she told me, speaking of the machine in an analgesic idiom.

The fact that machine gambling is used, as are most addictive substances, for purposes of self-medication makes it difficult to distinguish its effects from those of the remedies applied to treat it. It is not simply that the technologically enabled, self-medicating equilibrium of the zone and that of the recovery model just examined are alike, but that the two become intertwined. The following pages consider how addicts' machine gambling practices can play into and even abet their experience of therapy, and conversely, how their therapeutic practices can play into and sometimes intensify their experience of machine addiction.

Mollie approaches the project of self-recovery with the same combinatory drive at play in her self-loss, assembling an arsenal of tools and techniques to bring herself into balance:

> Some say I need different meds. Some say I should connect with the Anxiety and Social Phobia message boards. Some people tell me I need God in my life. Others say if I just do the Twelve Steps I'll be OK. They're all probably right. A combination of group and/or individual therapy, meds, GA, and virtual therapy on the Internet, is what counts.

Mollie's statement, posted to an online forum for gambling addicts, prompted other gamblers on the forum to share their own therapeutic assemblages. A man named Geoff had cobbled together the following techniques to manage the physical and psychological disquiet that drove his addiction: "Meditation—a simple breath-watching exercise—gets the mind-chatter under control for about two hours. Same with exercise. I need a large endorphin-rush, so I play handball now and then. I also lift weights and swim at a local gym. The gym also offers yoga classes. All of these help." Meditation, diverse forms of exercise, and yoga were all components of Geoff's custom-tailored armamentarium of self-care strategies, designed to bring his endorphins, mind chatter, and willpower into a state of balance that could keep him out of the zone and in the world.

For others responding to the thread, psychotropic medications figured prominently. Gambling addicts participating in online forums frequently exchange what amounts to quasi-professional advice on the different medications they have been prescribed—Xanax, Neurontin, Paxil, Zoloft, Prozac, Percocet, Ritalin. "It sounds like you should try adding an anti-anxiety medication to your recovery," writes one woman. "If I ever get medical insurance, I think I need Neurontin," writes another.[19] Many have developed exact insights into how to measure and modulate their dosages. "I keep a meticulous record of the medications I take," Rocky told me. "I've gotten to the point where I can cut my Xanax dosage in half and take it every four hours."

As gambling addicts describe it, addiction treatment is not unlike a user-oriented game whose elements can, like the machinic object of their addiction, be configured and reconfigured to accommodate their immediate affective requirements. Counterintuitively, equilibrium-oriented therapies like meditation, yoga, exercise, and pharmaceutical management may work for machine gamblers because of—and not despite—their skill at accessing the zone state of compulsive machine play.[20] The catch, as we will see next, is that these therapies can also provide a route back to the zone.

Given that their treatments so frequently operate according to virtually the same principle as their addiction—that is, ongoing technological self-modulation to maintain equilibrium—perhaps it is not surprising that gamblers like Mollie, Geoff, and Rocky are so devilishly difficult to treat; the very protocol that promises to lead them out of their addiction risks turning into a game in which they can become lost. "Sometimes I get so carried away with a certain exercise or [self-help] step that I lose track of where I'm going with it," said Mollie, noticing that her therapeutic practice can take on a compulsive quality similar to that of her machine play. At every moment her treatment trajectory is susceptible to diversion from its intended end, veering from mindful engagement to escapism. (Seen in this light, the distinction that Csikszentmihalyi draws between self-actualizing and self-destructive modalities of "flow" would appear to be less linear than he proposes; by "escaping forward" gamblers sometimes find themselves circling "backward." As Deleuze has observed of drug addiction, that which is vital can "turn" self-destructive: "the drug user creates active lines of flight. But these lines roll up, start to turn into black holes."[21])

This susceptibility is at the crux of the dilemma that confronted Maria, who was wary of using medication or meditation as recovery tools, fearing they could lead her back into addiction. She had begun gambling in order to dampen her distress over a divorce and an unwanted pregnancy. She experienced panic attacks when she attempted to stop and assumed these were part of her "withdrawal from the machines"; when they did not subside, she visited a doctor who offered pharmacological treatment. But Maria "refused to be medicated," worrying that she would become as addicted to the drugs as she had been to the machines. "Medication was liable to become part of the problem," she told me. Even the nonpharma-cological, meditative therapies that remained at her disposal struck her as dangerous, because of the way that she had "used" them during her addiction:

> One recovery step says "Seek through prayer and meditation to improve your conscious contact with God as you understand him." Spirituality plays a big role in the recovery steps but my dilemma is that gambling itself was linked to spirituality from the start. I would meditate at night to try to see the cards that were going to come up on the machine the next day. It was never an out-of-body experience, but I'd be flying and all of a sudden I'd be somewhere in front of a machine and it was like a vision: I'd see a certain card combination. So I was afraid to pray and meditate during my recovery because I made a connection to what I had done when I gambled. I'd think, *I'd better not do that step …*

In the very act of meditating, Maria ran the risk of addiction—for the activity risked producing a state she too closely associated with that of the machine zone.

Another example of this risk can be found in Mollie's relationship to the antianxiety medication Zoloft—a drug that was originally prescribed to help her cope with the social interactions she sought to avoid through her machine play but that ultimately enabled her further withdrawal from the world. Mollie, who wears a full prosthetic leg and walks with a cane, was frank in her admission that video poker functioned as a mechanism for escaping from others, and from her own body. She nevertheless found that play could stimulate pleasurable bodily sensations: "I would have what you might call mini-orgasms at the machines—kind of a tightness but just very small, an exciting kind of release. It would happen when I got certain card combinations." Within the protected space of play, Mollie was able to experience her body in a way that she found difficult to do in social situations or moments of intimacy with others. The Zoloft she took to help her overcome her social isolation ended up compounding it, for she learned that the medication prevented her from having orgasms during sex with her husband, further compromising their intimacy. After she began taking Zoloft, sex became "strictly mechanical"—which she pre-ferred given that sexual sensations left her feeling dangerously exposed and overstimulated, "too close." In this way, the very drug prescribed to help her reconnect with and abide social ties ended up working in tandem with the gambling technology she employed to disconnect from others and experience her body in a controlled and private manner.

Pharmaceutical drugs most clearly "turn" from conditions of recovery into elements of addiction when gamblers discover, in the course of administering them, how well they can supplement the act of gambling and even facilitate the zone experience. Patsy, for instance, first used the medication Paxil to "even out" her moods and regulate the anxiety that led her to play machines. "Before Paxil, I would medicate myself with machines—but then, after playing, I would have strange pains in my jaw and my ears, and my menstrual cycle and appetite were irregular. Paxil was wonderful, an absolute miracle—I could feel it go to my brain and stop the anxiety from forming, and all the pains stopped too." As she recounted, her machine gambling began as a kind of medication to treat her emotional and bodily disequilibrium; although video poker alleviated this disequilibrium to some extent, it had the effect of aggravating and even producing new imbalances and irregularities, amplifying the need for more "medicine"—this time, pharmaceutical rather than machinic. But what appeared initially as Paxil's successful therapeutic outcome became more complicated when the drug began to flatten her mood to a point where she found herself gambling without guilt; she also found that she could more easily access the zone state while on the medication. "On the drugs, it didn't take as long to get there."

An even more striking example of the way in which drugs prescribed to dampen cravings for machine play come to function as intensifiers of its effects presents itself in the case of Amy. A recently divorced small business owner in her late fifties, she was prescribed Xanax to counteract the same anxiety she sought to neutralize through gambling. Almost immediately, she incorporated the drug into her play:

> I'd get so anxious when I was playing machines, I'd have panic attacks. My doctor prescribed Xanax and I never felt so good in my life. I was hooked for eight years. I'd take them while I was gambling. I'd feel the panic if I'd start losing, and also if I'd win—it was like an overload of excitement—and I'd pop two Xanax, or three, and it would calm me right down. I was taking four a day. I was supposed to be taking one. The doctor never knew about the gambling and how I used the pills with it. I'd just have him call in my prescription. If my prescription ran out, I knew somebody who lived in North Las Vegas who could buy them for one or two dollars a pill.

Amy's story, in which the administration of a therapeutic drug originally prescribed by a doctor comes to augment the effects of an addictive one, illustrates what Anne Lovell has called "pharmaceutical leakage," whereby a prescription pharmaceutical migrates from a treatment context to "an informal, illicit network (the drug economy)."[22] In the course of this leakage, the two "drugs" are joined in mutually reinforcing action. When Amy learned that Xanax could efficiently cancel out the "the overload of excitement" that she felt upon winning or losing at machines (for her, the two events carried the same perturbing value of an affective remainder), the drug became part of her play process. At the same time, her machine gambling modulated the calming effect of Xanax and in so doing entered the pharmacological process.

The unexpected interdependencies that form between the affect-regulating properties of drugs and machines short-circuit distinctions between self-care and compulsion. The concept of the "*pharmakon*," as Jacques Derrida elaborated it, well describes this no-win predicament in which remedies double as poisons and vice versa. "The *pharmakon*," he wrote, "can never be simply beneficial ... [for] what is supposed to produce the positive and eliminate the negative does nothing but displace and at the same time multiply the effects of the negative, leading the lack that was its cause to proliferate."[23] As gamblers recognize, the therapeutic remedies they self-administer—medicinal and meditative alike—carry multiple, indeterminate, and ultimately risky effects. They can rupture the zone's equilibrium, reinforce the reasons it is being sought, or simply strengthen its effects in a vicious, anaesthetizing circle.

Although this chapter has focused on instances of therapeutic failure or "turning," it should be noted that gambling addicts' projects of self-care do not always or necessarily fail. Nevertheless, even their moments of triumph tend to bear the traces of the double bind at stake in our discussion. In a post to an Internet forum, for example, a gambler once addicted to online video poker observed that her computer had morphed from a vehicle of addiction into a vehicle of recovery. "I spent most of the last several months of my gambling in total isolation in front of the computer," she wrote. "That is where I reached my bottom and that is why the online recovery sites are so important to me." As she told it, the conditions of her recovery were rooted in the conditions of her addiction. Another gambler on the forum described the implicit challenge this double bind posed for him: "I tried filtering out gambling sites using key words such as *gamble*, *gambler*, etc., but that prevented access to online recovery sites such as this one which have become so very important to me and my own personal recovery. So it's a constant struggle."

Las Vegas locals carry out this struggle in everyday living spaces rather than online. As Terry commented earlier, "it would probably be good for me to move away from all the triggers, but then I'd be without all the support I have, so I'm kind of stuck here." At the close of our meeting she recounted a recent gambling episode in which she had walked a distance to Savon drugs with her oxygen tank to fill a prescription she needed for her lung condition. Having forgotten to bring cigarettes, by the time she arrived she was so desperate that she picked up a butt from the ground to smoke. "The only place to sit and smoke that butt was in front of a poker machine. Just going near that machine was unwise—before I got up I had dropped a 100-dollar bill and I was broke again. I couldn't get the medication I'd come for, couldn't get a cab home, couldn't walk home either, and I was almost out of oxygen." She asked a woman in the parking lot for a ride home, and it turned out they knew each other from Gamblers Anonymous. During their car ride the woman, who like Terry also had a lung condition, told her about a casino that offered its regular players free oxygen tank refills and another that gave away free prescription drug refills based on the number of credits players had "earned" on their slot club cards.[24] Terry was stuck, it seemed, between pharmacies that doubled as casinos, and casinos that doubled as pharmacies (see fig. 9.3).

As we have seen, gamblers' and treatment programs' wish to "filter out" the toxic from the vital, to remove links to illness while preserving links to cure, carries a high risk of failure. Recall the Consumer Lifestyle Index exercise recounted earlier, in which each new element of addiction that participants added rehearsed this wish to separate negative from positive, unhealthy from healthy. The final lesson of that exercise—unwittingly clinched when therapy itself was included in the list of perilous conduct—was that the two cannot be clearly distinguished in a context where addiction and the means to control addiction move on a continuous circuit.[25]

ACTUARIAL ADDICTS

Some months after my first meeting with Terry, I visited her home a second time. When I asked about developments in her life, she gestured at

Figure 9.3. Las Vegas drugstore signs advertising video poker, 2002. Photographs by the author.

the dim shapes crowding her apartment and answered by way of a technological inventory. She had a new oxygen tank from which she didn't dare venture far, but it was such an effort to drag around that she wasn't going out much. The car she had managed to buy had been stolen, making it difficult to refill her medical prescriptions. The microwave on which she "had become quite dependent" had quit a week earlier. She had no computer, only a broken typewriter, and her radio had stopped working. She didn't have the money to replace these appliances, but she was "learning to adjust." Only one of her three television sets worked, somewhat. "If it goes out—and I won't be surprised if it does—I'll have to learn to get along without that, too."

The technologies among which and through which Terry lived—some of them defunct, or nearly so—were alternately sources of depletion and resuscitation: video poker machines promised reward and control while draining her finances; the new oxygen tank kept her alive but restricted her movement; casinos offered her free meals and oxygen tank and prescription refills, but only if she racked up enough credits on her player card; the pharmacy provided medication and a place to rest in front of a machine. In a world where potentially addicting elements were tactical components in the task of self-care and palliative elements were potentially addicting, she was challenged to configure and reconfigure her technological interactions in order to "adjust."

The double bind of the recovering gambling-machine addict, this chapter has suggested, resonates with the more general predicament of consumers as they struggle to simultaneously make and manage choices from within a field of goods and services whose effects and interactions are often difficult to predict. Machine addicts exemplify the sort of adjustability required of actuarial selves in the face of this predicament. At first glance such a claim may seem counterintuitive, for addicts are typically defined as lacking the skills of self-adjustment that healthy selves require to successfully navigate the world; they are an "outcast sector," writes the sociologist Nikolas Rose, "unable or unwilling to enterprise their lives or manage their own risk, incapable of exercising responsible self-government."[26] "The government of addiction," he observes, thus takes the form of interventions that "enable the individual to reenter the circuits of everyday life, where he or she will re-engage with the cybernetics of control built into education, employment, consumption, and leisure."[27] Yet gambling-machine addicts' behavior, while certainly at odds with ideals of enterprise and responsibility, is by no means marginal to the "cybernetics of control" built into everyday life. In fact, their conduct—not only in their practice of recovery but also in their practice of addiction itself—makes them more fitting representatives of contemporary actuarial selfhood than the mythic figure of the "consumer sovereign" who masterfully and rationally maximizes a pristine, coherent, and unconflicted set of desires in a world whose chorus of consumptive appeals do not affect him.[28] Gambling addicts, like other consumers in "risk society," act not so much to maximize as to manage; to this end, they continually recalibrate their actions in response to environmental feedback, flexibly adjusting themselves to changing circumstances and contingencies.

10

FIX UPON FIX

Recipes for Regulating Risk

IN 2004, five years after I heard the Australian firm Aristocrat's Stuart Bull speak of the market's growing "tolerance for technology" in the conference rooms of the Las Vegas Convention Center, I heard another Australian gambling executive speak of a growing "intolerance" for his industry's technologies.[1] "Australian products are the best in the world technically—we lead the market in games. But we also lead in worry over what's good for people." He cautioned his North American colleagues: "Beware—there is real discussion in my country about slowing down reel speeds, making machines shut down after a certain period of time, screens that pop up and say *Okay, you've played for two hours now, you really need to have a think about whether you want to continue to play ...*" Laughter rippled through the audience. "I'm not joking," he protested facetiously, "we're actually going to make the machine shut down for ten minutes, run messages across the screen every ten minutes saying *Gambling can be dangerous, you really should have a pause ...*"

The amusement of the American audience notwithstanding, an independent federal commission in Australia five years earlier had resulted in several legislative acts seeking to mitigate gambling addictions by restricting or minimizing the use of certain features on slot machines.[2] Five years later, a second governmental commission would produce a two-volume, 1,110-page report recommending an extensive suite of adjustments to gambling environments and technologies.[3] Such adjustments have been recommended not only in Australia but also in Canada, Britain, Norway, Sweden, and Switzerland—all jurisdictions where machine gambling was liberalized in the 1990s for fiscal purposes (in some cases run by the state itself) and later became the object of widespread public discontent.

Even in the United States, where the private sector dominates commercial gambling and a deregulatory ethic reigns, the idea that the gambling industry and its products might share a portion of responsibility for problematic gambling behavior is on the rise. In some respects, this idea harkens back to the first quarter of the twentieth century, when slot machines were routinely seized and taken to Halls of Justice to await court orders for their destruction, whereupon they were publicly smashed or dumped en masse in waterways. Gambling machines themselves were treated as culpable entities, and quite literally put to trial (see fig. 10.1). Yet today in America and other free market democracies, the suggestion of culpability leads to relatively milder forms of regulation. Governments have become too reliant on the taxes machines generate to ban or harshly restrict them, and the public perception of gambling has shifted in line with the growing liberalization of everyday life such that the activity is considered one choice among others to which consumers are entitled—and for which they themselves are held responsible. In such a climate, prohibition and its performative rituals of denunciation have given way to harm minimization.[4] This regulative strategy assumes that consumers will continue to participate in the marketplace of gambling; its aim, like that of the therapeutic techniques discussed in the last chapter, is to manage rather than eradicate risk.

The exact shape that risk management should take, however, is hotly debated. Advocates of the so-called technological remedies mocked above by the Australian gambling executive would impose strict constraints on existing machine features, especially those regarded as most harm inducing. Unsurprisingly, the gambling industry aggressively dismisses the possibility that technology is part of the problem, or that adjusting its design might be part of the solution. "The problem is not in the products they abuse, but within the individuals," asserts the American Gaming Association.[5] Accordingly, the lobby's preferred form of risk management follows the same course of self-governance as the therapeutic approaches discussed in the last chapter.[6] Consumer advocates, for their part, argue that gamblers will be better able to achieve self-governance in the presence of "informational remedies" such as the posting of safety warnings, odds,

Figure 10.1. *Top*: Government agents smash slot machines in Chicago, 1910. *Bottom*: Senate Labor Rackets Committee meets to open its investigation of the coin-operated machine business in 1959. (In the foreground, from left to right: counsel Robert Kennedy, Chairman John L. McClellan, and Senator Frank Church.) Courtesy of Bettmann/Corbis.

and even probability lessons on machines. Going beyond mere information, some propose that "control aids" be designed to overlay existing machine functions, empowering players to protect themselves in the very process of play. Still another approach, largely motivated by gambling corporations' efforts to reduce their liability in future litigation by demonstrating duty of care, allocates the initial responsibility for monitoring and intervening in risky play to casinos' own player tracking and marketing systems.

Between the lines of this technocratic regulatory debate run deeper cultural and political tensions over who or what is in control in the machine gambling encounter, and who or what should be held accountable for loss of control: The machine? The player? Their interaction? Which should be regulated, and how?[7] As we will see, different ways of fixing blame lead to different ways of "fixing" problem gambling, and vice versa. As we will also see, despite their differences in attribution of responsibility, the majority of approaches treat individual behavior as the ultimate object of intervention and adjustment; even those approaches that seek to adjust machines' behavior do so in a way that facilitates consumers' self-regulation rather than fundamentally altering the terms of their consumption.

Responsibility Campaign

In 1996 the US federal government responded to the explosion of gambling across the country by creating the bipartisan National Gambling Impact Study Commission, allotting it $5 million to study legalized gambling and its associated social ills.[8] In response, Washington insider Frank Fahrenkopf founded the American Gaming Association (AGA) to protect and promote the gambling industry.[9] He recognized at the outset that a critical aspect of its mission should be to strategically position the industry in relation to the problem of gambling addiction. Soon after founding the AGA, Fahrenkopf gave a speech to high-ranking industry executives in Las Vegas in which he called problem gambling the "Achilles' heel" of their trade.[10] "The growth of our industry is certainly endangered by the issue," he warned, "and it is not hyperbole to say that the industry's very existence is at stake."

Fahrenkopf urged his colleagues to avoid the mistakes made by their counterparts in the tobacco industry, reminding them of the infamous scene in which a panel of prominent tobacco executives raised their hands before a 1994 congressional committee to unanimously disavow any link between nicotine and addiction. By the mid-1990s, the gambling industry had already grasped (as the alcohol industry had some decades earlier) that a medical diagnosis linked to the excessive consumption of its product by some individuals could serve to deflect attention away from the product's potentially problematic role in promoting that consumption, and onto the biological and psychological vulnerabilities of a small minority of its customers.[11] The late Shannon Bybee—whose career included stints as a casino regulator on the Nevada Gaming Control Board, a casino president, an executive for a slot machine manufacturer, and the first president of the Nevada Council on Problem Gambling—voiced this position in 1988: "Failure to resist impulses to gamble means to me that the problem—and the solution—is found within the individual. Those who can't control gambling must be suffering from a behavior disorder, perhaps even a disease."[12] His choice of words explicitly drew from the diagnostic language of "pathological gambling" that had been endorsed by the American Psychiatric Association in 1980.[13] Not only should the gambling industry admit that such a condition exists, Fahrenkopf ventured in his speech to AGA members, it should also lead research efforts in the area.[14]

A step in this direction was the AGA's creation of the National Center for Responsible Gaming (NCRG) in 1996, the same year that Congress convened the National Gambling Impact Study Commission. The NCRG was established to fund "research that someday will identify the risk factors for gambling disorders and determine methods for not only treating the disorder but preventing it, much like physicians can identify patients at risk from cardiovascular disease long before a heart attack."[15] This charter cast problematic gambling behavior as the expression of preexisting tendencies within a small, circumscribed group of "at risk" individuals rather than as an outcome of consumers' interactions with gambling environments or technologies. The center's first award went to professor of psychiatry Howard Shaffer at Harvard, resulting in what the industry dubbed "the first reliable statistic" on the rate of gambling disorders in the United States and Canada, indicating that between 1.14 and 1.60 percent of the adult population fulfilled the diagnostic criteria for pathological gambling. (As indicated in the introduction, the percentage is estimated to be far higher for the adult *gambling* population.) The figures were presented before the National Commission in 1998 and have since been vociferously touted by industry representatives in the rounded-down form of "one percent." "Recent research coming out of Harvard," Harrah's CEO Gary Loveman told a large audience of peers attending the Global Gaming Expo's 2003 "State of the Industry" keynote panel, "shows that some individuals are predisposed, and the vast majority of people are at virtually no risk of ever becoming addicted to gambling."[16] There is rarely mention of the study's additional findings—that nearly 4 percent of adults fit the looser criteria for "problem gambling" (a conservative estimate, according to some researchers), and that the "lifetime" (as opposed to "current") problem gambling rate among adults had doubled between 1977 and 1997.[17] "Gambling proponents tend to focus on the lower numbers," Shaffer has conceded.[18]

The board of directors for the NCRG, which since its establishment has financed most of the research conducted on gambling addiction in the United States, has included representatives from many of the largest companies in the industry (MGM-Resorts, Harrah's Entertainment, International Gaming Technology, Gaming Laboratories International, Station Casinos, WMS Gaming, Aristocrat, and Wynn Resorts, among others), as well as the executive director of the American Gaming Association. Boyd Gaming provided the start-up funds with a ten-year pledge of $875,000.[19] "More than $22 million has been committed to the NCRG, an unprecedented level of funding for gambling research from the private sector," boasted AGA's website in 2008.[20] Some researchers, ethicists, and critics of the industry are unsettled by the potential conflict of interest this scale of investment raises. Henry Lesieur and Richard Rosenthal, two leading scholars of problem gambling, resigned from NCRG's advisory board in 1997 when they became worried about the industry's influence over funding allocations. Specifically, they doubted that the center would fund research on topics such as the role of gambling accessibility or machine design in problem gambling.[21]

To defend itself against intimations of bias, in 2000 the AGA set up an entity called the Institute for Research on Pathological Gambling and Related Disorders, based at the Division on Addictions at Harvard Medical School, directed by Shaffer.[22] The institute's role was to review applications for research and disburse NCRG funds, thereby "further strengthening the existing firewall between the gaming industry and decisions about what research would be funded."[23] Although NCRG board members do not directly select projects or control their research outcomes, it is nevertheless abundantly clear that an industry-friendly ethos guides its funding priorities. "You don't see any research into the addictive nature of different games, and why people who play video machines seem to get addicted faster," Lesieur told a journalist in 2008.[24]

Not only does the institute fund virtually no research on the industry's products and the role they might play in problem gambling, it also explicitly denies that such a connection exists. "Things are not addictive, they're just not," insists executive director Christine Reilly. Just as alcoholism doesn't come in bottles, she argues, gambling addiction doesn't come in machines. "I play a slot machine for 10 minutes and I'm so bored I want to shoot myself. If you don't have [the] vulnerability, the odds are you won't get addicted."[25] As she sees it, the purpose of the institute is to pursue the root of that vulnerability—which she considers to be common to all addictions (rather than specific to gambling): "Wouldn't it be great to have an objective measure—a blood test, maybe a genetic marker, saying this person is predisposed to addiction?" In keeping with this quest, the lion's share of NCRG monies support investigations into the genetic, neuroscientific, and psychological determinants of the addiction.[26] The minimal portion of funding allocated to research on the social and environmental determinants of problem gambling goes to studies such as Shaffer's in 2004, proposing that initial spikes in addiction after the introduction of gambling to a new area resolve over time as exposed residents "adapt" to the novelty of its temptations.[27]

Before Shaffer was approached by NCRG's board, he "had voiced some of the harshest warnings in academia against the collateral damage of gambling's growth," the author of a 1998 exposé in the *Los Angeles Times* pointed out.[28] As we saw in the introduction, Shaffer was one of the first to have called video poker the "crack cocaine of gambling" and did so on repeated occasions. In fact, even after his involvement with the industry, he occasionally made comments to reporters suggesting that the design of gambling technology played a significant role in the development of gambling problems. "These are rapid games, quickly played, relatively private, and hold the greatest potential for addictive disorder because they work our neurobiological systems in the most threatening of ways," he said of slot machines in 2001. "These fast-acting games are like fast-acting drugs." In early 2004 he similarly commented: "The hard wiring that nature gave us didn't anticipate electronic gaming devices."[29] In his published writings since then, Shaffer has become more circumspect regarding technology's effects on gamblers, claiming that "psychopathology disproportionately precedes excessive involvement with the technology."[30] Despite his earlier recommendation that addiction be viewed as an interactive relationship between subjects and objects, his recent spoken and written statements have either deemphasized or explicitly disavowed the technological dimensions of addiction to gambling machines. "It's hard not to suspect that his reticence on the external factors has something to do with the support he receives from the industry," a former colleague of Shaffer's told me, on condition of anonymity. "These days he sounds more like a lobbyist than a researcher."

By 2003, when he appeared on G2E's closing keynote panel along with representatives from Harrah's and Aristocrat, former "harsh warnings" had turned to unequivocal defense. The panel was moderated by Republican pollster and public opinion shaper Frank Luntz, who had recently been commissioned to develop a report for the AGA on American perceptions of casino entertainment.[31] When Luntz asked Shaffer if fellow academics were hostile to his work, Shaffer responded: "There is a tendency to study only negative aspects [of gambling], but there are positive aspects as well—and not only economic." He cited emerging research indicating that games are not only important for children but also for adults and the elderly, providing the cardiovascular benefits of physiological stimulation as well as opportunities for cognitive and problem-solving exercise.[32] "It is quite likely that gambling serves a medicinal purpose in low doses," he told the audience.

In 2006 the NCRG permanently shifted its annual conference dates to coincide with those of the Global Gaming Expo as a way to heighten interaction among industry members, academic researchers, treatment providers, policy makers, and gaming regulators. "By aligning our event with G2E," said Phil Satre, then chairman of the NCRG (he had formerly been chairman and CEO of Harrah's Entertainment and would go on to be chairman of IGT), "we hope to foster a more lively exchange of ideas within the field of gambling research and, ultimately, expand the positive impact of this vital research within casino communities."[33] Yet as skeptics in the research community point out, the exchange that transpires is highly limited given that the conference consists entirely of invited speakers and includes only a small subset of academic researchers. Further solidifying its "alignment" with G2E, in 2007 the NCRG offered a specially priced combo-pass to both meetings and convened a number of its sessions at G2E headquarters in the Las Vegas Convention Center—only a few stops away from its headquarters at the Paris casino resort, on the same monorail line. That year Shaffer received a National Scientific Achievement Award from the board members. It was presented to him at a lavishly catered reception sponsored by IGT, during which the lights were dimmed to screen a ten-minute tribute video made by the production house of MGM-Mirage. The video lauded Shaffer as a man "devoted to science" and to data. It was clear that a strong industrial-academic alliance had formed around the understanding of gambling addiction as a discrete disease entity rooted in individual predisposition.

Although the determinist language of mental and biological pathology the NCRG uses to cordon off pathological gamblers implies that the rest of the population is immune to the problem, the center's educational programs—which include the Responsible Gaming National Education Campaign, the Responsible Gaming Resource Guide, Responsible Gaming Education Week, and the Responsible Gaming Lecture Series— contradictorily suggest that *any* of us might slide into the problem if we do not comport ourselves responsibly. The contradiction comes to the fore in a brochure titled "Keeping It Fun: A Guide to Responsible Gaming." The brochure presents five gamblers, each of whom bears a different message of responsibility. Three are Caucasian. A thin older woman smiles shyly: *Gambling's more fun when I set limits and stick to them.* A balding man in his forties wearing a navy sports jacket tells us: *Without setting limits, it's easy to get carried away* (see fig. 10.2). A confident young man in a dress shirt, one arm akimbo: *I never lose more than I can afford, which means I never lose.* A thirty-something Asian woman in casual dress strikes a confident pose: *Every player thinks they have a system. Mine is I only bring what I can afford.* An older black man in a polo shirt, hands on his hips and an easy smile on his face: *You don't have to take big risks to have big fun.*

Armed with the responsible gaming "codes of conduct," the self-limiting, budget-managing gamblers depicted in the brochure model exemplary consumer behavior (which happens to be the same self-monitoring, self-regulating behavior at which problem gamblers in recovery become so practiced, as we have seen). They take risks, and at the same time manage themselves; gambling becomes an exercise in risk management. Beneath each image appears the same message: "To keep it fun, set time and money limits and stick with them. Understand the odds. And please don't gamble when you're lonely, angry, or depressed. It clouds your judgment." Despite Loveman's statement above that "the vast majority of people are at

When you gamble for fun, you've already won.

" Without setting limits, it's easy to get carried away. "

KEEP IT FUN

WE'RE BANDING TOGETHER TO KEEP IT FUN.

To order responsible gaming awarness wristband, visit www.americangaming.org.

Proceeds benefit the National Center for Responsible Gaming.

Responsible gaming is a social activity, best enjoyed with family and friends. To keep it fun, set time and money limits and stick with them. Understand the odds. And please don't gamble when you're lonely, angry or depressed. It clouds your judgement.

For a free guide to responsible gaming go to americangaming.org

AMERICAN GAMING ASSOCIATION

Figure 10.2. Image from American Gaming Association's "Keeping It Fun" responsible gaming campaign. Available for download at American Gaming Association website.

virtually no risk of ever becoming addicted to gambling," these advertisements suggest that risk exists for all gamblers and must be vigilantly kept at bay.[34]

Shaffer goes so far as to claim that gambling and its risks offer individuals a valuable *opportunity* to cultivate and practice responsibility. "The value of tempting activities (e.g., gambling, investing, engaging in sex) is that enticements provide the opportunity to learn self-control and build character," he wrote in 2005. "Self-regulation emerges from the gentle interplay with temptation; absent such access, it is more difficult if not impossible for people to learn how to regulate themselves."[35] As he tells it, the "gentle interplay" between human and gambling machine leads naturally to responsibility and control rather than to irresponsibility and loss of control. His narrative follows a strongly moral logic according to which autonomous individuals are responsible for themselves.

"How do you know if you've gone beyond enough?" Luntz asked Shaffer during the 2003 keynote panel. "Are there any signs?" Warning signs, Shaffer responded, were spending more than you intended, going beyond your budget, and beginning to crave the activity. "Do casinos do enough to warn people of the signs?" Shaffer replied that he didn't think it was the casino's obligation to warn people. Luntz asked for the house lights to be turned up so that he could ask the same of the audience: "Is it the casino's responsibility to warn its patrons that they've reached a point of too much, or is it individual's responsibility to know when enough is enough?" Nearly all raised their hands for "individual's responsibility." As the scene demonstrates, the discussion around "responsible gambling" slips easily from scientific into moral and political terrain, with industry participants taking clear sides on the social debate over what sort of regulation should characterize the sphere of commercial consumption.

Whether the gambling industry is sincere in its campaign to promote responsible gambling, or whether the driving impetus behind this campaign (as behind similar campaigns by the alcohol and tobacco industries) is to insulate the industry's products and practices from blame for problematic consumer behavior, the fact remains that a grossly disproportionate percentage of its revenues happen to derive from precisely such behavior.[36] Gamblers who manage to follow "responsible gaming codes of conduct," one study found, contribute a mere 4 percent of gambling revenues.[37] "If responsible gaming were successful," an author of that study told a radio journalist, "then the industry would probably shut down for lack of income."[38] The conflict between the industry's responsibility rhetoric and the profit it reaps from irresponsibility leads some to the cynical conclusion that the promotion of responsible gambling, first and foremost, is a public relations strategy geared toward protecting revenue. As the Canadian gambling scholar James Cosgrave has commented, "responsible gambling is a form of risk management taught to individuals, for individuals, but it is also a method of risk management" for states and the gambling industry.[39]

Informing Consumer Choice

A consumer protection approach, while endorsing the model of the responsible consumer, maintains that the capacity to exercise responsible choice depends on full information.[40] So-called informational remedies for irresponsible gambling would "help gamblers be good shoppers" by using signs, displays, and pamphlets to educate them about gambling machine attributes whose operation and true cost might otherwise elude them. "To be rational consumers," writes Kurt Eggert, law professor and consumer protection advocate, "gamblers should be given adequate price information."[41]

Although machines present paytables detailing how much will be awarded for a particular combination of symbols or cards, they do not post the *odds* of hitting that combination, as table games do. A given machine may indicate its "theoretical payout percentage" or "return to player" (RTP) percentage (e.g., 89 percent), but never its *hold* percentage (otherwise known as "house advantage" or "house edge").[42] At a Starbucks kiosk off the lobby of the hotel hosting the 2007 International Conference on Gambling and Risk-Taking in Lake Tahoe, a group of industry entrepreneurs sat with their coffees, killing time between sessions. "I don't think it would hurt the industry to show odds on machines," said one, reflecting back on the topic of a panel he had attended earlier in the day, "because most people already know the odds aren't in their favor." "Yes but what people don't realize," said another, "is that when you bet *over and over again*, you have no chance." In other words, players do not easily grasp the *cumulative* nature of machines' hold. A "90% payback percentage" does not mean that a player who starts off with $100 is likely to lose only $10 by the end of a given session; it means that she is likely to lose 10% of her funds *every time she makes a bet*, resulting in the "churn effect" represented in chapter 4 (fig. 4.2), whereby her funds are gradually reduced to zero.[43]

Since it is nearly impossible for gamblers to track a machine's hold percentage on their own (a manufacturer can increase a game's hold by five times, Eggert reports, without consumers noticing[44]), some suggest that machine manufacturers be required to post games' average cost per hour and loss rates directly next to the buttons players push to gamble, much as alcohol manufacturers are required to disclose the alcohol content of their product (90 proof, 120 proof, etc.). Others suggest a "dynamic price display," since slot machine odds fluctuate depending on how many credits a gambler bets, or how many lines she bets on. Such a display would show the changing "price" of play in dollars and cents rather than payback or hold percentage, thus communicating in real time the financial effect of the "churn" on a player's budget.

Still others argue that information for consumers should not merely be posted, but also *explained*. This would happen through onscreen educational modules about randomness and the probabilities of winning, near misses, multiline slots' "losses disguised as wins," and virtual reel mapping. Roger Horbay, designer of Safe@Play educational software for gamblers, has proposed that the software be added to all machine units as a form of risk management. For traditional reel-spinning slots, he would include warnings that the number of blanks and symbols appearing on the reels are not representative of the odds of winning. For video slots featuring multiple simulated reels, a touchscreen link would graphically reveal the actual stop configuration of each reel, so that players could easily see the symbol distribution and weighting across reels. Machines without this kind of transparency, he argues, present consumers with misleading graphics that violate standards of consumer safety required of similar products.

Another "informational" approach to the management of problem gambling risk involves programming machines to periodically scroll messages across the screen, appealing to gamblers' reason through language similar to that used in NCRG's responsibility campaign: *You cannot control the outcome of games of chance; Gambling is entertainment, not a way of making income; There is a cost to play these games; They will take in more than you win; The more you play, the more you pay; Set a budget and stick to it; Don't spend money on things intended for other activities; Take regular breaks.* Horbay has likened the educational messages in his own risk-management interface to rumble strips on the highway, functioning to "wake people up before an accident happens" rather than containing them in the event of a crash as do seat belts or airbags. For gamblers already caught in problematic play patterns, information-ready machines would offer responsible gambling tips, guidelines for assessing their problem, and resources and referrals for counseling, hotline help, and self-exclusion and self-help services.[45]

All informational remedies—from the posting of hold percentages to dynamic price displays, educational modules to scrolling messages— share the conviction that problematic gambling can be addressed by facilitating consumers' rational choices. Yet advocates for these remedies part ways when it comes to their respective understandings of what undermines rational choices in the first place, falling into two camps: those who see information provision as a corrective to distorted cognition, and those who see it as a corrective to the deceptive distortions of machine design. The first camp, supported by the gambling industry, adheres to the dominant perspective in gambling addiction research that problematic play is a function of cognitive errors and defective heuristics—illusions of control, faulty evaluation of outcomes, irrational schemas of probability, false beliefs of control over random events, misattribution of causal connections, and other "erroneous perceptions."[46] As Shaffer and his colleagues write, "it is crucial for any informed choice program in gambling to target faulty cognitions."[47] (Proponents of this view typically leave unspecified how exactly those cognitions should be targeted, in favor of calls for future "evidence-based research" to determine which forms of information might actually work and which might be counterproductive.[48])

For the second camp of consumer protection, the gambling machine rather than the gambler is the target of reform. Following this view, problematic play is a function of machines' opacity and deceptive inner mechanisms—virtual reel mapping, near misses, and the like. "It's correct human processing—it's the lie of the technology that's the problem," Horbay tells me. Machines set up valid expectations in the human cognitive system, he argues, and then violate those expectations—thereby preying on gamblers' rationality, not their irrationality.[49] Accordingly, machines are not a blameless medium through which to educate gamblers and repair their distorted thinking, but are a strategically configured technology whose scripted distortions must be offset via product transparency, thus lessening the informational asymmetry inherent in the gambling exchange. Yet even this more radical version of consumer protection, although it considers machines accountable, ultimately targets consumer behavior; informational remedies unmask the workings of machines as a way to appeal to gamblers' rationality, leaving basic machine features and functions intact.

Most members of the gambling industry regard informational measures—especially the static, "passive" sort—as a worthwhile hedge against liability for problematic gambling rather than a significant threat to profits.[50] Some have expressed concern that information delivered during the course of play in an "active" form such as scrolling messages could "increase breaks [in play] and increase self-awareness" to the detriment of industry profits.[51] In other words, they worry that appealing to gamblers' rationality in too overt a manner would lower machine revenue.

Critics of informational remedies from the clinical side, however, question the idea that consumers, once informed, would actually alter their behavior during a session of continuous gambling. Bo Bernhard (who directs the International Gaming Institute at the University of Nevada, Las Vegas, and has long been associated with local problem gambling clinics) points out that onscreen messages, designed to give gamblers "the opportunity to consider their options and break the cycle of play," appeal to rationality at a time "when the rational parts of their brains are shut off"—much like trying to talk sense into alcoholics who are passed out.[52]

The psychologist Mark Dickerson has argued that machine gambling, whether or not its "price" is adequately disclosed, "erodes the player's ability to maintain a sequence of informed and rational choices about purchasing the next game offered by the machine."[53] Gambling machines and the way they configure experience, he suggests, are "in direct conflict with responsible gaming strategies" and thus undermine the potential efficacy of informational measures. Horbay reflects on his own past forays into the design of responsible gaming messaging for slot machines: "It's like asking gamblers to step on the gas and the brake at same time, or to stay in speed-control at 200 miles an hour."

TECHNOLOGICAL REMEDIES

Going a step further than advocates of informational remedies, some argue that machine design itself should be modified to protect gamblers. Instead of encouraging gamblers to step more lightly on the gas pedal, why not reduce the pedal's capacity to produce speed? Rather than seeking to enable gamblers' exercise of responsible behavior or to rectify their cognitive interpretations of play, technological remedies would intervene at the level of machines' script for faster, longer, and more intensive play—a script Dickerson has described as "an 'addictive' sequence" characterized by the "tendency to raise, increase and expand."[54]

Modifications to reduce *speed* of play would slow the rate at which video reels "spin," pause reels between spins, and increase the time interval between a bet and its outcome. Modifications to reduce *duration* of play would mandate time-outs at certain intervals, display a permanent on-screen digital clock, and present periodic pop-up reminders alerting players to the time and money they have spent (stricter time-based measures would require a mandatory cash-out at 145 minutes of continuous play, following a five- or ten-minute warning). To reduce *magnitude* of wagering, modifications would decrease maximum bet size per spin, remove bill acceptors (or restrict them to small bills), show bet amounts in actual cash value rather than as play credits, and dispense all wins in the form of cash, check, or electronic bank transfer rather than tokens or tickets that might be easily regambled; multiline, multicoin games would be required to decrease the number of betting lines and to remove the "bet maximum coins" feature.[55] Another set of modifications would address machines' mathematical sleights of hand by eliminating near-miss effects, restricting losses disguised as wins, phasing out virtual reel mapping on nonvideo reel slots, and requiring video slots to "balance their reels" so that all contain the same symbols, in accordance with player intuition. Still another set of modifications, known as "environmental," would require slot areas to have natural light, smoking bans, and "liquidity controls" to limit "impulsive withdrawals" (e.g., less proximate placement of ATMs, cash limits for ATMs, and restrictions on credit card access).[56]

Unlike the other "fixes" we have considered so far, these remedies for problem gambling focus on the material design features of gambling technologies and environments—not necessarily to fundamentally change or eliminate them, but to dampen their effectiveness. Like airbags in cars, their point is not to stop risky behavior, but to minimize its adverse consequences. How exactly and to what degree this harm minimization should proceed is a topic of mind-numbing technocratic minutiae: How slow should reels spin—2.14 seconds? 2.5 seconds? 5 seconds? Should the "idle time" between spins be set at a minimum of 1.5 seconds, or 2 seconds? Should bill acceptors on machines be limited to a maximum of $20, $50, or more? What about ATM withdrawal limits—should they be set at $200? $400? Should ATMs be placed within a certain distance from gambling machines? Banned from machine areas? Banned altogether from gambling establishments? In theory, the aim of each intervention is to find a balance that can discourage impulsive machine betting without driving away players who experience no trouble with gambling machines. For example, the hope is that "low cash input levels and irritation associated with them" will exact "a high price for dissociated gamblers or those playing at a frenetic pace" but go unnoticed by the casual player.[57]

The gambling industry finds this claim dubious, and is wary of where it could lead. At eight o'clock on the last Sunday morning of the 2006 G2E meetings, Bo Bernhard introduced a panel called "Bells, Whistles, and Warnings: The Safe Gambling Machine." Under consideration was what he described as "the first generation of seatbelts for gambling machines to protect people."[58] Connie Jones, director for Responsible Gaming at IGT (the first company to establish such a position), delivered the opening presentation. She proceeded through the exhaustive list of modifications that had been proposed for gambling machines, dismissing each as having no empirical evidence to support it—or, worse, as having the unintended consequence of encouraging rather than discouraging problematic play. She told of her visit to a problem gambling center, where she met a machine gambler who chuckled upon hearing of onscreen clocks and session time limits: "Boy, if I saw I was running out of time, I'd probably double my bet." By the same token, Jones surmised, limits on the number of credits bet per turn might prolong play rather than decrease expenditure, while slowing reel speed might cause more aggressive play, and random time-outs might provoke gamblers to jump to new machines. She was certain that problem gamblers would find ways to circumvent any limits programmed into machines and persist at their excessive behavior.

The next speaker, Christine Reilly of Harvard's NCRG-funded research institute, continued on the theme of unintended consequences, comparing safety modifications to airbags—devices meant to save lives that nevertheless sometimes severely injure or even kill small children. It was no coincidence that both speakers framed their presentations with the idea of "unintended consequences"; both had in mind moderator Bernhard's discussion of the sociological concept in his academic article of that title, subtitled "Potentially Sobering Consequences of Problem Gambling Policy."[59] The Canadian company Techlink Entertainment had commissioned Bernhard in 2006 to conduct a study of the various safety modifications it had developed for machines. One participant in the study astutely identified an unintended consequence of a modification that displayed gamblers' cumulative losses, surmising that the feature "might trigger chasing behavior in which the gamblers sought to gamble more money to 'win back those losses.'"[60] A display intended to provide gamblers with a realistic account of their spending, he warned, might inadvertently increase spending.

As Jones's and Reilly's presentations attest, the American Gaming Association has embraced the concept of unintended consequences as an argument against making safety modifications to machines. "Changing the machine does not help the person," wrote AGA representatives in their letter opposing Australia's Poker Harm Minimization Bill of 2008, since "gamblers will adjust their behaviors to compensate for technology-based attempts to limit their gambling."[61] To be effective, policies should "concentrate on helping the people who have the problem," they insisted, "rather than trying to modify their behavior indirectly."

Whether or not they are correct on this point, their words are starkly undermined by the fact that "trying to modify behavior indirectly" is exactly what the industry itself attempts to do at every step of product design—in the absence of evidence that there will be no harmful unintended consequences. To energetically invest in technologies that can guide consumer behavior while casting "normal" consumers as self-determining subjects whose responsibility holds strong throughout their interaction with those technologies raises a contradiction that is hard to ignore. "How can they expect people to gamble responsibly when they build machines that make them behave irresponsibly?" asked Shelly, stubbing out her cigarette in the ashtray at the Denny's where we had met to talk. "They say the problem isn't the gambling—it's our fault, because we can't gamble like normal people. I sit there and think, *You're so full of shit your eyes are brown*—what the hell is normal about sitting in front of a machine and pressing buttons to give your money away?"

Shelly's comment suggests that inducement to irresponsible behavior is built into the design of machine gambling. "By virtue of playing [gambling machines] as intended," a researcher points out, "a normal consequence is to overspend."[62] Australia's 2010 federal commission on gambling echoes this point in their final report, as quoted earlier: "The problems experienced by gamblers—many just ordinary consumers—are as much a consequence of the technology of the games, their accessibility and the nature and conduct of venues, as they are a consequence of the traits of the consumers themselves."[63] The technological remedies examined above are grounded in the acknowledgment that gambling products and environments play a significant role in problem gambling.

Yet, radical as these remedies may appear when considered alongside those based in consumer responsibility, they are part of the broader turn toward regulative strategies that attempt to manage risk rather than to eliminate it. Modified machines do not remove the potentially problematic features of machine gambling, but rather present gamblers with two competing "scripts"—one operating to get them to play longer, faster, and more intensively, and the other operating to slow them down, make them stop sooner, and wager less.

Responsible Gaming Device

Relatively new on the scene of fixes for problematic gambling is an approach that presents itself as a resolution to the contradictory scripts associated with technological remedies. Instead of seeking to *fix* the gambling machine in some way, it would *deploy* the machine as a vehicle for risk management and responsibility—as an instrument, rather than an object, of governance. Going beyond informational strategies that equip machines with the means to demystify their own technological workings, this approach equips machines with software through which players can perform voluntary acts of self-governance (such as budget management, self-exclusion, or personal risk evaluation). "There appears to be a developing interest," wrote two Australian researchers in a report related to their country's 2008 harm minimization bill, "in the [electronic gambling machine] technical system as a potential 'tool' that can be deployed in the interests of those with gambling problems, or those who may be at-risk of developing problems."[64]

The Canadian gambling machine manufacturer Techlink Entertainment designed the first of these tools in 2004, calling it the Responsible Gaming Device (RGD). The device took the form of a small touchscreen mounted above the play terminal through which gamblers could track, monitor, and manage the money and time they spent gambling. Techlink described it as an interactive, player-centric instrument that "seamlessly becomes part of the player's environment," functioning as a "personal navigator" that "reduces the likelihood of impulse play and getting 'lost' in the game."[65] (Rather incongruously, another page on the company's website advertises a game that "makes innovative use of bonus rounds allowing for extended play and an increased level of interactivity.") Techlink's website placed the invention in a broader social and political context:

> New technologies are spurring fresh fields of endeavor and transforming forever the social and economic character of nations. In this the opening decade of the new millennium, it is not business as usual. Nor is it gaming as usual. The need to embrace and adapt to change is evident. Society

requires nothing less and is growing manifestly intolerant of unfettered problem gambling.

Responding to the need for some sort of "fettering," Techlink's device "affords players a restraint that minimizes personal damages that inherently result from irresponsible play." At the same time it is "unobtrusive and allows for an unencumbered, satisfying and enjoyable gaming experience." In other words, it promises the seemingly impossible: to restore the maximizing rationality of the consumer without encumbering the maximizing economic drive of the gambling industry—even as the latter would seem to depend on consumers' self-abandon. By "empowering players to exercise self-control," it promises to leave gamblers' enjoyment—and industry profits—intact. The RGD amounts to a kind of compromise between consumer advocates' call for product transparency and the industry's call for personal responsibility—a compromise, that is, between those who believe in an unfettered free market and those who believe that consumers need some form of "fettering." The compromise takes the form of a machine equipped to help gamblers "self-fetter."

Activated by the insertion of a "smartcard" (which, ironically, also functions as a means of player tracking for the house), the system provides players "with a suite of digital tools that enhance [their] control of each gaming session." Unlike the previous approaches we have considered—responsible gaming codes of conduct, informational remedies that would educate gamblers on how machines function, and technological remedies that would modify the behavior of machines—the RGD and emerging systems like it enable gamblers to manage their own behavior through a reflexive interaction with the machine during the process of play itself. As two sociologists observe, "these measures seek to build a reflexive component into the relationship between gambling technologies and gamblers, providing the capacity for 'responsible' gamblers to be informed, self-monitoring, and self-governing consumers."[66]

The system's budget management tools include *My Account*, a program that tracks cumulative wagering activity, wins, and losses over time (by day, week, month, and year); *Live Action*, which tracks up-to-the-second expenditure for a current play session; and *My Money Limit*, which allows gamblers to set spending limits over a given period of time (when limits are reached, the system denies them machine play throughout the entire jurisdiction). Additional tools include *My Play Limit*, which allows players to lock themselves out of play for a given period (perhaps until closing, on paycheck day, a child's birthday, or Sundays), and the *Stop* feature, whereby they can enact an immediate twenty-four-, forty-eight-, or seventy-two-hour exclusion (or "cool-down" period) from gambling, which becomes effective and irreversible upon the touch of a screen (see fig. 10.3).[67] Those who believe they might be problem gamblers are given tools to self-administer an onscreen risk evaluation and choose among the program's various coping mechanisms; therapy can happen right at the machine console.

The provincial government in Nova Scotia, which itself runs gambling establishments, granted Techlink a $90 million contract to implement the system, altering its name to the "Informed Player Choice System." On condition of anonymity, one of the system's developers told me that legislators "had no choice" but to adopt it—for although they were dependent on gambling revenues, the fact of problem gambling called their "duty of care" into question and was too widespread to ignore. "So they figured, let's set it up so that players manage the problem themselves, like seatbelts that you can refuse to wear." As a set of researchers writes, Techlink's system replaces "involuntary 'air bag' safety component[s]" with "voluntary 'seat belt' type features that gamblers could choose to use."[68]

"This next generation of seat belts for gamblers preserve free choice," Bernhard told his G2E audience. "If you want, you can decide to click in and see your balance." His 2006 study of the device found that while players resisted some of its forced features, they embraced the voluntary ones. "It gives me great options," said one participant. "I mean, people in this world now, they like options."[69] Bernhard and his team applauded the system's "relative lack of features that are forced upon the entire gambling population" and its offer of opportunities for players to "'enact' personal responsibility."[70] Jones of IGT voiced similar approval for the system: "Features that allow you to self-exclude or self-limit don't try to police behavior—they put responsibility directly on the player." As Australia's 2010 commission notes, the approach "is consistent with consumer sovereignty, since each gambler has the choice about what limits are appropriate for him or her."[71]

Prior to Nova Scotia's adoption of the RGD, a 2007 field study monitored 1,854 adults who used the device over six months, recording 30,000 sessions of play.[72] As in Bernhard's study, players preferred the "voluntary

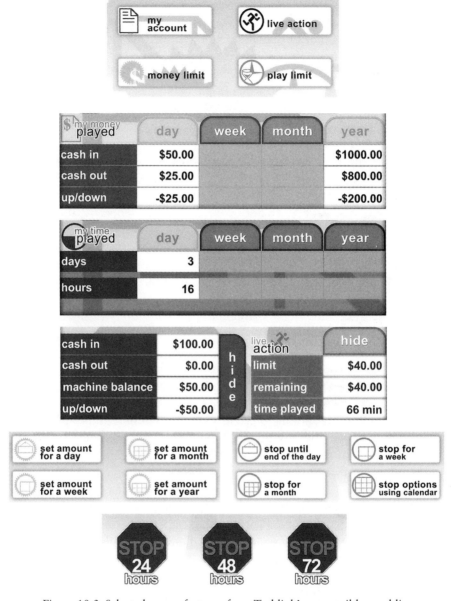

Figure 10.3. Selected screen features from Techlink's responsible gambling system, originally called the "Responsible Gaming Device," now called "Gameplan." Courtesy of Techlink Entertainment, Inc.

features" of *My Account* and *Live Action*. Curiously, use of the system was associated with 80 percent longer play sessions and a 132 percent increase in wagering activity. However, given that the system was also associated with a reduced rate of expenditure, researchers did not interpret the increases in time spent and wagering intensity as signs of failure. On the contrary, since "players were spending less than expected given their heightened level of engagement ... use of the features was associated with increased play value."[73] In this purely economic assessment, "play value" was construed as a function of the ratio of play cost to play time; since players were spending more time at play without spending more money, then the experience must have been a positive one for them. "Presumably," their report stated, "customers are receiving value if they continue to choose to use the feature"—an odd conclusion to draw in the case of addiction, where one cannot presume a link between the continuance or intensity of an activity and the value that activity confers upon an individual.

The report deemed the RGD a success, emphasizing that its "features were *not* structured to 'reduce the amount of time or money' spent gambling per se" but rather "to assist players in tracking and controlling expenditures ... through *information features* which can serve to inform and 'motivate' players to stay on budget, and optional *control features* to help players manage expenditure *if* they are motivated to use the feature."[74] The authors of the study concluded that although reduced expenditure by users of the system would certainly be beneficial, "finding evidence that players are effectively using the system to control their behavior ... is preferable as an indication of the system's value and impact."[75] The device was thus cast as a kind of control aid or rationality prosthetic that enabled gamblers to exercise their actuarial capacities—but only if they wished—in the interest of maximizing their gambling "value."

The RGD's responsibility features complement and extend a slew of freestanding techniques and technologies proffered to assist gamblers with the task of financial self-regulation. Global Cash Access, for instance, has implemented a Responsible Gaming partnership program in conjunction with the National Council on Problem Gambling, displaying "point-of-decision messages" on its cash advance devices (including a twenty-four-hour, toll-free helpline) and a Self-Transaction Exclusion Program (STEP) that offers problem gamblers a way to block their own access to ATM credit card and debit card cash advances.[76] An earlier, more primitive ver-

| DATE | TIME | PLACE | MACHINE | | AMOUNT SPENT | | AMOUNT WON | | NET LOSS | | NET GAIN | | WITNESSES / COMMENTS |
			TYPE	NO.									

Figure 10.4. Money management chart for machine gamblers. From *Slot Machine Mania*, by Dwight and Louise Crevelt, 1988, page 107.

sion of this so-called liquidity control is the kind of simple money management chart drawn up by a former machine designer and presented to readers in his popular 1988 book, *Slot Machine Mania*, with the instructions: "Carry a pocket calendar and enter the amount spent and the amount won on the appropriate day you play. Also, include such data as where and what type of game was played. Another efficient record could be a small notebook to carry in your purse or pocket with a form to easily record the necessary data" (see fig. 10.4).[77] Recording and tracking play data becomes a means of control.

Offering related advice on how to self-track gambling expenditures, a regular column by Bill Burton in the magazine *Strictly Slots* called "Controlling Your Cash" at one point urged gamblers to set up what he called a "401-G" account with their banks, dedicated solely to gambling funds, and to deposit money directly into it as one would into a retirement account. Burton offered formulae by which a yearly gambling budget could be broken down into weekly and daily deposits into such an account. His colleague Jim Hildebrand, another frequent contributor to *Strictly Slots*, developed a method by which gamblers could set "quit points" or cash out when their winnings equal 50 percent of a predetermined gambling session bankroll. "Managing your credit, your tickets and your put-aways is the easy part," he wrote, and continued:

> The tough part … is to quit, get off that stool, gather your winnings and walk. Stools are bad, are comfortable, are dangerous to bankroll and can

cause extensive losses. If I find it difficult to stop play when I've reached an established Quit Point, I find it helps to get off the stool, gather my ticket and then—if really necessary—play "one for the road."[78]

Much like the responsible gaming campaign discussed earlier, Hildebrand's column implicitly suggests that his entire readership—not just problem gamblers—are vulnerable to irresponsible gambling behavior and are candidates for risk-management remedies.

The line between problem gambling and gambling in general blurs further when one considers that the tips, tools, and techniques presented in *Strictly Slots* and countless other publications for regular gamblers function in much the same manner as the craving scales that recovering gamblers are encouraged to use in clinical and self-help settings. (Global Cash Access even calls its system STEP, in an eerie echo of 12-step terminology.) Designed to buttress the actuarial mindfulness necessary for self-accounting and self-regulation, these systems help gambler-consumers to "take inventory" of their losses, and to "track their balance," as it were. The RGD, as we have seen, integrates these approaches into the process of game play such that gamblers can reflexively monitor themselves from within the experience, not only from outside of it. In this sense, it functions as a tool for self-regulation.

Like all therapeutic tools, however, whether gamblers use these techniques as intended is another story. Randall told me:

> I like to keep track, keep a spreadsheet. I write down every win on the penny machines. I've got an account for each day I play: what casino, my list of winners for that day, how many reward points, etc. I keep track of all that and my top ten winners for each year so presumably it gives me an idea of what machines and what casinos I do well at.
>
> But mostly I just like to *know*. It lets me see my own progression, the increase in my gambling. I can see myself getting progressively more hooked in as the years go on.

Although Randall's meticulous budgeting does not increase his control over gambling, it does allow him to "know" that he is becoming "progressively more hooked" as the years pass. "Really what these budgetary tools do," Horbay comments, "is give players tools so they know how much they're spending and how long they stay there, and feel like they're the ones choosing to spend and stay." In this sense, Randall is a sort of "actuarial addict"—much like Daniel, whose careful log of gambling expenditure served to reveal his losses, and Julie, who "economized" to save up for gambling. As we saw in the last chapter, the tools of the self-monitoring, self-managing subject become implicated in the addiction circuit.

The RGD is no exception. As it happens, the problem gamblers in the Nova Scotian field study on Techlink's RGD demonstrated the highest activation rate of the system's features, using the *Live Action* feature three to four times as much as other gamblers. As one Techlink engineer observed in a conversation with me, *Live Action* and its constant stream of feedback seemed to become "an addictive strategy." Problem gamblers were not, however, as inclined to use the system's limit-setting tools. The authors of the study speculated on their curious findings:

> Problem Gamblers appeared to derive different value from the responsible gaming system ... The repetitious use of "Live Action" during a play session suggests that this feature was enhancing play value and the gambling experience in particular for the Problem Gamblers, [and that] *they used the system less often for controlling or monitoring their on-going gambling behavior than for obtaining feedback on their immediate play session.*[79]

Tracking financial balance in real time using *Live Action* appears to feed into the self-modulation and balance of the zone—as it did for Randall in his spreadsheets, and for Patsy, who called her bank ten times a day "to know the time frame of when checks cleared," and who continuously rebudgeted her wagering sum during play sessions. Real-time feedback on their behavior became a kind of "control" that only amplified the problem. Despite Bernhard's and Jones's conviction that control-lending features will be the ones that work, and that such features are somehow immune to unintended consequences, it is clear that these features carry risks as well. Earlier chapters showed how so-called capacitive game effects (i.e., those allowing users interactivity, control, and manipulative efficacy) were often associated with heightened absorption in play and loss of a sense of agency. In a similar fashion, the choice-based, self-tracking, budget-setting features of responsible gambling can ironically become a source of compulsive behavior, attenuating gamblers' self-control.

The failures of reflexive risk-management technologies such as the RGD ultimately stem from the fact that they attempt to limit harm by appealing to personal responsibility through the very same machine interface that short-circuits personal responsibility in the first place. Furthermore, like most of the remedies we have considered thus far, the RGD and other control aids target only one side of the human-machine interaction at stake in problem gambling. As a Canadian research group points out, although the RGD casts gambling machines as a tool for regulation, it continues to focus on "the transformation of *gamblers* rather than of fundamental gaming technologies (other than in relation to information, access or management)."[80] Once again, in keeping with regulatory trends in Western capitalist societies, risk and the duty to manage are downloaded onto individuals.[81]

Tracking Risk

The very latest technological approach to problem gambling, and the last one this chapter will consider, also depends upon reflexive information tracking—yet it delegates this task neither to players nor to the machine but, instead, to player tracking software running on a network into which both machines and players are plugged. As we saw in chapter 5, tracking capabilities began to expand the functional repertoire of gambling machines in the mid-1980s, turning them from mere games into surveillance monitors, data gatherers, and marketing tools. Inadvertently, these developments prepared them for yet another task: monitoring live play data so as to pick up on patterns that indicate problematic gambling behavior. A promotional pamphlet for the Canadian gaming company iView, which developed the software, elaborates:

> Traditional player reward programs provide casinos with access to patron play data from slot machines: how many hours a day they play, how much they spend, wins and losses, what machines they prefer and frequency of bets. Most casinos use this information for marketing initiatives, customizing reward programs based on play habits.

While the casino's player tracking system continues to crunch live data and generate ratings of "player value" for marketing purposes, the iView system draws upon the very same data to identify and rate players' risk for problem gambling.

These ratings are generated through a number of steps. First, the system gathers player card data. Next, a predictive algorithm called the Intelligent Gaming Measurement Index, or iGMind, conducts a depth analysis of this data in order to identify high-risk gambling patterns. Focal Research Consultants, the same Canadian firm the government of Nova

Scotia had commissioned to test the RGD, developed the algorithm. To build it they drew on two and a half years of rich player tracking data from Saskatchewan casinos, isolating over five hundred behavioral variables: the number of machines gamblers played, their total session times, their rates of machine betting, the days of the week on which they played, and so forth. The first automated risk assessment tool of its kind, the system compares a player's real-time data with his historical data: *What was his longest losing streak? Does he typically come back the day after a losing streak? How much money does he usually spend? How much time?* The program generates a risk index for each player, in the form of a score ranging from zero to three.

If any measure of risk is detected, the system communicates with the casino's automated marketing module (which triggers a freeze on all advertising to that player), with the casino management module (which triggers a freeze on a player's card), and with the casino's facial recognition module (which conducts constant real-time biometric surveillance to detect banned or self-excluded players). The system also sends casino managers a color-coded risk alert to flag the patron in question. Like thermal visualizations of slot floor activity, or Bally's handheld device whose animated face points up or down to indicate if a player is losing or winning, iView's technology "takes something nebulous and makes it concrete" (to quote company promotional literature). In this case, the "something nebulous" made legible for casino staff by technology is addictive behavior rather than marketing opportunities. Not unlike automatic external defibrillators, which reduced the fatality of heart attacks after casinos integrated them into surveillance systems and trained security guards to use them, iView's algorithm screens and intervenes for the less visibly detectable risk of problem gambling.[82]

While allocating the heavy lifting of risk detection to the software, the system also integrates the observations of trained employees who walk the casino floor looking for clues to risky behavior. Although problem gamblers are not clearly identifiable by physical markers (as drunken individuals are by slurred speech or an unsteady gait), Focal Research Consultants came up with a highly reliable "taxonomy of visual clues." Among this taxonomy's highest indicators of problematic play are repeated trips to ATMs or attempts to obtain cash through credit cards, gambling sessions over three hours, playing two machines at once, sighing and groaning, jamming the machine to allow for continuous automatic play (a practice described in chapter 6), nausea, trembling, and dry eyes.[83] When such behavioral observations are triangulated with a gambler's computed risk score, the confidence level in correctly identifying problem gamblers reaches an impressive 95 percent.

"Everyone is trained to recognize red-flag gaming behaviors, even the janitors on the floor," said Laurie Norman, whom I met at iView's expo booth at G2E 2007. Norman, a quick-talking, energetic woman in her thirties, is the in-house problem gambling counselor for a casino in Saskatchewan, a Canadian province that mandates use of the system (iView's Responsible Gaming module, iCare, entails "the establishment of responsible gaming centers with on-site health professionals hired to inform, educate and refer players").[84] When Norman is alerted to the detection of risky play, she approaches the gambler in question. The system "changes the site of intervention from the clinic to the slot floor," notes Tony Schellinck, a marketing professor and developer of the algorithm.

Norman's intervention tactics are diverse:

> I teach the players about the machines, about randomness, and how casinos make money. I tell them the more they gamble, the more they will lose. I show them the Safe@Play video and the inside of an actual machine. Sometimes I take pen and paper and draw randomness as a river—I tell them there is no set sequence of wins or losses, but an unending flow of chance, that they can never possibly know when to dip into.

Occasionally Norman's strategy is to present gamblers with information about the scale of their cumulative losses. One patron, a farmer who had put a quarter of a million dollars into machines, wasn't surprised to learn of his losses when the system verified them. "His problem wasn't unawareness or denial, so I tried to work with him on budgeting strategies." The goal of iCare intervention is not to convince players to stop gambling, but "to move them to more moderate play," as Norman put it. Like the other approaches examined in this chapter, the system follows a logic of risk management rather than pathology diagnosis. "It isn't a diagnosis, it's a detection of risk," she explained. "Like if you went to the doctor and learned that you were at risk for developing a high cholesterol problem, then you could change your behavior to prevent that, maybe stop eating McDonald's every day."

At the end of each encounter with a gambler, Norman enters her notes into the system, leaving messages for other staff and follow-up reminders. The system can "learn" if its interventions are working by tracking these notes along with a player's risk code, to see if it drops down to a lower risk level. As iCare's product brochure indicates, player risk scores are "dynamic in both directions ... subject to escalation or reduction based on associated dependencies and actions." The company explains that by tracking risk over time casino operators can "continuously measure, evaluate, monitor and improve their approach to problem gambling."[85] Although iView's tracking system ultimately works to fold gamblers into a program of self-regulation, it transfers the initial responsibility for reflexively monitoring and intervening in risk from gamblers to casinos.

Why would casino operators endorse such a transfer? In fact, many of them are quite unsettled by the prospect of using their player tracking data in this manner. Schellinck recounted the litany of anxieties they have expressed to him concerning the system: "*Are we going to find out that 70 percent of our revenue and 50 percent of our players are problem gamblers? Will all our best customers be identified as problem gamblers with this system? If we approach these people, will they duck and run, and will this negatively impact our profits?*" Yet the incentives to implement such a system outweigh these dangers. For one, casinos like the one where Norman works are locals-oriented establishments concerned with long-term player retention. "You want happy healthy social gamblers so they can be your customers for a whole lifetime—you don't want to tap them out so they hate you," she told me. As an iView press release states, "The iCare program is based on the concept that with expanded gaming around the world, to be sustainable, the gaming industry must maintain players for life."

The most immediately pressing incentive, however, is to put in place "an effective risk management strategy to deal with potential lawsuits related to problem gambling," as iView emphasizes in its promotional literature. The primary risk being managed by iView, it turns out, is not that of gamblers, but that of the industry. This risk lies in the very structure of casinos' tracking and marketing systems, which are set up such that the more a gambler plays, the more aggressively a casino will market to him. "Where inducements to gamble increase with increasing losses," explain a set of Canadian researchers, "the industry may be seen as 'actively soliciting gamblers with a high probability of dependency.'"[86] In an ironic twist on the theme of unintended consequences that the gambling industry has so embraced, the casino's database of tracked player behavior, amassed for marketing purposes, becomes a potential liability—especially when it is used to inform real-time appeals to gamblers in the form of immediate bonuses or other incentives to continue play. "It's a trove of potential fodder for litigation," Horbay comments. "Can you subpoena the tracked material? Who owns it? Could it be considered criminal negligence not to analyze it?"

In Australia, the gambling industry's fears over just these questions led to a scandal in which whistle-blower Phil Ryan, former corporate affairs manager for a leading gaming company, alleged that his company had colluded with others to shut down their player tracking systems after lawyers warned them of the liability they would incur from the power to identify problem gamblers. "Our lawyer suggested we cut the electronic link between collected data and individual player records so as to make all collected data anonymous," Ryan claimed. "It was his advice that if we didn't do so, we would end up with duty-of-care actions, and would consequently suffer reductions in profits as we became bound to eliminate problem gamblers from our network."[87]

When casino insurers in Canada recognized that their clients' real-time player data could demonstrate problematic patterns of play they withdrew coverage for lawsuits, pressing gaming corporations into exactly the sort of "duty-of-care actions" that their Australian counterparts had feared. "With insurance companies no longer willing to insure [casino] operators for problem gambling related claims," read a press release by the Saskatchewan Gaming Corporation, "[casino] operators must address their duty of care to manage risk." iView's documentation of the chain of interactions between machine and gambler, tracking program and staff, and staff and players promised to "give casinos the evidence to show they are protecting players while protecting themselves."[88]

Although demands for corporate duty of care are rare in the business-friendly United States, American gambling corporations are increasingly attuned to the legal risks of their tracking practices. Some have taken preliminary measures to protect themselves against future litigation. Harrah's, for instance, a company that draws heavily upon player tracking data in its marketing campaigns, has forbidden its executives from using gamblers' financial and banking information for marketing purposes, thereby attempting to shield itself against accusations that it might be encouraging play among those who cannot afford it or targeting those with high disposable income.[89]

The company also introduced a rudimentary version of iView's system by adapting the Luck Ambassadors marketing system examined in chapter 5 to a new set of aims; instead of tracking gamblers and approaching them when they are judged to need incentives to *continue* playing, this new squadron of ambassadors approaches gamblers when they are judged to be playing in self-destructive ways, inviting them to take a time-out and talk over their behavior. Like iView's tracking system and counselors, the ambassadors neither interfere with the mechanisms of gambling devices nor make demands on gamblers to manage themselves during a session of play; instead, they silently monitor play and only intervene at the moment when risk is discerned. Although the interventionist initiative of Harrah's ambassadors program appears to deviate from the US industry's typical emphasis on self-exclusion, self-help, and self-regulation, it is motivated primarily by a desire to preclude legal liability.[90] Once gamblers have been identified and approached, they are asked to participate in regulating their own behavior.

As with the other remedies examined in this chapter, risk-tracking measures share in the paradoxical attempt to build a protective program on top of the platform that solicits such behavior from gamblers in the first place—without altering that platform. iView's system embodies this paradox: its addiction-detection algorithm and the response network that it mobilizes work against the primary marketing purposes of the very player tracking system that enables them to run, and against the solicitations of the very gambling device whose operation triggers them into action.

The Fault Lines of Risk Management

Discordant narratives of accountability compete in the debate over how to regulate problem machine gambling that unfolds among industry representatives, regulators, researchers, consumer advocates, gamblers, and, increasingly, lawyers. The inner workings of gamblers, gambling machines, and gambling venues become matters of contention: Should consumers be expected to regulate their own play through the practice of responsibility (or, failing that, through therapeutic and pharmacological remedy)? Alternatively, should regulators require that machines bear messages informing consumers of programmed odds and illusions? Should "control aids" like the RGD be added to machines, helping consumers to reflexively monitor and regulate themselves more responsibly? Should the task be allocated to algorithms running in the background, tracking risky play to manage its multiple liabilities? Or should machine design be reconfigured to protect players from potential harm?

The debate around gambling machines expresses tensions that trouble the field of consumption more broadly in the West, where a free-market ethos and ideals of consumer sovereignty so often clash with the realities of harmful consumer-product interactions and stark asymmetries in the design-consumption chain. Yet despite their differences, all of the competing remedies written in, on, and around machines—taking the form of pop-up responsibility messages, posted odds, brakes on reels, budgeting charts, precommitment cards, and networked tracking software—follow a governance logic of risk management in which the goal is to minimize harm rather than to eliminate it, and in which individual consumer behavior is the ultimate object of concern. Of the remedies we have considered, only a handful address the behavior of machines themselves—and even then, the focus is on mitigating the harm of specific design elements rather than challenging the core modes of use programmed into machines. Consumers of gambling products are left in a fix similar to that of addicts in recovery: they are charged with the task of governing their own tendencies while participating in activities designed to stimulate those tendencies.

CONCLUSION

Raising the Stakes

THE 2007 MEETINGS of the National Center for Responsible Gambling opened with a town hall forum, held in a vast room in the conference facilities at the back of the Paris casino resort. Howard Shaffer presided over the gathering, whose purpose was to "challenge conventional wisdom" about problem gambling. Some four hundred were in attendance, a group comprising health professionals (24 percent), academic researchers (24 percent), gambling industry members (27 percent), government officials (14 percent), and representatives from other professional areas (11 percent). "It's good to have all the stakeholders in the same room," said Shaffer, neglecting to note the relative absence of gamblers.

Conference aides had distributed "Response Innovation" clicker technology at the entrance to the ballroom, and as Shaffer polled us on a number of widely held beliefs—the idea that the spread of legalized gambling leads to a spike in problem gambling, for instance—we pressed small buttons on the handheld devices. Our responses were transmitted, tallied, and posted on a large screen at the front of the room. After each polling, Shaffer invited audience members who represented the position of "conventional wisdom" to speak at the microphone in the center aisle, then promised that their beliefs would be challenged one by one in the upcoming panel sessions.

Some deviated from the format, returning the challenge to Shaffer. A middle-aged man voiced doubt over the industry's motivation to support research initiatives on problem gambling. "We had a tour of this casino earlier and learned that two million dollars come in per day. If the industry is making *that* much money, doesn't it make sense that they'd want to protect it, and that they'd have little incentive to encourage anything that could change that?" By way of answer, Shaffer asked the audience: "Isn't it possible to take in a huge amount of money *and* reduce gambling-related harms?" Dispensing with the clicker technology to pursue this unscripted line of questioning, he had people raise their hands in the air. "How many believe it is possible to take in large amounts of money and reduce gambling-related harms at the same time?"

Another audience member took the microphone. "Howard, it's not just about making a profit—it's about *maximizing* profit, and that's where the problems come in." Shaffer asked: "Is there a limit? What's the limit?" Someone in the back of the hall called out an answer: "*In the industry, there is no limit.*" A woman in the front row stood and pointed out that revenue was exploding and had grown to three times what it was only recently. "I don't disagree," Shaffer responded, "but it's not a criticism you're making, because Disney does it too." Still standing, she countered: "At Disney you have limits on the rides." Although many had their hands raised to speak, Shaffer stopped the conversation and moved on.

Maximization and Its Discontents

Shaffer's attempt to set up an ethical framework within which the gambling industry and its representatives could cleanly dissociate their revenue-maximizing practices from problematic gambling behavior was interrupted more times than he would have liked—presumably by nonindustry members of the audience. As we have seen, the majority of industry members tend to cordon off the problem of addiction from their own vocational practices. "Our game designers don't even think about addiction," IGT's Connie Jones told us in the introduction, "they think about beating Bally and other competitors. They're creative folks who want machines to create the most revenue."[1] When a journalist asked the company's leading designer, Joe Kaminkow, if he thought he might one day make machines that were too powerful, his response was simply: "What kind of a question is that?"[2]

Yet most of the game developers I spoke with in the course of my research were less cavalier than Kaminkow, and a good number seemed genuinely troubled by the potential sequelae of their creative revenue-maximizing efforts. Caught in the dissonance between their industry's concerted program of consumer preference-shaping and its insistence on the inviolability of consumer sovereignty, they toggled between prideful narratives of technological prowess and uneasiness over the power those technologies might hold. As the following pages illustrate, some became defensive or cynical when pressed to consider the possible links between problematic gambling behavior and their design, marketing, and management innovations, while others expressed an assuredly principled stance. Taken together, their varied attempts to navigate the murky terrain between ideals of individual freedom and their own practices of persuasion map the broader ethical fault lines of consumer society.

In December of 2001, before the National Center for Responsible Gambling had changed its conference dates to coincide with those of the Global Gaming Expo, its annual meeting was held at the Mirage convention center in Las Vegas. The agenda included a Gamblers Anonymous session to which conference participants were invited. "Wow, it really makes you think," a man sitting next to me remarked at the close of the session. "That's a side of things I rarely hear in my business." Denis was in his early forties, handsome, with glasses, a moustache, and a neatly shaven head to conceal the beginnings of male pattern balding. I expressed surprise on learning that he was a casino operator, since most at the meeting that year were researchers, clinicians, and counselors of problem gambling. "Yeah, I'm a mercenary, making money is *my* addiction, so it's weird for me to be here. But the market is evolving and those of us who are progressive need to stay on top of it. I don't need compulsives on my property, I don't need to destroy people's lives."

When we emerged from the sound-dampened, carpeted hallways of the convention facilities onto the busy Mirage casino floor, Denis's contemplative demeanor changed. He gestured animatedly at the walls, the carpets, and the slot machines, describing how he had laid out his own casino floor. As he spoke, it became evident that he had adhered closely to Bill Friedman's principles of interior design for casinos. "If you lay out a yellow brick road, people won't step off it into the gaming areas—they think they'll fall off some cliff. I set it up like a pinball game, I broke up the space into different areas, connected them with carpetry." Denis was good enough at what he did that casinos with revenue problems routinely called him in as a design consultant. "The casino is like a big washing machine—you swirl 'em around in there and take their budget from 'em." He had a patent in formulation for slot machines, having invented a way to progressively lower their odds as their jackpots progressively grow. "Technology is catching up to the gambler's paranoia," Denis told me.

As a cluster of participants from the GA meeting passed by the bank of machines where we had stopped, he switched seamlessly back to the topic of gambling addiction. "The key is to filter out the compulsives, the ones who are not there to have a good time, just in it for the fix, coming to lose everything they have." Denis had agreed to let a researcher use his property as "a testing site" for a study on problem gambling. "It's a sort of research laboratory anyway, so I might as well share it," he said of the casino he ran. "These researchers embrace me—I lead the charge from an ethical standpoint." For Denis there was no ethical conflict: compulsive gamblers came fully formed to his property and had to be "filtered out"; the rest he could "swirl around" with impunity, applying his self-professed mercenary tactics to extract their budgets.

Richard Mirman, senior vice president of business development at Harrah's, navigated the ambiguous ethical terrain of his field with less sure footing. At the helm of a franchise that draws 90 percent of its profits from 10 percent of its regular gamblers, he found himself worrying: "Are we doing the right thing? Is it right to incent[ivize] people to gamble?" When he approached a senior colleague with his concern, she invoked the ready-made ethical escape route of player responsibility examined in the preceding chapter: "*You can't make people do something they don't want to do.*" "She talked me off the ledge," he recalled.[3] Yet Mirman continued to find himself back on that ledge, especially when he came face to face with his customers. A journalist described a meeting between Mirman and three of his "best customers" in 2008. One of them, Robbie, drove to Harrah's in Tunica two or three times a week, often after work; she would gamble all night, then drive back to work early in the morning. During her sessions at the casino, casino employees would check in with her, sometimes bringing her food and drink so that she would not have to leave her machine. They would ring her cell phone: "*Robbie, do you need anything?*" Harrah's had actually *hired* one of the other best customers when she needed extra money, allowing her to schedule work hours around her gambling.[4] Mirman admitted to the journalist that he "started to feel queasy as he listened to [his] top customers describing their gambling habits."[5] "You start to see who's gambling," he said of spending time in locals' casinos in Louisiana and Indiana. "Especially our VIPs."[6]

Game developer Gardner Grout, whom one of his colleagues had described to me as "a genius at using emergent technologies to take advantage of people's weaknesses, to make them sit there for twenty-four hours instead of five," recalled a similar queasiness when meeting the gamblers who played his machines. As long as he was engineering gambling technology in his company's laboratory, he was able to sustain a sense that he was in the "entertainment" industry. "The hardest thing about the job for me was the focus groups," he remembered, "because that's when you saw who you were making these games for. You'd talk to some woman on welfare who would play your game for twenty-three hours. It would make some of us question why we were doing it, we'd get down on the whole thing. But we were really good at rationalizing it." By the time I spoke with him in 2001, Grout had left the gambling industry to work for a toy manufacturer.[7]

"Michelangelo of slots" Randy Adams took a different approach to the potential harm of his own design practices. Instead of rationalizing or denying it, he actively sought it out. In the 1980s, long before Denis attended the Gamblers Anonymous meeting at the Mirage, Adams regularly attended meetings for gambling addicts at a Charter Hospital program then run by Robert Hunter. "I enrolled in the groups, as if I was a compulsive gambler. I didn't say '*I design machines*'; I presented myself as one of them. I would sit and listen and talk to the addicted gamblers." I asked Adams what he had been there to learn. "This was back when I was doing a lot of game design," he told me. "I wanted to find out about the compulsive side, because I really didn't want to build addictive stuff. I am personally against that, totally. Morally. I was there to see what NOT to do, because I didn't want to make them like that."

Whether or not one is convinced of Adams's sincerity, his claim that he did not wish to "build addictive stuff" was a straightforward acknowledgment that product design played a key role in problematic gambling behavior. But on this point Adams was not consistent. He began by locating addiction within the person, stating that "*some people can't control the part that turns it from fun into addiction*." When pressed to specify "the part that turns it from fun into addiction," he replied: "*It's the design of the game*," and then added that this characteristic of design was "*not intentional on our part*, just the way it happened to evolve." After first implicating the person, and then implicating the product, he finished by delinking product design from human intention. As in the narratives of many other game developers, accountability for addictive behavior jumped from one position to another, never quite settling.

Nicholas Koenig, another of the game developers we met earlier in the book, was uncharacteristically consistent in his assumption of accountability. "I admit that the games I build are addictive. When I started out I had real reservations about the morality of what I was doing. I still do, I really wrestle with it." A woman in a purple velour pantsuit walked by as we sat on a cement island just outside the entrance to the Las Vegas Convention Center, where the 2009 G2E was in full swing. "This woman here is our prime demographic," he remarked.

> She's between fifty and seventy, has some money to spend, and I know how to hook her in. You know, I don't feel great preying on psychological weaknesses of little old ladies—I'll come right out and say that. I'm not proud of what it is. I can't sit here and say, *I only put the screws in the bomb, I only assemble the warhead*, because I'm sure that products I've made have destroyed people's lives somewhere.[8]

Another industry stakeholder who has distinguished himself with his frank acknowledgment of the harm produced by his practices is Richard Schuetz, one-time CEO of the Las Vegas Stratosphere hotel and casino. "Much has been discussed about the percentage of the gaming population that possesses some type of obsession, addiction, or problem with gambling," he said in the course of a starkly confessional luncheon address delivered at the 11th International Conference on Gambling and Risk Taking in 2000. "This was always a silly question to me as a marketer and a manager," he went on. "The question to me was revenues, plain and simple, and the fact of the matter was that a critically important segment of the revenues came from individuals who had some type of issue with gambling. These were my people and I went after them."[9] By way of stinging self-indictment, Schuetz points to the "plain and simple" fact that his industry's revenue seeking dictates its behavior, overriding other concerns. As a gambler told me, "The corporations have taken over, and they care only about money. I'm not saying they're evil, trying purposefully to turn people into compulsive gamblers—I don't believe that for a moment. But it *is* good for them to show a big bottom line." Echoing Schuetz, he summed up the problem: "They're trying to make money, and they want people to gamble. It's simple." Simple to diagnose, perhaps, but not simple to resolve.

It has become commonplace in public discussions to hear that purvey-ors of commercial gambling, along with the governments that draw taxes from them, have themselves become "addicted" to gambling revenue. "Given their fixation on maximizing and preserving gambling dollars," write two Canadian researchers, "gambling organizations are susceptible to acquiring an addictive worldview and behaving similarly to active in-dividual addicts."[10] Shelly drew a link between the uncontrolled behavior of gambling addicts like herself and the uncontrolled behavior of the commercial gambling enterprises that solicit her increased wagering ac-tion as a way to increase their own growth: "They talk about us gam-blers, how enough is never enough for us. But enough is never enough for *them*—they only care about making millions and millions of dollars." "We're drunk on gambling revenue," agreed a representative from Dela-ware. "The biggest addict turns out to be the state government that be-comes dependent on [gambling revenue]," said a senator from South Da-kota.[11] "They become just like the people playing the slot machines," commented Frank Quinn, director of the South Carolina Center for Gam-bling Studies. "They are looking for a quick fix to long-term problems. They start chasing their losses just like the addict docs. They suspend their own sense of reality."[12]

Some have gone so far as to enumerate the classic defense mechanisms of addiction by which industry stakeholders, caught in the maximizing momentum of a drive for revenues, rationalize their actions: "blaming others, belittling contrary viewpoints, disavowing responsibility for nega-tive outcomes, preferring to avoid conflict, and not tolerating straight talk, honesty, or directness."[13] Schuetz, himself a one-time addict, recalled his behavior as a casino executive:

> I had a great idea as to the extent of the nature of the problems, because I had access to the databases of the casino. But I employed minimization, rationalization, and denial—*It's only a small percentage of the gaming pop-ulation; It's an individual's RIGHT to choose how to spend his money; I'm in the "entertainment industry."* And research? You bet we needed research. Lots of it. My objective was to delay any change, not acquire any under-standing. If [the industry] appears to exist as if it has no conscience, that may make sense, for when I was an addict I had none.

Over the past few years, the term Corporate Social Responsibility (CSR for short) has come to stand for the "conscience" to which Schuetz al-luded. The G2E meetings added a new panel track of that name the same year that Shaffer held his town hall meeting a few miles down the Strip. "Years ago, Milton Friedman reigned supreme, and just by being a business and turning a profit you were doing what you were supposed to be doing," remembered the moderator for a panel called "What Is Corporate Social Responsibility?" Yet economic amoralism, he observed, was no longer the state of affairs in business: "The operating environment we're in now is like none we have ever seen." Some in the audience favored regulation as the method for coping with this new environment, expressing a wish that the government would "take a stronger hand" and "provide more guidance"—at the very least to maintain the public's trust in the industry's integrity. Others were wary of such an approach. "Don't mandate anything, don't hold a stick above our head—because as soon as you remove that stick, or when no one is looking, we're going to find a shortcut." Instead, they argued, the answer was incentives: "The government should *incentivize*; then we'll do it ourselves, from within." Yet no one ventured to articulate what the incentives could or should be. Still others refrained from all talk of oversight or incentives, persisting in their allegiance to Friedman's famous dictum that corporations are responsible only to their shareholders and should therefore strive for increased revenues by any means necessary.

This allegiance was the default position on the boldly titled panel, "Leave Us Alone: The Case for Regulatory and Legislative Relief." Industry researcher Richard Thalheimer managed to give the case for relief a player-centric spin, relating how one venue in West Virginia experienced a staggering 687 percent increase in slot take after state gaming regulations were relaxed such that venue managers could "respond to *what consumers want*—where they want machines, how many they want, what kind of machines, the bet limits." To his mind, the outcome was a "win-win" scenario in which "manager decisions match up with player preferences and generate huge revenue." In this cheerful account of the relationship between consumer demand and industry supply, the grossly disproportionate percentage of revenue that might derive from problem gambling went unremarked.[14]

Advocates for deregulation often point out that gambling is one of the most highly regulated industries there is. "As slot machines have evolved," writes the author of a recent progambling treatise, "regulation has become ever more stringent. Few industries are as heavily regulated as the gaming industry."[15] Yet his words lose much of their weight when one considers the specific content of the "exacting regulation by state agencies" to which he refers. In fact, regulatory agencies check machines only to make sure that they are tamper resistant (to prevent cheating), that their financial auditing systems run accurately (to facilitate accounting and taxation), and that they are "reliable and fair"—which means that their random number generators function properly, and, bewilderingly, that near misses show up only *six times more often* than they would by chance alone.[16] Despite the American Gaming Association's claim that "regulators carefully examine the impact on consumers of game innovations," in fact no tests are performed (such as those for consumer products such as food, drugs, cars, or children's toys) to evaluate the potential harmful impact of machine features or player tracking systems on users, and no safety guidelines exist to inform their design.[17] The profound effects of these features and systems on users' psyches and behaviors—effects that we have spent the length of this book examining—go utterly unexamined by regulators. The fact that machine gambling is "no ordinary commodity" but rather a product consumed in tiny increments, each following the next in a rapid, serial manner that dynamically affects a user's inclination to keep consuming, makes this lack of regulation particularly troubling.[18]

As has often been pointed out by journalists and industry critics, existing regulations function primarily to streamline and protect commercial gambling revenue, serving the interests of business and government rather than those of consumers.[19] The collusion between the gambling industry and its regulators is apparent in the cosponsorship of the aforementioned progambling article by the American Gaming Association and Gaming Laboratories International, the top slot machine regulatory agency in the country.[20] "It's a very symbiotic, help-us-help-you kind of thing," said the director of one regulatory approval laboratory, referring to the process by which the gambling industry and the state "benefit from an efficient approval process, so the [slot] machines can hit the floor and start earning money for each party."[21] At G2E 2007, an industry member elaborated on the nature of the symbiosis between machine manufacturers and regulatory laboratories: "We are constantly ratcheting up the technology, so we need to do a lot of education of regulators. We spend a great deal of time sitting with them…. [We ask] *How can we do this thing that we want to?* They come back and say, *If you do it that way, it might be a hard sell.* They give us advice."[22] "It is sometimes hard to convince the regulators," writes I. Nelson Rose, a leading authority on gambling and the law, "that their job is not to maximize the profit for casinos but rather to protect the public, and the casinos themselves, from self-destructing."[23]

Koenig draws a parallel between the practices and products of the gambling industry and the kinds of predatory lending practices and innovative financial products that led, in the absence of regulatory oversight, to the recent economic meltdown.[24] "What you've got going on in the current financial crisis," he told me in 2009, "is that the guys who might have become game mathematicians working with Reno slot makers instead became stockbrokers in New York and Chicago and invented all these exotic financial instruments, got regulators to permit them not to have escrows for payout, and so on." The gambling industry's shortsighted logic of revenue intensification, along with the close relationship it has cultivated with regulators, he suggested, is more systemic than it is exceptional:

> I've come to see the addictive proposition of gambling products in a whole lot of industries, and sometimes they're marketed much more deviously than in gaming. The insurance industry is the worst. *This thing we see going on in the gambling industry is happening on a much broader spectrum.* I'm not saying that to redeem myself, or to redeem the gaming industry—it's incredibly opportunistic and should be better regulated.

When I asked Koenig what exactly a better way to regulate the gambling industry and check its "additive proposition" might be, he raised the same question of limits that had come up in Shaffer's town hall.

> Well, some other countries have a healthier attitude toward gambling. They don't treat it like a straightforward consumer transaction; they treat it for what it is—something that could always go out of control. And as a result it's not as self-destructive, because there are limits placed on the activity. With those limits in place, the activity is tolerated as a natural form of human behavior, and it doesn't get out of hand the way it does here in the States, because there is a *net*. It has less dark energy there. Here, we let people destroy themselves.

After a pause, Koenig concluded on a cynical note: "But I don't think serious regulation will ever be part of the conversation here in the States. The industry is too entrenched, provides too large of a tax base, and the lobby is just too powerful. And if you do create a regulative loophole, guys like us will drive a truck through it."

Tapping New Markets

Rather than find ways to diminish the "dark energy" produced by its drive to maximize short-term profit, the US-based gambling industry seeks new markets to tap. The current economic recession has spurred on these efforts, extending the formula for intensive repeat machine gambling to new states, new countries, and new demographic markets. The gaming equipment manufacturing sector is "proving to be a growth area during these challenging economic times," reports the American Gaming Association.[25] Even as industry revenues as a whole have suffered since 2008 (they started to rebound in 2011), machine suppliers have achieved record financial performance domestically and worldwide.

Domestically, this robust performance is a result of cash-strapped states' push to legalize or expand machine gambling. "With every state facing severe budget deficits," read the advertisement for a 2008 G2E panel called "North American Emerging Markets," "gaming is likely to be passed in more states than ever before." "We're going to look back at this budgetary crisis and see a tremendous expansion," remarked a panelist for G2E's Slot Manufacturers Roundtable in 2010, by which point Illinois had legalized machine gambling, as had Ohio (whose governor, a Methodist minister, reversed his original resistance to video slots, explaining that they would net more than $760 million for his state).[26] As this book goes to press, Massachusetts is preparing to implement its recently passed gambling bill, while a number of other states are considering similar bills. Several states where gambling is already legal have increased their machine caps and bet limits; others have converted their faltering raceways into "racinos" that derive 90 percent or more of their income from slot machines.[27] "States are hemorrhaging and need money *now*," said a G2E speaker in 2008. "States are responding to what other states are doing—there's a lot of border anxiety. It's an arms race."[28] Some industry analysts have speculated that the rush for gambling machines will dilute their potential to generate quick proceeds; others believe that consumer demand for the machines will keep up with their spread.

To ensure this demand, the gambling industry has been ramping up its efforts to secure new foreign markets for its technology-driven gambling model. Mirroring the embrace of this model in the 1990s by formerly gambling-resistant regions in need of revenue (among them Canada, Australia, New Zealand, Scandinavia, South Africa, and Britain), an increasing number of jurisdictions in Africa, Eastern Europe, the Middle East,

Figure 11.1. International Gaming Technology production facilities in Reno, Nevada. Available for download from media bin at IGT.com.

and Latin America have opened their markets to machine gambling.[29] The burgeoning machine market in Mexico, for example, "is good news for US suppliers, who are shipping terminals by the truckload to south-of-the-border gaming venues," wrote an industry reporter in 2005.[30] That same year, another wrote of Russia: "It is a market that is hurtling toward maturity ... a clientele of high-repeat visitors who are gambling-savvy."[31]

Machine gambling takes on diverse configurations as it moves abroad, each jurisdiction adopting different game types, product standards, regulative specifications, and cultural attitudes toward the respective responsibilities of individuals and governments when it comes to problem gambling.[32] Yet despite local differences in games, marketing practices, and government policies, the core formula for machine gambling remains the same.[33] "Basically," said an executive for one supplier to Mexico, "what you're doing is *establishing player habits*. We get our machines down there, and the players start becoming familiar with them and they like them, and you keep those players."[34] According to this account, the formation of a new market proceeds from exposure to familiarity, and from familiarity to habit.

The Far East, with over 4 billion people and under 30,000 slots, has become a key frontier for the spread of machine gambling and the establishment of new player habits. According to the CEO of the Sands Corporation, Asia can accommodate "five to ten Las Vegases."[35] "The general feeling in the industry, particularly among slot vendors," wrote an industry analyst in 2006, "is that Asian players will enjoy slots almost as much, if not just as much, as their American brethren once they are exposed."[36] "Exposing" the traditionally table-loving Asian market to machines, however, has so far proved to be a considerable challenge. "We hoped we could figure out a way to pull people off the tables," said one casino executive, "but that's really complicated because there's a whole social aspect."[37] "Chinese culture does things communally, and it's not communal when you're alone in front of that machine," echoed AGA president Fahrenkopf while moderating a 2007 G2E panel called "Future Watch: Electronic Gaming in the 21st Century." "We have struggled to get people onto the product," reported the former director of slot operations at a casino in Macau, the center of the Far Eastern gambling scene. His own explanation was that local gamblers "play to win" and thus prefer high-volatility, high-stakes table games rather than low-stakes machines whose primary appeal is time-on-device.[38] Even more of a cultural obstacle to machine gambling than its low-stakes or solitary nature is its computerized interface. "Asian players have very strong doubts about anything related to electronic games," commented the president of a Taiwanese gaming company. "They think there is always something predetermined or calculated or computed behind every hand so they don't trust it."[39]

In radical contrast to gaming revenue ratios in the United States, machines pulled in just over 5 percent of revenue in Macau in 2010. Low as this figure is, it is an impressive gain from the 2003 figure of 0.8 percent, and industry analysts expect the jurisdiction's slot income to eventually surpass its table income as the market "finally starts trusting and becoming familiar with gaming machines."[40] In part, they believe, this trust will grow organically as younger players enter the market. "China is the fastest-growing electronically literate country in the world and that's going to breed a new generation of players who are exposed to electronic games," observed one gaming executive. "It's very early in the evolutionary process and we will continue to make inroads."[41]

To cultivate trust in the existing player market, the gambling industry has been investing in the development of "automated" table games in which traditional, group-oriented games like poker, blackjack, and even craps are rendered in an electronic format. Players gathered around these tables are equipped with individual video screens and consoles while live dealers are replaced by the center screen of the table itself, which sometimes features digitally simulated croupiers who verbally address and even make simulated eye contact with players.[42] Because electronic table games incorporate familiar, non-virtual elements (e.g., dice jumping, a ball floating, or cards being dispensed), they "can be an educational tool for players to accept the technology … a very good catalyst for us to transfer people from tables to video slots—a catalyst to change players' habits," said one Asian gambling executive.[43] Electronic table games placed in one Macau casino "drew crowds who gradually began to explore the other idle slot machines." The hope is that as local players "get used to machines," they will also get used to player tracking cards.[44] The ability to monitor and analyze players' behavioral data will allow the gambling industry to "win the hearts and minds of slot players," commented a Bally representative at G2E Asia in 2010.[45]

While in Asia gaming executives hope that electronic table games will serve as transitional devices to adapt the local market to a technologized gambling interface, in the United States they hope to draw a brand new segment of players, and to draw stubborn table players. "The player will be weaned over time to video screens," write the authors of the 2009 article, "Floor of the Future."[46] (Heralding this future, the first fully automated casino opened in 2009, called *Indiana Live!*.) Electronic tables create significantly more profit than their nonelectronic predecessors not only because they eliminate human mistakes (such as misread hands, accidentally flipped cards, inaccurate deals, or mistaken payouts), but also because they facilitate a much faster pace of play (in the case of poker, speed of play increases the house "rake").[47] Engineers for a company called PokerTek have enabled their automated poker tables to offer "side bets for players who have folded and are temporarily out of action."[48] These players, they explain, can "make small bets on what the next card the dealer turns over will be" or "bet on whether the three flop cards will

Figure 11.2. Conference attendees at the 2007 Global Gaming Exposition in Macau try out PokerTek's automated poker table. Photograph by days2think, available for download at flickr.com.

be red—or any of a number of possibilities." These side bets "will keep players involved with the game and keep them playing longer," and, because they are placed against the house rather than against other players, may render the game just as profitable as gambling machines.[49] As in Asia, another advantage that mechanized tables confer upon the house is their ability to track the details of players' real-time behavior, a feat not possible on conventional table games.

The gambling industry also hopes that electronic tables will help attract the significant contingent of online gamblers who have, over the last ten years, developed a taste for playing conventional casino games like blackjack and poker via the consoles of their personal computers.[50] Casino operators have found that players familiar with Internet gambling have "gravitated" toward electronic table games (as opposed to live table games) because "they tend to flow better, play faster and offer more aggressive betting."[51] The online market appreciates the fact that they "can play in privacy on their own screen without having to worry about other players."[52] One Internet gambler praised the devices in a blog: "The experience was almost identical to what I get from online casinos' blackjack offerings. The social aspect of player interaction didn't happen at all like it does at a live table."

Such comments make evident that online gambling, popular despite its ambiguous legality in the United States, has been a critical force in tilting gambling habits toward the asocial phenomenology of machine play. Even though the leading online games (e.g. poker) involve multiple players, each plays alone at his own individual terminal and can free himself from waiting for others by "multi-tabling" (playing at more than one table simultaneously).[53] The very same affordances of gambling machines—pace of one's own choosing, repetition, continuity, lack of cues for quitting, and a sense of modulatory control over one's internal state—are present in online table games, making them a more potently compelling medium than their live counterparts.[54] "Each hand interlocks with the next," wrote the author of a 2006 profile of online poker addiction. "Time slows down to a continuous present, an unending series of buildups and climaxes. The gains and losses begin to feel the same."[55] A consumer psychology study based at the University of Nevada sheds further light on the phenomenological characteristics of online gambling, finding that local Las Vegans who had shifted from live table play at casinos to online table play at home experienced the online play as "anonymous" rather than "social," "muted" rather than "exhilarating," and distinguished by "lack of touch" rather than "sensory stimulation." The online games also gave them a heightened illusion of control over their time commitment, monetary spending, and game outcomes.[56]

At the same time that electronic tables and online gambling help to expand consumer taste for the solitary absorption of machine gambling, a new type of slot machine helps to cultivate the "youth market" by importing the characteristics of contemporary video games into machine gambling. "The slot makers need to figure out how to develop these younger players," said George Maloof Jr., president of a Las Vegas venue popular among those under forty.[57] On a 2008 G2E panel called "Brave New World," an IGT product designer spoke of "breaking the reel paradigm" to achieve this goal.[58] WMS has developed an action-oriented, skill-based, immersive platform called Adaptive Gaming that offers "a game experience similar to those that players have become accustomed to with the internet, e-commerce and console-based video gaming."[59] The games involve players in a developing epic that allows them to progressively unlock new features as they play, move up in rank, save their progress, and resume play at a later time—even at a different casino, and even in another state. The recent wave of "communal gambling," in which players may compete against others at a bank of machines while interacting only with their own game terminal, likewise reflects an attempt to draw younger consumers to the atomized activity of machine gambling by combining it with screen-based formats more familiar to them.

Following this combinatory logic, some in the gambling industry envision consumers placing bets from their mobile phones and PDAs, media that would render the activity—and its tracking—even more continuous with the movements, transactions, and rhythms of everyday life. ("More and more people are using handheld devices and they are now becoming part of our culture," remarked a gambling executive.[60]) The realization of such a vision would amount to more than the simple expansion of a consumer market; at a more intimate scale, it would further entrench the technologically mediated practices of subjective withdrawal, affect modulation, and risk management that characterize machine gambling and other contemporary human-machine interactions. In this sense, the movement of electronic gambling into new domains of consumption—like its movement into new geographic jurisdictions—is as much an extension of the "machine zone" as it is an extension of technology.

THE GAMING OF CHANCE

At the start of this book I recalled earlier ethnographic treatments of gambling as a deeply meaningful social and existential drama. In America in the 1960s, Erving Goffman wrote of the activity as a character contest through which individuals could break from the bureaucratized homogeneity of their daily routines and engage in consequential action, opening themselves to the risks and possibilities of chance and life "on the wire." Like others writing before and after him, he dismissed machine gambling as a shallow, existentially inconsequential activity with nothing much of interest to tell us about ourselves or our world. My own ethnography began from a different premise, traveling along the circuit of environments, technologies, and practices encircling the human-machine encounter at the center of Mollie's map, in search of clues to the design logics, forms of experience, and cultural values at stake in that encounter, and what those might tell us about contemporary life more generally.

If Goffman's social gamblers sought out "fatefulness" as "the mark of the threshold between retaining some control over the consequences of one's actions and their going out of control," today's repeat machine gamblers could be said to retreat from that threshold, seeking instead a smooth, insulated zone where nothing unexpected or surprising can happen—the "eye of the storm," as Mollie described it in the first pages of this book.[61] Instead of the open and volatile affect of life on the wire, they gravitate toward the contained affect and "perfect contingency" of the zone. The draw of this zone, I have suggested, is more than a symptom of the extreme tendencies of individual gambling addicts; beyond that, it registers far-reaching anxieties around precarious economic and social circumstances, and ambivalence toward the prevailing cultural expectation that individuals be flexible, adaptable, and poised to adjust themselves to these ever-changing circumstances.

The material infrastructure of machine gambling caters to the zone. As we have seen, the slot floors of commercial casinos are arranged to provide spaces of protection and control in which gamblers can "take chances that are not really chances."[62] Gambling machines, along with their auxiliary financial and tracking technologies, are designed to facilitate affective balance and continuity of play—and thus, "continuous productivity." Like gamblers, the gambling industry seeks to manage chance through technology; its analytically informed design, management, and marketing techniques are geared to ensure certain gain by mitigating uncertainties, risks, and liabilities. "In the casino," writes the sociologist James Cosgrave, "the calculation of probabilities is the rule, the house has the edge and, as much as possible, nothing is left to chance."[63] It is not that the industry seeks to root out and eliminate contingency but that it seeks to cultivate and control it. We can understand its particular rationalization of the aleatory domain as a variation on "the taming of chance" that Ian Hacking detected in the rise of statistical calculative thinking in the nineteenth century, a variation we might term the "gaming of chance"—a form of rationalization that proceeds *through* rather than *against* contingency, play, and affect.[64]

Gamblers' and the gambling industry's desire to carve out a zone of certainty within risk is apparent in one entrepreneur's vision for what he calls "Gaming Insurance":

> Customers buy insurance against unexpected financially adverse events in almost every area of their life. Why not insurance for gaming losses that exceed a certain amount over a certain time period, or for unexpected runs of terrible luck? The casino wants players to be insured so as to capture a larger share of their wallet and not drive them to competitors when they experience the statistically inevitable rub of bad luck.[65]

Gaming Insurance and its protection against the losses of chance is cast as a mutually beneficial partnership between industry and player. Yet the seeming alignment between players and the industry around the quest to manage contingency, I have argued throughout this book, masks asymmetries of risk and reward, control and compulsion, loss and gain.

In the conjuncture of experiments in self-modulation (gamblers) and experiments in profitable behavioral engineering (the gambling industry), each partner comes to the table—or the machine, as it were—with very different stakes. Gambling addicts play machines to suspend themselves in a state of equilibrated affect rather than to maximize monetary payoff in the climax of a win; they recalibrate their play in response to the feedback of game outcomes, adjusting their pace and wagering intensity upon detection of any disequilibrium that disrupts the "machine zone" and its affective continuity.[66] The architects, managers, and technicians of the gambling industry work to facilitate this zone and at the same time devise game schedules and marketing systems that subtly and continuously introduce disequilibrium into the gambler-machine exchange, ratcheting up its intensity and duration—or "upping the ante," in gambling parlance.[67] To compensate for this disequilibrium and sustain the plateau-state of the zone, gambling addicts must make ever-escalating investments in machines. These investments do more than sustain the interior state of the zone; they also sustain the exterior assemblage of technologies, design practices, regulatory policies, and political-economic values that configure the human-machine relationship in which players become caught.

Mollie sketched her own vision of this assemblage in the map presented at the start of this book. In the chapters that followed I attempted to fill in the details and also to expand the frame, tracking the pathways that connect the architectural curves of casino floors to the ergonomic curves of machine consoles; the mathematical algorithms of game software to the patterns of gamblers' play; the volatile biographical turns and everyday events of gamblers' lives to the smooth zone of repetitive wagering in which they seek relief; narratives of addiction and self-care to corporate campaigns for consumer responsibility and policy debates over how to best regulate the gambling industry's products. At every step, I sought to draw out the dynamic linkages between experience and design. Beyond elucidating the singular case of addiction to machine gambling, such a mapping suggests a methodological and analytical framework for parsing the complexities, consequences, and challenges that emerge in and through the intimate entanglements between people and technology that have become such a defining feature of contemporary life.

Notes

1. Legato 2005b, 30.

2. "Slot Symphonies: The Importance of Peripherals," G2E 2009. Gambling machines can be seen as "heterogeneously engineered" artifacts (Law 1987, 113) that combine different forms of scientific knowledge and industrial innovation in an ongoing process of innovation, modification, and refinement (see also Woolley 2008).

3. See chapter 3 for a fuller genealogy of the contemporary gambling machine. There is substantial international variation in machine nomenclature. In North America, devices with physical reels are referred to as "slot machines" or "stepper slots" (referring to their use of stepper motors), while screen-based devices are "video reel slots" and "video poker." In Australia, machines are exclusively video reel games but are colloquially referred to as "poker machines" or "pokies." In Canada and some US jurisdictions, "video lottery terminals," or VLTs, offer diverse games in one unit (poker, video reels) and are called "terminals" because the outcome on each machine derives from a central system to which all units are linked, in the manner of a state lottery. In Britain, "fruit machines," "jackpot machines," "amusement with prizes," or AWPs, and "fixed odds betting terminals" typically refer to devices with four reels and one payline, featuring a low maximum spending rate and slow speed of play; such devices are found also in Germany, Spain, and Japan. In Japan, "pachinko" machines (pinball-like devices played with tiny metal balls) and "pachisuro" or "pachislo" are variants on slot machines that give out noncash prizes. To speak of gambling machines across type and region, industry representatives often use the term "electronic gambling machines" (EGMs for short) or "electronic gambling devices" (EGDs). Here I use the phrase "gambling machine."

4. Some machines additionally post their "theoretical payout percentage," also known as the "return to player" (RTP), which is the amount a player is likely to receive back over an extremely extended period of play—1 million spins, for example; in the short term, the return may deviate radically from this figure. The RTP is predetermined down to a decimal point by factory-generated computer chips that are randomly spot-checked by state gaming agents (Cooper 2004, 116). Different jurisdictions require different RTP minimums; in Las Vegas, the minimum is 75 percent. Manufacturers of electronic gambling machines typically offer casino operators a choice of five different payback percentages ranging from 88 to 97 percent. If a casino requests a 94 percent RTP on a game, the game's chip will be set accordingly; if they later wish to change the RTP, they must buy and insert a new chip. "From a labor standpoint," a game developer at a top manufacturing company told me, "the idea that casinos are always changing their chips is ludicrous—it's expensive and impractical." For more on RTP rates and what they actually mean for players, see relevant sections and notes in chapter 4 and chapter 10.

5. Todd Elsasser of Cyberview, panelist for "Server Based Gaming II: The State of the Industry," G2E 2007. In the terms of actor network theory, the electronic gambling machine has become a "thick node" in the larger networked system of the casino. As I will discuss in chapter 5, the slot machine becomes even more central to the casino with emerging systems of "networked gaming" (also called "downloadable gaming" and "server-based" gaming) in which game content, customer tracking applications, and other services exist on an online server and are downloaded to individual machine units.

6. Turdean 2012. In 1980, 45 percent of casino floor space in Nevada was dedicated to coin-operated gambling; by the late 1990s, the figure had risen to 80 percent (Thompson 1999; Garrett 2003), as it also had in Atlantic City (Marriott 1998, G7).

7. Despite an upswing in the popularity of live poker since 2003 (when, during the television broadcast of the World Series of Poker, an amateur won the 2.5 million dollar top prize), a mere 3 percent of consumers named it as their preferred casino game in 2007 (AGA 2008a, 3). Poker is often regarded by casinos as a waste of floor space because it is a skill-based game played between individuals rather than against the house, making it impossible for casinos to have an edge (instead, they take small buy-ins from players and "rake" a percentage from each pot). Historically, the few establishments in Las Vegas that kept poker rooms did so to attract wealthy clientele who wished to play against the local champions. Since poker went on TV, more casinos have offered the activity, but 2005 seemed to mark the height of its popularity (ibid.). As the author Marc Cooper writes, "Texas Hold 'em poker and other table games may be the latest gambling fad both on TV and in Ben Affleck's social circle, but for the casinos it's all about machines, machines, machines" (Cooper 2005, 121).

8. Panelist for "State of the Industry," G2E 2003. In Nevada gambling machines typically earn a lower percentage of gaming revenue than in other states (70 percent versus 83 to 92 percent) (AGA 2011).

9. Quoted in Rivlin (2004, 44).

10. Many view revenue generation through gambling as a "tax on stupidity"; others view it as a "regressive tax" in which funds are withdrawn from disadvantaged communities into the general revenue pool, following an upward redistribution of wealth (e.g., see Volberg and Wray 2007). Whatever the case, states' ongoing attempts to shore up budget deficits with gambling revenue has driven the expansion of gambling over the past thirty years in the United States. As recently as 1976 there were no casinos outside of Nevada, and only thirteen states had lotteries; today, one can make some sort of wager in every state except Hawai'i and Utah, and tribal gaming has grown into a nearly $27 billion industry since its inception in 1988, today featuring 442 casino operations in twenty-eight states (*North American Gaming Almanac* 2010).

11. "Gaming" and "gambling" were interchangeable terms in the United States until the mid-1800s, but afterward the latter term came to specifically denote the act of wagering on an uncertain event (although the word "gaming" was used in the Nevadan regulatory context since at least the 1920s [Burbank 2005, 4]). In the 1970s, responding to the industry's image-cleansing campaign, writers at the *Wall Street Journal* began to use the term "gaming" instead of "gambling"; by the late 1980s other media venues had followed suit, and by the late 1990s it had become widely accepted. To defend this semantic reform, the American Gaming Association makes reference to the *Oxford English Dictionary*, which indicates that the word "gaming" dates back to 1510, predating the use of "gambling" by 265 years (AGA website, americangaming.org/Industry/factsheets/general_info _detail.cfv?id=9, accessed February 2007). Nevertheless, English-language dictionaries consistently define games as activities involving skill, and gambling as activities involving chance. Given that the industry in question currently earns three-quarters of its revenue from machine games that involve little to no skill, and given that those machines are the topic of this book, I use the term "gambling"; I also use the term to reduce confusion with home computer video games, arcade games, and other games that do not involve wagering.

12. While in 1983 only 37 percent of casino players reported machines to be their favorite form of play, by 2005, this preference rose to 71 percent (Harrah's profile of American Casino Gambler 1991–2006). See chapter 4 for a discussion of the relationship between changing technology and changing player preferences. See Ernkvist 2009 for a business historian's account of the interaction between technological innovation and "demand-side changes in casino gambling."

13. *North American Gaming Almanac* 2010, 2. Illegal devices not included in official machine counts may include "8 liner machines" or "sweepstakes machines"; they return tickets to players, which are then in turn handed to the bartender or manager to be redeemed for money. See Plotz 1999 and Robertson 2009 for more on how machines can be configured to circumvent legal restrictions.

14. Comments made as moderator for "The Problem Gambler: Emphasis on Machine Gambling," 11th International Conference on Gambling and Risk-Taking, Las Vegas, 2000. See also Bernhard et al. 2007, 2.

15. The typical cost of a slot machine (in cases where establishments do not rent or profit-share with the manufacturers) is in the range of $10,000 to $15,000, depending on whether the game is a standard or premium game (Stewart 2010).

The typical "lifespan" of a game is seven years. In some markets, a game can pay for itself in less than one hundred days; in markets with more competition, it may take longer. As more casinos shift to "server-based" gaming (in which game content is downloaded to machine cabinets from an online menu), new pricing arrangements are likely to emerge.

16. Quoted in Cooper (2004).

17. Quoted in Anderson (1994).

18. In 1999, one set of sociologists saw movement in both directions: "Las Vegas is becoming a more typical American city, while the rest of the country is changing in ways that make it more like Las Vegas" (Gottdiener, Collins, and Dickens 1999, xiii).

19. For dystopic viewpoints, see Brigham 2002; Cristensen 2002; Moehring 2002; Epstein and Thompson 2010. These authors point to local social problems as an index of the city's disregard for human welfare, and its ongoing "crisis of greed, selfishness, and stupidity" (Epstein and Thompson 2010). Las Vegas scores exceptionally high on rates of poverty, crime, bankruptcy, automobile accidents, child abuse, addictions of all manner, and most infamously, suicide. At twice the national average, the city has the highest number of suicides in the country, a significant number of which are local residents ("Suicide Rates by State" 1997; Woo 1998; Wray et al. 2008).

20. Rothman and Davis 2002, 5.

21. The 1969 law came about at the behest of Howard Hughes, who assigned a coterie of lobbyists to win passage for the act and free him to purchase properties along the Las Vegas Strip. As one gambling scholar reports, by 1976, 70 percent of casino revenues were being generated by nineteen casinos run by twelve publicly traded corporations on the Strip (Schwartz 2003).

22. This building boom was triggered by the astonishing success of the Mirage, a $640 million, 3,400-room, tropical-themed resort financed with junk bonds in 1989 by Steve Wynn. Nevada maintains a growth-friendly climate by imposing no personal income or general business taxes (companies pay no corporate income, franchise, inventory, or unitary taxes), filling its coffers instead by modestly taxing the gambling revenue of its 340 casinos (by 1997, the 6.7 percent tax on the gambling industry generated 33 percent of the state's operating funds).

23. This population growth represented an increase of 60 percent between 1980 and 1990, and close to 90 percent between 1990 and 2000—the largest gain for any US metropolitan area during that time, and an astonishing 800 percent greater than the national average (The Center for Business and Economic Research, University of Nevada, Las Vegas, http://cber.unlv.edu/stats.html, accessed October 2009). From 1995 to the mid-2000s, Las Vegas maintained the highest new job growth in the country, garnering a reputation as "the most highly developed version of a low-skilled service economy in the nation and possibly the world" (Rothman and Davis 2002, 8). Newcomers to the city have been described as "castoffs of de-industrialization" (ibid., 14) and "a prolonged wave of new Okies" who, displaced from their rust belt vocations, "retooled themselves in the Nevada desert as hotel cooks and maids, if not construction drywallers and carpenters or casino craps dealers and parking valets" (Cooper 2004, 63). Las Ve-

gas's dependence on tourism, construction, and the housing market made the city more acutely vulnerable to the 2008 recession than any other state (in 2010 Las Vegas had the highest unemployment rate in the country).

24. "By the early 1980s," writes Robert Goodman in his study on the gambling explosion in America, "it was already estimated that roughly one-half of all jobs in Nevada were either directly or indirectly dependent on the gambling industry" (Goodman 1995b, 19). Currently fourteen of Las Vegas's top twenty employers are casinos and others include a gambling equipment manufacturer, a bank, a convention service, and a linen provider (www.nevadaworkforce.com, "largest employers," accessed February 2012).

25. Shoemaker and Zemke 2005, 395. A study by GLS Research (2009) similarly found that two-thirds of Las Vegas residents gamble "at least occasionally"; of those, 44 percent gamble at least once a week, and 27 percent do so twice a week or more (see also Woo 1998, 4; Volberg 2002, ii).

26. GLS Research 2011, 35 (67 percent of casino visitors in the United States use player club cards when they gamble [AGA 2010, 30]). Half the revenue generated by local gamblers is captured by Station Casinos, a publicly traded franchise founded in 1976 and acknowledged today as the leading purveyor of gambling for the locals market. Most residents live within a short driving distance of one of its ten full-service casinos or eight smaller gambling halls. Another major locals chain is Boyd Gaming, which owns nine casinos (Shoemaker and Zemke 2005; Skolnik 2011).

27. The term "convenience gambling" was used as early as 1995 (Goodman 1995b), to distinguish it from "destination gambling," or tourist gambling. One-fifth of Las Vegas area residents who gamble do so in convenience stores, grocery stores, or gas stations; one-quarter gamble in local bars or restaurants (GLS Research 2009, 6, 36–37). Many "convenience gambling" venues have restricted gaming licenses that limit them to a maximum of fifteen machines; in these cases, machine manufacturers typically rent or lease the location's space and collect all the machines' winnings, or provide the machines and share a percentage of the proceeds with the location operators.

28. GLS Research 1995, 14. In 2008 and 2010, the figure stood at 72 percent (GLS Research 2009, 4, 19; 2010, 4, 19).

29. There are currently 145,000 gambling machines on record at more than 1,400 venues in Clark County (which includes Las Vegas and its suburbs, but not McCarran International Airport, which operates over one thousand machines of its own) (gaming.nv.gov, accessed February 2012).

30. Brenda Boudreaux of Palace Station, panelist for "The Video Future," World Gaming Conference and Expo 1999.

31. Calabro 2006.

32. Kent Young of Aristocrat, quoted in Green (2006, 10). As I discuss in chapter 4, the rise of "multiline video slots" began primarily in Australia and came to the United States via Native American Casinos and the Midwest, temporarily unseating Las Vegas as the center of gambling trends.

33. Between 2009 and 2010, a total of thirty-seven states moved to either legalize new or expand existing forms of gambling (for a comprehensive review

of these regulatory efforts, see Skolnik 2011, 14–18). As in prior waves of gambling expansion, machine gambling in particular has played a leading role. As a 2010 gambling industry report notes, "When considering gambling expansion, public policymakers have favored electronic gaming machines over other forms of gambling, often because they can be approved under existing state authority to conduct a lottery" (Stewart 2010, 4).

34. In his introduction to Caillois's work, Barash (1979 [1958], ix) observes that Caillois regards games as "cultural clues." Caillois was building on the earlier work of Dutch historian and cultural theorist Huizinga (1950 [1938]), author of *Homo Ludens* (*Man the Player*), a treatise on the importance of the play element of culture and society. As Caillois points out at the start of his text, Huizinga was dismissive of games of chance (1979 [1958], 5). "In themselves," Huizinga wrote, "gambling games are very curious subjects for cultural research, but for the development of culture as such we must call them unproductive. They are sterile, adding nothing to life or the mind" (1950 [1938], 48). Caillois disagreed fundamentally, pointing out that uncertainty and risk are key aspects of all forms of play (1979 [1958], 7; see also Malaby 2007).

35. Goffman 1967, 260–61. As Gerda Reith notes, sociological accounts have often attempted to endow the unproductive activity of gambling "with some kind of utilitarian function" (1999, 8). Edward Devereux, for instance, wrote in his 1949 analysis that gambling was "a particularly convenient mechanism in which the psychological consequences of economic frustration, strain, conflict and ambivalence may be worked out without upsetting the social order" (1980 [1949], 955). The idea of gambling as a "safety valve" or "shock absorber" for the conflicts of a capitalist economic system persisted through the 1970s. Gambling was understood to be an escape from routine and the futility of working-class lives (e.g., Zola 1963). As Caillois had written earlier: "Recourse to chance helps people tolerate competition that is unfair or too rigged. At the same time, it leaves hope in the dispossessed that free competition is still possible in the lowly stations in life" (1979 [1958], 115).

36. Goffman 1961, 34.

37. Geertz 1973. The concept of "deep play" was first elaborated by Jeremy Bentham to describe play in which financial stakes run "irrationally" high despite the fact that chance will determine the outcome, indicating that more than just money is at stake (in ibid., 431).

38. Dostoyevsky 1972 [1867], 199. The semiautobiographical novel was written during a period when Dostoyevsky struggled with his own excessive gambling. The quoted passage carries echoes of Schiller's German romanticist view of gambling: "man only plays when in the full meaning of the word he is a man, and *he is only entirely a man when he plays*" (quoted in Caillois 1979 [1958], 163). For an existentialist perspective on gambling, see Kusyszyn 1990, 159.

39. "The development of slot machines in the modern world and the fascination or obsessive behavior that they cause is indeed astonishing," wrote Caillois in a footnote to his text, noting that there were 300,000 slot machines in cities throughout the United States in the mid-1950s. He followed with a long passage by a reporter in Times Square in 1957: "In an immense room without a door

dozens of multicolored slot machines are aligned in perfect order. In front of each machine a comfortable leather stool ... allows the player with enough money to sit for hours. He even has an ash tray and a special place for his hot dog and Coca Cola ... which he can order without budging from his place" (1979 [1958], 183). Caillois described how the mania for "pachinko" machines in Japan became so intense that they were installed in doctors' waiting rooms. He quoted an observer of these contraptions: "An absurd game, in which one can only lose, but which seduces those in whom the fury rages" (ibid.).

40. Goffman 1967, 270.

41. Geertz 1973, 435–36.

42. Lears 2003. The sociologist Robert Putnam, in his influential book *Bowling Alone*, uses the example of solitary machine gambling to illustrate the decline of social engagement in the United States. "Any visitor to the new mega casinos that dot the land," he writes, "has chilling memories of acres of lonely 'players' hunched in silence over one-armed bandits" (2000, 105).

43. Borrell 2008, 213.

44. See, for example, Giddens 1991; Beck 1992, 1994, 2006; Lupton 1999; Lakoff 2007.

45. Thinking in terms of risk "permeates into everyday life," writes the sociologist Anthony Giddens, forming "a general existential dimension of the contemporary world" (1991, 3). Scholars who have examined the existential fallout of contemporary risk society from an ethnographic perspective include Rapp 2000; Petryna 2002; Kaufman 2005; and Fullweily 2008. Those who have considered how technology serves as a form of affective management under circumstances of risk and uncertainty include Turkle 1984, 1997, 2011; Biehl, Coutinho, and Outeiro 2004; Martin 2004, 2007; Roberts 2006, 2007; Clough 2007; Biehl and Moran-Thomas 2009.

46. Latour 1999, 199. Ihde similarly writes that "existence is technologically textured," not just at the broad-scale level, but in the "rhythms and spaces of daily life" (1990, 1); see also Turkle 1984, 1997, 2011; Lurhman 2004, 526; Clough 2007; Biehl and Moran-Thomas 2009. Philosopher of technology Hans Jonas detected the movement toward affective self-modulation in 1979 when he wrote of the appearance of "the domestic terminals of the electronics industry" that accompanied the switch from power engineering to communication engineering: "catering to the senses and the mind," telephones, radios, televisions, and record players offered citizens "insubstantial, mind-addressed output" (2010 [1979], 19). Scholarly criticism of the subjective effects of such technology in contemporary capitalist societies both follows upon and departs from earlier criticisms of technology's alienating and dehumanizing effects during the industrial era (Marx 1992 [1867]; Marcuse 1982 [1941]; Heidegger 1977 [1954]; Ellul 1964; Winner 1977; Borgmann 1984).

47. Studies of addiction can illuminate broader social experiments and experiences—in domains of profit-making, social relations, self-care, and policymaking. As the editors of the forthcoming volume *Addiction Trajectories* argue, addiction can provide a lens through which to examine "distinctly modern forms of life, including patterns of consumption and production, sickness and health, normalcy

and pathology, neglect and intervention, belonging and alienation—in short, the very 'stuff' out of which the contemporary world is made" (Raikhel and Garriott, 2013). For recent anthropological monographs on addiction, see Bourgois and Schonberg (2009) and Garcia (2010). For historical and cultural work on the important place of addiction in modern capitalism, see Sedgwick (1992); Courtwright (2001, 2005); Brodie and Redfield (2002).

48. Comments made as moderator for "The Problem Gambler: Emphasis on Machine Gambling," 11th International Conference on Gambling, 2000 See also Bernhard et al. 2007. Studies based on other jurisdictions estimate that up to 70 percent of gamblers seeking treatment identify electronic gaming machines as their primary, if not exclusive, problem form of gambling (see, for example, Schellinck and Schrans 1998, 2003; Breen and Zimmerman 2002; Gorman 2003, A20).

49. APA 1980. Although pathological gambling was officially listed in the APA's *Diagnostic and Statistical Manual of Mental Disorders (DSM-III)* as an "Impulse Control Disorder Not Elsewhere Classified," most psychiatrists and clinicians felt that the condition was best conceived as an addiction, and the category of psychoactive substance dependence was used as a model when the criteria for pathological gambling were modified in a later revision of the manual (APA 1994, 4th ed.; see also Castellani 2000, 54; Lesieur and Rosenthal 1991). The DSM-V (anticipated for 2013) will change "pathological gambling" to "disordered gambling," and will classify it under "Addiction and Related Disorders."

50. Zangeneh and Hason 2006, 191–93.

51. APA 2000, 616. The earliest use of the word "addiction" was in Roman law, where it indicated a sentence of enslavement of one person to another, usually to pay off debts. (Because these debts were often incurred through gambling, some in gambling studies have claimed that gambling addiction was the very first addiction [Rosenthal 1992].) Later, the word was used to indicate a strong devotion to a habit or pursuit. It was only during the eighteenth century that "addiction" was used in association with psychoactive drugs (Shaffer 2003, 1). The term was extended to a wider and wider range of drugs during the twentieth century and eventually to all forms of human behavior (Sedgwick 1992, 584; see also Berridge and Edwards 1981; Courtwright 2001; Brodie and Redfield 2002; Vrecko 2010; Keane and Hamill 2010; Kushner 2010; and various essays in Raikhel and Garriott 2013).

52. Early writings on excessive gambling include France 1902; Freud 1966 [1928]; and Bergler 1957. For histories of the medicalization of gambling, see Collins 1969, 70; Castellani 2000.

53. Castellani 2000, 123.

54. Ibid., 132–34; Orford 2005.

55. Dickerson, Haw, and Shepherd 2003, described in Abbott 2006, 7 (see also Orford 2005, 1237; Cosgrave 2010, 118). The gambling industry's embrace of the diagnosis was motivated largely by the alcohol industry's success with such an approach, along with the tobacco industry's infamous rejection of the association between smoking and addiction (see chapter 10). For critical discussions of the pathological gambling diagnosis and its "individual susceptibility" framework,

see Wakefield 1997; Castellani 2000; Volberg 2001; Dickerson 2003; Abbott et al. 2004; Orford 2005; Livingstone and Woolley 2007; Reith 2007; Borrell 2008.

56. Shaffer, Hall, and Vander Bilt 1999. "Problem gamblers" are those who do not meet the requisite number of diagnostic criteria for pathological gambling (see fig. i.4), but who experience difficulties limiting money and time spent on gambling, with negative consequences for themselves, their families, and their communities. Problem gambling has been referred to by Shaffer, Hall, and Vander Bilt (1999) as "level 2" of disordered gambling. In his testimony to the National Commission, Shaffer estimated that one-third to one-quarter of level 2 gamblers would progress to level 3.

57. For good summaries of the many difficulties involved in measuring the prevalence of gambling problems, see Volberg 2001 (especially chapter 4), 2004; Reith 2003; 13–14; Dowling, Smith, and Thomas 2005; Abbott 2006; Doughney 2007; Smith, Hodgins, and Williams 2007. Recently the gambling industry has heavily cited research claiming that the percentage of Americans who suffer from pathological gambling has remained steady over the last twenty-five years, despite the expansion of commercial gambling during that same period (see Shaffer, LaBrie, and LaPlante 2004a; Shaffer 2005; LaPlante and Shaffer 2007; see also chapter 4 and chapter 10). There are a number of problems with this claim, not least of which is the fact that more stringent criteria are now used to assess whether a gambler has a problem than were used in the past. "Although it appears that the prevalence hasn't changed," observes Volberg, the leading expert on rates of pathological and problem gambling in the United States and abroad, "that actually has more to do with how problem gambling has been measured both in the past and more recently" (quoted in Green 2004). Another problem is that most prevalence screens examine only whether individuals have had a gambling problem in the last year, rather than asking whether they have *ever* had a problem. With growing evidence that gambling problems wax and wane over time for individuals (Slutske 2007; Abbott and Clarke 2007; Nelson et al. 2009)—which means that *lifetime* prevalence rates are much higher than *annual* prevalence rates—this method of sampling misses the full extent of the problem (Abbott and Volberg 2006).

Whatever the overall prevalence of problem gambling at any one time in the general population, Volberg points out that the majority of studies show "a link between the expansion of legal gambling opportunities and the prevalence of problem gambling" (2004, abstract). The 1999 National Gambling Commission, for instance, found that living within a fifty-mile radius of a casino meant twice the rate of pathological gambling (Gerstein et al. 1999), and a large-scale 2004 study found that living within ten miles of a large-scale gaming operation put individuals at a 90 percent increased risk for gambling problems (Welte et al. 2004). In 2002, Volberg found the prevalence of pathological gambling in Las Vegas to be between 75 and 85 percent higher than in the United States as a whole; the combined rate of pathological and problem gambling was 6.4 percent among Las Vegas area residents (2002, 136). Supporting this finding, a 2003 study reported that 31 percent of southern Nevadans said someone in the household had experienced a challenge with a gambling problem during the past year, and over 6 percent reported a major challenge (United Way of Southern Nevada and Nevada Community Foundation 2003).

58. PC 1999, 6.1; Abbott and Volberg 2000; Schellinck and Schrans 2004, xi; MacNeil 2009, 142; 154. As an independent governmental commission in Australia recently reported, "problem gambling prevalence rates expressed as shares of the adult population are misleading measures of the real risks when most of the adult population do not gamble regularly, or do not gamble at all" (PC 2009, xxi–xxii).

59. The first wave of these studies appeared in 1998. That year, Lesieur calculated that pathological and problem gamblers accounted for an average of 30.4 percent of total gambling expenditures in the four US states and three Canadian provinces he examined; the low was 22.6 percent, the high was 41.2 percent. He also identified the particular games associated with problematic play, placing video slot machines in this group (Lesieur 1998, 164–65). A report to the Montana Gambling Study Commission found that problem and pathological gamblers accounted for 36 percent of video gambling expenditures/revenues (compared to 25 percent for bingo and 11 percent for the lottery) (Polzin et al. 1998, see fig. 6, p. 25). A report to the Louisiana Gambling Control Board the following year similarly indicated that problem and pathological gamblers comprised 30 percent of all spending on riverboat casinos, 42 percent of Indian casino spending, and 27 percent of expenditures on gambling machines (Ryan and Speyrer 1999). A 1998 Nova Scotia study found that only 4 percent of net gambling machine (or video lottery) revenue came from "casual" players (although they comprised 75 percent of players), while a full 96 percent of the revenue came from under 6 percent of the population who classified as "regular gamblers" (Schellinck and Schrans 1998, 7). Approximately 16 percent of these regular gamblers were "problem gamblers," generating 53 percent of machine revenues although they constituted a mere 1 percent of the total population (ibid., 14). A large-scale epidemiological report to the Australian government estimated that severe and moderate problem gamblers made up only 4.7 percent of the population but contributed 33 percent of net gambling revenues and 42.4 percent of *gambling machine* revenue (PC 1999, 6.54; 7.46; appendix P, p. 16). A 2001 study similarly found that 37 percent of all commercial gambling revenue and 48.2 percent of gambling machine revenue was attributable to problem gamblers (AIGR 2001, table 25, 114), and a 2005 study found that 43 percent of gambling machine revenue came from problem players (Young, Stevens, and Tyler 2006, 46). A 2004 report in Ontario found that 35 percent of total gaming revenue came from moderate and severe problem gamblers, and that up to 60 percent of machine revenue came from problem gamblers (Williams and Wood 2004, 6, 42, 44). The Australian government's latest comprehensive study confirms that problem gamblers' share of expenditures "range around 40 percent, with some estimates raising the possibility that the share is as much as 60 percent and, in the most conservative case, still above 22 percent"; this study has additionally found that 16 percent of those who play weekly or more on gaming machines are problem gamblers, while an additional 15 percent are "moderate risk" for a gambling problem (PC 2010, 16).

60. One study determined that nearly half the individuals sitting in front of gambling devices at any one time exhibited "problematic" gambling behaviors (Schellinck and Schrans 1998; 2004, xi). For a discussion of the continuum approach to prevalence measures, see Dickerson 2003; Volberg 2004).

61. Smith and Wynne 2004, 54.

62. See Gerstein 1999; PC 1999, 2010; Dickerson, Haw, and Shepherd 2003; Smith and Wynne 2004; Dowling, Smith, and Thomas 2005; Abbott 2006; Smith and Campbell 2007, 86. "Product liability law," writes the anthropologist Sarah Jain, "offers two sites of explanation and blame within [the] slippery network of design and use, person and thing" (2006, 12). For a discussion of "person or product" debates around tobacco, see Brandt 2007; for such debates around addiction more generally, see Courtwright 2001, 94–97; for a fuller discussion of this debate regarding addiction to gambling machines in particular, see chapter 10.

63. Breen and Zimmerman 2002; Breen 2004. The shortening of the time it takes to become addicted is known as "telescoping."

64. Abbott 2006, 7 (describing the work of Dickerson, Haw, and Shepherd 2003). See also Schellinck and Schrans 1998; Griffiths 1999; Dickerson 2003; Turner and Horbay 2004, 32; Livingstone and Woolley 2008, 120; Hancock, Schellinck, and Schrans 2008. I consider this perspective more fully toward the close of chapter 10 and in the conclusion.

65. PC 2009, xxvii.

66. For the industry position, see Stewart 2010.

67. Shaffer 2004, 9.

68. Shaffer n.d. In 1996 Shaffer wrote that it is "the relationship of the addicted person with the object of their addiction that defines addiction" (1996, 465–66). Shaffer later revised his view, stating that "psychopathology disproportionately precedes excessive involvement with the technology" (Shaffer 2004, 10). For more on Shaffer's shift in view, which many have linked to his funding by the gambling industry beginning in the late 1990s, see chapter 10 and the conclusion.

69. Shaffer n.d. "Potency," writes Shaffer, "refers to the capacity of the drug or gamble to shift subjective experience" (Shaffer 2004, 15). He notes that "new technology" has increased slot machines' potency by enhancing their ability to "provide relatively reliable and potent contemporary vehicles for changing emotional states" (Shaffer 1996, 461).

70. For examples of neuroscientific research on how activities like gambling affect the brain, see Breiter et al. 2001; Lehrer 2007; Vrecko 2010; Keane and Hamill 2010; Kushner 2010. Some scientists have gone so far as to suggest that activity-based addictions, since they are unclouded by the confounding presence of an ingested psychoactive substance, "can serve as an informative model for substance dependence" (Bechara 2003, 44). As Shaffer testified to the 1998 National Gambling Impact Study Commission, "the study of disordered gambling holds greater potential to inform our understanding of drug addiction than the other way around."

71. Eggert 2004, 227. At this rate, a fast slot player can average approximately one thousand wagers an hour (Grochowski 2003).

72. Griffiths 1993, 1999. Event frequency is correlated with development of any addiction.

73. Henry Lesieur, quoted in Green (2004); Lesieur 1977.

74. The first statement is by Robert Breen (quoted in Green 2004); I heard the term "electronic morphine" used by Robert Hunter; both Hunter, Howard Shaffer, and others have used the "crack cocaine" metaphor when speaking of gambling machines (e.g., see Bulkeley 1992; Simurda 1994; Dyer 2001).

75. Quoted in Bacon (1999). "It's like crack was to cocaine," Shaffer said in 1994; "it's becoming too easy to gamble" (quoted in Simurda 1994; see also Dyer 2001; Rivlin 2004, 74). The specific game of video poker was the original "crack cocaine" of machine gambling (Bulkeley 1992), although the phrase quickly spread to all forms of video gambling.

76. Quoted in Rivlin (2004, 74).

77. Personal communication with Hunter (1999); see also Dickerson 2003; Shaffer 2004, 15; Parke and Griffiths 2006.

78. Quoted in Rivlin (2004, 74).

79. Reith 1999, chapter 3. Elster (1999) and Malaby (2003) have made similar observations.

80. Thomas, Sullivan, and Allen 2009, 3. Three researchers compiled a list of the top reasons machine gamblers gave for their heavy play: *To stop thinking about problems; Provides a break from worrying; Don't think about responsibilities; To distract from demands of life; Machines provide a focal point; Distracts from things that bother me; Somewhere to escape alone; Go when overwhelmed by demands; Distracts from issues outside the venue; No one knows I'm there; Somewhere to go alone; Be around people without talking; A place to unwind; Somewhere to go after an argument* (ibid, 8). See also Jacobs 1988; Wood and Griffiths 2007; Borrell 2008. The idea of gambling as a way to escape personal troubles and negative feeling states is often called the "need state theory."

81. The medical doctor and slot enthusiast David Forrest suggests that machine gambling produces a meditative, trancelike state because its pace and rhythm (three spins every ten seconds, or what he calls "basal slot play rate") coincides with that of human breathing (2012, 49).

82. The term "zone" is used in association with machine gambling in other English-speaking countries as well. One author reports that in Australia, no theme is as resonant among gamblers "as the idea of 'the zone,' a term used by many gamblers and counselors to describe the dissociated state that problem gamblers seem to enter during periods of intense play" (Livingstone 2005, 528). The zone, Livingstone elaborates, "is a particular space and time which is not consonant with the rest of life ... a place away from the world where nothing really mattered except the present, timeless moment" (ibid.; see also PC 2010, 11.16). As gamblers' descriptive vocabulary suggests, the zone of intensive machine play shares qualities with other states of subjective suspension and absence. Analogues in the anthropological literature include spirit possession and ritual trance; in religious studies, mysticism, meditation, and ecstatic prayer; and in the

psychological literature, hypnosis, depersonalization, dissociation, fugue, addiction states, and even the creative absorption that one psychologist has termed "flow" (Csikszentmihalyi 1975, 1994; see also Luhrmann 2000). Although these varied phenomena may involve similar or even identical psychophysiological shifts, they emerge from distinct social settings, cultural ideals, techniques of enactment, forms of expression, and material accessories. My analysis of the "machine zone" focuses more on its specificities than on the qualities it shares with other "altered states" (for an extended contrast between machine gambling and psychological "flow," see chapter 6).

83. Sojourner 2010, 149.

84. Woolley 2009, 187. Technological advance, the historian David Courtwright points out, has been a significant element of all addictions: "Inventions such as improved stills, hypodermic syringes, and blended cigarettes made for more, efficient, speedier, and more profitable ways to get refined chemicals into consumers' brains" (2001, 4).

85. Ihde 1990, 2002. Ihde describes the approach as "post-phenomenological" in that it does not seek to illuminate the authentic essence of being or reality, but instead seeks to illuminate the relationships between humans and their world. More recently (Ihde 2002), he has endorsed the phrase "post-subjectivist" to describe this relational approach to the project of phenomenology (see also Verbeek 2005a, 2005b).

86. Latour claims that nonhuman entities, while not alive and without purposeful intentions, can nevertheless act in and on the world; in this sense, Latour conceives of subjects and objects alike as "actants" (Latour 1988, 1992, 1994, 1999; Akrich 1992; Akrich and Latour 1992). Similar to Latour's notion of "actancy," albeit with subtle differences, are Ihde's idea of "technology intentionality" (1990, 141–43) and Andrew Pickering's idea of "machinic agency" (1993).

87. Gomart and Hennion 1999, 243. The term "affordance" alludes to the concept developed by psychologist James Gibson in the late 1970s to describe "the characteristics of objects and arrangements in the environment" that support interactive activity between an agent and a given system (in Greeno 1994, 341).

88. For analyses of addiction as a "coproduction" of objects and subjects, see Gomart 1999; Hennion and Gomart 1999.

89. Stewart 2010, 18. The gambling industry frequently defends its products by way of metaphors that equate slot machines to other products associated with consumer harm, such as alcohol ("alcoholism doesn't come in bottles, it comes in people") and automobiles ("[a] powerful car does not make the driver speed" [Blaszczynski 2005]).

90. The quotation is part of Australian gambling researcher Blaszczynski's expert testimony in support of the defense in a Canadian class action case that turned on the issue of whether VLTs are addictive (Blaszczynski 2008, 7). In his testimony Blaszczynski insisted that just as speeding "is ultimately dependent upon the psychological constitution and decisions made by the driver," slot machine addiction derives from "factors intrinsic to the individual rather than to [machines]" (Blaszczynski 2008, 12).

91. Roberts 2010.

92. Latour 1999, 179. Ihde independently developed a similar analysis of the gun example (1990, 26–27). For a discussion of the subtle differences and resonances between Latour and Ihde, see Verbeek 2005a.

93. Winner 1986; Latour 1994, 1999; Verbeek 2005a, 2005b; Poel and Verbeek 2006; Suchman 2007a. At once building upon and departing from actor network theory's call for greater symmetry in analyses of human-nonhuman relations, Suchman cautions that scholars should be mindful of asymmetries and dissymmetries in the ways that humans and nonhumans constitute each other (Suchman 2007b, 268–69). "Human and nonhuman agencies are not parallel and interchangeable in some larger system," Jain aptly notes in her analysis of product liability law (2006, 16).

94. Grint and Woolgar 1997, 71. See also Woolgar 1991; Akrich 1992, 205–24; Akrich and Latour 1992, 259–64; Latour 1992, 152; Latour 1999; Verbeek 2005a, 2005b; Poel and Verbeek 2006, 233; Suchman 2007a, 2007b.

95. Quoted in Rotstein (2009, n.p.).

96. Panasitti and Schüll 1993.

97. When I use the terms "compulsive" or "addicted," I do so not in a clinical or diagnostic sense, but in a colloquial, descriptive sense (as do gamblers themselves), to indicate behavior that has become excessive, out of control, difficult to stop, and destructive. It should be noted, however, that there are a number of technical differences among the terms I employ. For instance, although the group Gamblers Anonymous prefers the term "compulsive," many psychiatrists consider this descriptor a misnomer, pointing out that excess gambling actually has an *impulsive* structure. While compulsions are characterized by a feeling of being compelled by an external force at odds with one's own desires, impulses are characterized by an increasing sense of tension or arousal in anticipation of performing an act, followed by pleasure, gratification, or a sense of release upon completion. Impulses, in other words, are "ego-syntonic" (i.e., intentional, goal-oriented) while compulsions are "ego-dystonic" (involuntary, alien, purposeless). Given that gambling is an ego-syntonic and pleasurable activity (at least initially), the members of the original American Psychiatric Association diagnostic task force for pathological gambling collectively decided that the condition was better classified as an impulse control disorder than a compulsion (APA 1980). Some considered that decision debatable, since gambling typically becomes a problem only at the point when it feels involuntary and driven. The debate is likely to become obsolete with the recent decision to rename pathological gambling "disordered gambling" and to reclassify it as an addiction rather than an impulse control disorder.

98. The Las Vegas Trimeridian clinic, no longer in operation, was conceived in 1997. Investors believed that profit was to be made if insurance companies could be convinced that the pathological gambling diagnosis warranted coverage; they have yet to be convinced. Richard Rosenthal, a company board member and consultant psychiatrist, was familiar with my research project and invited me to intern at the new Las Vegas branch as part of my research. His colleague, Lori Rugle, coordinated the arrangement. In my capacity as an intern, I performed

detailed client intakes, sat in on group therapy sessions and staff meetings, and was put to use as minute taker. The internship led to my employment as an assistant to a clinical drug trial involving video poker addicts that Trimeridian had been commissioned to conduct by the pharmaceutical company Eli Lilly. In the process of enrolling subjects in the trial, I met and later interviewed gamblers who had never before participated in any form of individual or group therapy.

99. In 1990, Hunter reported that 95 percent of his female clients and 74 percent of his male clients played gambling machines exclusively; by 1995, when I began to visit GA meetings, the figure had shifted to 97 percent of women and 80 percent of men. Over the last fifteen years, the gender gap has closed even further. With the increasing popularity of machine play among men, it has become apparent that the two sexes are equally likely to become problematically involved with machines if exposed to them (Breen and Zimmerman 2002, 48; Breen 2004; see also Abbott 2006). In countries with different histories of gambling, gender differences in machine gambling either do not exist or skew in the opposite direction: in Australia, for example, men are more likely than women to have played machines; in Canada, younger men make up over 60 percent of the slot machine market; in Russia, 70 percent of the machine market is male (Schellinck and Schrans 1998; AIGR 2001, 9, 54; Rutherford 2005b, 22). In the United States, women's preference for machine gambling had to do with the fact that table gambling was the near-exclusive preserve of men prior to the 1970s; women played machines because it was not considered their place to sit at tables, and because they had not developed the knowledge to do so. Meanwhile, as slot machines became associated with women, men did not consider playing them. Yet once machines became computerized—and became more profitable for the industry— the association between machine gambling and women began to fade. Las Vegas's biannual Residents Surveys indicate that women were "much more likely" to say they played machines most often throughout the 1990s (GLS Research 1993; 1995; 1997; 1999), but only 7 to 10 percent more likely to do so by 2002 (GLS 2003). For more on gender and gambling, see chapter 7.

100. Robert Breen, a specialist in the treatment of gambling addiction at the Rhode Island Hospital, has remarked upon this continuum of experience: "I have seen people not even old enough to get into the casinos who were already hooked on the video slots, I have seen people in their 70s and 80s, black, white, well-to-do, impoverished, graduate school educations, not finished high school, people who don't have any prior psychiatric history—depression, alcoholism, any history of therapy, people who are gainfully employed, pay their taxes, raise their families, send their kids to college. I think given the right circumstances, almost anyone can get hooked on slots" (from video interview conducted by Elizabeth Massie in 2008, youtube.com/watch?v=jNL3FzU_glU, accessed January 2010). Gambling addiction is often called an "equal opportunity addiction," affecting even accomplished public figures like William Bennett, former director of the Office of National Drug Control Policy, who was known to play video poker for two to three days at a time (Green 2003). Nonetheless, certain social groups are disproportionately vulnerable to the condition: those with a high school education or less, those with low annual household incomes, the elderly, women, employees of the

gambling industry, and recent immigrants. For a discussion of how social differences mediate the outcomes and consequences of excessive gambling, and how they may lead certain minorities to be disproportionately labeled as "problem gamblers" (those with less wealth, for instance), see Volberg 2001, 55–57; Volberg and Wray 2007.

101. Over the course of this project I interviewed approximately eighty gamblers. The interviews were unstructured and open-ended, most lasting two hours or more. They took place in private homes, hotel rooms, chain restaurants, local bars, casino buffets, ladies' room lounges, and in cars in the parking lots of strip malls. I began each interview by asking gamblers how they had come to live in Las Vegas, and how their gambling had begun. This question tended to provoke long narratives, which I occasionally interrupted to request clarification or elaboration, but did not direct. Often I asked gamblers to describe particular sessions of play, and to describe the machines on which they played. I recorded the interviews on cassette tapes and also took notes. Some gamblers I met with two or three times; others I spoke with only once. Some kept in touch by telephone, letters, and e-mail.

102. Katrina, quoted in Borrell (2004, 183, 182).

103. Venturi, Izenour, and Brown 1972.

104. My choice to begin this book with Mollie's map was inspired by anthropologist Stefania Pandolfo's opening placement, in her own book, of a map depicting a Moroccan village drawn for her by a resident. She wrote that his drawing composed "a poetic reckoning of the spatio-temporal universe the reader is about to traverse.... The 'map' takes the introductory place that in ethnographies is conventionally reserved for the setting" (1997, 6).

105. "Encounters at the interface," notes Suchman, "invariably take place in settings incorporating multiple other persons, artifacts, and ongoing activities, all of which variously infuse and inform their course" (2007b, 284). Scholars of technology have used terms such as "socio-technical ensemble" and "socio-material assemblage" (Bijker and Law 1992; Latour 1999) to characterize the arrangements of persons, artifacts, and activities to which Suchman alludes. As conceptualized in social theory more generally, assemblages comprise artifacts, practices, desires, logics, and institutions bound into provisional configurations of association, each with their own dynamics of constraint and possibility, determination and contingency. Paul Rabinow has written of the assemblage as an "experimental matrix of heterogeneous elements, techniques, and concepts," defining the "anthropology of the contemporary" as the task of identifying emergent assemblages and setting them in their wider context (2003, 56). Here I approach this task from the starting point of the "zone"—a state that at once escapes from and can be empirically situated within a wider technological, social, and political-economic context (as Deleuze and Guattari write, every assemblage "always has a line of escape" [1986, 86]). (It should be noted that my use of the term "zone," which derives from gamblers themselves, accords more importance to the affective and phenomenological aspects of the zone than that of Barry [2006], who has proposed the term "technological zone" to indicate assemblages of common measurement, communication, and regulatory standards relating to technical artifacts and practices.)

PART ONE: DESIGN

1. Hellicker 2006.

CHAPTER 1: INTERIOR DESIGN FOR INTERIOR STATES

1. Venturi, Izenour, and Brown 1972. Today the book is regarded as an inaugural text on postmodern aesthetics and the built environment.

2. Ibid., 50.

3. Ibid., 49.

4. Reisman 1950.

5. The titans of "corporate splendor" in post-1980s Las Vegas, writes architectural scholar Alan Hess, "often erred on the side of stylistic safety when commissioning new architecture," erecting "look-alike slabs that reflect mass economics but not mass taste" (1993, 100, 102). "Although Las Vegas hotel and casino architecture seems to be designed in an exuberance of creativity and fantasy," writes another, it entails "purposeful planning and requires high levels of expertise and specific knowledge" (Ötsch 2003, 135). See also Gottdiener, Collins, and Dickens 1999, 92.

6. Jameson 1991. For further reflections on the text and its legacy, see Izenour and Dashiell (1990) and the anthology *Relearning from Las Vegas* (Vinegar and Golec 2008). For more on the importance of space to capitalism, see Lefebvre (1991 [1974], 21, 374–75), who writes that space entails a "productive consumption" that ultimately serves "dominant economic interests."

7. Michael Hong from the Jerde Partnership, in an interview with Ötsch 2003, 91, 93. Casino designers, like those of malls and other consumer spaces, conceive of space as a continuous storyboard that keeps the consumers in active, infinite motion and "encodes ideal consumer behavior." Frederic Jameson wrote in 1991 that "recent architectural theory has begun to borrow from narrative analysis in other fields and to attempt to see our physical trajectories through such buildings as virtual narratives or stories, as dynamic paths and narrative paradigms which we as visitors are asked to fulfill and to complete with our own bodies and movements" (42).

8. Sweephand website, www.divnull.com/lward/writing/sweephand.html, accessed May 2004.

9. Friedman 1982 [1974].

10. Friedman 2000, 63.

11. Ötsch uses this same term to describe Freidman's approach (2003, 135).

12. Friedman 2000, 64.

13. The major competing model for casino design is that of the gaming consultant David Kranes (1995). Unlike Friedman, Kranes emphasizes "legibility" over disorientation, relief from environmental stimulation over bombardment with stimuli, airy space over congestion, and natural over unnatural light. Tourist venues in which the architecture itself (and not just gambling) is part of the experience on offer often follow this design formula. One set of researchers proposes

that casinos designed according to Friedman's principles increase patrons' gambling impulses and intensity, while those who follow Kranes's model do the opposite by promoting cognitive clarity and rational decision making (Finlay et al. 2006).

14. Ibid., 42.

15. Ibid., 84.

16. Friedman 2000, 104.

17. Ibid., 105.

18. Panelist for "Casino Floor Layout: Variations from Around the World," G2E 2009.

19. Friedman 2000, 12. Thomas, Sullivan, and Allen similarly write that machine gamblers seek a "private oasis in which they could be undisturbed" (2009, 3).

20. Friedman 2000, 66. As Reith points out, the external setting of the casino may be one of formlessness and "labyrinthine confusion," yet the activity of gambling itself is a means through which the gambler can achieve control: "it is in this action that order and regularity emerge out of the sensory maelstrom of the casino floor. In the repetitive rituals of play, the world becomes organized again" (Reith 1999, 123). She describes machines as "oases of order." "As players gravitate towards them, their attention and actions become focused and the imperatives of the game gradually relieve them of the responsibility of deciding what to do."

21. Friedman 2000, 70.

22. Ibid., 46, 66. Friedman notes that the same rules apply to grocery stores and other consumer venues: people prefer to consume within "insulated enclaves" rather than exposed spaces.

23. Ibid., 51.

24. Ibid., 64.

25. Following an exhaustive "methodological study of the relation between ceiling height and player counts" that takes into account not only the variable of height but also the relationship of height to corresponding widths and depths, Friedman concludes that ceilings over twelve feet should be avoided (ibid., 20).

26. Ibid., 421. He is writing about a neighborhood casino called the Santa Fe.

27. Ibid., 331.

28. Ibid., 48.

29. Adopting the terminology of philosophers Deleuze and Guattari, one could describe the gambling zone as a "smooth space," or one that is open-ended and continuous, without interruption or demarcation (Deleuze and Guattari 1987, 480–81; Hardt and Negri 2001, 327). Friedman is a "technician of smooth space" in the sense that he is "someone who would try to make such space, to use it, to instrumentalize it" (Osborne and Rose 2004, 218). To cultivate "smoothness" in the gambling experience, he applies architectural strategies involving enclosure, segmentation, construction, and perceptual division.

30. The authors of a recent study in Australia write of casino architecture that creates player sanctuaries: "Some venues lay out their gaming room in a relatively open plan style, but many others arrange EGMs in such a way as to provide 'cover' for those who may not wish to be observed by others whilst playing them. It is not uncommon to observe a row of EGMs placed at the rear of a gaming

room, obscuring any players who may be using them" (Livingstone and Woolley 2008, 108). Another Australian researcher has explored the ways in which casino environments support the escape that gamblers seek by providing them with a retreat or hiding place (Thomas et al. 2011).

31. Friedman 2000, 22.

32. Ibid., 52.

33. Allen 1992, 6.

34. Interview conducted with Butler DeRhyter in 1992 (Panasitti and Schüll 1993). "The guiding principle in the interior design of the Mirage was to make the large appear smaller," said Kenneth Wynn, a designer who happens to be the brother of Steve Wynn (panelist for "Casino Design," World Gaming Congress and Expo 1990). Outside, the huge structure features triple-sized windows with giant shutters to give the building a homey and small-scaled appearance. This design strategy was carried over to the interior of Wynn's next major property, the Bellagio, where groups of six exterior windows are made to appear as one.

35. Friedman 2000, 82, 69.

36. Ibid., 79, 84. An analyst of casino design similarly writes that Friedman's typical "lack of open space may induce disorientation and impede a logical interpretation of the scene" (Finlay et al. 2006, 580).

37. Friedman 2000, 82, 284. As Jean Baudrillard notes, commodity displays can "mimic disorder to better seduce, but they are always arranged to trace out directive paths" (1988, 31). If this arrangement is not in place, Margaret Crawford writes in her study of malls, "the resulting disorientation leads to acute shopper paralysis" (1992, 17). Friedman has acknowledged the similarity between casinos and retail settings, invoking Woolworth's pioneering merchandising approach, in which "inventory is thrust in front of shoppers" (2000, 82; for more on spaces of consumption see Crawford 1992; Williams 1992; Benjamin 1999).

38. Friedman 2000, 56.

39. Ibid., 64, emphasis mine.

40. Ibid., 63–64.

41. Friedman writes dramatically of "the devastating impact of a combined raised entrance landing and the barn effect," in which patrons "look down into a huge undifferentiated expanse that resembles a deep cavern that seems to descend into the bowels of the earth" (ibid., 37–38).

42. "Cashless Slot Machines" 1985, 25, 26. The head of the design firm, DiLeonardo, added an environmental psychologist to his staff in the mid-1980s, explaining: "environmental psychology is a new category of science that studies why people react the way they do to the characteristics of a space" (quoted in Carroll 1987b, 20).

43. Zia Hanson, quoted in an interview with Ötsch (2003, 87). By contrast, exits "should be toned down, almost camouflaged, made to perceptually disappear into the interior environment" (Friedman 2000, 149).

44. Friedman 2000, 81.

45. CEO of Gasser Chairs quoted in Legato (1987, 15). "The grace of a curve," wrote the philosopher Gaston Bachelard in *The Poetics of Space*, "is an invitation to remain. We cannot break away from it without hoping to return. For the be-

loved curve has nest-like powers; it incites us to possession, it is a curved corner, inhabited geometry" (Bachelard 1969 [1958], 146).

46. Panelist for "Casino Floor Layout: Variations from Around the World," G2E 2009.

47. Friedman 2000, 147.

48. An early instance of using architecture to evoke pedestrians' propensity to gamble was William Harrah's decision to remove window glass from his Reno casino in 1967, replacing it with what he called an "air curtain" (a strip of filtered air circulating downward); pedestrians then not only saw into the casino but also heard the clinking of silver dollars and the calls of dice dealers. "Anybody walking past is practically part of the play," said one of Harrah's employees. "There's no barrier to slow down his impulsive response" (quoted in Sanders 1973, 106–7).

49. Friedman 2000, 81.

50. Ibid., 81.

51. Ibid.

52. Ibid., 84.

53. Mayer and Johnson 2003, 22.

54. Following Spinoza, Deleuze and Guattari (1988) define affect as the ability to affect and be affected. Massumi (1995; 2002) points out that affect is prior to and outside of consciousness, unlike emotions (which are sociolinguistic) and feelings (which are personal and biographical). Lyotard (1993) describes affects as "libidinal energies" and "intensities" that are available for interpretation and exploitation, and which *can only* exist within environments, systems, and structures. See also Negri 1999; Clough 2007. For anthropological literature on affect and subjectivity, see Desjarlais 2003; Biehl 2004; Luhrmann 2004, 2005; Pandolfo 2006; Biehl, Good, and Kleinman 2007; Stewart 2007; Masco 2008; Mazarella 2008; Biehl and Moran-Thomas 2009.

55. Massumi 1995; 2002. Countering Jameson's (1991) claim that the postmodern age is one of diminished or flat affect, Massumi argues that the contemporary capitalist world is characterized by a *surfeit* of affect (1995, 88; 2002, 27). For further discussion of the displacement of value-production onto affect, see Negri (1999), and Clough (2000, 2007).

56. Hirsch 1995. Hirsch is a psychiatrist and neurologist.

57. Ibid., 593.

58. Ibid., 585–86.

59. Friedman 2000, 136.

60. Ibid., 140.

61. Ibid., 101–2. Friedman criticizes Mirage's interior designers for decorative indulgences that hide the gambling equipment, including "lush plants, beautiful flowers, and a fantastic aquarium" (Friedman 2003, 82). The design model associated with such flourishes is that of Kranes (1995).

62. Ibid.

63. Friedman 2000, 7, emphasis mine.

64. Ibid., 135.

65. Ibid., 136.

66. Manager for Digigram (quoted in Holtmann 2004, 30), emphasis mine.

67. Ötsch 2003, 137.

68. Quoted in Holtmann (2004, 30, emphasis mine).

69. Ötsch 2003, 137.

70. Karen Finlay, quoted in Thompson (2009, n.p.). Gambling scholars Livingstone and Woolley have found that problem gamblers dislike jarring music and sounds on gambling machines (2008, 102).

71. As a factory engineer observed regarding the role of the physical setting on the flow of work in the early 1900s: "The design of the building should allow work to go forward as though the building does not exist at all" (Charles Day, quoted in Biggs 1995, S183). Biggs notes that historians of modern production have placed far more emphasis on factory machinery than on "the factory building—its design, layout, and construction," although some engineers, she points out, considered it to be the "master machine" or "the big machine containing and coordinating all the little machines" (Biggs 1995, S174, S181). She undertakes an analysis of the factory building not as a passive structure but as a "a dynamic element in the production process." This chapter undertakes a similar analysis with respect to the interior design of the casino.

72. Reith 1999, 143, 144. An interesting counterpoint to the casino floor is the stock trading floor, a related but distinct space of money and risk. Anthropologist Caitlin Zaloom (2006) describes the trading floor of the former Chicago Board of Trade as an "architecture of circulation" whose design facilitates hierarchy, status indication, relationality, and embodiment. An enormous clock hangs over the floor, reminding passers-by of the connection between time and money and fostering a sense of the future; wide-open spaces allow easy circulation; equal access to information facilitates rational decision making. Zaloom compares trading activity to Geertz's description of "deep play," in which selves are at stake in a relational field of risk. Traders' actions, she argues, embody a capitalist ethic of self-mastery.

73. "Design/Construction Firms" 1985, 25.

74. Foucault 1979, 172.

75. Ötsch 2003, 138; Klein 2002.

76. Although Deleuze loosely grouped forms of power into those of "sovereignty societies," "disciplinary societies," and "control societies," he did not draw a sharp divide between "new" and "old" forms of power; instead, he argued that they would intermingle, "with the necessary modifications" (1992, 7). From a Marxist perspective, Harvey (1989) and Jameson (1991) similarly argued that strategies of industrial Fordism had not been retired as much as they had been intensified within new forms of time-space compression; the underlying logic of capitalist accumulation remained the same.

CHAPTER 2: ENGINEERING EXPERIENCE

1. Cummings 1997, 64, 63.

2. Before the commoditization of gambling lent it a new, productive value within a changing economy, it was regarded as "an occasion of pure waste," as Caillois characterized play activities (1979 [1958], 5). The association of play

with nonproductivity had much to do with its lack of a material product (Malaby 2007), an association that has waned with the increasing prevalence of "immaterial" forms of labor and consumption within the service economy (Hardt 1999; Negri 1999; Terranova 2000; Courtwright 2001, 2005; Dibbell 2006, 2007, 2008; Andrejevic 2009). Cosgrave (2009) has called gambling a form of "productive consumption" (see also Reith 2006, 132; 2007, 39).

3. For discussions of time and energy techniques applied to manufacturing labor, see Marx 1992 [1867]; Taylor 1967 [1911]; Thompson 1967; Rabinbach 1992. Ironically, the infamous American management consultant Frederick Taylor developed many of his ideas at Bethlehem Steel in Pennsylvania, a factory that has been recently converted, with minimal renovations, into a "factory-themed" casino.

4. Dibbell 2008. "Any productive process that can be rendered as a computer program requiring human input," Dibbell observes in the course of his research on digital online gaming, "can also, theoretically, be designed to take that input via a program humans might want to *play*." An emerging literature on the conjuncture of play and labor in contemporary capitalist economies—sometimes called "playbor"—suggests that play is not antithetical to a logic of labor exploitation (see, for example, Hardt 1999; Negri 1999; Terranova 2000; Dibbell 2006, 2007, 2008; Andrejevic 2009).

5. Thrift 2006, 282. Thrift regards this mining of experience as a symptom of capitalist "desperation" to find new sources of commodification and profit (2006, 280–81). See also the literature on the "affective economy" (Massumi 1995, 2002; Hardt 1999; Negri 1999; Clough 2000, 2007; Terranova 2000).

6. Pine and Gilmore 1999, cited by Mark Pace of WMS, panelist for "CRM and Data Analytics: Make Me Money or Save Me Money," G2E 2009. The book uses the term "experience economy" to mark a form of economy that *follows* the service economy, while some use the expression to *characterize* the service economy (see, for instance, Callon, Méadl, and Rabeharisoa 2002).

7. Mark Pace of WMS, panelist for "Slot Appeal: Applying New Technologies," G2E 2007; Kathleen McLaughlin of Las Vegas Sands, panelist for "Harnessing the Market: The Potential of Server-Based Gaming," G2E 2008.

8. Christopher Strano of AC Coin, panelist for "Boosting Machine Productivity: Creating an Environment," G2E 2007. In behaviorist terms, these "auxiliary products" are examples of "secondary conditioning" or "classical conditioning"— elements that reinforce play behavior because they have become associated with a machine's pattern of reward delivery or "operant conditioning" (to be discussed in chapter 4).

9. Alexandra, a retired casino dealer, remembers: "My bosses loved me because they had a quota of 350 hands an hour and I dealt 500. When I started playing machines, I got pretty fast at that too." Josie, who works in an insurance office, makes a similar link between her work skills and play skill: "I could play a machine so fast you couldn't even keep up with watching me—it was like a typewriter and I've got every button memorized. My fingers are quite nimble and coordinate nicely with my eyes because of all the time I spent playing; if anyone wants to become a typist, I recommend video poker as an exercise."

10. Neil Nicastro, quoted in Bulkeley (1992, B1). Today, if "one-armed bandits" have arms at all, they are purely vestigial, "nothing more than a tribute to their evolution" (Cummings and Brewer 1994, 75).

11. Cummings 1997, 76; see also Lehman 2007a.

12. On multiplay video poker machines, which allow players to select cards for one hand and play those cards out on three, five, ten, fifty, or even one hundred decks simultaneously, this rate rises higher still (see chapter 4).

13. Harrigan and Dixon 2009, 83.

14. Hans Kloss of Bally Technologies, quoted in "A Slot Maker for All Seasons" 1996, 18.

15. Warren Nelson, quoted in Turdean (2012, 11).

16. Stuart Bull of Aristocrat, panelist for "The Video Future," World Gaming Conference and Expo 1999.

17. Jack O'Donnell, quoted in "Cashless Slot Machines" 1985, 14.

18. "Cashless Slot Machines" 1985, 14.

19. Palmeri 2003; Joseph Pitito, director of investor relations for Global Payment Technologies, quoted in Emerson (1998a, 31).

20. Foucault 1979, 152–54.

21. Marx 1992 [1867], 352.

22. Cummings 1997, 76. Taking the industry's logic of temporal maximization to its farcical limit, the editor for the trade journal *Global Gaming Business* writes, "Maybe they'll come up with some kind of technology that actually hooks your brain waves to a wagering device, so you can play slots while you're asleep. That seems like such wasted time, casino revenue-wise, when you're asleep" (Legato 2006, 114).

23. Benjamin 1968 [1939], 179n11.

24. Turkle 1984, 83.

25. Phantom Belle was part of Silicon Gaming's Odyssey line. The dynamic play rate is described in the company's US Patent No. 5758875. In an earlier version of the feature made for reel-spinning slot machines, a mechanical drive mechanism sped up the rotation of the reels depending on how fast a player pulled the handle, and electronic circuitry further improved this effect with the patented Variable Speed Gaming Device (see US Patent No. 4373727).

26. US Patent No. 5758875. Simplifying the "dynamic play rate" concept, some machines have since incorporated a simple speed gauge that picks up the pace of play depending on the player.

27. Historical precursors to player-centric slot machines appeared in the second half of the nineteenth century in the form of amusement devices (often called "coin-in-the-slots") that gave users "at least an illusion of agency, although within strictly predefined limits," observes the game historian Erkki Huhtamo (2005, 8). An advertisement for one such device claimed that its functioning was "entirely under [the user's] own control by the turning of the crank. He may make the operation as quick or as slow as fancy dictates" (ibid., 9). As Huhtamo points out, although these machines could be considered "the antithesis of the production machines in the factories and offices," in fact their goal "was to make the user

spend more and more coins at an increasing pace," and using them "was not far from the repetitive gestures the worker was forced to perform in a mechanized factory" (ibid., 6, 9). Like contemporary slot machines, they simultaneously provided users "an opportunity to step outside the capitalistic idea of constant productivity and scientifically regulated work routines" and "linked the working life and the spare time even more tightly together" (ibid., 10, 11).

28. Jim Medick, industry consultant, interview with the author.

29. Panelist for "Games and Expectations: The Slot Floor of the Future," G2E 2004.

30. Tony Testolin of Billy's West, quoted in Rutherford (1996, 83).

31. Cummings 1997, 71.

32. Ibid., 73.

33. Nicholas Koenig, an independent designer who has created gambling machines products for IGT and Silicon Gaming, among other manufacturing companies.

34. Cummings 1997, 68.

35. Witcher 2000, 25.

36. Thrift 2006, 288.

37. Rivlin 2004, 47.

38. Kranes 2000, 33. "The basic concept of my job is to make music that draws a player in quickly," said one senior sound designer for gambling machines. "It's my goal to draw players in and keep them interested long enough to play the game" (Daniel Lee, quoted in Villano 2009).

39. The industry consultant Kranes writes: "It goes back to Dr. Pavlov and his dogs, their salivating on cue: Conditioned response. The sounds of coins, dropping into metal trays, the theory reasons, will prompt players to salivate for the WIN" (2000, 32). When one Las Vegas manager lowered machine trays six to eight inches to amplify this noise in 1985, he reported a significant increase in machine revenue ("Cashless Slot Machines" 1985, 14; the properties he worked at were Sam's Town and the California Hotel).

40. Quoted in Rivlin (2004, 45).

41. Spencer Critchly, as paraphrased by his former colleague Nicholas Koenig in an interview with me in 2009.

42. Kranes 2000, 33. "Noise is *dis*-ordered sound," Kranes elaborates. "Noise inhibits activity. Noise, logically then, discourages play."

43. Immersion Corporation promotional material and press release from 3M news, November 13, 2007. Immersion and its haptic software was acquired by 3M Corporation and rereleased as the Microtouch Capacitive Touchscreen System.

44. Nicholas Koenig, creative director for IGT's 2003 AVP slant top machine cabinet (see www.nkadesign.net).

45. Croasmun 2003. Complementing ergonomic design measures are encouragements that gamblers comport themselves according to ergonomic guidelines. Echoing tips for office workers at computer stations, one gambling industry advisor composed a list of "simple exercises" that slot players can perform to protect

their eyes, wrists, and fingers from strain and repetitive stress injuries: "Look from left to right while you are playing instead of staring at the same spot on the screen. Take some deep, slow breaths while doing this.... Stop occasionally and flex your fingers and wrists.... Wiggle your fingers to get blood circulating again" (Burton, n.d.).

46. Quoted in Legato (1987, 15, emphasis mine). The emerging attention to player comfort extended to casino hotel rooms, whose garish, striped wallpaper and uncomfortable furniture was shed in exchange for subdued, suburban, residential decor. "Casino operators used to operate under the philosophy that the more uncomfortable the room, the less time the player will want to be in that room and the more time he will spend in the casino," a trade journalist wrote in 1987. "Today," he went on, "the feeling has shifted to a belief that ... you want to keep that player happy and comfortable so that he/she will want to return" (Carroll 1987b, 22).

47. Although contemporary ergonomics works to adapt tasks and their technologies to human behavioral and cognitive capacities and limitations, when the field formed in the early twentieth century "the machine assumed priority in design considerations, and the operator came last" (Tilley 2002, 158; see also Meister 1999). With the advent of wartime, it was no longer possible to select individuals perfectly fitted to a job, and it became necessary to take the variable masses into account in technology design. This shift grew with the transition to a consumer economy in the postwar years, when product designers were compelled to pay increasing attention to an unskilled public. With the rise of the personal computer came a demand for user-friendly hardware and software design, and by the 1980s a new branch of ergonomics had appeared, called "human factors ergonomics," or HFE. Distinguishing itself from the largely physical concerns of industrial ergonomics, this form of ergonomics is concerned with "how [to] build comfort and satisfaction ... into machines" (Meister 1999, 19). Important precursors to HFE were "motivation research" and a concern with "industrial relations" in the postwar management literature (see Dichter, 1960; McGregor, 1960).

48. Chairs are built not only to last, wrote the author of a piece called "Please Remain Seated," but "must also convince players to sit and stay" (Knutson 2006, 32).

49. Ibid.

50. Frankhouser, director of slot operations at Red Rock Casino, quoted in Wiser (2006, 36).

51. Lars Klander of Tech Results, moderator for "CRM and Data Analytics: Make Me Money or Save Me Money," G2E 2009.

52. IGT 2005, 43.

53. Royer 2010.

54. Examples of ticket-in/ticket-out (TITO) systems are IGT's EZ-pay and Bally's e-ticket. Customers were resistant to the technology until low-denomination games came on the scene, at which point they embraced the opportunity to do away with the hassles of inserting one penny at a time, carrying large coin buckets

around the casino floor, and dirty hands (Emerson 1998b, 34). By 2005, TITO was running on 70 percent of US slot machines (today nearly all slots feature TITO).

55. Lehman 2007a.

56. When a play session has terminated, players with remaining credits head to self-redemption kiosks that convert their tickets into cash.

57. Eadington 2004, 10–12.

58. Steven Kile of Imperial Bank and Richard Lightowler of Bank of America, quoted in Parets 1996, 65.

59. The total cash dispersed to gaming patrons by Global Cash Access in 2006 was $17 billion, and over $21 billion in 2007.

60. Emphasis mine. The Arriva executive notes: "The reason patrons like the kiosks is because they don't need to face the embarrassment of being declined at the cage. With us they are approved or declined in privacy. This is especially important to people who do this for the first time" (quoted in www.macaubusiness.com/newsadmin/preview.php?id=804, accessed July 2007).

61. By 2008 the Arriva Card was operable in one thousand casinos and other gaming properties worldwide and had dispensed nearly 40 billion dollars in cash advances. Global Cash Access discontinued the card given the fragility of the larger economic climate ("in this environment, no consumer credit product will be immune to losses," a spokesperson noted), but promised to "continue [its] pursuit of innovative new products and services aimed at delivering more cash to the casino floor" ("Global Cash Access to Discontinue" 2008).

62. Parets 1996, 64.

63. Eadington 2004, 10–12.

64. Company promotional material (www.cashsystemsinc.com/powercash.asp, accessed January 2008); see also Hodl 2008. At the time of this book's writing, the system, which was developed in 2007, was in place at California and Colorado casinos but had yet to be approved for use in Nevada.

65. TODD (developed in 2004) was formerly known as the QuikPlay ATM, a name that did not bode well for regulatory approval given laws against incorporating ATM functions into slot machines (Parets 1996, 64).

66. Hodl 2008; Stutz 2007a; Grochowski 2006.

67. Aaron Righellis, marketing manager for Cash Systems, quoted in Grochowski (2006, 32).

68. Stutz 2007a.

69. Legato and Gros 2010, 14.

70. Neal Jacobs, CEO of Automated Currency Instruments, quoted in McGarry (2010).

71. Foucault 1979, 153.

72. Deleuze 1992; see chapter 1. Elaborating on this mutation in the mid-1990s, Castells (1996) wrote of contemporary capitalism as a "space of flows" in which spatial boundaries are smoothed, markets are opened, and production is "deterritorialized" (using the term that Deleuze and Guattari coined to describe the uprooting of capital to seek new markets and labor sources). Hardt and Negri have similarly written: "Capital tends towards a smooth space defined by uncoded flows, flexibility, continual modulation" (2001, 327).

73. Dibbell 2008, 3. Andrejevic (2009) has argued that both autonomy and exploitation are involved in immaterial, affective forms of labor. Ritzer writes that consumers, like producers, have become an exploitable mass in their own right, with certain key differences: "Although they may not be subject to much, if any, overt coercion, consumers are the objects of a variety of softer, more seductive controlling techniques" (2005, 53). He regards Las Vegas casino-resorts (along with shopping malls, cruise ships, and fast-food chain restaurants) as paradigmatic of the "new means of consumption," which combine bureaucratic processes of rationalization (to expedite consumption) with elements of enchantment (to lure and captivate consumers). The historian David Courtwright likewise views Las Vegas as an exemplary site of what he calls "limbic capitalism" (or "the reorientation of capitalist enterprise [around] providing transient but habitual pleasures, whether drugs or pornography of gambling or even sweet and fatty foods") (2005, 121).

74. Terranova 2000.

75. Thrift 2006, 284, 279.

76. Callon, Méadl, and Rabeharisoa 2002, 202, emphasis mine. Callon and his colleagues describe the iterative process of customization as one of "qualification" and "requalification," in which product qualities are progressively attributed, stabilized, objectified, and arranged. They are interested in the "relays and relations between the predilections and passions of the individual and the attributes and image of the product," as Nikolas Rose puts it in his own work (1999, 245).

77. Callon, Méadl, and Rabeharisoa 2002, 202. Although Callon and his co-authors allow that consumer preferences are shape-shifting, to my mind they overemphasize the power of contemporary consumers to "clarify their preferences" and "define product characteristics" through their interactions with products, and underemphasize the ways in which product design can strategically steer consumer preference formation. As chapter 4 will show, insufficient attention to the latter leaves their analysis unable to account for various forms of consumer addiction.

78. This is how the psychologist Mihaly Csikszentmihalyi has described the autotelic nature of "flow" activities (1985, 490; see chapter 6 for a fuller discussion of flow and its relationship to machine gambling). The anthropologist Gregory Bateson similarly wrote of the type of activity that, "rather than being purposive, i.e. aimed at some deferred goal, is valued for itself" (Bateson 1972, 117).

79. Heidegger 1977 [1954], 15.

80. Sylvie Linard, panelist for "Slot Systems: New Innovations, New Experiences, New Efficiencies," G2E 2005. Linard uses the term "extinction" in a behaviorist sense, to indicate the termination of a conditioned response—but in this case, the behavior terminates not because the activity has ceased to be compelling to the subject, but because the subject's means to continue it have dried up. "Playing to extinction" thus means extinction of the play behavior, rather than extinction of the *drive* to play.

81. Cummings 1997, 65.

82. Deleuze 1992.

CHAPTER 3: PROGRAMMING CHANCE

1. "The player may win or lose in the short term," writes technology columnist and game designer John Wilson, but the [purveyor] is there for the long haul" (2009a). As the "law of large numbers" in probability theory dictates, a game's cumulative outcomes over millions of plays will align with its programmed "hold percentage," or house edge. "If a player continues to play for a long time," note three consultants to the industry, "there is no chance for the player to be ahead of the casino" (Singh, Cardno, and Gewali 2010; see also Turner 2011). In the temporal asymmetry of the gambling exchange, time is on the side of the house.

2. Coser 1977, 233.

3. Weber 1946 [1922], 139. Weber introduced the concept of "disenchantment" to describe the decline of ancient cosmological traditions and the rise of mechanistic thinking and modern science.

4. Woolley and Livingstone 2009, 48; Weber 1946 [1922], 139.

5. Bauman 1991, 125; Weber 1946 [1922], 216.

6. The term "manufactured incalculability" is used by Beck (1994, 11) in his discussion of "risk society." At once building upon and departing from Weber, scholars of risk society argue that as humans interact more with technologies, and as these technologies have more extensive effects in our world, risks proliferate, spin out of control, and become increasingly difficult to calculate and manage; in effect, technologies designed to rationalize and gain certainty produce new uncertainties and irrationalities. Beck considers this to be a breach at the core of modernity, "not in its marginal zones" (Beck 1994, 10; see also Giddens 1991, 1994; Beck 1992; Beck, Giddens, and Lash 1994).

7. Malaby 2007. An example of "contrived contingency" would be the use of dice to cultivate randomness in play, or the running of a random number generator.

8. Jenkins 2000, 18. As the financial success of gambling enterprises demonstrates, the historian Richard Jenkins continues, "neither desire nor playfulness are necessarily at odds with the schemes and strategies of organized, utterly rationalized and disenchanted, capitalism." For additional work on the persistence of enchantment alongside rationalization in capitalism, see Williams 1982, Campbell 1987, and Schneider 1993. Ritzer (2005) notes that recreation and its escape routes have become rationalized, and at the same time are "re-enchanted" to attract customers.

9. Weber 1946 [1922], 139. Weber uses the term "technical" to denote rationalities, technologies, and techniques specific to modernity, yet the premodern historical record contains instances in which "technical means and calculations" play a key role in spiritual and magical practices. The early Islamic automata that the art historian Gunalan Nadarajan describes, for example, were considered conduits for the capricious movements of God's will and a visible manifestation of divinity (2007, 13).

10. See Falkiner and Horbay 2006.

11. Commissioner Hyte quoted in Harrigan (2009b, 73). Technically, horse racing and sports are also games of unknown odds, for both players and the house.

12. Joe Kaminkow, quoted in Rivlin (2004, 44). Kaminkow was then vice president of IGT's central design team.

13. Malaby 2007, 108.

14. Woolley 2008, 143.

15. King 1964; Costa 1988, 21; Nassau 1993; Huhtamo 2005. "The introduction of large-scale machine production was accompanied by an avalanche of different devices that provided amusement, including gameplay," notes the game historian Huhtamo. "The proliferation of automated slot machines in the cityscape took place simultaneously with this development" (2005, 3).

16. "Slot Machines and Pinball Games" 1950, 62.

17. Fey 1983, 13.

18. Fruit symbols did not appear on slot machines until Fey's second model, called the Operator Bell. He used the fruit symbols to disguise the devices as gum vending machines and thereby circumvent antigambling laws.

19. Collier 2008.

20. Fey 1983, 1. For a discussion of the key role that pinball gambling machines played in the ongoing success of the slot industry, see King 1964.

21. In 1964 Bally developed the first fully electromechanical slot machine called *Money Honey*. The device allowed unprecedented automatic payouts of five hundred coins instead of a mere twenty coins, as did all prior devices.

22. Until then it had been possible to cheat on the machines by manipulating their mechanics. One method, called "rhythm play," involved pulling the lever in such a way as to influence the stopping of the reels; "stringing" involved pulling a coin in and out of the slot with each spin; "handle slamming" attempted to disable the payout control mechanisms on old machines; and "spooning" required a special device (Friedman 1982 [1974]; Turdean 2012, 15–16). Some slot cheats used "slugs" or fake coins, "shims" or wire pieces that were inserted into holes made in the machine's case or glass, or simply poured substances into the pay slot to fix its handle into play mode. Others attempted to stop the reels in certain positions with help from magnets.

23. Turdean 2012, 46.

24. US Patent No. 4095795, emphasis mine.

25. Technically, the RNG is "pseudorandom" which means that since it is a designed program, it can never truly be random in its functioning (unless it draws its numbers by sampling random noise in the environment). Slot machine RNGs sample a real-time internal computer clock to establish a "seed" value, and starting there they derive each random number from the previous one, following a recursive function. Given that their cycles contain approximately 4.3 billion distinct values, they are virtually unpredictable—especially when one takes into account the contribution the gamblers make by initiating plays at unpredictable intervals.

26. The algorithm works by taking the random number that has been generated and dividing it by the number of stops on a given virtual reel until there is a remainder; that remainder indicates the reel position to select.

27. Rogers 1980, 25.

28. Ellul 1964, 333.

29. Rogers 1980, 25.

30. President of Bally's gaming machine division, quoted in "The New Generation of Slots" 1981, 28.

31. Mark Pace of WMS, panelist for "Slot Appeal: Applying New Technologies," G2E 2007.

32. Hodl 2009, 15.

33. Reiner 2009.

34. Harrigan and Dixon 2009, 84. For a video demonstration, see "Illusion of Control" online at http://problemgambling.uwaterloo.ca/video-stories/. Stop features exist on machines in some jurisdictions of Canada, and on Japanese "pachislo" games. A similar "skill stop" button appeared in Atlantic City when gambling was legalized, to satisfy New Jersey gaming laws that required an element of actual player control. Since then, US gaming regulations have outlawed skill features in gambling machines (aside from video poker, which requires skill to play optimally). Game developers have long hoped this would change, so that they might incorporate small skill factors into games and in this way enhance players' illusion of control. In 2007 WMS Gaming's PONG, offering bonus rounds in which player dexterity is involved, was granted regulatory approval, suggesting the start of a regulatory shift with respect to skill features on gambling machines. In 2010 IGT and Konami introduced games whose bonus features required actual hand-eye coordination using pinball-like flippers and a joystick, not just "perceived skill."

35. Two studies on stop devices were conducted by Ladouceur and Sévigny (2005). In the first, 87 percent of players believed that the timing of their activation of the stopping device affected the symbol display on the video reel, over half believed they could control game outcomes through the stopper device, and nearly half believed skill was involved in using it. In the second, gamblers on machines with the stop feature played twice as many games as a control group without it. IGT's 2009 "REEL Edge" game series allows players when to stop each video reel, as a press release describes: "When the player presses the "stop" button, the reels decelerate and stop within 150 milliseconds."

36. "IGT product profile" 2000, 39.

37. Scoblete 1995, 5.

38. Ibid.

39. Suchman 2007b; see also Turkle 1984, 2011; Ihde 1990; Nadarajan 2007.

40. Turkle 1984, 29.

41. Nadarajan's work on early Islamic automata is pertinent to contemporary gambling machines and the way they "contrive contingency," to use Malaby's related idea (2007). The devices, Nadarajan writes, involved "deliberate and elaborate programming for untoward rather than predictable behavior," giving their movements "an order that was within certain predefined but not completely controlled parameters" (2007, 15).

42. Dancer 2001, 26.

43. Randy Adams of Anchor Gaming, quoted in Legato (1998b, 74).

44. Crevelt and Crevelt 1988, 17.

45. Robison 2000.

46. US Patent No. 4448419. Telnaes developed the software in the late 1970s when he was working for Bally Distributing. He filed for a patent in 1982, and the patent was granted in 1984.

47. Turner and Horbay 2004, 16.

48. Ibid., 11. US Patent No. 4448419.

49. Turner and Horbay 2004, 21.

50. Wilson 2004a. Telnaes was the first to own the patent for virtual reel mapping; IGT bought it in 1989, and then licensed it to others (Ernkvist 2009, 169).

51. Legato 2004.

52. US Patent No. 4448419.

53. Ernkvist 2009, 166–68.

54. Ibid.

55. Harrigan 2007, 2008.

56. See Falkiner and Horbay 2006. A software engineer posted his reaction to their article on an online discussion forum for technology insiders: "I think that they have valid points with regards to near misses and weighted virtual stop reels. Consider Roulette as a virtual slot. The player would walk up to the table to play. The wheel would be hidden under a cover, except for a small space that showed the final resting place of the ball, and the casino would have the right to install a wheel that was weighted any way they pleased, as long as each of the numbers appeared at least once. They would not have to disclose to the patron any details about their wheel other than the fact that it paid back at least 75% as required by law, and every roulette table would be different, including those within the same casino" (newlifegames.net/nlg/index.php?topic=6532.msg58188;topicseen, accessed May 2010).

57. Regulations 465.015 and 465.075 (Nevada Gaming Commission 2010b).

58. Regulation 14.040 (Nevada Gaming Commission 2010a).

59. Nevada State Gaming Control Board, 1983, 39, emphasis mine.

60. Ibid., 41. In this comment, IGT's lawyer, Raymond Pike, was specifically referring to the machine's capacity to produce near miss effects by presenting more winning symbols above and below the payline, as I discuss in the next section.

61. Nevada Gaming Commission 1989, 280.

62. Nevada Gaming Commission 1983, 88. "Maybe part of the intrigue is part of the deception," echoes Connie Jones, director of responsible gaming for International Game Technology (quoted in Green 2004). Her claim would appear to contradict the recent claim by a gambling industry journalist that "there is no sleight of hand or trickery involved in the slot machine business" (Roberts 2010).

63. Turdean 2012, 31; see also Davis 1984, 18.

64. "Gaming Laboratory International: The Testing Standard" 2007, 72. GLI is run by James Maida, named one of the top twenty-five most influential people in gaming by the industry trade publication *International Gaming, Wagering, and Business* in 1996. See also Maida 1997; Bourie 1999; Wilson 2003, 2004a, 2004b, 2004c, 2004d, 2004e, 2004f. For a discussion of the "triangular" relationship among machine manufacturers, testing agencies, and the government in Australia, see Woolley 2008.

65. For a detailed historical study of the corporate politics involved in the switch from an electromechanical paradigm to a digital paradigm, see Ernkvist 2009 (especially chapter 7). As he explains, IGT's rise to prominence (at its height in 2006, the company supplied 70 percent of the gambling machines in the United States) was due also to the company's development of Wide Area Progressive (WAP) technology in 1986 in the form of Megabucks, a system that combined virtual reel technology with nascent telecommunications technology, linking gambling machines in multiple properties to a central system. A portion of every player's wager was dedicated to a collective jackpot pool that rose in real-time on a large display, becoming far larger than it could ever be on a single machine. Other slot machine manufacturers later introduced their own versions.

66. Maida 1997, 45. In Australia and New Zealand, where virtual reel mapping is banned, machines are exclusively video based and entail their own set of "perceptual distortions," which I discuss in the next chapter. Some slots in Britain are unique in that their odds are constantly adjusted to conform with a target payout percentage, following a form of negative feedback control called "adaptive logic" or "compensation" (see Turner and Horbay 2004).

67. Bourie 1999.

68. The informal rule that American and Canadian slot machine manufacturers follow is that blanks with near misses directly above or below them should appear no more than twelve times more often than they would by chance alone (six times above, and six times below); some tribal casinos apply a more liberal ratio (Stewart 2010, 13).

69. Harrigan 2007; Burbank 2005, 114. For a comparative report of different games based on anonymously provided PAR sheets and intensive empirical research, see http://wizardofodds.com/slots/slotapx3.html.

70. Nevada State Gaming Control Board 1983, 44, emphasis mine.

71. Cote et al. 2003.

72. Blaszczynski, Sharpe, and Walker 2001, 86. For more work on the efficacy of near misses in extending play, see Skinner 1953, 397; Dickerson 1993; Delfabbro and Winefield 1999; Kassinove and Schare 2001; Blaszczynski and Nower 2002, 491; Dixon and Shreiber 2004; Parke and Griffiths 2004; Haw 2008a; Harrigan 2009b.

73. Harrigan 2009b; Reid 1986.

74. Skinner 1953, 397. Slot machine makers take care not to produce too many near misses, since their effect will be diluted above a certain threshold (Collier 2008).

75. See Burbank (2005, 104–27) for a more detailed discussion of the near miss hearings and the corporate politics behind them, which was largely driven by IGT's quest for industry dominance.

76. After determining that a player had lost, Universal's machines referenced a predetermined table of losing hands that included jackpots symbols (Rose 1989).

77. Thompson 2009; see also Rose 1989; Turner and Horbay 2004, 29; Burbank 2005, 104–27.

78. Raymond Pike, quoted in Reich (1989).

79. Burbank 2005, 107, xvii. Burbank provides a detailed history of Nevada's gaming regulatory agencies and its struggle to keep up with the complex computerized technology of gambling machines.

80. Rose 1989.

81. Regulation 14.040 (Nevada Gaming Commission 2010a). Until this regulation was drafted, there were "no written regulations governing the concept of what would become known as randomness" (Burbank 2005, 107, xvii).

82. Falkiner and Horbay 2006, 10. Placing less winning symbols on the second reel, and even fewer on the third, is a design tactic that dates back to early mechanical reel slots.

83. On New Life Games Tech Forum, an online "information sharing site for those of us in the amusement and gaming industry," a gambling industry electronics engineer explains: "the strips you see rolling past during the game are not the same strips you see when the reels stop. They are 'teaser' strips that show lots of jackpots and high-pay symbols while the game runs, then as each reel stops, the machine cuts in the percentage strips for the last few strips." A software engineer responded to his post: "psst—I won't tell about the video slot tactic if you don't" (http://newlifegames.net/nlg/index.php?topic=6532.msg58188;topicseen, accessed May 2010).

84. Weber goes on: "The savage knows incomparably more about his tools. Increasing intellectualization and rationalization do *not*, therefore, indicate an increased and general knowledge of the conditions under which one lives" (Weber 1946 [1922], 139).

85. PAR sheets contain the configuration of a game's reels (including a listing of every symbol that appears on the reels, and its position), pay combinations, payback percentages, hit frequency, volatility index, confidence level statistics, and more.

86. More recently, Canadian researchers Harrigan and Dixon (2009) obtained PAR sheets through the Freedom of Information and Protection of Privacy Act.

87. The software is available online at www.gameplanit.com/Slot_tutorial.html. Horbay and Harrigan have since developed similar software for the "multiline" video slots that I will discuss in the next chapter.

88. Suchman 2007b, 42. See also Turkle 1984, 272; 2011, 111.

89. Livingstone and Woolley 2007, 369.

90. Borrell 2004, 181.

CHAPTER 4: MATCHING THE MARKET

1. Stuart Bull of Aristocrat, panelist for "The Video Future," World Gaming Conference and Expo 1999.

2. Michael Pollack of *The Gaming Observer* , moderator for "The Video Future," World Gaming Conference and Expo 1999.

3. Clues to this script are found in games' "paytable and reel strip sheets" or PAR sheets, also called "probability accounting reports" (see chapter 3).

4. A study of gambling behavior by Delfabbro and his colleagues, for instance, concluded that "frequency [of reinforcement] was generally found to be more important than magnitude" (Delfabbro, Falzon, and Ingram 2005, 20). This is evident in the playing style that most gamblers follow, which is to bet minimum or medium credits on maximum lines (the "mini-maxi" approach), thus lowering the size of prizes but ensuring their steady stream (Livingstone and Woolley 2008, 25; Legato 2005a, 74). While steady small wins have been shown to increase gamblers' rate of play, larger wins have actually been shown to *disrupt* it (Dickerson et al. 1992; Delfabbro and Winefield 1999).

5. Jeffrey Lowenhar was the IGT representative (he has since left the company to become a casino executive, and now consults for gambling operations worldwide). The book he directed me to was *Reward and Punishment* (Logan and Wagner 1965). Skinner's theory included "operant conditioning" (the schedule of reinforcement) as well as "classical conditioning" or "secondary conditioning" (the sounds, music, visual graphics, and other environmental cues that become associated with rewards and thus contribute to their reinforcement). "The schedule is the important characteristic" of behavioral conditioning, he emphasized (Skinner 1953, 104).

6. A number of scholars have discussed gambling machines in relation to the phenomenon of reinforcement (Dickerson et al. 1992; Dickerson 1993; Delfabbro and Winefield 1999; Kassinove and Schare 2001; Blaszczynski and Nower 2002; Dixon and Shreiber 2004; Parke and Griffiths 2004; Delfabbro, Falzon, and Ingram 2005; Haw 2008a, 2008b; Livingstone and Woolley 2008; Harrigan 2009b). Although some refer to the payout structure of gambling machines as following the "variable ratio" schedule of reinforcement (in which the probability of a reward increases with every unrewarded chance, because the ratio is based on a predetermined number of rewards), in fact it follows the "random-ratio" schedule (in which every round is independent of the previous round and therefore carries the same probability of a reward) (see Haw 2008a). The intermittent wins of gambling machines can "produce states of arousal often described as equivalent to a "drug-induced high" and spur prolonged play, write Blaszczynski and Nower (2002, 491).

7. Skinner 2002 [1971], 35.

8. Ibid., emphasis mine.

9. Chris Satchell, quoted in Fasman (2010, 10).

10. Prater is now president of the Association of Gaming Equipment Manufacturers, the international trade group that represents the manufacturers of gambling technology.

11. As an industry-commissioned report called "Demystifying Slot Machines," indicates, high volatility, low hit frequency games tend to "generate lower amounts of customer time" since "customers will spend their gambling budgets more rapidly in return for the excitement of playing for higher stakes" (Stewart 2010, 10). See also Eisenberg 2004.

12. Ibid. Although the properties of low volatility and high hit frequency do not have a one-to-one relationship, they generally go together. High volatility

games (i.e., those with large jackpots) typically have far lower hit frequencies than low volatility games, because it is easier to configure their math in this way. (In order to achieve good hit frequency on a volatile game, it is necessary to increase the game's hold percentage as well as increase its "lines of play," as in the video slots formula I will discuss further along in this chapter.) The lower a game's "volatility index," the more players' immediate experience will conform to that game's indicated payout percentage; the higher its volatility, the more their experience may deviate from this percentage (Harrigan 2009a, 3–4; see also Lehman 2007a; Wilson 2009a, 2009b; 2010a; 2010b; Singh and Lucas 2011; Turner 2011).

13. Wilson 2009a.

14. IGT 2005, 48, 49.

15. As gambling has become increasingly commercialized, gamblers' aim has shifted from wanting to win to wanting "to lengthen participation"—that is, to get more of the commodity for the money (Reith 1999, 133; see also Findlay 1986).

16. Jay Walker of Walker Digital, quoted in Legato (2007a).

17. Kent Young, panelist for "Content Is King: Developing the Games," G2E 2008.

18. Author's interview with Butler DeRhyter in 1993.

19. The casino attribute that turns out to be most critical to capture a local market is not promotional giveaways, check-cashing services, or child-care facilities, but "an easy drive from home." Others at the top of the list include "feel safe there," "friendly and courteous staff," and "convenient parking" (Shoemaker and Zemke 2005, 403).

20. A black and white version of video poker called Poker Matic had been built by Dale Electronics in 1967. Si Redd at Bally Distributing made a version in 1976, but took the rights to the patent with him when he split with the company to join Fortune Coin, where in 1977 Stan Fulton developed the first color video poker model, called Draw Poker. Fortune Coin was acquired by IGT (called SIRCOMA—for "Si Redd Coin Machines"—until 1981) in 1978. Until IGT released its version of the game, it had remained a novelty within a niche market.

21. Ernkvist 2009, 146.

22. Although five-card and seven-card stud versions of the game have been tried, nearly all versions of video poker in use today are variations on five-card draw poker.

23. Len Ainsworth, quoted in Rutherford (2005a, 17).

24. The payback percentage on video poker machines is typically 96 percent or higher, yet this percentage is calculated with an assumption of perfect strategy; the actual rate can drop to an abysmal 34 percent if a player is not familiar with the rules and strategies of poker (interview with Dom Tiberio at Bally; Stacy Friedman at Silicon). Even for relatively knowledgeable players, the actual payback rate tends to be 2–4 percent less than the maximum payback based on perfect play.

25. Si Redd, quoted in Ernkvist (2009, 147). As Rivlin reports, top IGT designer Joe Kaminkow later carried on Redd's insight that players would spend more at games that allowed them longer play. After spending time in locals casi-

nos, he asked his mathematicians to lengthen the speed at which games took player's money (specifically, he instructed that a 20 dollar bill should last at least 15–20 minutes) (Rivlin 2004, 46).

26. Reinforcement schedules involving frequent small or moderate payoffs create a high "event frequency," or number of opportunities to gamble in a given time frame. The "loss period is brief, with little time given over to financial considerations," such that players may immediately regamble their winnings (Dickerson et al. 1992, 246; Griffiths 1993, 101, 107; 1999, 268).

27. Si Redd, quoted in Ernkvist (2009, 147).

28. Hevener 1988, 10. At the Gold Coast Casino, for instance, 84 percent of gambling devices were video poker in 1988, attesting to the game's economic importance to local casinos.

29. Ernkvist 2009, 142. From the mid- to the late 1990s, IGT supplied 90 percent of North American video poker games; today, the company supplies 95 percent. For a discussion of video poker's role in IGT's ascent to a position of industry dominance, see Ernkvist 2009.

30. IGT website (www.igt.com, accessed June 2007).

31. Colin Foster, quoted in "IGT Unveils" 1983, 31.

32. Woo 1998, 4. The Las Vegas Convention and Visitors Authority calculated the local preference for video poker that year to be 44 percent.

33. Nevada gaming law requires machine games that imitate live dice and card games to carry the same odds as the live versions.

34. Friedman 1982 [1974], 235.

35. The "learning" of which Hunter speaks is sometimes literal. Sixty to eighty thousand residents, for example, have enrolled in Bob Dancer's classes on video poker (see his website: www.bobdancer.com/seminars.html, accessed May 2010). As Dancer told me: "The level of knowledge is much higher; the downside is that games have become tighter as the population has learned. This is a cat and mouse between casinos and players."

36. Buckeley 1992, B1.

37. As indicated in the introduction to this book, Hunter and others have found that the players of contemporary video poker and slot machines reach a debilitating level of involvement with gambling three times as rapidly as those who play live games, even if these individuals have gambled regularly on other forms of gambling in the past without a problem (Breen and Zimmerman 2002; Breen 2004, 48).

38. Gambling machines had been legal in Australia since the mid-1950s, but were restricted. The 1990s deregulation changed that. Today, there are over 200,000 machines throughout the country, in every state except for Western Australia. The vast majority of these are located in neighborhood "clubs" and cater to the local population.

39. Dettre 1994, 3.

40. PC 1999, 12.

41. Ibid., 2.11

42. A number of small countries dominated by tourism (e.g., Monaco, Aruba, Macau) have a higher adult to machine ratio than Australia. Although the Aus-

tralian gambling industry argues that Japan also has a higher ratio (see TNS Consultants 2011), pachinko and pachislo devices technically do not count as slots given certain unique attributes and the fact that they are played with tokens rather than money (although clever marketing allows people to play for prizes they may exchange for cash).

43. Although Australians call their slot machines "poker machines" or "pokies," they do not feature the game of video poker (they are called pokies in reference to early mechanical gambling devices based on poker).

44. Although the first coin multiplier was introduced as early as 1941 by Bally, the design did not become popular until 1967 when the company married it with electromechanical technology.

45. The Keeney Company had developed a mechanical "multiline" slot machine as early as 1941, but it never became popular (Fey 2006, 237).

46. Aristocrat website (www.aristocrat.com.au/history.aspx, accessed February 2009).

47. Ibid.

48. Stuart Bull of Aristocrat, panelist for "The Video Future," World Gaming Conference and Expo 1999.

49. On one popular game, it was found that a player who bet on maximum lines would experience a "win" on one-third of his or her spins; of these "wins," the majority (60 percent) were actually for less than the amount wagered (Harrigan and Dixon 2009, 102).

50. Wilson 2010a.

51. Harrigan and Dixon 2009, 102; Dixon et al. 2010. For online video demonstrations see problemgambling.uwaterloo.ca/other/losses-disguised-as-wins/ldw-intro-video/ and problemgambling.uwaterloo.ca/other/losses-disguised-as-wins/examples-of-ldws/. Dixon, Harrigan, and colleagues conducted experiments in laboratories equipped to take physiological measurements (including heart rate, perspiration, blood pressure, pupil dilation) while gamblers played slot machines. They found that players "react physiologically to LDWs as though they are wins.... Although LDWs are obviously losses, the myriad of sights and sounds that occur during slots play may serve to camouflage this fact." They suggest that "despite being losses, LDWs engender the reinforcing arousal that is a key factor in the development of problem gambling" (Dixon et al. 2010, 1820, 1824).

52. For studies showing that small wins increase gamblers' persistence and rate of play while larger wins disrupt it, see Dickerson et al. 1992 and Delfabbro and Winefield 1999.

53. As two Australian scholars of gambling write, "gamblers have choices to make, options to pursue. This confers a sense of agency—despite the fact that [the] devices are entirely random and nothing a gambler does can influence the outcome of the operation of the technology" (Woolley and Livingstone 2009, 51). A scholar of video games similarly writes: "Games offer a variety of participatory means of affecting mood as well as allowing players to tweak game settings to bring about the desired affective changes" (Calleja 2007, 244–45).

54. Haw 2008a, 11. He goes on: "This could promote the belief in the player that they can control the betting outcomes (e.g., "If I buy more lines I get more

wins and less losses"), which is true regarding the frequency of (small) wins, but actually leads to an increase in the rate of net loss" (ibid.); see also Delfabbro, Falzon, and Ingram 2005; Delfabbro 2008, 11; Haw 2008a, 11; Livingstone and Woolley 2008, 25.

55. Livingstone and Woolley 2008, 29; Woolley and Livingstone 2009, 44. See also Delfabbro, Falzon, and Ingram 2005; Delfabbro 2008, 11; Haw 2008a, 11.

56. Michael Pollack of *The Gaming Observer*, moderator for "The Video Future," World Gaming Conference and Expo 1999.

57. Stuart Bull of Aristocrat, panelist for "The Video Future," World Gaming Conference and Expo 1999.

58. Frank Neborsky of Mohegan Sun, panelist for "The Video Future," World Gaming Congress and Expo 1999.

59. The first multiline game approved in Nevada was WMS's Reel 'Em In, a five-reel, five-payline game that applied an American blue-collar fishing theme to the Australian multiline model. WMS (formerly Williams) is the leading American company in video technology today, largely because IGT pushed them in that direction during the period when it had exclusive rights to the Telnaes patent (see Ernkvist 2009).

60. Brenda Boudreaux of Palace Station, panelist for "The Video Future," World Gaming Conference and Expo 1999. Boudreaux went on to become IGT's senior vice president of product development.

61. Panelist for "Get Real: Reel Slots vs. Video Slots," Global Gaming Expo 2005.

62. Aristocrat website (www.aristocratnz.co.nz/AUS/What/Games.asp, accessed July 2008).

63. There are twenty paylines per reel and players may bet on these as a block, for ten credits per block (WMS website description of "Wrap Around Pays," wms.com/wraparound/, accessed October 2009). Another of WMS's innovations, called Cascading Reels, removes the winning combinations after the first spin, while the other symbols remain present; on a second spin, new symbols cascade down into the empty spots to form new winning combinations. An inverse variation called Spinning Streak freezes winning combinations on the screen after the first spin, while nonwinning symbols are respun.

64. Reiner 2009.

65. Michael Pollack of *The Gaming Observer*, moderator for "The Video Future," World Gaming Congress and Expo 1999.

66. John Giobbi of WMS, panelist for "The Video Future," World Gaming Congress and Expo 1999. An Australian study determined that the average bet size for nickel games was between fifteen and twenty-four nickels (while the average bet on games of one cent is thirty-three to fifty times the single penny credit value) (Livingstone and Woolley 2008, 54). An additional factor to take into account when assessing the profitability of nickel versus dollar gambling machines is the higher hold percentage the latter carry (nickel games hold an average of 7 percent while dollar games hold an average of 3 percent (Lehman 2009).

67. Ernkvist 2009, 221. The percentage of penny denomination machines in Las Vegas's *locals* casinos is much higher (by 2005 one third of the slots at Stations Casinos were penny machines) (Legato 2005a, 74).

68. Weinert 1999, 77.

69. Jerald Seelig of AC Coin and Slot, quoted in Green (2006).

70. Leading consultants to the gambling industry have encouraged a move away from high-volatility games, especially those configured to produce high hit frequency at the same time, for these devices have such a massive range of possible outcomes that years could pass before they reach their theoretical hold percentages and produce a profit for the casino (Wilson 2010a, 2009b; Lehman 2007a). Reducing the volatility on low-denomination, high hit frequency games produces a "smoother," less volatile revenue stream that more quickly approximates casinos' expected returns.

71. Kent Young, quoted in "Aristocrat Technologies to Display 140 Innovative Games" 2000.

72. Kent Young, quoted in Legato (2005b, 52, 50).

73. The Las Vegas Convention and Visitors Authority has tracked local gambling preferences since 1992, when 53 percent of gambling locals preferred video poker and only 18 percent slots (GLS Research 1993). With the introduction of Australian-format video slots to the market this imbalance gradually evened out, and by 2004 equal percentages of local gamblers preferred video poker and slots (GLS Research 2005). However, a 2005 study using a different methodology found that half of resident gamblers played video poker while only 18 percent played slots (Shoemaker and Zemke 2005, 395).

74. Legato 2005a, 74.

75. GLS Research 2007, 5; 2009, 20, 21; 2011, 20, 21.

76. Woolley 2009, 187.

77. "The overwhelming majority of problem gamblers," reported Livingstone and Woolley, "gamble small amounts on multiple or maximum lines.... This 'style' of play can be understood as to a significant extent formatted by the core reinforcement schedule technology of gaming machines" (2008, 25).

78. Ibid., 104.

79. Cooper 2005, 128. The turn to escape in gambling—and, in its extreme form, to addiction—might be understood within the framework of the "ecological niche," as sociologist Ian Hacking uses the metaphor; that is, as a way to understand how "mental illnesses of the moment" (e.g., chronic fatigue syndrome, attention deficit hyperactivity disorder) find "a temporary home" and flourish in particular social, economic, and technological settings (Hacking 1998, 13).

80. Those who play video poker tend to play heavily (twice a week or more, with session lengths of four hours or more) or moderately (one to four times a month, with session lengths of one to four hours), while those who prefer slots most often play lightly (defined by a frequency of once a month or less, and session length of one hour or less) (Shoemaker and Zemke 2005, 395).

81. See IGT's website for its current video poker variations (www.igt.com).

82. Legato 2007a.

83. In Triple Play video poker, the top two rows are dealt face down while the bottom row is dealt face up. Players choose the cards they wish to hold from the bottom hand, and those same cards automatically appear in the corresponding spaces in the two top hands. After hitting the Draw button, the player gets three different draws from three different decks.

84. IGT website (www.igt.com, accessed May 2010).

85. Legato 2007b.

86. Grochowski 2000.

87. A version of video poker called Multi-Strike takes the game even further by allowing gamblers to proceed through four *different* hands of poker each round; if a player wins at the first hand, the next carries double the odds of winning, and so on to the fourth hand (if he or she does not win on the first hand, the entire bet, up to twenty credits, is lost). "The beauty of Multi-Strike," a writer notes, "at least from the casino point of view, is that although it theoretically pays back the same as any other video poker machine, its play is so complicated, there is so much happening on the screen, the betting must be so strategic, that it requires NASA-level concentration to play perfectly" (Cooper 2005, 130). It is possible to lose $250 an hour at the twenty-five-coin level. He comments: "If video poker is the crack cocaine of machines, the Multi-Strike game is the mound of snow that Tony Montana sticks his face in at the end of Scarface."

88. Linard of Cyberview, panelist for "Slot Systems: New Innovations, New Experiences, New Efficiencies," G2E 2006.

89. In contrast with my own argument that players' adaptation to game algorithms can follow an addictive pathway, the "adaptation hypothesis" proffered by Howard Shaffer and his colleagues (see endnote in chapter 10) makes the somewhat different claim that players develop a kind of protective resistance or immunity to the games to which they have been exposed, leading to the curious conclusion that "this is one reason the gaming industry constantly introduces new games, suggesting that both players and purveyors of gambling know that it is not inherently dependence producing" (Shaffer, LaBrie, and LaPlante 2004a, 46). The fact of game innovation strikes me as an odd defense against the potential for addiction, given that innovation typically involves complexifying or intensifying prior games (rather than introducing qualitatively different games) and thus serves just as well to illustrate the classic addiction phenomenon of tolerance formation in which more of something is needed to produce the same subjective shift.

90. The name Katrina was given to this gambler by Jennifer Borrell (2004), another scholar to whom she wrote, who published another of her letters.

91. Bonus features began exclusively on video slots but have now migrated to reel spinners and video poker. While the gambling industry stands to gain nothing during the bonus round (the player either wins or loses nothing), the money dispensed to gamblers as bonuses is considered a tax-deductible marketing expense; thus bonus features are a financially prudent way to provide gamblers with the extended "time-on-device" they desire (Lehman 2009). Harrigan and Dixon (2009) note that bonus games amount to a secondary reinforcement schedule.

92. "The cognitive, emotional, and kinesthetic feedback loop that is formed between the game process and the player makes games particularly powerful means

of affecting players' moods and emotional states," writes a scholar of video games (Calleja 2007, 244–45).

93. It is important to note that although machine gamblers like Katrina seek a zone in which rhythm, comfort, and habituation hold sway over risk, perturbation, and surprise, the zone cannot exist without the presence of the latter elements. If contingency is too thoroughly evacuated from the gambling exchange, players are not drawn in and access to the zone is blocked. This became apparent in the failure of a new sales formula for machine gambling that came on the scene in 2006. The formula, designed both for repeat players who were after time-on-device and for risk-averse novices who needed "training wheels" to get used to the uncertainty of the gambling commodity, appeared in two versions: IGT's was called Guaranteed Play; Cyberview's was called Time Play ("Cyberview Technology" 2007; Green 2007; Legato 2007a; Reiner 2007). In Guaranteed Play, gamblers purchased a set number of hands or spins in advance, for a set price, and started out with a zero balance on the credit meter while another meter ticked off the hands or spins remaining. "Play does not stop—no matter how far below zero the credit meter goes," notes IGT's website. "As long as hands or spins remain [on the guaranteed purchase], the player simply keeps trying to win to return the credit balance to positive territory." "Basically, it's about giving the gambler an even smoother ride," the self-described "math guy" in attendance at IGT's G2E booth told me in 2007. In Time Play, players prepurchased *time* rather than hands, quite literally buying "time-on-device." In this formula, the credit meter never dipped into the negative, but instead remained at zero until a win came along and returned to zero in the event of a loss; meanwhile, a clock steadily ticked toward the end of the session. In both systems, the logic of appeal was the same: the contingencies of losses and wins would no longer determine the length of a play session; instead, players would know for sure how long their session will last. The hypothesis was that this certainty would grant them more continuous play, and thus, easier absorption: "If you KNOW you have 500 hands, you can get absorbed more easily." When I asked the system representative what became of chance in this setup, he explained: "We sell a block of guaranteed time and inside that block, you would still have chance." Yet the removal of temporal contingency from the encounter evidently went too far, for gamblers were not drawn to the system.

94. For a similar discussion of the relations of supply and demand in machine gambling, see Woolley and Livingstone (2009, 38), and Cosgrave (2010, 124), who has written of this relation as one of "dynamic behaviorism." See also chapter 2.

95. Two gambling scholars have developed a compelling model of gambling addiction as the interaction between two systems of feedback: "When the [gambler's] system encounters a context or situation that causes 'discomfort' or 'problematic' input,' the positive feedback loop is activated until a more 'comfortable' state is attained.... If the positive feedback loop does not return to a resting position after the required changes have occurred, the system will continue into a maladaptive spiral, thereby creating further deviation-increasing behaviors" (Zangeneh and Haydon 2004, 27; for a related cybernetic conception of addiction, see Bateson 1972, 448, 109).

CHAPTER 5: LIVE DATA

1. Anchor Gaming was acquired by IGT in 2001.

2. See chapter 4.

3. IGT advertisement, in *Casino Gaming* , April 1988, 42.

4. Panelist for "Cashless Cow: The Next Step in Ticket-In/Ticket-Out," G2E 2004.

5. Gregg Soloman of IGT, panelist for "Sensory Overload: Light, Sound and Motion in Slot Machines," G2E 2005.

6. Wilson 2008.

7. Eadington and Cornelius 1992, xxv.

8. Cardno, Singh, and Thomas 2010.

9. Nickell 2002.

10. The club was called The Captain's Circle and managed to enroll 15,000 patrons within a few months of its introduction. The system was developed by Electronic Data Technology, a subsidiary of IGT.

11. Casinos have long "tracked" the play of table games by having employees fill out sheets noting the amount bet by players, so managers could later discover who its high-rolling customers were and provide them with complimentary services corresponding to their level of betting, such as meals, hotel rooms, or transportation. Those who bet and risked more received better complimentary services, or "comps," to induce them to return to the casino.

12. "Player Tracking" 1990, 6.

13. Crary 1999, 76. See Andrejevic 2007 for a study of contemporary "methods for the management of attention that use partitioning and sedentarization, rendering bodies controllable and useful simultaneously, even as they simulate the illusion of choices and 'interactivity'" (75); see also Deleuze 1992.

14. See Foucault 1979 for a discussion of panoptic technology. The surveillance infrastructure of Las Vegas casinos provides a present-day example of such technology. Cameras monitor every area, and a single gaming table may have up to sixty cameras trained on it, transmitting digital images directly to the Nevada Gaming Commission. Cameras are either hidden or tinted, such that it is difficult to tell where they are being aimed at any given moment; in this way, customers and employees are subjected to a perpetual gaze meant to deter theft.

15. Deleuze 1992. See Andrejevic 2007 for an extended analysis of contemporary consumer surveillance and tracking technology.

16. Ed McDonald of SAS Customer Intelligence, panelist for "Casino Operations: Leveraging Analytics Technology," G2E 2007.

17. Quoted in Binkley (2008, 193). Mirman has since left the gambling industry.

18. Cummings 1997, 68.

19. The extension of tracking methods beyond the physical boundaries of single casinos has proceeded in step with advancements in telecommunications and the military. Craig Fields, former science and technology advisor to the CIA and director of the Pentagon Defense Advanced Research Projects Agency (DARPA) during the period when it funded the creation of the Internet, became vice chair-

man and technological savant of Alliance Gaming Corporation in Las Vegas, where he worked on refining linkages between games and across casinos. An industry journalist reported: "Fields quit DARPA when he concluded that the greatest number of users of high technology were not to be found in the military but in the entertainment industry" (Rutherford 1996, 81; see also Kaplan 2010).

20. Harrah's Total Rewards website (https://Harrah's.com/TotalRewards/Total Rewards, accessed November 2010). The Total Rewards program began as Total Gold in 1998 and changed names in 2000 with the addition of "player tiers." By 2004, 30 million cardholders were signed up in the program, and today the number stands at 40 million.

21. Press release for G2E institute conference, February 7, 2006.

22. See Andrejevic 2007 for a discussion of the use of RFID in the domain of commerce (89–90, 122–23).

23. Barrett and Gallagher 2004.

24. Brock, Fussell, and Corney 1992.

25. Compudigm International website (www.compudigm.com, accessed June 2007).

26. Javier Saenz of Mariposa (who would become vice president of "strategy for network systems" at IGT), panelist for "Increasing Slot Revenue: New Techniques," G2E 2007.

27. Tracey Chernay of Transact Technologies, panelist for "CRM Part II: Technology and Applications," G2E 2008.

28. Scheri 2005, 145; IGT 2007, 47. The Mariposa system, acquired by IGT in 2007, was developed under the auspices of Venture Capitalist, Inc., by Javier Saenz.

29. Mariposa website (http.mariposa-software.com/software_datavis.html, accessed June 2007).

30. Founder and chief technology officer of Compudigm Andrew Cardno, quoted in "Harrah's Sees Success" 2003.

31. Compudigm press release, August 31, 2005. Compudigm executive Rob Berman quoted in "Harrah's Sees Success" 2003.

32. Andrejevic 2007, 4, 33.

33. Thomas Soukup of Konami, panelist for "Casino Operations: Leveraging Analytics Technology," G2E 2007.

34. Panelist for "Bonus Bonanza: How Bonusing Software Is Changing," G2E 2005.

35. Brian Macsymic of Progressive Gaming International Corporation, panelist for "Patron Rating: The New Definition of Customer Value," G2E 2008.

36. Andrejevic 2007, 4. Slavoj Žižek similarly notes that "today's progressive computerization of our everyday lives" means that people are "more and more 'mediatized,' imperceptibly stropped of [their] power, under the false guise of its increase" (in Andrejevic 2007, 22).

37. Reiner 2009.

38. Tim Stanley of Harrah's, panelist for "CRM Part II: Technology and Applications," G2E 2008.

39. Bruce Rowe of Bally, panelist for "Increasing Slot Revenue: New Techniques," G2E 2007.

40. Jeff Cohen of Konami, panelist for "Patron Rating: The New Definition of Customer Value," G2E 2008. "Recency," "frequency," and "monetary" values combine in what is often called the "RFM" value score, which is used to predict future customer behavior.

41. Richard Mirman, quoted in Nickell (2002).

42. Binkley 2008, 174, 194.

43. Ibid., 175.

44. Ibid., 177; Kontzer 2004; Freeman 2006.

45. Quoted in Freeman (2006).

46. Kontzer 2004. Following Nevada state law, casinos may change the odds on a machine only after the machine has been idle for four minutes, and four additional minutes must pass before a new player can gamble.

47. Mariposa's "player contact" component has incorporated a similar feature that color codes players' floor icons to indicate whether they are expected to increase in value (green), decline in value (red), or remain the same (yellow).

48. Wilson 2007. Despite the argument for the emotion-removing capacities of visual analytic tools, it should be noted that such tools can also be a source of anxiety and other forms of affect on the part of analysts, as the anthropologist Zaloom (2009) has pointed out in the case of the "yield curve." For more work on how financial professionals have used visual tools to model the market and thus better intervene in it, see Knorr Cetina and Breugger 2002; Mackenzie 2006; Preda 2006; Zaloom 2006. Tools for visualizing the market are part of a more general contemporary trend in which "narrative, models, and scenarios [are devised to] capture in useful ways the uncertainties, contingencies, and calculations of risk that complex technologies and interactions inherently generate" (Fischer 2003, 2).

49. IGT's Andy Ingram, quoted in Green (2007, 34). MGM-Mirage's Treasure Island tested downloadable gambling in 2006, and the company's 2009 Aria casino marked the first large-scale rollout of the technology. European jurisdictions have moved more quickly to downloadable gambling. Although originally conceived for video formats, it is now possible to download content to reel-spinning slot machines via ingenious technology that convincingly projects video images onto blank mechanical reels (as discussed in chapter 2).

50. Richtel 2006.

51. Macomber and Student 2007a, 28.

52. Quoted in Green (2007, 34).

53. Legato 2005b, 47.

54. Neil Crossman of IGT, panelist for "Evolution or Revolution: How Technology Will Impact Asian Casinos," G2E Asia 2010.

55. For discussions of flexible specialization and related changes to the organizing principles of capitalism, see Piore and Sabel 1984; Harvey 1989; Martin 2004.

56. This responsiveness is already "built in" to machine cabinets like Game King's, which offer players dozens of different games. Flex Play Poker allows players to choose the type of poker and number of hands they would like to play at once (one, two, three, five, or ten hands). As the game's advertisement reads: "Flex Play Poker: It's all about freedom of choice" (www.actiongaming.com, accessed August 2009).

57. Justin Beltram, quoted in Richtel (2006).

58. Todd Elsasser of Cyberview Technology, panelist for "Server Based Gaming II: The State of the Industry," G2E 2007.

59. Macomber and Student 2007a, 28.

60. Ibid., 30.

61. Ibid., 28. Macomber and Student write of these mini-environments: "Food outlets nearby would be developed to align with the culture or market segment targeted, as well as the piped-in music played. Consequently, there could be anything as broad-based as Asian and Latino areas to more micro-areas such as those designed to cater to Vietnamese or Mexicans" (ibid., 30). In these mini-areas, game manufacturers envision games such as a "latino machino" with Spanish-language options, a "matzo ball bonus game" for the Jewish market, and a "soul train" themed game to target the African American market. "We have a large customer base that is a black player and looks at things that have been developed in this industry and says *I have no interest in this stuff, it doesn't pluck my responsive chord*," remarked a panelist at G2E 2005. "We have to be willing to press the envelope and be culturally sensitive but not be accused of racism, like the fortune cookie game," he went on, referring to a failed game that had targeted the Chinese market. There is also talk of games for blind players using Braille buttons and songs by Ray Charles (Cooper 2004, 121).

62. Macomber and Student 2007a, 30.

63. Peter Ing, director of slot operations at Fallsview Casino Resort and Casino Niagara, panelist for "Boosting Machine Productivity: Creating an Environment," G2E 2007.

64. Javier Saenz of IGT, panelist for "Server-Based Gaming: Beginning to Begin," G2E 2008.

65. Christopher Strano of AC Coin, panelist for "Boosting Machine Productivity: Creating an Environment," G2E 2007.

66. Todd Elsasser of Cyberview Technology, "Slot Systems: New Innovations, New Experiences, New Efficiencies," G2E 2006.

67. Sylvie Linard of Cyberview, panelist for "Slot Systems: New Innovations, New Experiences, New Efficiencies," G2E 2006.

68. Macomber and Student 2007b.

69. David Durst of IGT, panelist for "Slot Systems: New Innovations, New Experiences, New Efficiencies," G2E 2006. Andrejevic notes a general shift away from methods of marketing that treat consumers as a homogeneous mass, or even as an aggregation of crudely distinguishable preference groups, toward methods of "personalized feedback" that "seek to exert control at the individual level" (2007, 37).

70. Macomber and Student 2007b.

71. Rich Schneider of IGT, panelist for "Slot Systems: New Innovations, New Experiences, New Efficiencies," G2E 2006.

72. Sylvie Linard of IGT, panelist for "Slot Systems: New Innovations, New Experiences, New Efficiencies," G2E 2006.

73. Butch Witcher, moderator for "Games and Expectations: The Slot Floor of the Future," G2E 2004.

74. Mick Roemer, moderator for "Slot Appeal: Applying New Technologies," G2E 2007.

75. Panelist for "Games and Expectations: The Slot Floor of the Future," G2E 2004.

76. Bruce Rowe of Bally, panelist for "Server-Based Gaming III: The Potential," G2E 2007.

77. Al Thomas of WMS, panelist for "Brave New World: Emerging Games and Alternative Technologies," G2E 2008. Callon and colleagues write of e-commerce vendors: "Since they are able to record customers' previous purchases and their reactions to new offers, suppliers end up knowing as much as consumers themselves do about what they want and expect. This shared knowledge, which evolves as new experiences accumulate, is based on consumers' engagement in a sociotechnical device with which they interact and evolve" (Callon, Méadl, and Rabeharisoa 2002, 210).

78. Green 2010, 28.

79. Larry Hodgson, quoted in Grochowski (2010).

80. Velotta 2009. John Acres's patent for Talo's "volatility device" (US Patent No. 20100004047) works with casinos' tracking capacities such that that gaming conditions can be monitored to determine optimal volatility levels: "tracked gaming conditions may include player selected wagering patterns, recent game event outcome patterns, time-based considerations, or other conditions relating to player characteristics or game play." For example, "the gaming device may automatically alter the volatility level for gaming events to match the general player preferences at specific times." The patent suggests that the device could be used not only to match the preferences of the general market but also to match the preferences of individual gamblers by changing a game's volatility mid-course. For instance, if a player is suffering a run of play without any wins, "a lower volatility (higher hit frequency) paytable may be used for a predetermined number of future games or until the player receives a winning combination. The player may receive an option of accepting or rejecting the change in volatility, or the paytable substitution may be done automatically by the gaming device." Changing the paytable in the middle of a play session would be legal because it can be done in a way that does not alter the overall odds or "payback percentage" of the game.

81. Rich Schneider of IGT, panelist for "Server-Based Gaming III: The Potential," G2E 2007.

82. Kathleen McLaughlin of The McLaughlin Gaming Group, moderator for "Host in a Box: Interface to the World," G2E 2010.

83. Mark Pace of WMS, panelist for "The Possibilities: The Impact of Networked Gaming, Part II," G2E 2009.

84. The Nevada Gaming Control Board approved wireless handheld devices developed by Cantor Gaming (based on software used for wireless interactive bond trading on Wall Street) in 2006, whereupon the devices were given a limited trial run at the Venetian in Las Vegas (Weingarten 2006, 4). International Game Technology has also been granted manufacturer and distributor licenses. "We see the mobile gaming applications fitting into the whole suite of products that will

be part of our server-based gaming initiative," said IGT spokesperson Ed Rogich, quoted in Stutz (2007b).

85. Robert Bittman of IGT, panelist for "Future Watch: Electronic Gaming in the 21st Century," G2E 2007.

86. Kevin Kerr of Microsoft, panelist for "Future Watch: Electronic Gaming in the 21st Century," G2E 2007.

87. Casino representatives' vision for mobile gaming is part of a larger move in the world of commerce toward time- and location-specific marketing enabled by GPS capabilities within personal mobile devices—a trend that calls to mind Deleuze's observation that "giving the position of any element within an open environment at any given instant (whether [an] animal in a reserve or a human in a corporation, as with an electronic collar) is not necessarily ... science fiction" (1992, 6).

88. "Player Tracking" 1990, 6. The phrase "control in steering" evokes the field of cybernetics, whose name derives from the Greek *kybernetikos* or "good at steering." This evocation is apt, given the field's concern with "circular causal" or feedback relationships.

89. Deleuze elaborates on the idea of control as something at once directive and unrestrictive: "In making freeways, for example, you don't enclose people but instead multiply the means of control. I am not saying that this is the freeway's exclusive purpose, but that *people can drive infinitely and 'freely' without being at all confined yet while still being perfectly controlled* . This is our future" (1998, 18, emphasis mine). "Rather than restricting movement," Andrejevic notes in his study of contemporary forms of monitoring and surveillance, the aim is that of "exploiting the productive potential of mobility" (2007, 106).

90. Parets 1999, 19.

91. For example, casinos were the first to use biometric systems for surveillance, far ahead of law-enforcement agencies, airport security, and mainstream business (Schwartz 2003, 216–17). Non-obvious relationship awareness (NORA) software used to discover cheating collusion in casinos was only later adopted by Homeland Security to investigate connections between terrorist suspects (see Kaplan 2010). Yet the exchange goes both ways: server-based gambling, for instance, adopts the same cryptography system as the government's National Security Agency.

92. Lars Klander of Tech Results, moderator for "CRM and Data Analytics: Make Me Money or Save Me Money," G2E 2009.

93. This recursive process aligns with Beck's vision of contemporary capitalist society as one in which the effects of technical systems are continuously fed back into the systems themselves, informing their refinement (Beck, Giddens, and Lash 1994). As Thrift notes, today product designers seek to "draw customers much more fully into the process, leaching out their knowledge of commodities and adding it back into the system" (Thrift 2006, 282; see also Callon, Méadl, and Rabeharisoa 2002). "The configuration of the [electronic gambling machine] technical system," write two Australian scholars, "appears likely to shape and condition the consumption patterns and experiences of gamblers. At the same

time, gambling behavior is likely to feed back into the configuration of the technical system" (Livingstone and Woolley 2008, 156). See Andrejevic (2007) for an extended discussion of the cybernetic "steering" of behavior enabled by contemporary techniques of consumer data capture.

Chapter 6: Perfect Contingency

1. Csikszentmihalyi 1993, 184; see also 1985; 1994 Csikszentmihalyi regards flow as a universal phenomenon: "Regardless of culture, stage of modernization, social class, age, or gender, the respondents described it in very much the same way" (1994, 48). Flow as he sees it is not merely the key to our own happiness, but to collective well-being. Citing the work of Émile Durkheim on collective effervescence, Victor Turner on ritual, and Albert Einstein on the value of art and science as forms of escape that create new realities, he argues that culture evolves through flow experience. Early on in his formulation of the concept, Csikszentmihalyi used the word "zone" to describe flow (1975).

2. Csikszentmihalyi clarifies: "in a flow state one is not, in fact, in complete control.... Rather, what happens is that one knows that control is possible *in principle*. In daily life, there are too many things happening for anyone to feel that control is possible" (1993, 182).

3. Griffiths 1993, 1999; Morgan et al. 1996; Parke and Griffiths 2006. The game scholar Calleja has similarly noted that "the concept of flow is particularly relevant to digital games as core aspects of their design, such as the ability to adjust challenges to player skill, the existence of clearly defined goals, and the provision of immediate feedback, [which] make them ideal vehicles for experiencing flow" (Calleja 2007, 255).

4. Csikszentmihalyi 1994, 62–66.

5. Flow might be described as a kind of "becoming" in the sense that the philosopher Deleuze elaborates: "To become is not to attain a form (identification, imitation, mimesis) but to find the zone of proximity, indiscernibility, or indifferentiation where one can no longer be distinguished from *a* woman, *an* animal, or *a* molecule" (Deleuze 1997, 1; see also Deleuze and Guattari 1987, 262). Becoming entails movement outside of the self, dissolution of bodily grounding, and unmooring from the chronometric order of time; beings lose their texture as subjects and become points of intersection of different speeds, affects, intensities, flows, and forces. Like flow, "becoming" is associated with exuberance, affirmation, invention, transformation, and open-endedness. Machine gambling, by contrast, is a kind of petrifaction—an activity whose uninterrupted repetition no longer opens out onto life and its events, and from which no creative action is likely to emerge. (For a study of pathological gambling involving the concept of flow, see Wanner et al. 2006.)

6. Csikszentmihalyi 1985, 495; 1994, 69, 61. Csikszentmihalyi defines psychic entropy as "noise in the information-processing system [that is] experienced as fear, boredom, apathy, anxiety, confusion, jealousy" (1988, 24). Flow reduces this

noise, given that participants are "using psychic energy in a harmonious pattern" (1993, 176). This harmony produces "a structured experience ... almost addictive in its fascination" (1975, xii). "One might say that, as a species, we are addicted to flow," he writes (1993, 198).

7. Csikszentmihalyi 1993, 30. "It is not the objective, external conditions that determine the quality of experience, but how we respond to them," Csikszentmihalyi writes (ibid., 203). His emphasis on the subjective can be read in part as a reaction to the mechanistic orientation and stimulus-response paradigm of behaviorism, the leading branch of psychology at the time when he first formulated the concept of "flow" (1975, 7).

8. Csikszentmihalyi 1975, 18; 1994, 5. Csikszentmihalyi's work on television with coauthor Robert Kubey (1990; 2003) is an exception to his reticence on the objective conditioning of flow.

9. Cummings 1997, 74.

10. Kent Young, former CEO of Aristocrat, quoted in "Super Slots" 2005, 50.

11. Mick Roemer, quoted in Legato (2005b, 58).

12. Gregg Soloman of IGT, panelist for "Sensory Overload: Light, Sound and Motion in Slot Machines," G2E 2005 .

13. Panelist for "Games and Expectations: The Slot Floor of the Future," G2E 2004.

14. Anonymous executive, interview with the author, 2005. In a short op-ed piece on the concept of "unintended consequences," a casino marketing consultant recalls that when he and his team decided to approach slot players, introduce themselves, and offer to assist them with any needs they might have, "many guests just wanted to be left alone to play their slot machine" (Conrad 2009, 40).

15. Kathleen McLaughlin, panelist for "Harnessing the Market: The Potential of Server-Based Gaming," G2E 2008.

16. Bruce Rowe of Bally, panelist for "Server-Based Gaming III: The Potential," G2E 2007. "The more time the players waste looking at all the intrusive messaging that is streamed to their machines," echoes an industry analyst, "the less time they spend putting money into the machine, which, in turn, means fewer spins and less money for both the casino and the manufacturer" (Royer 2010)

17. Rameesh Srinivasan of Bally, panelist for "Host in a Box: Interface to the World," G2E 2010.

18. Kathleen McLaughlin, panelist for "Harnessing the Market: The Potential of Server-Based Gaming," G2E 2008.

19. Dickerson 1996, 147. For a similar observation, see Walker 1992, 259.

20. Calleja 2007, 256. "In the flow state," writes Csikszentmihalyi, "action follows upon action according to an internal logic that seems to need no conscious intervention by the actor" (1975, 36). A similar sense of merging and loss of self unfolds in the activity of financial trading, as the anthropologist Zaloom describes: "Traders often speak of being 'in the zone' or of a 'flow' experience. In the zone, economic judgments and actions seem to come without effort from the instincts of the trader. The market and the trader merge, giving him special access

to the natural rhythms of financial fluctuations" (2006, 135–36). As traders move from the rich interpersonal and embodied spatial matrix of the open outcry pit to the video screens of online trading, this "special access" becomes more tightly framed and formatted. "In contrast to the overpowering sensory information in the pits," observes Zaloom, "screen-based technologies actually narrow the scope of information available to traders" (2006, 151; See also Knorr Cetina and Bruegger 2000, 2002; Zwick 2005; Zaloom 2010). This narrowing of information, accompanied by a narrowing of physical movement and social exchange, produces a disembodied, asocial form of absorption that resembles the fusion with onscreen processes that machine gamblers describe.

21. Ito 2005, 85.

22. Ibid., 96. Zwick (2005) writes that the technological interface and processes of online financial trading lend the stock market the characteristics of a video game, creating a "change in the phenomenological apperception of the stock market" in which "the aesthetics of the screen constitute [it] as an interactionally or response-present object of consumption ... enabling the individual online investor to gain a sense of (consumer) agency and self-actualization." As Ito tells us, repeated interaction with a response-present object can turn a sense of agency into a sense of merging.

23. Turkle 1984, 4, 14.

24. Winnicott 1971. According to Winnicott, the task of relating inner and outer is never complete; adults find relief from this task in areas of experience such as art and addiction. The disillusionment that infants experience as they transition from a state of merger to a relational existence is akin to the alienation of the "mirror stage," a concept proposed by Jacques Lacan (1977) to describe the child's introduction into the symbolic world of exchange (language, otherness, relating).

25. Children who repeatedly experience a sudden loss of control in parenting or social interactions tend also to retreat into self-based "perfect contingencies" as a mode of affect regulation, yet unlike autistic children, their disengagement is temporary rather than constitutional.

26. Calleja 2007, 241. An earlier, mechanical example would be pinball, as portrayed in the rock musical film *Tommy* (Ken Russell, 1975) about a character by that name who plays the game with magical perfection despite being "deaf, dumb, and blind." As the song titled "Pinball Wizard" narrates, Tommy "becomes part of the machine." It is no small irony that an Internet search for "pinball wizard" today reveals that the name has been trademarked by IGT for one of its themed slot machines.

27. Post by William Huber on March 31, 2004, at http.ludonauts.com/archives/000038.shtml, accessed April 2008. Players of World of Warcraft use the term "grinding," for instance, to describe the repetitive, circular actions they must perform to obtain a certain object or power, such as killing a creature "over and over and over again," as the sociologist Daniel Sahl wrote in a personal communication. "There is absolutely no challenge or skill involved for a highly ranked character to repeatedly kill these virtual monsters; players will just execute the same three or four commands to their avatar over and over again." The fact that

players cease to engage in social or narrative cognition and become caught up in interactive loops such as this ties into the so-called narratology-ludology debate in game studies. The central question in this debate is whether video game players are invested in the progression of narrative meaning or whether they play for the play itself—for the "gameness" of games. Endorsing the latter position, "ludologists" stress the importance of taking into account the material and interactive specifics of particular game activities, not just their narrative elements (Malaby 2007; see also Calleja 2007).

28. Ito 2005, 95.

29. Turkle 1984, 70.

30. Tim Stanley of Harrah's, panelist for "Future Watch: Technology and the Drive for Improved Customer Experience," G2E 2006.

31. Tim Stanley of Harrah's, panelist for "CRM Part II: Technology and Applications," G2E 2008.

32. Ihde 1990.

33. Ibid., 74. The art historian and media theoretician Oliver Grau similarly writes that "immersion arises when the artwork and technical apparatus, the message and medium of perception, converge into an inseparable whole. As a general rule, one can say that the principle of immersion is used to withdraw the apparatus of the medium of illusion from the perception of the observers to maximize the intensity of the message being transported. The medium becomes invisible" (2003, 349).

34. Deleuze and Guattari have written of drug addicts as "bodies without organs"; as opposed to "full" bodies without organs, which the authors positively value, they are "empty"—characterized by petrifaction rather than flow (1987; see also Keane 2002, 34).

35. Turkle 1984, 4.

36. The use of autohold on video poker speeds up play by increasing the number of hands that can be played per hour and also ensures the optimal play strategy for winning (although in the past autohold was programmed to follow a "less than perfect" strategy, as Bob Dancer told me: "Casinos would offer the feature to 'teach' the players how to play badly").

37. All games, Malaby proposes, involve "contriving and calibrating multiple contingencies to produce a mix of predictable and unpredictable outcomes" (2007, 106). The contingencies he considers include *performative contingency*, or the unpredictability that accompanies one's strategic moves; *social contingency*, or the unpredictability of others' strategies; *semiotic contingency*, or the unpredictability of meaning that may arise from a game's outcome; and finally, *pure contingency* , or the uncontrollable randomness of the game. Following this terminology (which Malaby derives in part from MacIntyre 1984), one could say that pure or "perfect" contingency prevails in machine gambling, while performative, social, and semiotic contingencies are absent or greatly diminished.

38. Haraway 1991. For more literature on cyborgs, see Gray 1995; Balsamo 1996; Downey and Dumit 1997; Jain 1999.

39. Analysts of digital media and other present-day technologies have often celebrated Haraway's vision of what a cyborgic world *could* be without taking her

caution into account or scrutinizing the harms of existing human-machine mergers. One exception, Suchman notes, is Jain's work (1999) on product design and human injury, which "provides a restorative antidote to any simplistic embrace of the pros- thetic, in considering the multiple ways in which prostheses are wounding at the same time that they are enabling. In contrast to the easy promise of bodily augmen- tation, the fit of bodies and artifacts is often less seamless and more painful than the trope would suggest. The point of such a recognition is not to demonize the prosthetic where formerly it was valorized, but rather, to recognize the misalignments that inevitably exist within human/machine syntheses" (Suchman 2007a, 148–49).

40. Comments made as moderator for "The Problem Gambler: Emphasis on Machine Gambling," 11th International Conference on Gambling, 2000.

41. Livingstone and Woolley 2008, 18.

42. Csikszentmihalyi 1985, 491. In his study of chess, the anthropologist Rob- ert Desjarlais distinguishes between live and online chess. While live chess is a medium through which players can actively "rework the experiential grounds of their lives" and "remake a challenging world on their own terms," he suggests that "online chess promotes recursive loops of fixed alertness" and that "the repetitive movements, the focused attentiveness, the easy slide into game after game can in- duce trancelike states." The technological format of online chess makes it an inter- action in which the "player is played by the game" (Desjarlais 2010, 43, 191).

43. Legato 1998a, 98. For a humorous documentary account of slot players' crass bodily behavior, written by a former casino slot attendant, see Goldberg 2006.

CHAPTER 7: GAMBLED AWAY

1. Huizinga 1950 [1938], 8; see also Caillois 1979 [1958], 43.

2. Goffman 1961, 27, 34.

3. Csikszentmihalyi and Bennet 1971, 49.

4. Malaby 2003, 147. Malaby understands "economic fluctuations, social ten- sions, personal crises, and the games themselves" as indeterminacies of the same order.

5. Malaby 2009, 208.

6. Rose 1999, 164. See also Burchell 1993; Miller 2001; Martin 2002; Reith 2007.

7. Rose 1999, 152, 214. See also Weber 1978 [1956], 86–90; Miller 2001; Martin 2002.

8. O'Malley 1996, 198. For more on rise of risk thinking in contemporary society, see Giddens 1991, 1994; Beck 1992, 1994, 2006; Luhmann 1993; Lupton 1999. It is not that life has become measurably more precarious than in times past, but rather that there are new kinds of uncertainties afoot which get framed in terms of "risk" and new expectations for how people should be responsible for managing those uncertainties. "If we are a risk society it is because we have come to be more conscious of the risks that we run and more intensely engaged

in attempts to measure and manage them," writes the sociologist David Garland (2003, 71).

9. Engin Isin describes the actuarial self as a "bionic citizen" who is "sufficient, calculating, responsible, autonomous, and unencumbered; he is "a subject whose rational and calculating capacities enable him to calibrate his conduct" (2004, 217, 222). The model of the risk-assessing self can be understood as a variant of what anthropologist Emily Martin calls the "flexible self" (1994). Such a self, she argues, corresponds to broader political and economic circumstances of insecurity, including flexible accumulation as a mode of contemporary capitalism that involves accelerated product innovation, specialized niche creation, dramatic restructuring and even disposability of markets, short-term labor contracts, chronic job insecurity, and the replacement of social protections with an ethic of personal responsibility (see also Harvey 1989; Lears 2003, 21, 321).

10. Hunt 2003, 169. "The significance of these choices," he elaborates, "is compounded by ... mechanisms of responsibilization demanding that we ... treat our lives as a project over which we should exercise a deliberate and long-term calculative effort."

11. Rose 1999, 87. See also Giddens 1991, 3; 1994, 76 and Beck 1994, 14, 20, 25. Alberto Melucci (1996, 44) has similarly written that "choosing is the inescapable fate of our time."

12. Schwartz 2005, 44. Schwartz argues in his best-selling book *The Paradox of Choice* (cited earlier in this book by representatives of the gambling industry) that despite strong positive cultural associations between choice and freedom among economists, policy makers, social scientists, and citizens, added options do not necessarily enhance societies. Elsewhere, Schwartz notes that upper- and middle-class citizens in America tend to associate choice with freedom, action, and control, while working-class citizens tend to associate choice with fear, doubt, and difficulty (Schwartz, Markus, and Snibbe 2006, 14–15). See also Rosenthal 2005.

13. Along these lines, Slavoj Žižek identifies and questions the implicit assumption of theorists that citizens of "risk society" actually comport themselves as rational actors in the face of economic and existential contingencies (1998, 1999; see also Giddens 1991, 1994; Lash 1994). Finding similar fault with scholars who approach risk through the Foucauldian framework of "governmentality," Isin suggests that "the subject at the center of governing practices [should be] less understood as a rational, calculating and competent subject who can evaluate alternatives with relative success to avoid or eliminate risks and more as someone who is anxious, under stress and increasingly insecure and asked to manage its neurosis"—a subject, that is, whose governance proceeds as much "through affects that manage its anxieties" as through the mobilization of its rational capacities (2004, 225). See also Hunt 2003.

14. Goffman 1961, 18.

15. Bell 1973.

16. Hochschild 1983, 5, 11. Others have extended this analysis to the broader domain of "affective" or "immaterial" labor, terms intended to bring together

service labor, nonremunerated forms of care, and intellectual or cognitive forms of labor (Hardt 1999; Negri 1999; Terranova 2000; Dibbell 2006, 2007, 2008; Andrejevic 2009).

17. Quoted in Benston (2009).

18. Davis 2002.

19. Goffman 1967; Lesieur 1977; Custer 1984, 35–38. Women were largely ignored in the literature on problematic gambling until machine gamblers began to present themselves for treatment in the 1980s. Pathological gambling "appeared to affect only white, middle-aged, middle-class businessmen, who were more often Jewish than Catholic or Protestant, married, and the father of three children." Typically, they wagered on "horse races, cards, commodities or options, or casino games" (Lorenz 1987). An exception was Bergler's 1957 psychoanalytic account, in which he cast female gamblers as "frigid hysteric women who seem to treat gambling as they treat men, coldly and spongingly" (cited in Mark and Lesieur 1992, 553; for another exception see Reik's 1951 case study of a female compulsive poker player).

20. Lesieur (1988) first made the distinction between action-seeking and escape-seeking gamblers after he conducted interviews with fifty female gamblers in the late 1980s (for additional work on escape gambling see Jacobs 1988, 2000; Lesieur and Blume 1991; Mark and Lesieur 1992; Diskin and Hodgins 1999, 18). Hing and Breen (2001) compared female to male patterns of machine play and found that women were drawn to continuous forms of gambling and preferred to maximize playing time rather than the chances of winning. Others have found that women are typically drawn to gambling that provides safe and predictable environments, giving respite from daily life (Dixey 1987; Brown and Coventry 1998). While men have been increasingly shown to engage in escapist modes of play, women have not moved to action play in the same numbers. For additional work on gender and gambling, see Koza 1984; Lesieur and Blume 1991; Specker et al. 1996; Trevorrow and Moore 1998; McLaughlin 2000; Boughton and Falenchuk 2007.

21. Anthropologists and game scholars have found that online, virtual worlds can be rich social arenas replete with transactional commerce, governance, romance, vocations, shared meanings and values (Dibbell 2006; Malaby 2006; Taylor 2006; Boellstorff 2008; Turkle 2011). The zone of machine play is not a parallel world of exchange, but rather a world in which conventional value fades away.

22. Reith 1999, 146. As Baudrillard has written, "the secret of gambling is that money does not exist as value" (1990, 86).

23. Participants in a qualitative study on slot machine play in Australia argued that "winning straight away is no good." One said, "Hell, I don't want to win, I want to keep playing!" (Livingstone and Woolley 2008, 107). For behavioral research on the way in which big wins disrupts the flow of machine play, see Dickerson et al. 1992, 246.

24. Reith 2007, 42. Kocurek (2012) argues that the phenomenon of coin-operated video arcade gaming of the 1970s and 80s reflected the rise of credit culture and the new spending practices it demanded.

25. Livingstone 2005, 533.

26. Adams n.d., 35.

27. Livingstone 2005, 530; see also Adams, n.d.

28. The "chase" is gamblers' shorthand for "chasing losses," an expression that describes the race to regain what has been lost through further wagering (the opposite of "cutting losses"). For an extended discussion of the gambler's "chase" see Lesieur's book of that title, in which he wrote: "It is the chase that provides the initial push for the spiral the gambler becomes committed to and that gives the spiral velocity" (1977, 2). Lesieur's description of gamblers' narrowing "spiral of options" evokes Devereux's earlier phrase, "circle of despair." Devereux wrote of the gambler: "He sees himself getting in deeper and deeper; yet if he quits now, all this is irretrievably lost. The only way to get it back is to keep on playing" (Devereux 1949, 729).

29. Livingstone 2005, 533.

30. Lears 2003, 8; see also Lears 2008.

31. "This peculiar form of consumption appears as the consumption of nothing at all," writes Reith of gambling (2007, 51).

32. Contemporary machine gamblers are less involved in illegal money-acquisition schemes than the card and sports gamblers that Lesieur (1977) described, most likely because they are not part of a gambling social network or culture of bookmaking. The day-to-day life of machine addicts is more isolated, and their methods for acquiring money are more integrated with legitimate systems of consumer banking and credit.

33. For recent ethnographic accounts of how high-finance practices can cut value loose from its everyday social moorings, see LiPuma and Lee 2004; Zaloom 2006, 2009; Ho 2009; Lepinay 2011.

34. Livingstone 2005, 527.

35. Deleuze and Guattari 1987, 262.

36. Csikszentmihalyi 1994, 66, 67.

37. Reith 1999, 124, 122.

38. Ibid., 140.

39. Benjamin 1968 [1939], 178–79n11.

40. Goffman 1967, 156.

41. Borrell 2008, 213.

42. Thompson 1967.

43. See Harvey 1989; Giddens 1990; Virillio 1995; Castells 1996; Wacjman 2008.

44. Lesieur 1977, 14, emphasis mine.

45. Benjamin 1968 [1939], 155–200.

46. In 1984, Turkle made a similar observation of video games, noting that they "appeal because there are rules, a program, structure; play is structured according to an 'either/or' scheme that simplifies life" (Turkle 1984, 5, 13). One of the game players she spoke with told her: "You know what you are supposed to do. There's no external confusion, there's no conflicting goals, there's none of the complexities that the rest of the world is filled with. It's so simple. You either get through this little maze so that the creature doesn't swallow you up or you don't."

47. France 1902, 397, emphasis mine. A follower of Csikszentmihalyi has ventured to connect the desire for certainty to certain social contexts, noting that "if daily routines are threatening, uncertain, if existence in the world is insecure, then

recreation will be sought in another realm—in situations where … actors are largely freed from the necessity of choice" (Mitchell 1988, 45). He goes on to rephrase his insight in terms of the sociological concepts of alienation and anomie: "those who experience a surplus of certainty in their lives, those who are alienated, will seek uncertainty in play. On the other hand, those who view the world as mainly uncertain, that is, anomic persons, will seek certainty in recreation."

48. Goffman 1961, 261.

49. Terranova 2000, 54.

CHAPTER 8: OVERDRIVE

1. With Isabella's permission, I reprint an excerpt from her handwritten biographical exercise here.

2. Burke 1969, 14.

3. Freud 1961 [1920]. The problematic transhistoricism and universal psychologizing of psychoanalysis notwithstanding, Freud's work on repetition compulsion offers useful insights for thinking about the material in this chapter, and I draw upon it in that spirit. It should be noted that the analysis I offer departs from Freud's own interpretation of compulsive gambling as a reflection of fear and guilt around masturbation (Freud 1966 [1928]).

4. Freud 1961 [1920], 9–15.

5. Ibid., 55–56. Despite frequent misreadings, "the death drive cannot be equated with a simple death wish," notes Loose (2002, 135).

6. William Burroughs evokes the death drive when he writes that heroin "suspends the whole cycle of tension, discharge, and rest" (2004 [1959], 31). As Loose notes of Burroughs, "the regulating and containing effect of the pleasure principle was insufficient to pacify something in him. He did not want relief only from tension; *he wanted relief from the whole life-process*" (2002, 185, emphasis mine). In this sense, "addiction incarnates—and openly demonstrates—the beyond of pleasure" (ibid., 110).

7. Freud 1961 [1920], 32.

8. Although some scholars of gambling addiction have interpreted the zone as a richly symbolic interior space for the play of desire and imagination, the gambling addicts I spoke with described it along the lines of the death drive—something that is pure process and merging, with no corresponding space of interiority, relationality, or signification (Livingstone 2005; Adams n.d.). In Lacanian terms, they reject "the detour through the Other" (or the long and winding road of language) and instead seek direct access to "the One" (or "pure chance"), demanding an immediate answer "to the question of the destiny of life" (Loose 2002, 159). "Aiming for the One rather than the Other is a death drive," Loose goes on, "in the sense that reaching this aim would annihilate the Other and—therefore—the subject who is constituted in this field" (ibid.).

9. Loose 2002, 153.

10. "Loss has to win in their game," writes Loose of gambling addicts. "The end of the game will eventually arrive, and this end is the answer they desire.

Death is the radical answer to the question of their destination, which is what the game will eventually reveal for them" (2002, 157).

11. In one qualitative study of problem gamblers in Australia, "no respondents reported having a successful strategy for bringing a gambling session to a close. A clear majority of participants reported that a gaming session would only conclude when they had run out of money. 'You just go and get more money and come back,' and '[I'm] not satisfied until I've used everything' were typical of participants' comments. Most participants told us it was rare or uncommon for them to leave a venue with money, and those who had the self-control to leave with winnings, generally reported that they would come back the next day or the next opportunity (often on the same day) and gamble it all" (Livingstone and Woolley 2008, 106).

12. Bataille 1991, 25–26.

13. Addicts' lives, Loose notes, are "profoundly mixed-up with death"—yet not in a way that is wholly foreign to nonaddicts (Loose 2002, 138).

14. As Latour has described, artifacts' operational mechanisms, typically concealed, come to the fore when those artifacts break (1994; 1999). The computer scientist Rosalind Picard found this to be true in one of her studies on "affective computing," which showed that the biggest jump in user affect occurred not in the course of interaction with a game but when the technology suddenly stopped or malfunctioned, disrupting the flow of game play (Picard 1997, 163).

15. Harkening back to my discussion in the introduction on the degree to which addiction is attributable to subjects' internal dynamics or to the external mechanics of the substances and activities with which they interact, Loose reflects: "Drugs do have an effect. That is impossible to deny. The question is: Where is the effect located? Is it located in the drug or is it located in the psyche? If it is located in the psyche, what is it in the psyche that drugs react to or indeed interact with?" (Loose 2002, 116). While my own answer to this question emphasizes the interaction between machine and psyche (along with the environment in which that interaction unfolds), he concludes that the effect of a drug is ultimately located within the subject: "the force, once set in motion, acquires its own dynamic which is dependent on the energy characteristics of the individual" (119).

CHAPTER 9: BALANCING ACTS

1. Although Las Vegas has the most robust Gamblers Anonymous group nationally, state funding for problem gambling programs is only a fraction of that provided in many other states, and was not implemented until 2005, when a two dollar annual fee on each slot machine was contributed to treatment and prevention programs (Skolnik 2011). Recently, senators have moved to redirect these funds toward plugging the budget deficit and providing other services to citizens. The funds to problem gambling programs have been cut in half (Coolican 2009).

2. Meetings are offered from as early as 8 a.m. to as late as 9 p.m. Fifteen meetings are in Spanish. They are held at hospitals, strip malls, VA clinics, churches, and even power plants.

3. See the introduction. "As in many a capitalistic country," wrote one of the company's spokespeople in a press release, "the private sector has stepped to the forefront in treatment design and implementation" (Franklin n.d.).

4. Although Zyprexa (olanzapine) was not shown to reduce gambling behavior among video poker addicts and the results of the study were never published, Trimeridian accomplished its chief aim of proving to a major drug company (Eli Lilly) that it could run a competent drug trial.

5. Simpson 2000; Strow 2000. The clinic, which offers a six-week treatment program that runs four nights a week, received a $50,000 start-up grant from Station Casinos.

6. The handout Taber authored in the 1990s had been inspired by "a need to take an inventory of all addictive behaviors," as he put it (Taber 2001). His use of the word "inventory" echoes the tradition of the "moral inventory" in Alcoholics Anonymous and the financial inventory as a means of "taking stock" of one's worth.

7. In an edited volume titled *I Shop Therefore I Am: Compulsive Buying and the Search for Self*, authors similarly distinguish between disorders of spending and disorders of buying, among other forms of pathological shopping (Benson 2000).

8. Hunt 2003, 185. By the 1990s, over two hundred self-help groups modeled on Alcoholic Anonymous had been formed to help those who believed they were addicted to such activities as shopping, watching TV, exercising, eating, using computers, and having sex. A number of scholars have approached the expansion of addiction as a lens through which to consider the broader predicaments of late capitalism. Eve Sedgwick, in her essay "Epidemics of the Will," notes "the peculiarly resonant relations that seem to obtain between the problematic of addiction and those of the consumer phase of international capitalism" (1992). Along similar lines, Frederic Jameson has written of America that "no society has ever been quite so addictive, quite so inseparable from the condition of addictiveness as this one, which did not invent gambling, to be sure, but which did invent compulsive consumption" (2004, 52).

9. The concept of equilibrium as Rocky uses it here evokes a diverse set of expert meanings, from thermodynamics in physics, to economic concepts like the Nash equilibrium, to cybernetic theories of control and regulation, to ecological notions of systemic balance, to psychoanalytic understandings of how the pleasure principle and the death drive work to extinguish excitation and restore a state of rest (Freud 1961 [1920]; Bateson 1972). Although the state of equilibrium would seem at first glance to be contrary to the condition of addiction (which is associated with excess), in fact it plays a critical role in the addictive process (see chapter 4).

10. The idea of addiction as a liability continuous with normal human propensities is reflected in contemporary neuroscience, where dependency is increasingly understood as a potential all humans possess. This scientific normalization of addiction proposes that drugs and certain activities addict because they stimulate or "hijack" the same reward pathways as survival-linked behavior like sex, eating, and the formation of attachments to people and places (Bozarth 1990; Breiter

et al. 2001; Vrecko 2010). As Nikolas Rose (2003) argues, there has been a "mutation in the logic of the norm" such that addiction no longer carries the moral weight of deviancy but, rather, is understood as an error in neurochemical machinery (419).

11. Reith 2007, 48. The anthropologist Emily Martin (2004, 2007) makes a similar argument in her work on therapeutic engagements by individuals with mood disorders. The responsible citizen must engage in a "constant monitoring of health," writes Rose (1999, 234).

12. "Twelve-step" programs require recovering addicts to take certain steps to overcome their addictions. The first step, for example, is "to admit one has a problem."

13. The self-modulation that recovering gamblers are expected to pursue is different from the self-transformation expected in classical Greek and Christian regimes of self-care as Foucault has described them, involving "technologies of the self" that allowed individuals to "transform themselves in order to attain a certain state of happiness, purity, wisdom, or immortality" (Foucault 1988, 1990). Rose has noted the shift from self-transformation to self-modulation (2003). For further discussion of the way in which the classical ethical question of "how to live" gets reposed in contemporary technological societies, see Collier and Lakoff's (2005) discussion of "regimes of living" (see also Rabinow 1996; 1999; Fischer 1999, 2003; Biehl, Coutinho, and Outeiro 2004; Ong and Collier 2005, 8).

14. Dumit 2002, 126. For a similar argument using the term "neurochemical self," see Rose 2003. As Vrecko notes, contemporary psychotropic medications are not meant to *cure*, but to modulate the intensity and frequency of impulses (2010, 45).

15. In her analysis of mood charts as a means of self-regulation for individuals with mood disorders, Martin described how a visiting guest introduced himself at a support group, following the protocol that speakers choose a number on a scale from -5 to 5 to indicate their present mood status: "I'm Brad and I guess I must be zero" (Martin 2007, 187). His statement expressed the conception of health as a kind of zero state.

16. Valverde 1998, 175; see also Miller 2001. Peter Miller (2001) has described how the inculcation of management accounting practices has extended to the subjective domains of life, such that individuals deploy them to manage their inner states in a kind of responsible "self-accounting" (see also Martin 2004, 2007). The self-auditing that therapist Taber's inventory-taking exercise encourages exemplifies this.

17. Upon intake, each new client underwent a battery of tests that were used to code, evaluate, and manage their behavior. The dossier included the Human Behavior Questionnaire, the Addiction Severity Index, the Family Environment Scale, the Barratt Impulsivity Scale, the State-Trait Anxiety Inventory, the Beck Depression Inventory, the Dissociative Experiences Scale, and a variety of gambling-specific testing instruments.

18. As the anthropologist and cybernetic theoretician Gregory Bateson noted in his research among alcoholics in the 1960s, their use of alcohol was a "short cut to a more correct state of mind" (Bateson 1972, 309). Bateson's idea that

equilibrium is related to addiction shares qualities with the "need state" theory of gambling addiction (see Jacobs 1988, 2000), which proposes that gamblers seek to escape personal troubles and self-medicate negative feelings through gambling.

19. The medications gamblers mention target symptoms ranging from anxiety to depression to pain to attention disorders. There was not yet mention of opiate antagonists (such as "naltrexone") that were beginning in the 1990s to be tested and prescribed specifically to manage addictions, including pathological gambling; as Vrecko has noted, this latest development has been "paradigm-shifting" (Vrecko 2010, 42; see also Potenza 2001; Grant, Kim, and Potenza 2003; Grant et al. 2006). Trimeridian's drug trial, in which Zyprexa was tested on video poker addicts, was the only application of an antipsychotic medication to gambling addiction that I came across during my research (and even in this case, it was not clear whether the drug's antipsychotic properties or its mood-altering side effects were those that the trial's designers hoped could alleviate compulsive gambling).

20. For a similar analysis concerning the case of anorexia nervosa, see Gremillion 2001. The same self-control and calculative practices that allow the disorder to flourish (calorie counting, choosing from menus, constant surveillance, and manipulation of intake) are those called upon in the treatment process. As she notes, "medical practices can recreate forms of bodily control that help constitute anorexia in the first place" (ibid., 385).

21. Deleuze 2007, 153.

22. Lovell 2006, 138. The anthropologist Philippe Bourgois similarly describes how methadone patients "mix" the drug with a range of others, including "cocaine, wine, prescription pills, and even heroin" (2000, 170): "by strategically varying, supplementing, or destabilizing the effects of their dose with poly-drug consumption, methadone addicts can augment the otherwise marginal or only ambiguously pleasurable effects of methadone" (ibid., 180; see also Lovell 2006, 153).

23. Derrida 1981, 100.

24. See Rivlin 2004, 45. Given that seniors comprise 20 percent of the Las Vegas area population, many locals-oriented casinos find it in their interest to operate jitneys that shuttle back and forth to assisted living centers; one property transports 8,000 to 10,000 seniors per month. "We're happy to take the people that are handicapped in any way, oxygen tanks, walkers. We do a lot of that. We have a lot of wheelchairs," said a casino shuttle driver for Arizona Charlie's (quoted in Rivera 2000).

25. In his history of "limbic capitalism," Courtwright draws our attention to the many new goods and services that derive secondary profit from bad habits associated with consumer products such as food and drugs (e.g., the diet industry, drug rehabilitation, nicotine patches, and the like), noting that "logically, the demand curves for the two sorts of products are correlated" (2005, 212).

26. Rose 1999, 259, 263. Keane has similarly characterized addiction as the "constitutive outside to domains of health" (2002, 8).

27. Rose 2003, 431. Vrecko calls such interventions "civilizing technologies," for they work to "produc[e] states in which individuals are healthier, more re-

sponsible and more able to adhere to the duties, expectations and obligations of their families and societies" (2010, 45).

28. As the historian Colin Gordon reminds us: "Whereas homo economicus originally meant that subject the springs of whose activity must remain forever untouchable by government, the American neo-liberal *Homo economicus* is manipulable man, man who is perpetually responsive to modifications in his environment" (1991, 43). We might call this model *Homo addictus*, in pointed distinction to the self-interested figure of *Homo economicus* (Schüll 2006).

CHAPTER 10: FIX UPON FIX

1. Panelist for "Games and Expectations: The Slot Floor of the Future," G2E 2004. As Jan McMillen (2009) describes, in Australia the question of gambling's morality has not had the same weight as in North America; instead, the focus has been on "which forms of gambling should be permitted and which should be restricted" (93).

2. PC 1999. In 2001 Queensland's government decreed that electronic gambling machines could not accept denominations over $20. Victoria's Gaming Legislation Act of 2002 banned $100 note acceptors, banned autoplay features, prohibited machine spin rates over 2.14 seconds, mandated a 1.5 second "idle time" between spins, set maximum bet limit at $10, and required that machines display information on odds of winning as well as amount of time and money a player had spent (see Blaszczynski, Sharpe, and Walker 2001; SACES 2005; Livingstone and Woolley 2008). The state of South Australia instituted the Game Approval Guidelines in 2003, requiring the assessment of any new game features or characteristics "likely to lead to an exacerbation of problem gambling" (www.iga .sa.gov.au, Appendix 5.0, accessed July 2008).

3. PC 2010. Current regulatory measures in Australian states include caps on machine numbers, overnight closing of gambling establishments, episodic shutdowns of slot areas, mandatory twenty-minute breaks after every two hours of straight play, limits on maximum bet amounts, limiting or banning the number of ATM machines, lowering ATM withdrawal limits, reimbursing winnings over $300 in the form of a check (rather than allowing immediate rebetting), and more.

4. For more on the rise of a "risk management" regulative philosophy in contemporary capitalist societies, see Ewald 1991; Castel 1991; O'Malley 1996; Garland 2003. For discussions of this philosophy in relation to gambling in particular, see Reith 2008; Cosgrave 2009, 2010.

5. This statement appeared in a 2010 white paper called "Demystifying Slot Machines" (Stewart 2010, 18), authored by a lawyer in the firm that represents the AGA.

6. See Reith 2008, 150; Volberg and Wray 2007, 67; Borrell 2008.

7. Ulrich Beck, the preeminent sociologist of modern "risk society," poses a similar set of questions in his own reflections: "Who is to define and determine the harmfulness of products, the danger, the risks? Where does the responsibility lie—with those who generate the risks, those who benefit from them, those who

are potentially affected by them, or with public agencies?" (Beck 2006, 78; see also Orford 2005).

8. At the close of its research, the commission recommended a moratorium on the expansion of legalized gambling to permit more research on its consequences (Gerstein et al. 1999). As a result of pressure from industry lobbyists and groups such as the AGA, along with lack of leadership by members of the commission after disbanding, its recommendations went unheeded. For a more detailed discussion, see Volberg 2001.

9. Frank Fahrenkopf was long-standing chairman of the Republican National Committee. Under his leadership (for which he is paid a salary and compensation package of over $2 million per year), the gambling industry has become one of the biggest political players in the country, through intensive lobbying efforts and by bankrolling political campaigns. Between 1992 and 2002, the gambling industry increased its contributions to political campaigns tenfold, to $15 million. After the passage of campaign refinance reform in 2002, soft money contributions were replaced by increased donations from individuals, and from political action committees (Smith 2003; Benston 2004). In 2008 the industry spent $26 million on federal lobbying and $17 million in campaign contributions to PACs and to federal legislative candidates (the top three spenders were MGM-Mirage, Harrah's, and Station Casinos) (Skolnik 2011). Fahrenkopf (2010) notes that recent Supreme Court rulings have undone campaign finance reform, expanding the sort of political advocacy in which the industry can engage. "Going forward," he notes, "the America Gaming Association can indirectly support political candidates without regard to contribution limits imposed on the AGA political action committee. In addition, the AGA can participate in or support coalitions that sponsor independent political advertisements" (18).

10. AGA website (www.americangaming.org/Press/speeches/speeches_detail.cfv ?ID=88, accessed January 2008). Industry analysts and critics often use the "Achilles heel" terminology in reference to gambling addiction.

11. "The arrangements for gambling research in the USA today," notes one scholar of gambling, "are reminiscent of those for the alcohol field in the 1940s and 1950s, when the alcohol industry and academic entrepreneurs seeking funding from it were able to reach an implicit agreement to limit the research focus to the causes of 'alcoholism', a mysterious disease confined to a small fraction of the population" (Room 2005; see also Volberg 2001, 87–91). That fraction has been kept small in part, he points out, by incremental increases in the threshold number of criteria required to meet the pathological gambling diagnosis—from three in 1980, to four in 1987, to five in 1994 (APA 1980; 1987; 1994). A 299-page report by a group of respected scholars notes of the industry's position: "The usual stance is that pathological gambling is a rare mental disorder that is predominantly physically and/or psychologically determined" (Abbott et al. 2004, 53). See also Vrecko 2007, 57.

12. Bybee 1988, 304; Castellani 2000, 130, 125.

13. While the 1980 version of the DSM used the language "*unable* to resist impulses," this was changed to "*failure* to resist impulses" in the 1987 revision of the manual (APA 1987). As Castellani discusses, this change in language (not

to mention the initial classification of the condition under "Impulse Control Disorders") had to do with concerns that the diagnosis could be used as the basis for insanity pleas in courts of law (2000, 125). For more on the "pathological gambling" diagnosis, see the introduction.

14. See Brandt (2007) for an exhaustive history of the tobacco industry and its strategic positioning toward the question of smoking addiction. One aspect of this positioning was the establishment of the Tobacco Industry Research Council, set up in 1954 as an "industry shield" (ibid., 333). Later the council encouraged research on the genetics of nicotine addiction, hoping that a hereditary link would turn attention away from factors of exposure and use.

15. NCRG website (www.ncrg.org/, accessed January 2009).

16. Gary Loveman, speaker for keynote panel "State of the Industry," G2E 2003.

17. Shaffer, Hall, and Vander Bilt 1999. See introduction endnotes for a discussion of the challenges involved in accurately measuring the prevalence of gambling problems, including whether to measure for "current" or "lifetime" problems.

18. Howard Shaffer, quoted in Gold and Ferrell (1998, A1, A8–A10).

19. Although the AGA touts its board as a balance between industry and non-industry members, "four of ten non-industry representatives have financial ties to the industry that are not disclosed in the NCRG publications or federal tax forms," the *Boston Globe* found in 2004 (Mishra 2004).

20. AGA website (www.americangaming.org/programs/responsiblegaming/history.cfm, accessed January 2009).

21. Personal communication with Lesieur (2008) and Rosenthal (2000); see also Mishra (2004).

22. Critics point out that Harvard's "arrangement with the gambling industry is in a different class" than arrangements involving pharmaceutical funding of research at medical schools, since, in the latter case, there is "a common interest in finding treatments" (Mishra 2004). The gambling industry's product, by contrast, "has nothing to do with healing patients."

In 2009, NCRG changed the name of its grant-making body to the Institute for Research on Gambling Disorders. The institute is no longer run from Shaffer's division at Harvard (it is now housed in Washington, DC, in the same building as the AGA, not far from the White House), although he continues to receive substantial funding as one of a handful of designated "Centers of Excellence in Gambling Research."

23. NCRG fact sheet (http.ncrg.org/press_room/factsheet.cfm, accessed January 2009). Despite its emulation of the National Institute of Health's (NIH) peer-review and funding structure, the NCRG has repeatedly declined to support a congressional bill that would have given the NIH $20 million for research on gambling addiction and $50 million more for treatment and prevention.

24. Henry Lesieur, quoted in Strickland (2008). As Vrecko points out, although other research is not explicitly ineligible, there is a fundamental structural bias at work such that "projects which seem likely to produce findings supportive of the agenda of the NCRG, and the gambling industry, are those which become possible to carry out" (Vrecko 2007, 59).

25. Christine Reilly, quoted in Strickland (2008).

26. At the same time that the NCRG was founded, Howard Shaffer and his staff at Harvard became the editors for the *Journal of Gambling Studies*, the most established of the field's journals. A 2000 statistical analysis of articles published in the journal found that very little attention was paid to psychological, sociological, economic, political, and cultural factors; instead, "the gambling object of investigation created is the neurotransmitter, the neurological tangle, the biochemical imbalance, the cognitive impairment" (Castellani 2000, 51–52; 60; see also Borrell 2008, 69–71). For a contemporary sociological analysis of the relationship between the gambling industry and neuroscience, including a discussion of the role of the NCRG in funding research, see Vrecko 2007.

27. Shaffer, Hall, and Vander Bilt 1999; Shaffer, LaBrie, and LaPlante 2004a; Shaffer 2005; LaPlante and Shaffer 2007. The "adaptation hypothesis" is presented as an alternative to the "exposure hypothesis" (also called the "access" or "availability" hypothesis), which predicts that the prevalence of problem gambling increases with increasing exposure to gambling machines. The adaptation hypothesis allows that there will be spikes in the development of gambling problems when individuals in a given area are newly exposed to gambling, but argues that "after the novelty of initial exposure, people gradually adapt to the risks and hazards associated with potential objects of addiction" (Shaffer 2005, 1228). The majority of research, however, continues to find that problem gambling prevalence is directly related to the availability and accessibility of gambling. In a recent meta-analysis by three researchers, one of whom is a former proponent of the adaptation hypothesis, "strong statistically meaningful relationships were found for an increase in prevalence with increasing per capita density of [gambling machines], consistent with the access hypothesis" (Storer, Abbott, and Stubbs 2009, 225). Although the authors found a marginal decrease in prevalence when there was no change in the density of machines (an effect some have linked to a rise in treatment and prevention programs rather than "natural adaptation"), they did not find that prevalence would plateau or decline in the face of increasing access to machines (ibid., 239). See also Abbott and Volberg 1996; Volberg 1996; Room, Turner, and Ialomiteanu 1999; National Research Council 1999; PC 1999; Gerstein et al. 1999; Grun and McKeigue 2000;Gambling Review Body 2001; Welte et al. 2004; Orford 2005. For more on how prevalence measurements confound this debate, see the introduction.

28. Gold and Ferrell 1998, A-1.

29. Quoted in Dyer (2001); Rivlin 2004, 47.

30. Shaffer 2004, 10.

31. Luntz, owner of a company called The Word Doctors, defines his skills as those of "testing language and finding words that will help his clients sell their product or turn public opinion on an issue" ("Interview with Frank Luntz," 2007, PBS Frontline, www.pbs.org/wgbh/pages/frontline/shows/persuaders/interviews/luntz.html, accessed March 2007).

32. The research he cites is that of Vander Bilt et al. 2004; see also Shaffer 2005. As a critic points out, "I am sure there are many other ways of increasing heart rate, not all of them to be encouraged" (Orford 2005).

33. Phil Satre, quoted in AGA (2006, n.p.). Starting in 2011, the NCRG and the G2E were located in the very same exposition space.

34. Gambling researchers besides myself have pointed out that the discourse of responsible gambling runs counter to the notion of problem gambling as a disease in its suggestion that "anyone is at risk of gambling irresponsibly," and that "normal gambling" is something that must be practiced by consumers (Campbell and Smith 2003, 14; Cosgrave 2009, 60; 2010, 128). The determinist language of medicalization and the agent-based language of responsibility, although contradictory, both contribute to the individualizing discourse of problem gambling presented by the gambling industry.

35. Shaffer 2005, 1229; appears also in LaPlante and Shaffer 2007, 621. For a criticism of the way in which the responsible gaming discourse seeks to shape gamblers' comportment by inculcating a certain orientation to risk, see Cosgrave 2009. As Rose (1999) discusses, the logic of risk requires the "responsibilization" of the individual; the downward diffusion of responsibility to gamblers, notes Reith (2008), echoes broader political and fiscal policies that focus on "the choices, freedoms, preferences, and habits of individual consumers" rather than product design, supply, or availability; "the party who emerges as the main subject of notions of responsibility is the individual gambler" (151; see also Campbell and Smith 2003).

36. See the introduction.

37. Schellinck and Schrans 1998, 11.

38. Tracy Schrans, interviewed by Lane, 2006.

39. Cosgrave 2009, 60.

40. "To make optimal choices, individuals must have the opportunity to be fully informed of the set of alternative choices available to them," write four proponents of the approach (Blaszczynski et al. 2008).

41. Eggert 2004, 286.

42. See chapter 3. Eggert 2004, 220, 233–38, 266. Typically, the theoretical payout or return to player percentage is based on one million spins.

43. Eggert 2004, 267. When Australia's 2010 governmental commission tested one video slot machine, they determined that "just moving from 1 hour to 16 hours of play" reduced the rate of winning from 30 percent to 7 percent, while "at 64 hours of play, less than 1 percent of people win—and when they do, not by much" (PC 2010, 11.8). Although the churn effect will not happen if a gambler wins a "life-changing jackpot" too large to gamble back in the same session, the more likely scenario is that wins are relatively small and will be played back until they are gone (see also Turner and Horbay 2004, 20; Turner 2011; chapter 4).

44. See Weatherly et al. 2004; Turner 2011.

45. Blaszczynski et al. 2008, 114–15. Lawyer and consumer protection advocate Eggert concedes that educational disclosure and its "informational remedies," while they can prevent individuals from becoming problem gamblers in the first place, might not help those already caught in machines. Nevertheless, there is some evidence of the success of treatments for gambling addiction involving cognitive restructuring to modify irrational expectations (e.g., Ladouceur et al. 2001; Ferland, Ladouceur, and Vitaro 2002).

46. For examples and criticisms, see Gaboury and Ladouceur 1989; Walker 1992; Ladouceur and Walker 1996; Eggert 2004, 255–56; Delfabbro 2004; Livingstone and Woolley 2008, 139; Blaszczynski et al. 2008; Bennis n.d.; Adams n.d. As sociologist Reith notes: "Cognitive explanations of problem gambling,

and the forms of treatment that are based on them, are founded on a model of rational economic action in which individuals make informed decisions based on calculations of the benefits and risks of various forms of activity" (2007, 43).

47. Blaszczynski et al. 2008, 112.

48. Ibid., 109. For an argument in favor of "precautionary" over "evidence-based" approaches to the regulation of slot machine gambling, see MacNeil 2009; PC 2010, Overview. The precautionary approach follows the idea that "action should be taken to protect consumers and communities in advance of conclusive evidence that harm will occur" (McMillen 2009, 111) and that it is those who profit from a product, rather than the public, who should bear the onus of proving product safety.

49. One researcher has developed this idea in relation to gambling environments and technologies, writing that "careful study of the structure of the environment shows that many judgments that have been labeled errors are in fact adaptive.... [T]he mistakes are promoted by misleading characteristics of the environment rather than substandard thinking" (Bennis n.d., 3). The same author and his colleagues elsewhere write that the source of gamblers' cognitive shortcomings "lies not so much in biased or irrational thinking, but rather in the gamblers' environment and their interactions with it. Specifically, there is a mismatch between the (otherwise usually adaptive) heuristics used by gamblers on the one hand, and the structure of the casino environment on the other." They suggest that this mismatch arises "because it is in the casinos' interest for this mismatch to exist, and they construct the gamblers' environment so that it does" (Bennis et al. n.d.).

50. Although informational measures such as product warning labels can imply retroactive industry liability, they can serve to protect product manufacturers as much as consumers (Jain 2006, 164n31; Brandt 2007, 277, 322). "Once the purchaser is informed of a danger," a lawyer for the tobacco industry once noted, "the burden of any injuries incurred from that danger would shift to him" (quoted in Brandt 2007, 322).

51. Two researchers reported that industry members had voiced these concerns upon hearing their presentation on pop-up messaging (Monaghan and Blaszczynski 2009).

52. Bernhard, Lucas, and Jang 2006, 516. Bernhard and coauthor Fred Preston write: "If it is true that problem gamblers suffer from substantial and irrational cognitive distortions during their gambling activities, it follows that this is not the most opportune time to intervene upon them by introducing rational mechanisms" (2004, 1402–03). See also Sharpe et al. 2005; Borrell 2008, 210. Ladouceur finds that "two distinctive cognitive sets about gambling can be present in the gambler's mind, one rational outside the game session and an irrational one triggered by the characteristics of the game" (2004, 557).

53. Dickerson 2003, 40. Some products "contravene the definition of rational behavior," the anthropologist Jain notes in her study on product liability law, compromising the capacities of consumers to behave responsibly; such products' "bending of options and preferences sits uneasily with the invocation of free choice," she goes on (2006, 127, 17). "When the product turns out to have addictive properties," Brandt asks in his work on nicotine, "how does this change our

perception of responsibility?" (2007, 355). As Reith points out, responsibility is defined as "being in charge or control; capable of rational conduct" (2008, 149).

54. Dickerson 2003, 40. Livingstone and Woolley 2008, 29.

55. For studies on harm minimization strategies, see Blaszczynski, Sharpe, and Walker 2001, 2003; SACES 2005; Sharpe et al. 2005; Livingstone and Woolley 2008.

56. IPART 2003; PC 2010, 13.4.

57. PC 2010 11.38.

58. Comments made as moderator for "Bells, Whistles, and Warnings: The Safe Gambling Machine," G2E 2006. Bernhard has drawn the comparison to automobiles elsewhere: "Much as the automobile industry did a generation ago, the global gaming industry is increasingly looking for research-based strategies that provide safety measures to protect those who need it" (quoted in Allen 2006). In his written study of safety modifications, Bernhard has voiced the fears of the industry, speculating that "these mechanisms could so frustrate the majority of "normal" gamblers that they decide to quit playing entirely" (Bernhard and Preston 2004, 1403). "Many of the do-gooders seem to assume that the answer to problem gambling lies in forcing the gaming industry to design machines that people do not want to play," commented the executive officer of the Australian Gaming Machine Manufacturers Association (Ferrar 2004, 29).

59. Bernhard and Preston 2004.

60. Bernhard 2006, 22.

61. AGA 2008b, 1, 5.

62. Tracy Schrans, interviewed by Lane, 2006. Schrans's reference to "using as intended" evokes the language of product liability law.

63. PC 2009, xxvii.

64. Livingstone and Woolley 2008, 154. See also Hancock, Schellinck, and Schrans 2008, 61, 64.

65. Techlink website (www.techlinkentertainment.com, accessed June 2007). Techlink now calls the RGD "Gameplan," and the Nova Scotia Gaming Corporation has adopted it as the "Informed Player Choice System."

66. Livingstone and Woolley 2008, 31.

67. Norway has implemented a similar system, requiring that all gamblers register for an account (which can be revoked) through which they may set their own time and money limits. The difference in Norway is that the government itself sets a default limit above which gamblers cannot spend ($70 a day; $400 a month) and cuts them off when that limit has been reached. The company Aristocrat has also produced gambling machines with responsible gambling features, as required by certain Australian jurisdictions. Like Techlink's system, these features focus on information- and self-management for gamblers rather than machines' structural characteristics. For other such systems on the horizon internationally, see PC 2010, chapter 10.

68. Hancock, Schellinck, and Schrans 2008, 65. See also Schellinck and Schrans 2007, 101–4.

69. Bernhard 2006, 27. A Canadian study of the system likewise found that players more frequently used the voluntary features—yet when asked, those same gamblers were in favor of more involuntary requirements such as restrictive limit

setting and fewer ways to opt out of the features. They suggested, for instance, that they should be *shown* their account instead of choosing to see it, and that pop-up reminders should remain fixed on the screen for a certain length of time, or until they had responded to them (Omnifacts Bristol Research 2007, 66–68).

70. Bernhard 2006, 11, 20.

71. PC 2010, xxx.

72. Schellinck and Schrans 2007.

73. Ibid., 48; vii (see also 44, 53). See also Hancock, Schellinck, and Schrans 2008, 65.

74. Schellinck and Schrans 2007, 12, emphases in the original.

75. Ibid., 49.

76. Global Cash Access website (www.globalcashaccess.com/press_apr19_06 .html, accessed July 2007).

77. Crevelt and Crevelt 1988, 106.

78. Hildebrand 2006, 39.

79. Schellinck and Schrans 2007, 83, 84, emphases mine. Another report on the RGD similarly found that users preferred features that conveyed information about their play rather than those that "actively controlled their play" (Omnifacts Bristol Research 2007, 21).

80. Ibid., 34.

81. As electronic gambling spreads internationally, responsible gambling programs and their attendant regulatory logics are traveling as well, even to the East. A major Chinese lottery operator whose products include gambling machines, for example, has approached IGT for help designing a responsible gambling policy, specifically asking them to create technological mechanisms to encourage responsible gambling and help players "to cultivate disciplined gaming habits through the use of advanced software that can manage and effectively limit their expenses" (China LotSynergy website, www.chinalotsynergy.com/en/Social.html, accessed July 2009).

82. Sweden has implemented a system for its state-run online gambling network that works in the same manner as the risk-tracking algorithm operating in Saskatchewan. In anticipation of imminent widespread legalization of Internet gambling, similar systems have been developed to run on popular online gambling sites.

83. Hancock, Schellinck, and Schrans 2008, 61.

84. Austin 2007, 4.

85. Ibid., 13.

86. Hancock, Schellinck, and Schrans 2008, 63 (quoting Sasso and Kalajdzic 2007).

87. Ferguson 2008.

88. Austin 2007, 8. In its promotional literature iView warned the gambling industry: "The onus in the future will be on gaming operators to demonstrate to the public, as well as potentially to a court of law, that they have implemented all reasonable responsible gaming 'best practices' to protect the 'vulnerable.' They must be prepared to show due diligence and a duty of care to their customers [so as to] mitigate liability associated with problem gambling."

89. Binkley 2008, 192. Some casinos in the United States, after divorcing themselves from direct knowledge of patrons' banking information in this manner, purchased from ATM vendors the names of patrons making withdrawals at their casinos, to use this information in marketing campaigns. One casino in Illinois was fined $800,000 when its managers sent marketing promotions to problem gamblers who had voluntarily banned themselves from casinos; they defended their actions by pointing out that they had bought the list of names from the casino ATM vendors.

90. Benston 2006. Unlike its "Luck Ambassadors" system, Harrah's responsible gaming ambassadors do not use player tracking data to guide their patron "intercepts"; instead, they rely on more subjective impressions of gamblers' condition.

Conclusion: Raising the Stakes

1. Quoted in Rotstein (2009).
2. Quoted in Rivlin (2004, 74).
3. Quoted in Binkley (2008, 184, 197).
4. Binkley 2008, 194–95.
5. Ibid., 198.
6. Ibid.
7. Grout reflected on his job change: "One thing that was weird going from designing slot machines to designing software games for little kids was that it wasn't that big of a leap, in fact it was very similar. That really struck me. I saw it as appealing to the same part of the mind, a really simplistic instinct for distraction. Similar types of customers—toddlers and gamblers."

8. For a related discussion of how nuclear weapons scientists tolerate knowledge of the harmful effects of weapons they built, see Gusterson 1996. Unlike weapons, the products of the gambling industry are presented as playful and innocuous, lending themselves to a rhetoric of entertainment and a healthy economy.

9. Schuetz 2000.
10. Smith and Campbell 2007, 98.
11. Butterfield 2005. See also Goodman 1995b.
12. Quoted in Green (2004).
13. Smith 2008. See also Borrell 2008, 213.
14. See the introduction.
15. Stewart 2010, 2. The industry, he goes on, "is regulated more rigorously than banks, brokerage houses or insurance companies" (ibid., 5).
16. Ibid., 13. For more on near misses, see chapter 3.
17. Stewart 2010, 12.
18. The phrase "no ordinary commodity" is used by Babor (2003) in the title of his book on alcohol.
19. See chapter 3.
20. Borrell (2008, 116, 152) has used the term "system collusion" to describe the close relationship the gambling industry and its regulators.

21. Michael Cruz at the Pennsylvania gaming lab, quoted in Mangels (2011).

22. Mark Pace of WMS, panelist for "Slot Appeal: Applying New Technologies," G2E 2007.

23. Rose 1989.

24. In the absence of counteractive regulative mechanisms, systems that value maximization "will clearly operate at a greater and greater rate or intensity," the anthropologist Gregory Bateson wrote in his work among addicts in California; like steam engines without governors, they are liable to enter a state of runaway growth, and even to self-destruct (Bateson 1972, 447). Bateson saw this tendency not only in the California addicts among whom he conducted research, but also in the capitalist economic system and in global political affairs such as the armaments race. Scholars and journalists have since returned to his cybernetic-ecological framework to illuminate the systemic dynamics of modern-day problems such as addiction, obesity, global warming, and oil dependency. Although it would be remiss to subsume these richly distinctive phenomena under one diagnostic or analytic umbrella, each is sustained by the same sort of maximizing logic and infrastructure that Bateson described.

25. This statement has appeared repeatedly in the AGA's annual reports since 2009, and on its website (http.americangaming.org/industry-resources/research/fact-sheets/gaming-equipment-manufacturing, accessed May, 2011).

26. Panelist for "Selling the Sizzle: Slot Manufacturers Roundtable," G2E 2010.

27. In 2012, twelve states had racinos.

28. Panelist for "Gaming Expansion: Push and Pull Factors in 2008 and Beyond," G2E 2008.

29. For more on the globalization of the gambling industry in the 1990s, see McMillen 1996. For a similar account of the exportation of cigarette consumption to the developing world in the wake of domestic regulation, see Brandt 2007, part V.

30. Burke 2005. To accommodate restrictions against slot machines, the Mexican government classifies them as "video bingo terminals" and describes them as "technological aids for playing bingo" rather than stand-alone gaming devices (18). There is debate over whether these machines are bingo terminals, or actually Vegas-style slot machines, known as "tragamonedas."

31. Rutherford 2005b, 20. In Russia in the late 1990s, local authorities issued gambling licenses very liberally in anticipation of huge tax revenues; only a decade after their introduction, the country had some 500,000 machines, which could be found in public settings such as railroad stations, bus stops, grocery stores, clinics, community centers, and even apartment building lobbies. In 2009, to counter the rampant epidemic of problem machine gambling, Vladimir Putin reimposed state regulation over gambling, sweeping casinos and slot machines from the streets of Russian cities and concentrating gambling into four regional gaming colonies in remote areas.

32. In the last chapter we closely examined regulatory policies in Australia and Canada; also notable for its regulatory approach is England, which strictly curtails casino promotion and marketing (in accordance with a philosophy of "unstimulated demand") and Norway, where the government sets stringent default time and money limits on play in its state-run casinos. In 2005, Switzerland com-

pletely removed slot machines from the wider community after their wide rollout in the 1990s. Singapore enforces gamblers' self-exclusion as in the States, but also allows regulators and police officers to ban individuals who have been on welfare or declared bankruptcy. Additionally, the government mandates a policy of "family exclusion" whereby individuals can exclude their relatives from casinos; all other citizens must pay steep entrance fees. In South Korea only one of fourteen casinos is open to locals, and it features a gambling treatment center in the parking lot. North Korea and Egypt ban their own citizens from casinos. In many other parts of the world, regulations are far more lax than in the United States. In these diverse regulatory climates, slot machine manufacturers and gambling companies exercise what anthropologist Adriana Petryna, writing on another topic, has called "ethical variability" (Petryna 2009).

33. As Hancock and colleagues note, despite state, regional, or national specifications in regulatory standards and guidelines for machine gambling, "the cross-jurisdictional similarities outweigh the differences in gaming products" (Hancock, Schellinck, and Schrans 2008, 63; see also McMillen 2009).

34. Mike Macke of Cadillac Jack casino, quoted in Burke (2005, 19, emphasis mine).

35. Sheldon Adelson, quoted in Fasman (2010, 5).

36. Anderer 2006, 4.

37. Panelist for "Future Watch: Electronic Gaming in the 21st Century," G2E 2007.

38. Lindsey Stewart, panelist for "A Growing Game: Slot Operators Roundtable," G2E Asia 2010.

39. Simon Liu, Vice President of Business Development at Jumbo Technology, panelist for "Faux Tables: New Intersection of Electronic Gaming," G2E 2010. Machines are regarded as "hungry tigers" whose hidden, internal processes are not to be trusted (see also Jalal 2008).

40. Legato 2008. The revenue statistics are from Macau Gaming Inspection and Coordination Bureau.

41. Lindsey Stewart, panelist for "A Growing Game: Slot Operators Roundtable," G2E Asia 2010.

42. Grochowski 2007, 36.

43. Simon Liu, vice president of Business Development at Jumbo Technology, panelist for "Faux Tables: New Intersection of Electronic Gaming," G2E 2010.

44. Jasbir Hsu, president of Jumbo Technology, panelist for "Evolution or Revolution: How Technology Will Impact Asian Casinos," G2E Asia 2010.

45. Catherine Burns, vice president and managing director of Asia Pacific Bally Technologies, panelist for "Evolution or Revolution: How Technology Will Impact Asian Casinos," G2E Asia 2010.

46. Macomber and Student 2007b.

47. Shuffle Master's table machines Table Master and Lightning Poker, for instance, double the number of hands played per hour. Table machines are additionally profitable in jurisdictions where properties are restricted in the number of machines they are allowed to own, because these machines often count as one giant slot machine despite their multiple seats.

48. Downey 2007.

49. Ibid.

50. AGA 2009; see also Skolnik 2011, especially chapter 5. The first online gambling site launched in 1995 and within ten years there were over two thousand in operation. Although the legality and governance of online gambling has been highly controversial in the United States and continues to remain so at the Federal level, a 2011 policy change at the Department of Justice makes it legal for states to institute online poker. Industry analysts expect that the recent financial crisis will drive a push for the legalization of online gambling.

51. Grochowski 2007, 37.

52. Ibid., 36.

53. In addition to playing multiple tables at one time, online gamblers may also spin slot machine reels in between hands, in the right hand corner of their screens—a scenario that electronic table games mimic. "This multitasking thing is how you can keep your six year old son future gamer interested; it's really compelling to the player," said Peter Shoebridge of Blue Yonder Gaming, panelist for "Networked Gaming, Part II: State of the Industry," G2E 2010.

54. See Shaffer 2004 for a study on Internet gambling. In another study, one out of every four online gamblers in the group of college students fit the clinical definition of pathological gambler (Griffiths and Barnes 2008).

55. Schwartz 2006, 55.

56. Cotte and Latour 2009. Aside from this study, there has been little research on the consumer experience of online gambling.

57. Quoted in Rivlin (2007). See also Roemer 2007, 40; Russell 2007, 94.

58. Ryan Griffin of IGT, panelist for "Brave New World: Emerging Games and Alternative Technologies," G2E 2008. "For generations raised in relatively high-technology environments and used to immersion in computer-generated games," predicted industry expert Andrew MacDonald, "games of the future will be tailored ... with an eye toward delivering customers back to their childhood" (quoted in Ward 2005, 26). In a reverse movement, children's toys imitate adult gambling; at Toys-R-Us one finds "big screen poker" and "big screen slot" toys for ages eight and up, and video slot versions featuring "5 reels and 9-line betting plus an animated bonus round for big points." The toys put "the fun of casino slot machine play right in the palm of your hand" (company website, accessed June 2007).

59. "WMS Showcases" 2008.

60. Gene Johnson Spectrum Gaming, moderator for "The Hand-Held Casino: How Wireless Gaming Can Increase Revenues," G2E 2010.

61. Goffman 1967, 27.

62. Hannigan 1998, 71. "The attraction of gambling is not risk but certainty; it is an escape into order," write the authors of the book *The Business of Risk* (Abt, Smith, and Christiansen 1985, 122). We recall the suggestion made by the psychologist Clemens France in 1902 that despite seeming evidence to the contrary, the impulse to gamble expresses a desire to dispel uncertainty with "a longing for the firm conviction of assurance for safety" (France 1902, 397).

63. Cosgrave 2008, 3, 85. "The gambling industry *does not gamble*," writes Turner (2011, 609) See also Smith and Campbell 2007, 97.

64. Hacking 1990. Lears makes a similar observation in his historical analysis of twentieth-century industrial managers, noting that their attempts to "minimize risk and to control a steady stream of profitability" did not mean that they shied away from risk and economic uncertainty, but instead, that they transferred "real risk" onto workers and thereby safely insulated themselves from it (Lears 2003, 322). The scenario he describes is not unlike the asymmetrical transfer of risk from gambling industry to gambler.

65. Reiner 2007, 3; see chapter 4. It should be noted that gambling and insurance have not always been distinguished in the law. It was not until the 1870s that life insurance was viewed as a legitimate investment rather than a form of gambling (Zelizer 1979; O'Malley 2003). As O'Malley writes: "Risk and certainty appear to be distinct species of governmental technology, but ones that are readily capable of being braided together and perhaps even hybridized" (2003, 250).

66. Ibid., 124, 125.

67. Philosopher of technology Jonas has noted that technological "innovation is disequilibrating rather than equilibrating with respect to the balance of wants and supply" (Jonas 2010 [1979]).

References

Abbott, Max. 2006. "Do EGMs and Problem Gambling Go Together like a Horse and Carriage?" *Gambling Research* 18: 7–38.

Abbott, Max, and D. Clarke. 2007. "Prospective Problem Gambling Research: Contribution and Potential." *International Gambling Studies* 7 (1): 123–44.

Abbott, Max, and R. Volberg. 1996. "The New Zealand National Survey of Problem and Pathological Gambling." *Journal of Gambling Studies* 12 (1): 43–160.

———. 2000. "Taking the Pulse on Gambling and Problem Gambling in New Zealand: A Report on Phase One of the 1999 National Prevalence Survey." Wellington, New Zealand: Department of Internal Affairs.

———. 2006. "The Measurement of Adult Problem and Pathological Gambling." *International Gambling Studies* 6 (2): 175–200.

Abbott, Max. M., R. Volberg, M. Bellringer, and G. Reith. 2004. "A Review of Research on Aspects of Problem Gambling: Final Report." Prepared for the Responsibility in Gambling Trust, UK. Auckland, New Zealand: Gambling Research Centre, Auckland University of Technology.

Abt, Vicki, J. F. Smith, and E. M. Christiansen. 1985. *The Business of Risk: Commercial Gambling in Mainstream America.* Lawrence: University Press of Kansas.

Adams, Peter. N.d. "Gambling, Finitude, and Transcendence: Explaining the Psychological 'Zone' Generated during Frequent Gambling." Unpublished article.

AGA (American Gaming Association). 2003. "State of the States: The AGA Survey of Casino Entertainment." A survey prepared by Luntz Research Co. and Peter D. Hart Associates, Washington, DC.

———. 2006. "NCRG Conference to Focus on Turning Research into Best Practices." *Responsible Gaming Quarterly,* Fall, www.americangaming.org/rgq/rgq_detail.cfv?id=411, accessed July 2007.

———. 2007. "State of the States: The AGA Survey of Casino Entertainment." A survey conducted for the American Gaming Association, Washington, DC.

———. 2008a. "State of the States: The Survey of Casino Entertainment." A survey conducted for the American Gaming Association, Washington, DC.

———. 2008b. "Comments of the American Gaming Association Poker Machine Harm Minimization Bill." Community Affairs Committee of the Australian Senate, www.aph.gov.au/senate/committee/clac_ctte/poker_machine_harm _minimisation/submissions/sub02.pdf, accessed August 2008.

———. 2009. "State of the States: The AGA Survey of Casino Entertainment." A survey conducted for the American Gaming Association, Washington, DC.

———. 2010. "Taking the Mystery out of the Machines: A Guide to Understanding Slot Machines." A brochure produced by the AGA, Washington, DC.

———. 2011. "State of the States: The Survey of Casino Entertainment." A survey conducted for the American Gaming Association, Washington, DC.

AIGR (Australian Institute for Gambling Research). 2001. *Survey of the Nature and Extent of Gambling and Problem Gambling in the ACT.* University of Western Sydney, Australia.

Akrich, Madeline. 1992. "The Description of Technical Objects." In *Shaping Technology / Building Society: Studies in Sociotechnical Change*, edited by W. Bijker and J. Law, 205–24. Cambridge, MA: MIT Press.

Akrich, Madeline, and B. Latour. 1992. "A Summary of a Convenient Vocabulary for the Semiotics of Human and Nonhuman Assemblies." In *Shaping Technology / Building Society: Studies in Sociotechnical Change*, edited by W. Bijker and J. Law, 259–64. Cambridge, MA: MIT Press.

Allen, Todd D. 1992. "Successful New Gambling Entries: Planning, Execution, and Competitive Response." In *Essays in Business, Economics, Philosophy and Science*, edited by W. Eadington and J. Cornelius, 3–12. Reno: University of Nevada Press.

Allen, Tony. 2006. "High Stakes Research." *Innovation* (Winter): 20–23.

Anderer, Charles. 2006. "As the World Turns." *International Gaming and Wagering Business* 27 (2): 4.

Anderson, Kurt. 1994. "Las Vegas, USA." *Time*, January 10.

Andrejevic, Mark. 2007. *iSpy: Surveillance and Power in the Interactive Era.* Lawrence: University Press of Kansas.

———. 2009. "Exploitation in the Digital Enclosure." Paper presented at The Internet as Playground and Factory, The New School for Social Research. New York City.

APA (American Psychiatric Association). 1980. DSM-III: *Diagnostic and Statistical Manual of Mental Disorders*, 3rd ed. Washington, DC: American Psychiatric Association.

———. 1987. DSM-III-R: *Diagnostic and Statistical Manual of Mental Disorders*, 3rd ed., rev. Washington, DC: American Psychiatric Association.

———. 1994. DSM-IV: *Diagnostic and Statistical Manual of Mental Disorders*, 4th ed. Washington, DC: American Psychiatric Association.

———. 2000. DSM-IV-TR: *Diagnostic and Statistical Manual of Mental Disorders*, 4th ed., text-revision. Washington, DC: American Psychiatric Association.

Arendt, Hannah. 1958. *The Human Condition*. Chicago: University of Chicago Press.

"Aristocrat Technologies to Display 140 Innovative Games and Products at 2003 Global Gaming Expo." 2003. *PRNewswire*, August 18, http2.prnewswire.com/cgi-bin/stories.pl?ACCT=104&STORY=/http/story/08-18-2003/0002002765&EDATE=, accessed June 2007.

"Aristocrat Technologies, Inc. Receives Key Product Approvals in Nevada, GLI Jurisdictions." 2005. *PRNewswire*, April 26, http.prnewswire.com/news-releases/aristocrat-technologies-inc-receives-key-product-approvals-in-nevada-gli-jurisdictions-54413047.html, accessed June 2007.

Austin, Michelle. 2007. "Responsible Gaming: The Proactive Approach / Integrating Responsible Gaming into Casino Environments." Prepared by iView Systems in Cooperation with the Saskatchewan Gaming Corporation, www.iviewsystems.com/assets/products/iCare_Responsible_GamingWhitepaper_V2.pdf, accessed August 2008.

Australian Bureau of Statistics. 2008. "Population by Age and Sex Australian States and Territories." Cat. No. 32010. A report prepared by the Office of Economic and Statistics, Queensland, Australia.

Australian Gambling Council. 2008. *Australian Gambling Statistics 1981–82 to 2006–07, 25th edition*. Australian Gambling Statistics, Queensland, Australia.

Babor, Thomas. 2003. *Alcohol and Public Policy: No Ordinary Commodity*. Oxford: Oxford University Press.

Bachelard, Gaston. 1969 [1958]. *The Poetics of Space*. Boston: Beacon Press.

Bacon, Katie. 1999. "The Net's Next Vice." *The Atlantic Online*, www.theatlantic.com/unbound/citation/wc990729.htm, accessed June 2007.

Balsamo, Anne. 1996. *Technologies of the Gendered Body: Reading Cyborg Women*. Durham, NC: Duke University Press.

Barash, Meyer. 1979 [1958]. Foreword to *Man, Play, and Games*. New York: Free Press of Glencoe.

Barrett, Larry, and S. Gallagher. 2004. "What Sin City Can Teach Tom Ridge." *Baseline Magazine*, April, http.baselinemag.com/c/a/Past-News/What-Sin-City-Can-Teach-Tom-Ridge/, accessed June 2007.

Barry, Andrew. 2006. "Technological Zones." *European Journal of Social Theory* 9 (2): 239–53.

Bataille, Georges. 1991. *The Accursed Share*. Vol. 1, *Consumption*. Translated by R. Hurley. New York: Zone Books.

Bateson, Gregory. 1972. *Steps to an Ecology of the Mind: Collected Essays in Anthropology, Psychiatry, Evolution, and Epistemology*. New York: Ballantine Books.

Baudrillard, Jean. 1988. "The System of Objects." *Art Monthly* 15 (April): 5–8.

Bauman, Zygmunt. 1991. *Modernity and Ambivalence*. Oxford: Polity.

Baumeister, Roy F. 1991. *Escaping the Self: Alcoholism, Spiritualism, Masochism, and Other Flights from the Burden of Selfhood*. New York: Basic Books.

Bechara, A. 2003. "Risky Business: Emotion, Decision-Making, and Addiction." *Journal of Gambling Studies* 19: 23–52.

Beck, Ulrich. 1992. *Risk Society: Towards a New Modernity*. London: Sage.

———. 1994. "The Reinvention of Politics: Towards a Theory of Reflexive Modernization." In *Reflexive Modernism: Politics, Tradition, and Aesthetics in Modern Social Order*, edited by U. Beck, A. Giddens, and S. Lash, 1–55. Stanford, CA: Stanford University Press.

———. 2006. "Risk Society Revisited: Theory, Politics, and Risk Programmes." In *The Sociology of Risk and Gambling Reader*, edited by J. F. Cosgrave, 61–84. New York: Routledge.

Beck, Ulrich, W. Bonss, and C. Lau. 2003. "The Theory of Reflexive Modernization: Problematic, Hypotheses, and Research Programme." *Theory, Culture, and Society* 20 (2): 1–33.

Beck, Ulrich, A. Giddens, and S. Lash. 1994. *Reflexive Modernism: Politics, Tradition, and Aesthetics in Modern Social Order*. Stanford, CA: Stanford University Press.

Becker, Howard. 1986. "Consciousness, Power, and Drug Effects." In *Doing Things Together: Selected Papers*, edited by H. Becker. Evanston, IL: Northwestern University Press.

Bell, Daniel. 1973. *The Coming of Post-Industrial Society: A Venture in Social Forecasting*. New York: Basic Books.

———. 1976. *The Cultural Contradictions of Capitalism*. New York: Basic Books.

Benjamin, Walter. 1968 [1939]. "On Some Motifs in Baudelaire." In *Illuminations: Essays and Reflections*, edited by H. Arendt, translated by H. Zohn, 155–200. New York: Schocken.

———. 1999. *The Arcades Project*. Translated by H. Eiland and K. McLaughlin. Prepared on the basis of the German volume edited by R. Tiedemann. Cambridge, MA: Belknap Press of Harvard University Press.

Bennett, William. 1996. *The Book of Virtues: A Treasury of Great Moral Stories*. New York: Simon and Schuster.

Bennis, William. N.d. "Environmental Design and Rational Choice: The Case of Casino Gambling," northwestern.academia.edu/WillBennis/Papers/111745/Environmental_Design_and_Rational_Choice_The_Case_of_Casino_Gambling, accessed November 2010.

Bennis, W. M., K. V. Katsikopoulos, D. G. Goldstein, A. Dieckmann, and N. Berg. N.d. "Designed to Fit Minds: Institutions and Ecological Rationality. In *Ecological Rationality: Intelligence in the World*, edited by P. M. Todd, G. Gigerenzer, and The ABC Research Group. New York: Oxford University Press. Forthcoming.

Benson, April Lane, ed. 2000. *I Shop, Therefore I Am: Compulsive Buying and the Search for Self*. Northvale, NJ: Jason Aronson.

Benston, Liz. 2004. "Political Donations Flow from Gaming Industry." *Business Las Vegas* October 15: 1.

———. 2006. "When Casinos Decide You're Losing Too Much Money." *Las Vegas Sun*, August 28, http.casinocitytimes.com/news/article/when-casinos-decide-youre-losing-too-much-money-160709, accessed November 2009.

————. 2009. "Illness Theory Gaining Ground for Gambling Addiction." *Las Vegas Sun*, November 23, http.lasvegassun.com/news/2009/nov/23/illness-theory -gaining-ground/, accessed November 2009.

Bergler, Edmund. 1957. *Psychology of Gambling.* New York: Hill and Wang.

Bernhard, Bo, D. R. Dickens, and P. D. Shapiro. 2007. "Gambling Alone: An Empirical Study of Solitary and Social Gambling in America." *Gaming Research and Review Journal* 11 (2), 1–13.

Bernhard, Bo, A. Lucas, and D. Jang. 2006. "Responsible Gaming Device Research." A report prepared by the Las Vegas International Gaming Institute. Las Vegas: University of Nevada.

Bernhard, Bo, and F. W. Preston. 2003. "On the Shoulders of Merton: Potentially Sobering Consequences of Problem Gambling Policy." *American Behavioral Scientist* 47 (11): 1395–405.

Berridge, Virginia, and G. Edwards. 1981. *Opium and the People: Opiate Use in Nineteenth-Century England.* London: St. Martin's Press.

Biehl, João. 2005. *Vita: Life in a Zone of Social Abandonment.* Berkeley: University of California Press.

Biehl, João, D. Coutinho, and A. L. Outeiro. 2004. "Technology and Affect: HIV/ AIDS Testing in Brazil." *Culture, Medicine, and Psychiatry* 25: 87–129.

Biehl, João, B. Good, and A. Kleinman, eds. 2007. *Subjectivity: Ethnographic Investigations.* Berkeley: University of California Press.

Biehl, João, and A. Moran-Thomas. 2009. "Symptom: Subjectivities, Social Ills, Technologies. *Annual Review of Anthropology* 38: 267–88.

Biggs, Lindy. 1995. "The Engineered Factory." *Technology and Culture* 36 (2): S174–S188.

Bijker, Wiebe E., and John Law, eds. 1992. *Shaping Technology / Building Society: Studies in Sociotechnical Change.* Cambridge, MA: MIT Press.

Binkley, Christina. 2008. *Winner Takes All: Steve Wynn, Kirk Kerkorian, Gary Loveman, and the Race to Own Las Vegas.* New York: Hyperion Press.

Blaszczynski, Alex. 2005. "Harm Reduction, Secondary Prevention and Approaches, and Trying to Make a Machine a Safer Product." *Journal of Gambling Issues* 15, jgi.camh.net/doi/full/10.4309/jgi.2005.15.4, accessed August 2008.

————. 2008. "Expert Report of Professor Alex Blaszczynski: In the Matter of Jean Brochu v. Loto Québec et al.—Class action. Available online at media. cleveland.com/metro/other/Blaszczynski%20expert%20deposition%20on %20slots%20addictiveness.pdf, accessed October 2011.

Blaszczynski, Alex, R. Ladouceur, L. Nower, and H. Shaffer. 2008. "Informed Choice and Gambling: Principles for Consumer Protection." *Journal of Gambling Business and Economics* 2 (1): 103–18.

Blaszczynski, Alex, N. McConaghy, and A. Frankova. 1990. "Boredom Proneness in Pathological Gambling." *Psychological Reports* 67 (1): 35–42.

Blaszczynski, A. and L. Nower. 2002. "A Pathways Model of Problem and Pathological Gambling." *Addiction* 97 (5): 487–99.

Blaszczynski, Alex, L. Sharpe, and M. Walker. 2001. "The Assessment of the Impact of the Configuration on Electronic Gaming Machines as Harm Minimization Strategies for Problem Gambling." A report prepared for the Gaming Industry Operator's Group. Sydney: University Printing Service.

————. 2003. "Harm Minimization in Relation to Gambling on Electronic Gaming Machines." Submission to the IPART (Independent Pricing and Regulatory Tribunal) Review. Sydney: University of Sidney Gambling Research Unit.

Boellstorff, Tom. 2008. *Coming of Age in Second Life: An Anthropologist Explores the Virtually Human*. Princeton, NJ: Princeton University Press.

Borrell, Jennifer. 2004. "Critical Commentary by an EGM Gambler." *International Journal of Mental Health and Addiction* 4 (2): 181–88.

Borgmann, Albert. 1984. *Technology and the Character of Contemporary Life: A Philosophical Inquiry*. Chicago: University of Chicago Press.

Borrell, Jennifer. 2008. "A Thematic Analysis Identifying Concepts of Problem Gambling Agency: With Preliminary Exploration of Discourses in Selected Industry and Research Documents." *Journal of Gambling Studies* 22: 195–217.

Boughton, Roberta, and O. Falenchuk. 2007. "Vulnerability and Comorbidity Factors of Female Problem Gambling." *Journal of Gambling Studies* 23: 323–34.

Bourgois, Philippe. 2000. "Disciplining Addictions: The Bio-Politics of Methadone and Heroin in the United States." *Culture, Medicine, and Psychiatry* 24: 165–95.

Bourgois, Philippe, and Jeffrey Schonberg. 2009. *Righteous Dopefield*. Berkeley: University of California Press.

Bourie, Steve. 1999. "Are Slot Machines Honest?" *American Casino Guide*, http://americancasinoguide.com/Tips/Slots-Honest.shtml, accessed December 2006.

Bozarth, Michael. 1990. "Drug Addiction as a Psychobiological Process." In *Addiction Controversies*, edited by D. Warburton, 112–34. London: Harwood Academic.

Brandt, Allan M. 2007. *The Cigarette Century: The Rise, Fall, and Deadly Persistence of the Product That Defined America*. New York: Basic Books.

Breen, Robert B. 2004. "Rapid Onset of Pathological Gambling in Machine Gamblers: A Replication." *eCommunity: The International Journal of Mental Health and Addiction* 2 (1): 44–49.

Breen, Robert B., and M. Zimmerman. 2002. "Rapid Onset of Pathological Gambling in Machine Gamblers." *Journal of Gambling Studies* 18 (1): 31–43.

Breiter, H. C., I. Aharon, D. Kahneman, A. Dale, and P. Shizgal. 2001. "Functional Imaging of Neural Responses to Expectancy and Experience of Monetary Gains and Losses." *Neuron* 30: 619–39.

Brigham, Jay. 2002. "Lighting Las Vegas: Electricity and the City of Glitz." In *The Grit beneath the Glitter: Tales from the Real Las Vegas*, edited by H. Rothman and M. Davis, 99–114. Berkeley: University of California Press.

Brock, Floyd J., G. L. Fussell, and W. J. Corney. 1992. "Predicting Casino Revenue Using Stochastic Migration Simulation." In *Gambling and Commercial Gaming: Essays in Business, Economics, Philosophy, and Science*, edited by W. Eadington and J. Cornelius. Reno: University of Nevada Press.

Brodie, Janet F., and M. Redfield, eds. 2002. *High Anxieties: Cultural Studies in Addiction*. Berkeley: University of California Press.

Brown, Sarah., and L. Coventry. 1997. "Queen of Hearts: The Needs of Women with Gambling Problems." Melbourne: Financial and Consumer Rights Council.

Bulkeley, William. 1992. "Video Betting, Called Crack of Gambling, Is Spreading." *Wall Street Journal*, July 14, B1.

Burbank, Jeff. 2005. *License to Steal: Nevada's Gaming Control System in the Megaresort Age*. Las Vegas: University of Nevada Press.

Burchell, Graham. 1993. "Liberal Government and the Techniques of the Self." *Economy and Society* 22 (3): 266–82.

Burke, Anne. 2005. "Que Pasa en Mexico? Quite a Lot." *International Gaming and Wagering Business* (December): 16–19.

Burke, Kenneth. 1969. *A Grammar of Motives*. Berkeley: University of California Press.

Burroughs, William. 2004 [1959]. *Naked Lunch*. New York: Grove Press.

Burton, Bill. N.d. "Slot Machine Ergonomics: Preventing Repetitive Stress Injury," casinogambling.about.com/od/slots/a/Ergonomics.htm, accessed June 2010.

Butterfield, F. 2005. "As Gambling Grows, States Depend on Their Cut." *New York Times*, March 31.

Bybee, Shannon. 1988. "Problem Gambling: One View from the Gaming Industry." *Journal of Gambling Studies* 4 (4): 301–8.

Caillois, Roger. 1979 [1958]. *Man, Play, and Games*. Translated by M. Barash. New York: Free Press of Glencoe.

Calabro, L. 2006. "Station Casino's Glenn Christenson," *CFO Magazine*, July 1, www.cfo.com/printable/article.cfm/7108950/c_7129649?f=options, accessed June 2007.

Calleja, Gordon. 2007. "Digital Game Involvement: A Conceptual Model." *Games and Culture* 2: 236–60.

Callon, Michel, and B. Latour. 1981. "Unscrewing the Big Leviathan: How Actors Macrostructure Reality and How Sociologists Help Them to Do So." In *Advances in Social Theory and Methodology: Toward an Integration of Micro- and Macro-Sociologies*, edited by K. Knorr-Cetina and A. V. Cicourel, 277–303. Boston: Routledge and Kegan Paul.

Callon, Michel, C. Méadl, and V. Rabeharisoa. 2002. "The Economy of Qualities." *Economy and Society* 31 (2): 194–217.

Campbell, Colin. 1987. *The Romantic Ethic and the Spirit of Consumerism*. New York: Blackwell.

Campbell, C. S., and G. J. Smith. 2003. "Gambling in Canada: From Vice to Disease to Responsibility: A Negotiated History." *Canadian Bulletin of Medical History* 20: 121–49.

Cardno, Andrew, A. K. Singh, and R. Thomas. 2010. "Gaming Floors of the Future, Part 1: Downloadable Games." *Casino Enterprise Management*, July, http.casinoenterprisemanagement.com/articles/july-2010/gaming-floors-future-part-1-downloadable-games, accessed February 2011.

Carroll, Amy. 1987a. "Casino Construction: The Nuts and Bolts of the Industry." *Casino Gaming Magazine*, November: 15–19.

———. 1987b. "Step Inside: A Look at Interior Design in the Casino Industry." *Casino Gaming Magazine*, October: 18–22.

Casey, Maura. 2002. "An Equal Opportunity Addiction." *The Day: A Special Report on Problem Gambling*. Reprinted from the edition of March 17.

"Cashless Slot Machines: The Industry's View." 1985. *Casino Gaming Magazine*, August: 11–16.

Castel, Robert. 1991. "From Dangerousness to Risk." In *The Foucault Effect: Studies in Governmentality*, edited by G. Burchell, C. Gordon, and P. Miller, 281–98. Chicago: University of Chicago Press.

Castellani, Brian. 2000. *Pathological Gambling: The Making of a Medical Problem*. New York: University of New York Press.

Castells, Manuel. 1996. *The Rise of the Network Society*. Cambridge, MA: Blackwell Publishers.

Clough, Patricia Ticineto. 2000. *Autoaffection: Unconscious Thought in the Age of Teletechnology*. Minneapolis: University of Minnesota Press.

———. 2007. *The Affective Turn: Theorizing the Social*. Durham, NC: Duke University Press.

Collier, Roger. 2008. "Doctored Spins," *Ottawa Citizen*, July 26, http.canada.com/ottawacitizen/news/observer/story.html?id=df9b06d4-005a-4303-b351-794c75171a05, accessed October 2009.

Collier, Stephen, and Andrew Lakoff. 2005. "On Regimes of Living." In *Global Assemblages: Technology, Politics, and Ethics as Anthropological Problems*, edited by A. Ong and S. Collier, 22–39. Oxford: Blackwell.

Collins, A. F. 1969. "The Pathological Gambler and the Government of Gambling." *History of the Human Sciences* 9: 69–100.

Conrad, Dennis. 2009. "Marketing: Unintended Consequences." *Casino Journal*, November: 40.

Coolican, Patrick. 2011. "Severing Lifeline for Gambling Addicts Would Be a Shame." *Las Vegas Sun*, February 18, http.lasvegassun.com/news/2011/feb/18/severing-lifeline-gambling-addicts-would-be-shame/, accessed February 2011.

Cooper, Marc. 2004. *The Last Honest Place in America: Paradise and Perdition in the New Las Vegas*. New York: Nation Books.

———. 2005. "Sit and Spin: How Slot Machines Give Gamblers the Business." *Atlantic Monthly* 296: 121–30.

Coser, Lewis. 1977. *Masters of Sociological Thought: Ideas in Historical and Social Context*. New York: Harcourt Brace Jovanovich.

Cosgrave, James F. 2008. "Goffman Revisited: Action and Character in the Era of Legalized Gambling." *International Journal of Criminology and Sociological Theory* 1 (1): 80–96.

———. 2009. "Governing the Gambling Citizen: The State, Consumption, and Risk." In *Casino State: Legalized Gambling in Canada*, edited by J. F. Cosgrave and T. Klassen, 46–68. Toronto: University of Toronto Press.

———. 2010. "Embedded Addiction: The Social Production of Gambling Knowledge and the Development of Gambling Markets." *Canadian Journal of Sociology / Cahiers Canadiens de Sociologie* 35 (1): 113–34.

Cosgrave, James F., ed. 2006. *The Sociology of Risk and Gambling Reader*. New York: Routledge.

Costa, Nic. 1988. *Automatic Pleasures: The History of the Coin Machine*. London: Kevin Francis.

Cote, Denis, A. Caron, J. Aubert, V. Desrochers, and R. Ladouceur. 2003. "Near Wins Prolong Gambling on a Video Lottery Terminal." *Journal of Gambling Studies* 19: 380–407.

Cotte, June, and K. A. Latour. 2009. "Blackjack in the Kitchen: Understanding Online versus Casino Gambling." *Journal of Consumer Research* 35: 742–58.

Courtwright, David T. 2001. *Forces of Habit: Drugs and the Making of the Modern World*. Cambridge, MA: Harvard University Press.

———. 2005. "Mr. ATOD's Wild Ride: What Do Alcohol, Tobacco, and Other Drugs Have in Common?" *Social History of Alcohol and Drugs* 20: 105–40.

Coventry, Kenny R., and B. Constable. 1999. "Physiological Arousal and Sensation-Seeking in Female Fruit Machine Gamblers." *Addiction* 94 (3): 425–30.

Crary, Jonathan. 1999. *Suspensions of Perception: Attention, Spectacle, and Modern Culture*. Cambridge, MA: MIT Press.

Crawford, Margaret. 1992. "The World in a Shopping Mall." In *Variations on a Theme Park: The New American City and the End of Public Space*, edited by M. Sorkin, 3–30. New York: HarperCollins.

Crevelt, Dwight E., and L. G. Crevelt. 1988. *Slot Machine Mania*. Grand Rapids, MI: Gollehon.

Cristensen, Jon. 2002. "Build It and the Water Will Come." In *The Grit beneath the Glitter: Tales from the Real Las Vegas*, edited by H. Rothman and M. Davis, 115–25. Berkeley: University of California Press.

Croasmun, Jeanne. 2003. "Ergonomics Makes the Slot Player More Productive." *Ergonomics Today*, September 26, www.ergoweb.com/news/detail.cfm?id=806, accessed June 2007.

Csikszentmihalyi, Mihaly. 1975. *Beyond Boredom and Anxiety: Experiencing Flow in Work and Play*. San Francisco: Jossey-Bass.

———. 1985. "Reflections on Enjoyment." *Perspectives in Biology and Medicine* 28 (4): 489–97.

———. 1988. "The Flow Experience and its Significance for Human Psychology." In *Optimal Experience: Psychological Studies of Flow in Consciousness*, edited by M. Csikszentmihalyi and I. S. Csikszentmihalyi, 15–35. Cambridge: Cambridge University Press.

———. 1993. *The Evolving Self: A Psychology for the Third Millennium*. New York: HarperCollins.

———. 1994. *Flow: The Psychology of Optimal Experience*. New York: HarperCollins.

Csikszentmihalyi, Mihaly, and S. Bennet. 1971. "An Exploratory Model of Play." *American Anthropologist* 73 (1): 45–58.

Cummings, Leslie E. 1997. "A Typology of Technology Applications to Expedite Gaming Productivity." *Gaming Research and Review Journal* 4 (1): 63–79.

Cummings, Leslie E., and K. P. Brewer. 1994. "An Evolutionary View of the Critical Functions of Slot Machine Technology." *Gaming Research and Review Journal* 1 (2): 67–78.

Custer, R. 1984. "Profile of the Pathological Gamblers." *Journal of Clinical Psychiatry* 45: 35–38.

"Cyberview Technology Introduces New Gaming Cabinet and Operating Systems at G2E." 2007. *Global Gaming Business*, November 9.

Dancer, Bob. 2001. "Beginners Corner: How Do You Know When to Quit?" *Strictly Slots*, October, 26.

Davis, M. P. 1984. "A 'Virtual' Success." *Gaming and Wagering Business*, October 18.

Davis, Mike. 2002. "Class Struggle in Oz." In *The Grit beneath the Glitter: Tales from the Real Las Vegas*, edited by H. Rothman and M. Davis, 176–85. Berkeley: University of California Press.

Deleuze, Gilles. 1990. *The Logic of Sense*. Translated by M. Lester and C. Stivale. New York: Columbia University Press.

———. 1992. "Postscript on the Society of Control." *October 59*: 3–8.

———. 1997. *Essays Critical and Clinical*. Translated by D. W. Smith and M. A. Greco. Minneapolis: University of Minnesota Press.

Deleuze, Gilles. 1998. "Having an Idea in Cinema." In *Deleuze and Guattari: New Mappings in Politics, Philosophy, and Culture*, edited by E. Kaufman and K. J. Heller, translated by E. Kaufman, 14–22. Minneapolis: University of Minnesota Press.

———. 2007. "Two Questions on Drugs." In *Two Regimes of Madness*, edited by D. Lapoujade, translated by A. Hodges and M. Taormina, 151–55. Cambridge, MA: MIT Press.

Deleuze, Gilles, and Félix Guattari. 1987. *A Thousand Plateaus: Capitalism and Schizophrenia*. Translated by Brian Massumi. Minneapolis: University of Minnesota Press.

Delfabbro, Paul. 2004. "The Stubborn Logic of Regular Gamblers: Obstacles and Dilemmas in Cognitive Gambling Research." *Journal of Gambling Studies* 20 (1): 1–21.

———. 2008. "Australian Gambling Review June 2007." A report prepared for the Independent Gambling Authority of South Australia.

Delfabbro, P. H., K. Falzon, and T. Ingram. 2005. "The Effects of Parameter Variations in Electronic Gambling Simulations: Results of a Laboratory-Based Pilot Study." *Gambling Research* 17: 7–25.

Delfabbro, P. H., and A. H. Winefield. 1999. "Poker-Machine Gambling: An Analysis of Within-Session Characteristics." *British Journal of Psychiatry* 90: 425–39.

Derrida, Jacques. 1981. "The Pharmakon." In *Dissemination*, by Jacques Derrida, edited by B. Johnson, 95–116. Chicago: University of Chicago Press.

"Design/Construction Firms: Providing a Return on Casino Investment." 1985. *Casino Gaming Magazine*, November: 24–26, 39–41.

Desjarlais, Robert. 2003. *Sensory Biographies: Lives and Deaths among Nepal's Yolmo Buddhists*. Berkeley: University of California Press.

———. 2010. *Counterplay: An Anthropologist at the Chessboard*. California: University of California Press.

Dettre, Stephen. 1994. "Profile: Big Changes at Aristocrat." *Slotworld* (3): 3–4.

Devereux, E. C. 1980 [1949]. *Gambling and the Social Structure*. New York: Arno Press.

Dibbell, Julian. 2006. *Play Money; Or, How I Quit My Day Job and Made Millions Trading Virtual Loot*. New York: Basic Books.

———. 2007. "The Life of the Chinese Gold Farmer." *New York Times Magazine*, June 17: 36–40.

———. 2008. "The Chinese Game Room: Play, Productivity, and Computing at Their Limits." *Artifact* 2 (3): 1–6.

Dichter, Ernest. 1960. *The Strategy of Desire*. New York: Doubleday Press.

Dickerson, Mark. 1993. "Internal and External Determinants of Persistent Gambling: Problems in Generalizing from One Form to Another." In *Gambling Behavior and Problem Gambling*, edited by W. R. Eadington and J. Cornelius. Reno, NV: Institute for the Study of Gambling and Commercial Gaming.

———. 1996. "Why 'Slots' Equals 'Grind' in Any Language: The Cross-Cultural Popularity of the Slot Machine." In *Gambling Cultures: Studies in History and Interpretation*, edited by J. McMillen, 140–52. London: Routledge.

———. 2003. "Exploring the Limits of Responsible Gambling: Harm Minimization or Consumer Protection?" *Gambling Research: Journal of the National Association for Gambling Studies* (Australia) 15: 29–44.

Dickerson, M., J. Haw, and L. Shepherd. 2003. *The Psychological Causes of Problem Gambling: A Longitudinal Study of At Risk Recreational EGM Players*. Sydney: University of Western Sydney, School of Psychology, Bankstown Campus, www.austgamingcouncil.org.au/images/pdf/eLibrary/1575.pdf, accessed June 2007.

Dickerson, M., J. Hinchy, S. L. England, J. Fabre, and R. Cunningham. 1992. "On the Determinants of Persistent Gambling Behaviour. I. High-Frequency Poker Machine Players." *British Journal of Psychology* 83: 237–48.

Diskin, Katherine M., and D. C. Hodgins. 1999. "Narrowing of Attention and Dissociation in Pathological Video Lottery Gamblers." *Journal of Gambling Studies* 15: 17–28.

Dixey, Rachael. 1987. It's a Great Feeling When You Win: Women and Bingo. *Leisure Studies* 6 (2): 199–214.

Dixon, M. J., K. A. Harrigan, R. Sandhu, K. Collins, and J. A. Fugelsang. 2010. "Losses Disguised as Wins in Modern Multi-Line Video Slot Machines." *Addiction* 105 (10): 1819–24.

Dixon, M. R., and J. E. Schreiber. 2004. "Near-Miss Effects on Response Latencies and Win Estimations of Slot Machine Players." *Psychological Record* 54 (3): 335–48.

Dostoyevsky, Fyodor. 1972 [1867]. *The Gambler*. Translated by H. Alpin. London: Hesperus Press.

Doughney, James R. 2002. *The Poker Machine State: Dilemmas in Ethics, Economics, and Governance*. Melbourne: Common Ground.

———. 2007. "Ethical Blindness, EGMs, and Public Policy: A Tentative Essay Comparing the EGM and Tobacco Industries." *International Journal of Mental Health and Addiction* 5 (4): 311–19.

Dowling, N., D. Smith, and T. Thomas. 2005. "Electronic Gaming Machines: Are They the 'Crack-Cocaine' of Gambling?" *Addiction* 100: 33–45.

Downey, G. L., and J. Dumit, eds. 1997. *Cyborgs and Citadels: Anthropological Interventions in Emerging Sciences and Technologies*. Santa Fe, NM: School of American Research Press.

Downey, John. 2007. "PokerTek Betting on Expansion." *Charlotte Business Journal*, October 19, bizjournals.com/charlotte/stories/2007/10/22/story1.html?page=2, accessed July 2009.

Dumit, Joseph. 2002. "Drugs for Life." *Molecular Interventions* 2: 124–27.

Dyer, Scott. 2001. "Professor Says Video Poker 'Crack Cocaine' of Gambling." *Capital City Press, The Advocate*, February 16.

Eadington, William R. 2004. "Gaming Devices, Electronic Money, and the Risks Involved." *GamCare News* 19 (Winter): 10–12.

Eadington, William R., and J. Cornelius, eds. 1992. *Gambling Commercial Gaming: Essays in Business, Economics, Philosophy, and Science*. Reno: University of Nevada Press.

Eggert, K. 2004. "Truth in Gaming: Toward Consumer Protection in the Gambling Industry." *Maryland Law Review* 63: 217–86.

Eisenberg, Bart. 2004. "The New 'One-Arm Bandits': Today's Slot Machines Are Built like PCs, Programmed like Video Hames." *Software Design*, January, gihyo.jp/admin/serial/01/pacific/200402, accessed March 2006.

Ellul, Jacques. 1964. *The Technological Society*. Translated by J. Wilkinson. New York: Knopf.

Elster, Jon. 1999. "Gambling and Addiction." In *Getting Hooked: Rationality and Addiction*, edited by J. Elster and O. J. Skog, 208–34. Cambridge: Cambridge University Press.

Emerson, Dan. 1998a. "Virtual Money." *Casino Executive Magazine*, January 31.

———. 1999b. "Will Cashless Be King?: Casino Gambling Debates a Future without Bills and Coins." *Casino Executive Magazine*, October 3.

Ernkvist, Mirko. 2009. "Creating Player Appeal: Management of Technological Innovation and Changing Pattern of Industrial Leadership in the U.S. Gaming Machine Manufacturing Industry, 1965–2005." PhD diss., Department of Economic History, School of Business, Economics and Law, University of Gothenburg.

Epstein, William M., and W. N. Thompson. 2010. "The Reluctance to Tax Ourselves: Nevada's Depravity." *Las Vegas Review*, May 2, http://lvrj.com/opinion/nevada-s-depravity-92614189.html, accessed January 2011.

Ewald, Francois. 1991. "Insurance and Risk." In *The Foucault Effect: Studies in Governmentality*, edited by G. Burchell, C. Gordon, and P. Miller, 197–210. Chicago: University of Chicago Press.

Fabian, Ann. 1999. *Card Sharps and Bucket Shops: Gambling in Nineteenth-Century America*. New York: Routledge.

Fahrenkopf, Frank J. 2003. "State of the Industry Keynote Panel." Global Gaming Expo (G2E), Las Vegas, Nevada.

———. 2010. "The Changing Game in D.C." *Global Gaming Business*, March: 18.

Falkiner, Tim, and Roger Horbay. 2006. "Unbalanced Reel Gaming Machines," www.gameplanit.com/UnbalancedReels.pdf, accessed June 2007.

Fasman, Jon. 2010. "Shuffle Up and Deal: A Special Report on Gambling." *The Economist*, July 8, www.economist.com/node/16507670, accessed July 2010.

Ferguson, Adele. 2008. "Screw Problem Gamblers: Tatts." *The Australian*, February 13, http.theaustralian.news.com.au/story/0,25197,23205436-2702,00.html, accessed April 2008.

Ferland, F., R. Ladouceur, and F. Vitaro. 2002. "Prevention of Problem Gambling: Modifying Misconceptions and Increasing Knowledge." *Journal of Gambling Studies* 18: 19–29.

Ferrar, Ross. 2004. "Challenging Times Ahead for Australia: Jobs and Tax Revenues on the Line as Governments in Oz Crackdown." *Global Gaming Business*, August: 28–29.

Ferster, C. B., and B. F. Skinner. 1957. *Schedules of Reinforcement*. New York: Appleton-Century-Crofts.

Fey, Marshall. 1983. *Slot Machines: An Illustrated History of America's Most Popular Coin-Operated Gaming Device*. Reno: Nevada Publications.

———. 2006. *Slot Machines: America's Favorite Gaming Device*. Reno, NV: Liberty Belle Books.

Findlay, J. M. 1986. *People of Chance: Gambling in American Society from Jamestown to Las Vegas*. New York: Oxford University Press.

Finlay, Karen, V. Kanetkar, J. Londerville, and H. Marmurek. 2006. "The Physical and Psychological Measurement of Gambling Environments." *Environment and Behavior* 38: 570–81.

Fischer, Michael. 1999. "Wording Cyberspace: Toward a Critical Ethnography in Time, Space, and Theory." In *Critical Anthropology Now: Unexpected Contexts, Shifting Constituencies, Changing Agendas*, edited by G. E. Marcus, 245–304. Santa Fe, NM: School of American Research Press.

———. 2003. *Emergent Forms of Life and the Anthropological Voice*. Durham, NC: Duke University Press.

Forrest, David V. 2012. *Slots: Praying to the Gods of Chance*. Harrison, NY: Delphinium Books.

Foucault, Michel. 1979. *Discipline and Punish: The Birth of the Prison*. Translated by. A. Sheridan. New York: Vintage Books.

———. 1988. "Technologies of the Self." In *Technologies of the Self: A Seminar with Michel Foucault*, edited by L. H. Martin, H. Gutman, and P. H. Hutton, 16–49. Amherst: University of Massachusetts Press.

———. 1990. *The History of Sexuality*. Vol. 3, *The Care of the Self*. New York: Vintage Books.

France, Clemens, J. 1902. "The Gambling Impulse." *American Journal of Psychology* 13: 364–407.

Franklin, Joanna. N.d. Press release, www.responsiblegambling.org/articles/Problem_and_Pathological_Gambling_A_view_from_the_States.pdf, accessed October 2011

Freeman, Mike. 2006. "Data Company Helps Wal-Mart, Casinos, Airlines Analyze Customers." *Consumer Reports / San Diego Union-Tribune*, February 4, www.signonsandiego.com/uniontrib/20060224/news_1b24teradata.html, accessed June 2007.

Freud, Sigmund. 1961 [1920]. *Beyond the Pleasure Principle*. New York: W. W. Norton.

———. 1966 [1928]. "Dostoevsky and Parricide." In *Standard Editions of the Complete Psychological Works of Sigmund Freud*. Vol. 11. Edited by J. Strachey. London: Hogarth.

———. 1989. *Introductory Lectures on Psychoanalysis*. Translated by J. Strachey. New York: W. W. Norton.

Friedman, Bill. 1982 [1974]. *Casino Management*. New York: Lyle Stuart Publishers.

———. 2000. *Designing Casinos to Dominate the Competition*. Reno, NV: Institute for the Study of Gambling and Commercial Gaming.

———. 2003. "Casino Design and Its Impact on Player Behavior." In *Stripping Las Vegas: A Contextual View of Casino Resort Architecture*, edited by K. Jaschke and S. Otsch. Weimar: Bauhaus Weimar University Press.

Fullweily, Duana. 2008. "The Biologistical Construction of Race: 'Admixture' Technology and the New Genetic Medicine." *Social Studies of Science* 38 (5): 695–735.

Gaboury, A., and R. Ladouceur. 1989. "Erroneous Perceptions and Gambling." *Journal of Social Behavior and Personality* 4: 411–20.

Gambling Review Body. 2001. "Gambling Review Report." A report prepared for the UK government. Norwich: The Stationary Office.

"Gaming Laboratory International: The Testing Standard." 2007. Company Profile: G2E Overview, 72.

Garcia, Angela. 2010. *The Pastoral Clinic: Addiction and Dispossession along the Rio Grande*. Berkeley: University of California Press.

Garland, D. 2003. "The Rise of Risk." In *Risk and Morality*, edited by R. V. Ericson and A. Doyle, 48–86. Toronto: University of Toronto Press.

Garrett, T. A. 2003. "Casino Gambling in America and Its Economic Impacts." August, www.stls.frb.org/community/assets/pdf/CasinoGambling.pdf, accessed January 2004.

Geertz, Clifford. 1973. *The Interpretation of Cultures: Selected Essays*. New York: Basic Books.

Gerstein, D., et al. 1999. "Gambling Impact and Behavior Study." A report to the US Congress National Gambling Impact Study Commission. Chicago: National Opinion Research Center.

Giddens, Anthony. 1990. *The Consequences of Modernity*. Cambridge: Polity.

———. 1991. *Modernity and Self-Identity*. Cambridge: Polity.

———. 1994. "Living in a Post-Traditional Society." In *Reflexive Modernization: Politics, Tradition, and Aesthetics in the Modern Social Order*, edited by U. Beck, A. Giddens, and S. Lash, 56–109. Stanford, CA: Stanford University Press.

"Global Cash Access to Discontinue Arriva Credit Card." 2008. *Business Wire*, February 28, findarticles.com/p/articles/mi_m0EIN/is_2008_Feb_28/ai_n24354292, accessed October 2009.

"Global Games 2005." 2005. *Global Gaming Business*, September: 58–76.

GLS Research. 1993. "1992 Clark County Resident's Study: Survey of Leisure Activities and Gaming Behavior." A report prepared for the Las Vegas Convention and Visitors Authority.

———. 1995. "1994 Clark County Resident's Study: Survey of Leisure Activities and Gaming Behavior." A report prepared for the Las Vegas Convention and Visitors Authority.

———. 1997. "1996 Clark County Resident's Study: Survey of Leisure Activities and Gaming Behavior." A report prepared for the Las Vegas Convention and Visitors Authority.

———. 1999. "1998 Clark County Resident's Study: Survey of Leisure Activities and Gaming Behavior." A report prepared for the Las Vegas Convention and Visitors Authority.

———. 2001. "2000 Clark County Resident's Study: Survey of Leisure Activities and Gaming Behavior." A report prepared for the Las Vegas Convention and Visitors Authority.

———. 2003. "2002 Clark County Resident's Study: Survey of Leisure Activities and Gaming Behavior." A report prepared for the Las Vegas Convention and Visitors Authority.

———. 2005. "2004 Clark County Resident's Study: Survey of Leisure Activities and Gaming Behavior." A report prepared for the Las Vegas Convention and Visitors Authority.

———. 2007. "2006 Clark County Resident's Study: Survey of Leisure Activities and Gaming Behavior." A report prepared for the Las Vegas Convention and Visitors Authority.

———. 2009. "2008 Clark County Resident's Study: Survey of Leisure Activities and Gaming Behavior." A report prepared for the Las Vegas Convention and Visitors Authority.

———. 2011. "2010 Clark County Resident's Study: Survey of Leisure Activities and Gaming Behavior." A report prepared for the Las Vegas Convention and Visitors Authority.

Goddard, L. 2000. "S. C. Video Poker Ban Energizes Gaming Friends, Foes," September 7, www.stateline.org/live/printable/story?contentId=14114, accessed June 2007.

Goffman, Erving. 1961. "Fun in Games." In *Encounters: Two Studies in the Sociology of Interaction*, edited by E. Goffman. Indianapolis: Bobbs-Merrill Educational Publishing.

———. 1967. *Where the Action Is: Three Essays*. London: Allen Lane.

Gold, Matea, and D. Ferrell. 1998. "Casino Industry Fights an Emerging Backlash." *Los Angeles Times*, December 14, articles.latimes.com/1998/dec/14/news/mn-54012, accessed June 2007.

Goldberg, David. 2006. *Stupidity and Slot Machine Players in Las Vegas*. Maryland: Publish America.

Golub, Alex, and K. Lingley. 2008. "Just Like the Qing Empire." *Games and Culture* 3: 59–75.

Gomart, E. 1999. "Surprised by Methadone: Experiments in Substitution." PhD thesis, Centre de Sociologie de l'Innovation, École des Mines, Paris.

Gomart, Emilie, and A. Hennion. 1999. "A Sociology of Attachment: Music Amateurs, Drug Users." In *Actor Network Theory and After*, edited by J. Law and J. Hassard, 220–47. Malden, MA: Blackwell Publishers.

Goodman, Robert. 1995a. "Gamble Babble." *Washington Post*, November 12.

———. 1995b. *The Luck Business: The Devastating Consequences and Broken Promises of America's Gambling Explosion*. New York: Free Press.

Gordon, Colin. 1991. "Governmental Rationality: An Introduction." In *The Foucault Effect: Studies in Governmentality*, edited by C. Gordon, G. Burchell, and P. Miller, 1–52. Chicago: University of Chicago Press.

Gorman, Tom. 2003. "Casinos Bet on High-Tech Slots to Improve Returns." *Los Angeles Times*, February 16, articles.latimes.com/2003/feb/16/nation/na-slots16, accessed June 2007.

Gottdiener, Mark, C. C. Collins, and D. R. Dickens. 1999. *Las Vegas: The Social Production of an All-American City*. Malden, MA: Blackwell Publishers.

Grant, J. E., S. W. Kim, and M. N. Potenza. 2003. "Advances in the Pharmacological Treatment of Pathological Gambling." *Journal of Gambling Studies* 19 (1): 85–109.

Grant, J. E., M. N. Potenza, E. Hollander, R. Cunningham-Williams, T. Nurminen, G. Smits, and A. Kallio. 2006. "Multicenter Investigation of the Opioid Antagonist Nalmefene in the Treatment of Pathological Gambling." *American Journal of Psychiatry* 163 (2): 303–12.

Grau, Oliver. 2003. *Virtual Art: From Illusion to Immersion*. Cambridge, MA: MIT Press.

Gray, C. H. 1995. *The Cyborg Handbook*. New York and London: Routledge.

Green, Joshua. 2003. "The Bookie of Virtue: William J. Bennett Has Made Millions Lecturing People on Morality and Blown It on Gambling." *Washington Monthly*, June, www.washingtonmonthly.com/features/2003/0306.green.html, accessed July 2007.

Green, Marian. 2006. "Player's Choice." *Slot Manager* (Winter): 8–13.

———. 2007. "Station Casinos Carefully Rolls Out Guaranteed Play Option to Video Poker Crowd." *Slot Manager*, November/December.

———. 2009. "Top 20 Most Innovative Gaming Technology Products of 2009." *Casino Journal*, May, www.casinojournal.com, accessed July 2010.

———. 2010. *Casino Journal* (May): 24–30.

Green, Rick. 2004. "Long-Shot Slots, Part I." *Hartford Courant*, May 9, articles. courant.com/2004-05-09/news/0405090003_1_gambling-machines-long-shot -slots-problem-gambling/2, accessed July 2007.

Greeno, James. 1994. "Gibson's Affordances." *Psychology Review* 101 (2): 336–42.

Gremillion, Helen. 2001. "In Fitness and in Health: Crafting Bodies in the Treatment of Anorexia Nervosa." *Signs: Journal of Women in Culture and Society* 27 (2): 381–414.

Griffiths, Mark. 1993. "Fruit Machine Gambling: The Importance of Structural Characteristics." *Journal of Gambling Studies* 9 (2): 101–20.

———. 1996. "Gambling on the Internet: A Brief Note." *Journal of Gambling Studies* 12: 471–73.

———. 1999. "Gambling Technologies: Prospects for Problem Gambling." *Journal of Gambling Studies* 15 (3): 265–83.

———. 2003. "The Environmental Psychology of Gambling." In *Gambling: Who Wins? Who Loses?*, edited by G. Reith, 277–92. Amherst, NY: Prometheus Books.

Griffiths, Mark, and A. Barnes. 2008. "Internet Gambling: An Online Empirical Study among Student Gamblers." *International Mental Health Addiction* 6: 194–204.

Grint, Keith, and S. Woolgar. 1997. *The Machine at Work: Technology, Work, and Organization.* Cambridge: Polity Press.

Grochowski, John. 2000. "Video Poker Drawn Into a Multihand Revolution." *Casino City Times,* January 12, grochowski.casinocitytimes.com/articles/791 .html, accessed October 2006.

———. 2003. "The Faster the Game, the Faster You Stand to Lose Your Bankroll." *Detroit News,* January 23.

———. 2006. "Technology Spurs Improved Functionality in Next Generation ATMs." *International Gaming and Wagering Business* 27 (5): 28, 32.

———. 2007. "Beyond the Green Felt Jungle: Electronic Multiplayer Games Broaden the Appeal of Traditional Table Products, Finding a Home on the Slot Floor as well as the Pit." *Slot Manager,* November 1.

———. 2010. "Slots Let You Choose Volatility." *Casino City Times,* February 16, grochowski.casinocitytimes.com/article/slots-let-you-choose-volatility-57751, accessed May 2010.

Grun, L., and P. McKeigue. 2000. "Prevalence of Excessive Gambling before and after Introduction of a National Lottery in the United Kingdom: Another Example of the Single Distribution Theory." *Addiction* 95: 959–66.

Gusterson, Hugh. 1996. *Nuclear Rites: A Weapons Laboratory at the End of the Cold War.* Berkeley: University of California Press.

Hacking, Ian. 1990. *The Taming of Chance.* Cambridge: Cambridge University Press.

———. 1998. *Mad Travelers Reflections on the Reality of Transient Mental Illnesses.* Charlottesville: University Press of Virginia.

Hancock, Linda, T. Schellinck, and T. Schrans. 2008. "Gambling and Corporate Social Responsibility (CSR): Re-Defining Industry and State Roles on Duty of Care and Risk Management." *Policy and Society* 27: 55–68.

Hannigan, John. 1998. *Fantasy City: Pleasure and Profit in the Postmodern Metropolis.* New York: Routledge.

Hanson, Zia, and M. Hong. 2003. "Interview with Ötsch." In *Stripping Las Vegas: A Contextual Review of Casino Resort Architecture,* edited by K. Jaschke and S. Ötsch. Weimar: Bauhaus Weimar University Press.

Haraway, Donna. 1991. "A Cyborg Manifesto: Science, Technology, and Socialist-Feminism in the Late Twentieth Century." In *Simians, Cyborgs, and Women: The Reinvention of Nature,* edited by D. Haraway, 149–81. New York: Routledge.

Hardt, Michael. 1999. "Affective Labor." *Boundary* 2 (26): 89–100.

Hardt, Michael, and A. Negri. 2001. *Empire.* Cambridge, MA: Harvard University Press.

"Harrah's Sees Success with Compudigm's Advanced Retail Visualization Solution Running on Teradata." 2003. *Business Wire,* June 10, http.businesswire .com/news/home/20030610005463/en/Harrahs-Sees-Success-Compudigms -Advanced-Retail-Visualization, accessed June 2007.

Harrigan, K. A. 2007. "Slot Machine Structural Characteristics: Distorted Player Views of Payback Percentages." *Journal of Gambling Issues* (June): 215–34.

———. 2008. "Slot Machine Structural Characteristics: Creating Near Misses Using High Symbol Award Ratios." *International Journal of Mental Health and Addiction* 6: 353–68.

———. 2009a. "Comments and Suggestions Regarding $120 Hourly Losses." A report to Australian Government, Productivity Commission.

———. 2009b. "Slot Machines: Pursuing Responsible Gaming Practices for Virtual Reels and Near Misses." *International Journal of Mental Health and Addiction* 7: 68–83.

Harrigan, Kevin A., and M. Dixon. 2009. "PAR Sheets, Probabilities, and Slot Machine Play: Implications for Problem and Non-Problem Gambling." *Journal of Gambling Issues* 23: 81–110.

Harvey, David. 1989. *The Condition of Postmodernity: An Enquiry into the Origins of Cultural Change.* Oxford: Blackwell.

Haw, John. 2008a. "Random-Ratio Schedules of Reinforcement: The Role of Early Wins and Unreinforced Trials." *Journal of Gambling Issues* 21: 56–67.

———. 2008b. "The Relationship between Reinforcement and Gaming Machine Choice." *Journal of Gambling Studies* 24: 55–61.

Heidegger, Martin. 1977 [1954]. *The Question concerning Technology and Other Essays.* New York: Harper.

Hellicker, Kevin. 2006. "How a Gamble on Defibrillators Turned Las Vegas into the Safest Place to Have Your Heart Give Out." *Wall Street Journal,* January 28, A1.

Hess, Alan. 1993. *Viva Las Vegas: After Hours Architecture.* San Francisco: Chronicle Books.

Hevener, Phil. 1988. "Video Poker." *International Gaming and Wagering Business,* October 10.

Hildebrand, James. 2006. "Knowledge Is Power: The More You Know, the Better Off You Are." *Strictly Slots,* January: 38–39.

Hing, Nerilee, and H. Breen. 2001. "Profiling Lady Luck: An Empirical Study of Gambling and Problem Gambling amongst Female Club Members." *Journal of Gambling Studies* 17 (1): 47–69.

Hirsch, Alan R. 1995. "Effects of Ambient Odors on Slot-Machine Usage in a Las Vegas Casino." *Psychology and Marketing* 12: 585–94.

Ho, Karen. 2009. *Liquidated: An Ethnography of Wall Street.* Durham, NC: Duke University Press.

Hochschild, Arlie. 1983. *The Managed Heart.* Berkeley: University of California.

Hodl, James. 2008. "Cashing Out." *Casino Journal,* November 1, http.casino journal.com/Articles/Products/2008/11/01/Cashing-Out.

———. 2009. "World of Slots 2009: The Great Game Search Is On." *Slot Manager,* November/December.

Holtmann, Andy. 2004. "The Sound of Music: Hi-Tech Audio Systems Are Giving Casinos a Wider Variety of Musical Offerings to Choose From; and More Control over Them." *Casino Journal,* July: 3–49.

Huhtamo, Erkki. 2005. "Slots of Fun, Slots of Trouble: An Archaeology of Arcade Gaming." In *Handbook of Computer Game Studies*, edited by J. Raessens and J. Goldstein, 3–23. Cambridge, MA: MIT Press.

Huizinga, Johan. 1950 [1938]. *Homo Ludens: A Study of the Play Element in Culture*. Boston: Beacon Press.

Hunt, Alan. 2003. "Risk and Moralization in Everyday Life." In *Risk and Morality*, edited by R. V. Ericson and A. Doyle, 165–92. Toronto: University of Toronto Press.

IGT (International Gaming Technology). 2005. "Introduction to Slots and Video Gaming," media.igt.com/Marketing/PromotionalLiterature/IntroductionTo Gaming.pdf, accessed July 2007.

———. 2007. "SlotLine: Special Show Edition." Company promotional material G2E 2007, 47.

———. 2008. "The Right Choice." Company Annual Report, homson.mobular .net/thomson/7/2831/3632/, accessed August 2009.

"IGT Product Profile." 2000. *Casino Journal* (February): 39.

"IGT Unveils New Line of Video Gaming Equipment." 1983. *Public Gaming Magazine* (November): 31.

Ihde, Don. 1990. *Technology and the Lifeworld*. Bloomington: Indiana University Press.

———. 2002. *Bodies in Technology*. Minnesota: University of Minnesota Press.

IPART (Independent Pricing and Regulatory Tribunal). 2003. "Review into Gambling Harm Minimization Measures Issues Paper." New South Wales, Australia, www.ipart.nsw.gov.au/welcome.asp, accessed July 2007.

Isin, Engin F. 2004. "The Neurotic Citizen." *Citizenship Studies* 8 (3): 217–35.

Ito, Mitzuko. 2005. "Mobilizing Fun in the Production and Consumption of Children's Software." *Annals of the American Academy of Political and Social Science* 597 (1): 82–102.

Izenour, Steven, and D. A. Dashiell III. 1990. "Relearning from Las Vegas." *Architecture* 10: 46–51.

Jacobs, D. F. 1988. "Evidence for a Common Dissociative-Like Reaction among Addicts." *Journal of Gambling Behavior* 4: 27–37.

———. 2000. "Response to Panel: Jacob's General Theory of Addiction." The 11th International Conference on Gambling and Risk-Taking. Las Vegas, Nevada.

Jain, Sarah S. Lochlann. 1999. "The Prosthetic Imagination: Enabling and Disabling the Prosthesis Trope." *Science, Technology, and Human Values* 24: 31–54.

———. 2006. *Injury: The Politics of Product Design and Safety Law in the United States*. Princeton, NJ: Princeton University Press.

Jalal, Kareen. 2008. "A New Slot." *International Gaming and Wagering Business*, February, http.igwb.com/Articles/Games_And_Technology/BNP_GUID_9-5 -2006_A_1000000000000261686, accessed July 2011.

Jameson, Frederic. 1991. *Postmodernism; Or, the Cultural Logic of Late Capitalism*. Durham, NC: Duke University Press.

———. 2004. "The Politics of Utopia." *New Left Review* 25: 35–54.

Jaschke, Karin. 2003. "Casinos Inside Out." In *Stripping Las Vegas: A Contextual Review of Casino Resort Architecture*, edited by K. Jaschke and S. Ötsch. Weimar: Bauhaus Weimar University Press.

Jaschke, Karin, and S. Ötsch, eds. 2003. *Stripping Las Vegas: A Contextual Review of Casino Resort Architecture*. Weimar: Bauhaus Weimar University Press.

Jenkins, Richard. 2000. "Disenchantment, Enchantment, and Re-Enchantment: Max Weber at the Millennium." *Max Weber Studies* 1 (1): 11–32.

Jonas, Hans. 2010 [1979]. "Toward a Philosophy of Technology." In *Technology and Values: Essential Readings*, edited by C. Hanks, 11–25. Malden, MA: Wiley-Blackwell Publishing.

Kaplan, Michael. 2010. "How Vegas Security Drives Surveillance Tech Everywhere." *Popular Mechanics*, January 1, http.popularmechanics.com/technology/how-to/computer-security/4341499, accessed August 2009.

Kassinove, J., and M. Schare. 2001. "Effects of the 'Near Miss' and the 'Big Win' at Persistence in Slot Machine Gambling." *Psychology of Addictive Behavior* 15: 155–58.

Kaufman, Sharon R. 2005. *And a Time to Die: How American Hospitals Shape the End of Life*. New York: Scribner.

Keane, Helen. 2002. *What's Wrong with Addiction?* New York: New York University Press.

Keane, H., and K. Hamill. 2010. "Variations in Addiction: The Molecular and the Molar in Neuroscience and Pain Medicine." *Biosocieties* 5 (1): 52–69.

King, Rufus. 1964. "The Rise and Decline of Coin-Machine Gambling." *Journal of Criminal Law, Criminology, and Police Science* 55 (2): 99–207.

Klein, N. K. 2002. "Scripting Las Vegas: Noir Naïfs, Junking Up, and the New Strip." In *The Grit beneath the Glitter: Tales from the Real Las Vegas*, edited by H. Rothman and M. Davis, 17–29. Berkeley: University of California.

Kleinman, Arthur, and E. Fitz-Henry. 2007. "The Experimental Basis for Subjectivity: How Individuals Change in the Context of Societal Transformation." In *Subjectivity: Ethnographic Investigations*, edited by J. Biehl, B. Good, and A. Kleinman, 52–65. Berkeley: University of California Press.

Knorr Cetina, Karin, and U. Bruegger. 2000. "The Market as an Object of Attachment: Exploring Post-Social Relations in Financial Markets." *Canadian Journal of Sociology* 25 (2): 141–68.

———. 2002. "Traders' Engagement with Markets: A Postsocial Relationship." *Theory, Culture and Society* 19 (5–6): 161–85.

Knutson, Chad. 2006. "Please Remain Seated." *Casino Enterprise Management* (March): 32.

Kocurek, Carly. 2012. "Coin-Drop Capitalism: Economic Lessons from the Video Game Arcade." In *Before the Crash: An Anthology of Early Video Game History*, edited by Mark J. P. Wolf. Detroit, MI: Wayne State University Press.

Kontzer, Tony. 2004. "Caesars and Harrah's Have Big Plans—If Their Merger Gets Approved." *Information Week*, August 23, http.informationweek.com/news/global-cio/showArticle.jhtml?articleID=29112699, accessed August 2008.

Korn, David A., and H. J. Shaffer. 1999. "Gambling and the Health of the Public: Adopting a Public Health Perspective." *Journal of Gambling Studies* 15 (4): 289–365.

Koza, J. 1984. "Who Is Playing What: A Demographic Study (part 1)." *Public Gaming Magazine.*

Kranes, David. 1995. "Playgrounds." *Journal of Gambling Studies* 11: 91–102.

———. 2000. "The Sound of Music: Is Your Slot Floor a Deafening Experience?" *Casino Executive Magazine* 6 (5): 32–33.

Kubey, Robert, and Mihaly Csikszentmihalyi. 1990. *Television and the Quality of Life: How Viewing Shapes Everyday Experience.* Mahwah, NJ: Lawrence Erlbaum.

———. 2002. "Television Addiction Is No Mere Metaphor." *Scientific American:* 48–55.

Kuley, Nadia B., and Durand F. Jacobs. 1988. "The Relationship between Dissociative-Like Experiences and Sensation Seeking among Social and Problem Gamblers." *Journal of Gambling Behavior* 4 (3): 197–207.

Kushner, H. I. 2010. "Toward a Cultural Biology of Addiction." *Biosocieties* 5 (1): 8–24.

Kusyszyn, Igor. 1990. "Existence, Effectance, Esteem: From Gambling to a New Theory of Human Motivation." *Substance Use and Misuse* 25 (2): 159–77.

Lacan, Jacques. 1977. "The Mirror Stage as Formative of the Function of the I." In *Écrits: A Selection*, translated by A. Sheridan, 3–9. New York: W. W. Norton.

Ladouceur, R. 2004. "Perceptions among Pathological and Nonpathological Gamblers, Addictive Behavors." *Addictive Behaviors* 29, 555–65.

Ladouceur, R., and S. Sévigny. 2005. "Structural Characteristics of Video Lotteries: Effects of a Stopping Device on Illusion of Control and Gambling Persistence." *Journal of Gambling Studies* 21 (2): 117–31.

Ladouceur, R., C. Sylvain, C. Boutin, S. Lachance, C. Doucet, J. Leblond, and C. Jacques. 2001. "Cognitive Treatment of Pathological Gambling." *Journal of Nervous and Mental Disease* 189 (11): 774–80.

Ladouceur, R., and M. Walker. 1996. "A Cognitive Perspective on Gambling." In *Trends in Cognitive and Behavioural Therapies*, edited by P. M. Salkovskis. London: John Wiley and Sons.

Lakoff, Andrew. 2007. "Preparing for the Next Emergency." *Public Culture* 19 (2): 247–71.

Lane, Terry. 2006. "Canadian Pokie Lessons." Radio interview with Tracy Schrans on ABC National Radio, Australia, January 8.

LaPlante, D. A., and H. J. Shaffer. 2007. "Understanding the Influence of Gambling Opportunities: Expanding Exposure Models to Include Adaptation." *American Journal of Orthopsychiatry* 77 (4): 616–23.

Lash, Scott. 1994. "Reflexivity and Its Doubles: Structure, Aesthetics, Community." In *Reflexive Modernization: Politics, Tradition, and Aesthetics in the Modern Social Order*, edited by Ulrich Beck, A. Giddens, and S. Lash. Stanford, CA: Stanford University Press.

Latour, Bruno. 1988. "The Prince for Machines as Well as Machinations." In *Technology and Social Process*, edited by B. Elliott, 20–43. Edinburgh: Edinburgh University Press.

———. 1992. "Where Are the Missing Masses? The Sociology of a Few Mundane Artifacts." In *Shaping Technology / Building Society: Studies in Sociotechnical Change*, edited by W. E. Bijker and J. Law, 225–58. Cambridge, MA: MIT Press.

———. 1994. "On Technical Mediation." *Common Knowledge* 3 (2): 29–64.

———. 1997. "The Trouble with Actor-Network Theory." *Philsophia* 25: 47–64.

———. 1999. "A Collective of Humans and Non-Humans." In *Pandora's Hope: Essays on the Reality of Science Studies*, edited by B. Latour, 174–215. Cambridge, MA: Harvard University Press.

———. 1999. *Pandora's Hope: Essays on the Reality of Science Studies*. Cambridge, MA: Harvard University Press.

Law, John. 1987. "Technology, Closure, and Heterogeneous Engineering: The Case of the Portuguese Expansion." In *The Social Construction of Technological Systems: New Directions in the Sociology and History of Technology*, edited by W. E. Bijker, T. P. Hughes, and T. J. Pinch, 111–34. Cambridge, MA: MIT Press.

Lears, J. 2003. *Something for Nothing: Luck in America*. New York: Viking Press.

———. 2008. "Fortune's Wheel." *Lapham's Quarterly, About Money* 1 (2): 192–99.

Lefebvre, Henri. 1991 [1974]. *The Production of Space*. Edited by R. Tiedeman. Translated by H. Eiland and K. McLaughlin. Oxford: Blackwell.

Legato, Frank. 1987. "Right Down to the Finest Detail." *Casino Gaming Magazine* (October): 14–16.

———. 1998a. "Future Shock." *Strictly Slots* (December): 98.

———. 1998b. "Weighing Anchor." *Strictly Slots* (December): 74.

———. 2004. "The 20 Greatest Slot Innovations." *Strictly Slots* (March), www.strictlyslots.com/archive/0403ss/SS0304_Innovative.pdf, accessed June 2007.

———. 2005a. "Penny Arcade." *Strictly Slots* (June): 68–76.

———. 2005b. "Super Slots." *Global Gaming Business (*September): 30–76.

———. 2006. "Newfangled Gadgetry: The Brave New World of Techno-Slots Is Here." *Strictly Slots* (May): 114.

———. 2007a. "Paying to Play: 'Guaranteed Play' Gives Video Poker Fans Their Money's Worth, Win or Lose." *Casino Player Reprint*, November.

———. 2007b. "Triple Play Poker: The First Real Change to Video Poker Revolutionized the Game." *Strictly Slots*, www.strictlyslots.com/archive/0707ss/hall.htm, accessed August 2009.

———. 2008. "Tough Crowd: Operating and Selling Slots in Table-Heavy Macau Is a Tall Order—but Things Are Improving." *Global Gaming Business*, August, ggbmagazine.com/issue/vol__7_no__8__august_2008/article/tough_crowd, accessed August 2009.

Legato, Frank, and Roger Gros. 2010. "Ten Years of Innovation: Marketing and Game Technology during the First Decade of G2E." An IGT White Paper.

Lehman, Rich. 2007a. "Game Selection Criteria, Part IV: Payout Frequency." *Casino Enterprise Management*, December, http.casinoenterprisemanagement.com/articles/december-2007/game-selection-criteria-part-iv-payout-frequency, accessed May 2010.

———. 2007b. "Time, TITO, and Bonus Games: Where Do We Go from Here?" *Casino Enterprise Management*, June, http.casinoenterprisemanagement.com/articles/july-2007/time-tito-and-bonus-games-where-do-we-go-here, accessed May 2010.

————. 2009. "How Can Free Play Be So Misunderstood?" *Casino Enterprise Management*, November, http.aceme.org/articles/november-2009/how-can-free -play-be-so-misunderstood, accessed May 2010.

Lehrer, Jonah. 2007. "Your Brain on Gambling: Science Shows How Slot Machines Take Over Your Mind," Boston Globe, August 19, www.boston.com/news/ globe/ideas/articles/2007/08/19/your_brain_on_gambling/, accessed May 2010.

Leibman, Bennet. 2005. "Not All That It's Cracked Up to Be." *Gaming Law Review* 9 (5): 446–48.

Lepinay, Vincent. 2011. *Codes of Finance: Engineering Derivatives in a Global Bank*. Princeton, NJ: Princeton University Press.

Lesieur, H. R. 1977. *The Chase: Career of the Compulsive Gambler*. Garden City, NY: Anchor Press.

————. 1988. "The Female Pathological Gambler." In *Gambling Research: Proceedings of the Seventh International Conference on Gambling and Risk-Taking*, vol. 5, edited by W. R. Eadington. Reno: Bureau of Business and Economic Research, University of Nevada.

————. 1998. "Costs and Treatment of Pathological Gambling." *Annals of the American Academy of Political and Social Sciences* (March): 153–71.

Lesieur, H. R., and S. B. Blume. 1991. "When Lady Luck Loses: Women and Compulsive Gambling." In *Feminist Perspectives on Addictions*, edited by N. Van Den Bergh, 181–97. New York: Springer.

Lesieur, Henry R., and R. Rosenthal. 1991. "Pathological Gambling: A Review of the Literature." *Journal of Gambling Studies* 7 (1): 5–39.

Lipton, Michael, and Kevin Weber. 2010. "Ontario Court Rejects Certification of Class Action." *Gaming Legal News* 3 (11), law-articles.vlex.com/vid/gaming -legal-news-volume-number-199183983, accessed January 2011.

LiPuma, E. and B. Lee. 2004. *Financial Derivatives and the Globalization of Risk*. Durham, NC: Duke University Press.

Littlejohn, David. 1999. "Epilogue: Learning More from Las Vegas." In *The Real Las Vegas: Life beyond the Strip*, edited by D. Littlejohn, 281–90. Oxford: Oxford University Press.

Livingstone, Charles. 2005. "Desire and the Consumption of Danger: Electronic Gaming Machines and the Commodification of Interiority." *Addiction Research and Theory* 13 (6): 523–34.

Livingstone, Charles, and R. Woolley. 2007. "Risky Business: A Few Provocations on the Regulation of Electronic Gaming Machines." *International Gambling Studies* 7 (3): 361–76.

————. 2008. "The Relevance and Role of Gaming Machine Games and Game Features on the Play of Problem Gamblers." A report to Independent Gambling Authority of South Australia.

Logan, Frank A., and A. R. Wagner. 1965. *Reward and Punishment*. Boston: Allyn and Bacon.

Lorenz, Valerie C. 1987. "Family Dynamics of Pathological Gamblers." In *The Handbook of Pathological Gambling*, edited by T. Galski, 71–88. Springfield, IL: Charles C. Thomas.

Loose, Rik. 2002. *The Subject of Addiction: Psychoanalysis and the Administration of Enjoyment*. London: Karnac Press.

Lovell, Anne M. 2006. "Addiction Markets: The Case of High-Dose Buprenorphine in France." In *Global Pharmaceuticals: Ethics, Markets, Practices*, edited by A. Petryna, A. Lakoff, and A. Kleinman, 136–70. Durham, NC: Duke University Press.

———. 2007. "Hoarders and Scrappers: Madness and the Social Person in the Interstices of the City." In *Subjectivity: Ethnographic Investigations*, edited by J. Biehl, B. Good, and A. Kleinman, 215–39. Berkeley: University of California Press.

Luhmann, Niklas. 1993. *Risk: A Sociological Theory*. Berlin: Walter De Gruyter.

Luhrmann, Tanya. M. 2000. *Of Two Minds: The Growing Disorder in American Psychiatry*. New York: Alfred A. Knopf.

———. 2004. "Metakinesis: How God Becomes Intimate in Contemporary US Christianity." *American Anthropologist* 106 (3): 518–28.

———. 2005. "The Art of Hearing God: Absorption, Dissociation, and Contemporary American Spirituality." *Spiritus: A Journal of Christian Spirituality* 5 (2): 133–57.

———. 2006. "Subjectivity." *Anthropological Theory* 6 (3): 345–61.

Lupton, Deborah. 1999. *Risk*. New York: Routledge.

Lyng, S. G. 1990. "Edgework: A Social Psychological Analysis of Voluntary Risk Taking." *American Journal of Sociology* 95: 851–86.

Lyotard, Jean François. 1993. *Libidinal Economy*. Bloomington: Indiana University Press.

MacIntyre, Alasdair. 1984. *After Virtue: A Study in Moral Theory*. South Bend, IN: University of Notre Dame Press.

Mackenzie, Donald. 2006. *An Engine, Not a Camera: How Financial Models Shape Markets*. Cambridge, MA: MIT Press.

MacNeil, Ray. 2009. "Government as Gambling Regulator and Operator: The Case of Electronic Gambling Machines." In *Casino State: Legalized Gambling in Canada*, edited by J. F. Cosgrave and T. Klassen, 140–60. Toronto: University of Toronto Press.

Macomber, Dean, and R. Student. 2007a. "Floor of the Future I." *Global Gaming Business* 6 (11).

———. 2007b. "Floor of the Future II." *Global Gaming Business* 6 (12), www.ggbmagazine.com/articles/Floor_of_the_Future_part_II, accessed August 2009.

Maida, J. R. 1997. "From the Laboratory: No More Near Misses." *International Gaming and Wagering Business* (July): 45.

Malaby, Thomas M. 2003. *Gambling Life: Dealing in Contingency in a Greek City*. Urbana: University of Illinois Press.

———. 2006. "Parlaying Value: Capital in and Beyond Virtual Worlds." *Games and Culture* 1 (2): 141–62.

———. 2007. "Beyond Play: A New Approach to Games." *Games and Culture* 2 (2): 95–113.

———. 2009. "Anthropology and Play: The Contours of Playful Experience." *New Literary History* 40: 205–18.

Mangels, John. 2011. "Pennsylvania's Gaming Lab Improves Accountability of Slot Machines." *The Plain Dealer*, May 15, blog.cleveland.com/metro/2011/05/pennsylvanias_gaming_lab_impro.html, accessed May 2011.

Marcus, George E. 1998. *Ethnography through Thick and Thin*. Princeton, NJ: Princeton University Press.

Marcus, George E., and M. Fischer. 1986. *Anthropology as Cultural Critique: An Experimental Moment in the Human Sciences*. Chicago: University of Chicago Press.

Marcuse, Herbert. 1982 [1941]. "Some Social Implications of Modern Technology." In *The Essential Frankfurt School Reader*, edited by A. Arato and E. Gebhardt, 138–62. New York: Continuum.

Mark, Marie E., and H. R. Lesieur. 1992. "A Feminist Critique of Problem Gambling Research." *British Journal of Addiction* 87: 549–65.

Marriott, Michel. 1998. "Luck Be a Microchip Tonight: Gambling Goes Digital," *New York Times Magazine*, December 17.

Martin, Emily. 1994. *Flexible Bodies*. Boston: Beacon Press.

———. 2004. "Taking the Measure of Moods." Paper presented at the Society for Social Studies of Science annual meeting. Paris, France.

———. 2007. *Bipolar Expeditions*. Princeton, NJ: Princeton University Press.

Martin, Randy. 2002. *Financialization of Daily Life*. Philadelphia, PA: Temple University Press.

Marx, Karl. 1992 [1867]. *Capital: A Critique of Political Economy*, vol. 1. Edited by B. Fowkes. Translated by E. Mandel. New York: Penguin Classics.

Masco, Joseph. 2008. "Survival Is Your Business: Engineering Ruin and Affect in Nuclear America." *Cultural Anthropology* 23 (2): 361–98.

Massumi, Brian. 1995. "The Autonomy of Affect." *Cultural Critique*, no. 31, *The Politics of Systems and Environments, Part II* (Autumn): 83–109.

———. 2002. *Parables for the Virtual: Movement, Affect, Sensation*. Durham, NC: Duke University Press.

Mayer, K. J., and L. Johnson. 2003. "Casino Atmospherics." *UNLV Gaming and Review Journal* 7: 21–32.

Mazarella, William. 2008. "Affect: What Is It Good For?" In *Enchantments of Modernity: Empire, Nation, Globalization*, edited by S. Dube, 291–309. New Delhi and New York: Routledge.

McGarry, Caitlin. 2010. "Casinos & Cash." *Global Gaming Business* 9 (5), ggbmagazine.com/issue/vol-9-no-5-may-2010, accessed June 2010.

McGregor, Douglas. 1960. *The Human Side of Enterprise*. New York: McGraw-Hill.

McLaughlin, S. D. 2000. "Gender Differences in Disordered Gambling." Paper presented at the National Council on Problem Gambling, Philadelphia.

McMillen, Jan. 1996. "From Glamour to Grind: The Globalisation of Casinos." In *Gambling Cultures: Studies in History and Interpretation*, edited by J. McMillen, 240–62. London: Routledge.

McMillen, Jan. 2009. "Gambling Policy and Regulation in Australia." In *Casino State: Legalized Gambling in Canada*, edited by J. F. Cosgrave and T. Klassen, 91–118.

Meister, David. 1999. *The History of Human Factors and Ergonomics*. Mahwah, NJ: Lawrence Erlbaum.

Melucci, Alberto. 1996. *The Playing Self: Person and Meaning in the Planetary Society*. Cambridge: Cambridge University Press.

Miers, David. 2003. "A Fair Deal for the Player? Regulation and Compensation as Guarantors of Consumer Protection in Commercial Gambling." In *Gambling: Who Wins? Who Loses?*, edited by G. Reith, 155–74. Amherst, NY: Prometheus Books.

Miller, Peter. 2001. "Governing by Numbers: Why Calculative Practices Matter." *Social Research* 68 (2): 379–96.

Mishra, Raja. 2004. "Gambling Industry Link to Harvard Draws Questions." *Boston Globe*, November 6, www.boston.com/news/local/articles/2004/11/06/gambling_industry_link_to_harvard_draws_questions/, accessed August 2008.

Mitchell, Richard. 1988. "Sociological Implications of the Flow Experience." In *Optimal Experience: Psychological Studies of Flow in Consciousness*, edited by M. Csikszentmihalyi and I. S. Csikszentmihalyi, 36–59. Cambridge: Cambridge University Press.

Moehring, Eugene. 2002. "Growth, Services, and the Political Economy of Gambling in Las Vegas, 1970–2000." In *The Grit beneath the Glitter: Tales from the Real Las Vegas*, edited by H. Rothman and M. Davis, 73–98. Berkeley: University of California Press.

Monaghan, Sally, and A. Blaszczynski. 2009. "Impact of Responsible Gambling Signs for Electronic Gaming Machines on Regular Gamblers: Mode of Presentation and Message Content." Paper presented at the 14th International Conference on Gambling and Risk Taking. Lake Tahoe.

Morgan, Timothy, L. Kofoed, J. Buchkoski, and R. D. Carr. 1996. "Video Lottery Gambling: Effects on Pathological Gamblers Seeking Treatment in South Dakota." *Journal of Gambling Studies* 12 (4): 451–60.

Nadarajan, Gunalan. 2007. "Islamic Automation: A Reading of al-Jazari's *The Book of Knowledge of Ingenious Mechanical Devices* (1206)," MediaArt HistoriesArchive, hdl.handle.net/10002/469, accessed September 2009.

Nassau, David. 1993. *Going Out: The Rise and Fall of Public Amusements*. New York: Basic Books.

National Research Council. 1999. "Pathological Gambling: A Critical Review." A report prepared by the Committee on the Social and Economic Impact of Pathological Gambling. Washington, DC: National Academy Press.

Negri, Antonio. 1999. "Value and Affect." *Boundary* 2 (26): 2.

Nelson, S. E., L. Gebauer, R. A. Labrie, and H. J. Shaffer. 2009. "Gambling Problem Symptom Patterns and Stability across Individual and Timeframe." *Psychology of Addictive Behaviors* 23 (3): 523–33.

Nevada Gaming Commission. 1989. Hearing to Consider: Universal's Motion for Reconsideration/Rehearing of the Decision of Nevada Gaming Commission Made on December 1, 1988 in the Matter of Universal Company, Ltd. and Universal Distributing of Nevada, Inc., Case No. 88-4, pp. 256–300. February 23. Sierra Nevada Reporters. Las Vegas.

———. 2010a. "Manufacturers, Distributors, Operators, of Intercasino Linked

Systems, Gaming Devices, New Games Inter-Casino Linked Systems and Associated Equipment." *Regulations of the Nevada Gaming Commission and State Gaming Control Board*. Regulation 14.040, gaming.nv.gov/stats_regs .htm#regs, accessed July 2008.

————. 2010b. "Provision on Unlawful Acts and Equipment within Chapter on Crimes and Liabilities concerning Gaming." *Regulations of the Nevada Gaming Commission and State Gaming Control Board*. Regulation 465.015, gaming.nv.gov/stats_regs.htm#regs, accessed July 2008.

Nevada State Gaming Control Board. 1983. Agenda Item 6, "New Games/Devices (Request for Approval) Device: Virtual Reel Slot Machine." Transcript of discussions, i, ii, iii, 2–97, August 10. Sierra Nevada Reporters. Carson City, Nevada.

"The New Generation of Slots." 1981. *Public Gaming Magazine*, March: 26–38.

Nickell, Joe A. 2002. "Welcome to Harrah's: You Give Us Your Money. We Learn Everything about You. And Then You Thank Us and Beg for More. How's That for a Business Model?" *Business 2.0*, April, faculty.msb.edu/homak/homahelp site/webhelp/Harrahs_-__Welcome_to_Harrah_s_Biz_2.0_April_2003.htm, accessed August 2008.

North American Gaming Almanac. 2010. Casino City Press.

O'Malley, Pat. 1996. "Risk and Responsibility." In *Foucault and Political Reason: Liberalism, Neo-Liberalism, and Rationalities of Government*, edited by A. Barry, T. Osborne, and N. Rose, 189–208. Chicago: University of Chicago Press.

————. 2003. "Moral Uncertainties: Contract Law and Distinctions between Speculation, Gambling, and Insurance." In *Risk and Morality*, edited by R. V. Ericson and A. Doyle, 231–57. Toronto: University of Toronto Press.

Omnifacts Bristol Research. 2007. "Nova Scotia Player Card Research Project: Stage III Research Report." A report prepared for the Nova Scotia Gaming Commission.

Ong, Aihwa, and S. Collier. 2005. Introduction to *Global Assemblages: Technology, Politics, and Ethics as Anthropological Problems*, edited by A. Ong and S. Collier, 1–2, 8. Malden, MA: Blackwell.

Orford, Jim. 2005. "Complicity on the River Bank: The Search for the Truth about Problem Gambling: Reply to the Commentaries." *Addiction* 100: 1226–39.

Osborne, Thomas, and N. Rose. 2004. "Spatial Phenomenotechnics: Making Space with Charles Booth and Patrick Geddes." *Environmental and Planning D: Society and Space* 22: 209–28.

Ötsch, Silke. 2003. "Earning from Las Vegas." In *Stripping Las Vegas: A Contextual Review of Casino Resort Architecture*, edited by K. Jaschke and S. Ötsch. Weimar: Bauhaus Weimar University Press.

Palmeri, Christopher. 2003. "Hit a Jackpot? You Won't Need a Bucket." *Business Week Online*, www.businessweek.com/magazine/content/03_13/b3826076.htm, accessed August 2006.

Panasitti, Mike, and N. Schüll. 1993. "A Discipline of Leisure: Engineering the Las Vegas Casino." Honors thesis, Anthropology, University of California, Berkeley.

Pandolfo, Stefania. 1997. *Impasses of the Angels: Scenes from a Moroccan Space of Memory*. Chicago: University of Chicago Press.

———. 2006. "Nibtidi mnin il-hikaya [Where Are We to Start the Tale?]": Violence, Intimacy, and Recollection." *Social Science Information* 45 (3): 349–71.

Parets, Robyn Taylor. 1996. "Cash Is No Longer King." *International Gaming and Wagering Business* 17 (12): 64–65.

———. 1999. "Advances in Linked Gaming Technology." *International Gaming and Wagering Business* (Special Issue for World Gaming Congress and Expo) (September): 19–20.

Parke, J., and M. Griffiths. 2004. "Gambling Addiction and the Evolution of the 'Near Miss.'" *Addiction Research and Theory* 12 (5): 407–11.

———. 2006. "The Psychology of the Fruit Machine: The Role of Structural Characteristics (Revisited)." *International Journal of Mental Health and Addiction* 4: 151–79.

Parke, Jonathan, J. Rigbye, and A. Parke. 2008. "Cashless and Card-Based Technologies in Gambling: A Review of the Literature." A report prepared for the Gambling Commission, Great Britain.

Patterson, Judy. 2002. "Harm Minimization: A Call to Action for the International Gaming Community," June 28, www.americangaming.org/Press/speeches/speeches_detail.cfv?id=111, accessed October 2006.

PC (Productivity Commission). 1999. "Australia's Gambling Industries." A report prepared for the Australian Government.

———. 2009. "Australia's Gambling Industries: Draft Report." A report prepared for the Australian Government.

———. 2010. "Australia's Gambling Industries." A report prepared for the Australian Government.

Petryna, Adriana. 2002. *Life Exposed: Biological Citizens after Chernobyl.* Princeton, NJ: Princeton University Press.

———. 2009. *When Experiments Travel: Clinical Trials and the Global Search for Human Subjects.* Princeton, NJ: Princeton University Press.

Picard, Rosalind. 1997. *Affective Computing.* Cambridge, MA: MIT Press.

Pickering, Andrew. 1993. "The Mangle of Practice: Agency and Emergence in the Sociology of Science." *American Journal of Sociology* 99: 559–89.

Pine, J., and J. Gilmore. 1999. *The Experience Economy.* Boston: Harvard Business School Press.

Piore, Michael J., and C. F. Sabel. 1984. *The Second Industrial Divide: Possibilities for Prosperity.* New York: Basic Books.

"Player Tracking … It's a Service Business." 1990. *Casino Gaming Magazine* (April): 6–7.

Plotz, David. 1999. "Busted Flush: South Carolina's Video-Poker Operators Run a Political Machine." *Harpers* (August): 63–72.

Poel, Ibo van de, and Peter-Paul Verbeek. 2006. "Editorial: Ethics and Engineering Design." *Science, Technology, and Human Values* 31: 223–36.

Polzin, P. E., J. Baldridge, D. Doyle, J. T. Sylvester, R. A. Volberg, and W. L. Moore. 1998. *The 1998 Montana Gambling Study: Final Report to the Montana Gambling Study Commission.* Helena: Montana Legislative Services Division.

Potenza, M. N. 2001. "The Neurobiology of Pathological Gambling." *Seminars in Clinical Neuropsychiatry* 6: 217–26.

Preda, Alex. 2006. "Socio-Technical Agency in Financial Markets: The Case of the Stick Ticker." *Social Studies of Science* 36: 753–82.

Putnam, Robert. 2000. *Bowling Alone: The Collapse and Revival of American Community*. New York, NY: Simon & Schuster.

Rabinbach, Anson. 1992. *The Human Motor: Energy Fatigue, and the Origins of Modernity*. Berkeley: University of California Press.

Rabinow, Paul. 1996. *Essays on the Anthropology of Reason*. Princeton, NJ: Princeton University Press.

———. 1999. *French DNA: Trouble in Purgatory*. Chicago: University of Chicago Press.

———. 2003. *Anthropos Today: Reflections on Modern Equipment*. Princeton, NJ: Princeton Press.

Raikhel, Eugene, and W. Garriott. 2013. "Addiction Trajectories: Tracing New Paths in the Anthropology of Addiction." In *Addiction Trajectories*, edited by E. Raikhel and W. Garriott. Durham, NC: Duke University Press.

Rapp, Rayna. 2000. *Testing Women, Testing the Fetus: The Social Impact of Amniocentesis in America*. New York: Routledge.

Reich, Kenneth. 1989. "Misleading Slot Machines Retrofitted, Nevada Says." *Los Angeles Times*, June 4, articles.latimes.com/1989-06-04/news/mn-2501_1_slot -machines-international-game-technology-near-miss, accessed June 2007.

Reid, R. L. 1986. "The Psychology of the Near Miss." *Journal of Gambling Behavior* 2: 32–39.

Reik, Theodor. 1951. *Dogma and Compulsion: Psychoanalytic Studies of Religion and Myths*. Translated by B. Miall. New York: International Universities Press.

Reiner, Krista. 2007. "Jay Walker: A Step Ahead." *Casino Enterprise Management*, October 31, http.casinoenterprisemanagement.com/articles/november -2007/jay-walker-step-ahead, accessed August 2008.

———. 2009. "The 2009 Casino Enterprise Management Slot Floor Technology Awards." *Casino Enterprise Management*, April 30, http.casinoenterprise management.com/articles/may-2009/2009-cem-slot-floor-technology-awards, accessed May 2010.

Reisman, David. 1950. *The Lonely Crowd: A Study of the Changing American Character*. In collaboration with N. Glazer and R. Denney. New Haven, CT: Yale University Press.

Reith, Gerda. 1999. *The Age of Chance: Gambling in Western Culture*. New York: Routledge.

———. 2003. "Pathology and Profit: Controversies in the Expansion of Legalized Gambling." In *Gambling: Who Wins? Who Loses?*, edited by G. Reith, 9–29. Amherst, NY: Prometheus Books.

———. 2006. "The Pursuit of Chance." In *The Sociology of Risk and Gambling Reader*, edited by J. F. Cosgrave, 125–43. New York: Routledge.

———. 2007. "Gambling and the Contradictions of Consumption: A Genealogy of the 'Pathological' Subject." *American Behavioral Scientist* 51 (1): 33–55.

———. 2008. "Reflections on Responsibility." *Journal of Gambling Issues* 22: 149–55.

Richtel, Matt. 2006. "From the Back Office, a Casino Can Change the Slot Machine in Seconds." *New York Times*, April 12, www.nytimes.com/2006/04/12/technology/12casino.html.

Ritzer, George. 2001. *Explorations in the Sociology of Consumption: Fast Food, Credit Cards, and Casinos*. London: Sage.

———. 2005. *Enchanting a Disenchanted World: Revolutionizing the Means of Consumption*. Thousand Oaks, CA: Pine Forge Press.

———. 2007. *Culture and Enchantment, and Enchanting a Disenchanted World*. Thousand Oaks, CA: Pine Forge Press.

Rivera, Geraldo. 2000. "Geraldo Rivera Reports: Las Vegas, the American Fantasy." National Broadcast Company.

Rivlin, Gary. 2004. "The Tug of the Newfangled Slot Machines." *New York Times Magazine*, May 9: 42–81.

———. 2007. "Slot Machines for the Young and Active." *New York Times*, December 10, www.nytimes.com/2007/12/10/business/10slots.html, accessed December 2007.

Roberts, Elizabeth. 2006. "God's Laboratory: Religious Rationalities and Modernity in Ecuadorian In-Vitro Fertilization." *Culture Medicine and Psychiatry* 30 (4): 507–36.

———. 2007. "Extra Embryos: The Ethics of Cryopreservation in Ecuador and Elsewhere." *American Ethnologist* 34 (1): 188–99.

Roberts, Patrick. 2010. "Slot Sense." *Global Gaming Business* 9 (8), August 2, ggbmagazine.com/issue/vol-9-no-8-august-2010/article/slot-sense, accessed September 2010.

Robertson, Campbell. 2009. "Video Bingo Has Alabamians Yelling Everything But." *New York Times*, November 12, www.nytimes.com/2009/11/12/us/12bingo.html, accessed November 2009.

Robison, John. 2000. "Ask the Slot Expert: Casino Random Number Generators." *Casino City Times*, robison.casinocitytimes.com/articles/349.html, accessed March 2005.

Roemer, Mick. 2007. "Guest Column: Skill-Based Gaming—the New Frontier." *Slot Manager*, November, www.roemergaming.com/articles.html, accessed December 2007.

Rogers, Michael. 1980. "The Electronic Gambler." *Rocky Mountain Magazine*, 19–30.

Room, Robin. 2005. "The Wheel of Fortune: Cycles and Reactions in Gambling Policies." *Addiction* 100: 1226–39.

Room, Robin, N. E. Turner, and A. Ialomiteanu. 1999. "Community Effects of the Opening of the Niagara Casino." *Addiction* 94: 1449–66.

Rose, I. Nelson. 1989. "Nevada Draws the Line at Near-Miss Slots." *Casino Journal* (July): 51. Also available at *Gambling and the Law Columns*, www.gamblingandthelaw.com/columns/13.htm.

Rose, Nikolas. 1996. *Inventing Our Selves: Psychology, Power, and Personhood*. Cambridge: Cambridge University Press.

———. 1999. *Powers of Freedom: Reframing Political Thought*. Cambridge: Cambridge University Press.

———. 2003. "The Neurochemical Self and Its Anomalies." In *Risk and Morality*, edited by R. V. Ericson and A. Doyle, 407–37. Toronto: University of Toronto Press.

Rosenthal, Edward C. 2005. *The Era of Choice: The Ability to Choose and Its Transformation of Contemporary Life*. Cambridge, MA: MIT Press.

Rosenthal, Richard J. 1992. "Pathological Gambling." *Psychiatric Annals* 22 (2): 72–78.

Rothman, Hal. 2003. *Neon Metropolis: How Las Vegas Started the Twenty-First Century*. New York: Routledge.

Rothman, Hal, and M. Davis, eds. 2002. *The Grit beneath the Glitter: Tales from the Real Las Vegas*. Berkeley: University of California Press.

Rotstein, Gary. 2009. "Some Say Slots Gambling Most Addictive." *Pittsburgh Post-Gazette*, September 6, http.post-gazette.com/pg/09249/995723-455.stm.

Royer, Victor. 2010. "Manufacturer Maladies." *Casino Enterprise Management*, March, http.casinoenterprisemanagement.com/articles/march-2010 /manufacturer -maladies.

Russell, Rob. 2007. "Fun and Games: Convergence of the Slot Machine with the Arcade Experience." *Global Gaming Business*, November/December.

Rutherford, James. 1996. "Creative Alliance." *Casino Journal* 9 (3): 80–85.

———. 2005a. "Games of Choice." *International Gaming and Wagering Business*, January.

———. 2005b. "Russia Grows Up: Political Uncertainty Clouds the Future, but It Hasn't Dimmed the Possibilities." *International Gaming and Wagering Business* (December): 16–22.

Ryan, T. P., and J. F. Speyrer. 1999. "Gambling in Louisiana: A Benefit/Cost Analysis 99." A report prepared for the Louisiana Gambling Control Board.

SACES (South Australian Centre for Economic Studies). 2003. "Community Impact of Electronic Gaming Machine Gambling." Discussion Paper 1: Review of Literature and Potential Indicators. Victoria: Gambling Research Panel.

Sanders, Barbara. 1973. "A History of Advertising and Promotion in the Reno Gaming Industry." Master's thesis, Journalism, University of Nevada, Reno.

Sasso, W. and J. Kalajdzic. 2007. "Do Ontario and Its Gaming Venues Owe a Duty of Care to Problem Gamblers?" *Gaming Law Review* 10 (6): 552–70.

Schellinck, Tony, and T. Schrans. 1998. "The 1997/98 Nova Scotia Regular VL Players Study Highlight Report." A report prepared by Focal Research Consultants, Ltd., Nova Scotia.

———. 2002. "The Nova Scotia Video Lottery Responsible Gaming Features Study." A final report prepared by Focal Research Consultants, Ltd., for the Atlantic Lottery Corporation, Nova Scotia.

———. 2003. "Nova Scotia Prevalence Study: Measurement of Gambling and Problem Gambling in Nova Scotia." A final report prepared by Focal Research Consultants, Ltd., Nova Scotia, for the Atlantic Lottery Corporation, Nova Scotia.

———. 2004. "The Nova Scotia Video Lottery Self-Exclusion Process Test, NS VLSE Responsible Gaming Features Enhancements." A report prepared for the Nova Scotia government.

———. 2007. "VLT Player Tracking System: Nova Scotia Gaming Corporation Responsible Gaming Research Device Project." A final report prepared by Focal Research Consultants, Ltd., Nova Scotia, for the Atlantic Lottery Corporation, Nova Scotia.

Scheri, Saverio. 2005. *The Casino's Most Valuable Chip: How Technology Changed the Gaming Industry*. Institute for the History of Technology.

Schneider, Mark A. 1993. *Culture and Enchantment*. Chicago: University of Chicago Press.

Schrans, Tracy. 2006. Interview with Terry Lane. ABC Radio National, January 8, www.abc.net.au/rn/nationalinterest/stories/2006/1533815.htm, accessed July 2006.

Schuetz, Richard. 2000. "In Search of the Holy Grail (in Las Vegas): Love and Addiction from Both Sides of the Table." Keynote speech delivered at the 11th International Conference on Gambling and Risk-Taking, Las Vegas.

Schüll, Natasha. 2006. "Machines, Medication, Modulation: Circuits of Dependency and Self-Care in Las Vegas. *Culture, Medicine, and Psychiatry* 30: 1–25.

Schwartz, Barry. 2005. *The Paradox of Choice: Why More Is Less*. New York: ECCO.

Schwartz, Barry, H. R. Markus, and A. C. Snibbe. 2006. "Is Freedom Just Another Word for Many Things to Buy? That Depends on Your Class Status." *New York Times Magazine*, February 26: 14–15.

Schwartz, David G. 2003. *Suburban Xanadu: The Casino Resort on the Las Vegas Strip and Beyond*. New York: Routledge.

Schwartz, Mattathias. 2006. "The Hold-'Em Holdup." *New York Times*, June 11: 55–58.

Scoblete, Frank. 1995. "The God in the Machine." *Casino Player* (March): 5.

Sedgwick, Eve. 1992. "Epidemics of the Will." In *Incorporations*, edited by J. Crary and S. Kwinter, 582–95. New York: Zone Books.

Shaffer, Howard. 1996. "Understanding the Means and Objects of Addiction, the Internet, and Gambling." *Journal of Gambling Studies* 12 (4): 461–69.

———. 2003. "Shifting Perceptions on Gambling and Addiction." *Journal of Gambling Studies* 19: 1–6 (editor's introduction).

———. 2004. "Internet Gambling and Addiction." A report prepared for Mark Mendel and Robert Blumenfeld, of Mendel Blumenfeld, LLP, www.division onaddictions.org/html/publications/shafferinternetgambling.pdf.

———. 2005. "From Disabling to Enabling the Public Interest: Natural Transitions from Gambling Exposure to Adaptation and Self-Regulation." *Addiction* 100: 1227–30.

———. N.d. "What Is Addiction? A Perspective," www.divisiononaddictions.org/html/whatisaddiction.htm, accessed November 2009.

Shaffer, Howard, M. N. Hall, and J. Vander Bilt. 1999. "Estimating the Prevalence of Disordered Gambling Behavior in the United States and Canada: A Research Synthesis." *American Journal of Public Health* 89: 1369–76.

Shaffer, Howard, and D. A. Korn. 2002. "Gambling and Related Mental Disorders: A Public Health Analysis." *Annual Review of Public Health* 23: 171–212.

Shaffer, Howard, R. A. LaBrie, and D. LaPlante. 2004a. "Laying the Foundation for Quantifying Regional Exposure to Social Phenomena: Considering the Case of Legalized Gambling as a Public Health Toxin." *Psychology of Addictive Behaviors* 18 (1): 40–48.

———. 2004b. "Toward a Syndrome Model of Addiction: Multiple Expressions, Common Etiology." *Harvard Review of Psychiatry* 12: 367–74.

Sharpe, Louise, M. Walker, M. Coughlan, K. Emerson, and A. Blaszcynski. 2005. "Structural Changes to Electronic Gaming Machines as Effective Harm Minimization Strategies for Non-Problem and Problem Gamblers." *Journal of Gambling Studies* 21: 503–20.

Shoemaker, S. and D.M.V. Zemke. 2005. "The 'Local Market': An Emerging Gaming Segment." *Journal of Gambling Studies* 21: 379–410.

Simpson, Jeff. 2000. "Evening the Odds: Station Casinos Helps Fund Clinic for Problem Gamblers." *Las Vegas Review Journal*, February 7.

Simurda, Stephen J. 1994. "When Gambling Comes to Town: How to Cover a High-Stakes Story." *Journalism Review* (January/February): 36–38.

Singh, A. K., A. Cardno, and A. Gewali. 2010. "The Long and Short of It: Slot Games from a Player's Perspective." *Casino Enterprise Management*, April, www.bis2.net/LinkClick.aspx?fileticket=2PieHrl5%2FAU%3D&tabid=1974.

Singh, A. K., and A. F. Lucas. 2011. "Estimating the Ability of Gamblers to Detect Differences in the Payback Percentages of Reel Slot Machines: A Closer Look at the Slot Player Experience." *UNLV Gaming Research and Review Journal* 15 (1): 17–36.

Skinner, B. F. 1953. *Science and Human Behavior*. New York: Free Press.

———. 2002 [1971]. *Beyond Freedom and Dignity*. New York: Knopf.

Skolnik, Sam. 2011. *High Stakes: The Rising Costs of America's Gambling Addiction*. Boston: Beacon Press.

"Slot Machines and Pinball Games." 1950. *Annals of the American Academy of Political and Social Science* 269: 62–70.

"A Slot Maker for All Seasons." 1996. *International Gaming and Wagering Business*, September 18.

Slutske, W. S. 2007. "Longitudinal Studies of Gambling Behavior." In *Research and Measurement Issues in Gambling Studies*, edited by G. Smith, D. C. Hodgins, and R. J. Williams, 127–54. London: Elsevier.

Smith, Garry. 2008. "Accountability and Social Responsibility in the Regulation of Gambling in Ontario." Paper presented at the Alberta Gaming Research Institute Annual Conference. Banff.

Smith, Garry, and C. S. Campbell. 2007. "Tensions and Contentions: An Examination of Electronic Gaming Issues in Canada." *American Behavioral Scientist* 51: 86–101.

Smith, Garry, D. Hodgins, and R. Williams, eds. 2007. *Research and Measurement Issues in Gambling Studies*. Boston: Elsevier/Academic Press.

Smith, Garry, and H. J. Wynne. 2004. "VLT Gambling in Alberta: A Preliminary Analysis," hdl.handle.net/1880/1632, accessed August 2008.

Smith, Rod. 2003. "Seeking Power and Influence, Gaming Interests Contribute Increasingly to Election Campaigns." *Las Vegas Review Journal*, February 9,

http.reviewjournal.com/lvrj_home/2003/Feb-09-Sun-2003/news/20655447
.html, accessed May 2010.

Sojourner, Mary. 2010. *She Bets Her Life: A Story of Gambling Addiction*. Berkeley: Seal Press.

Specker, S. M., G. A. Carlson, K. M. Edmonson, P. E. Johnson, and M. Marcotte. 1996. "Psychology in Pathological Gamblers Seeking Treatment." *Journal of Gambling Studies* 12: 67–81.

Stewart, David. 2010. "Demystifying Slot Machines and Their Impact in the United States." American Gaming Association White Paper, http.american gaming.org/industry-resources/research/white-papers, accessed May 2011.

Stewart, Kathleen. 2007. *Ordinary Affects*. Durham, NC: Duke University Press.

Storer, John, M. W. Abbott, and J. Stubbs. 2009. "Access or Adaptation? A Meta-Analysis of Surveys of Problem Gambling Prevalence in Australia and New Zealand with Respect to Concentration of Electronic Gaming Machines." *International Gambling Studies* 9 (3): 225–44.

Strickland, Eliza. 2008. "Gambling with Science: Determined to Defeat Lawsuits over Addiction, the Casino Industry Is Funding Research at a Harvard-Affiliated Lab." June 16, www.salon.com/news/feature/2008/06/16/gambling _science/.

Strow, David. 2000. "Station Casinos Grant Aids in Opening Problem Gambling Clinic." *Las Vegas Sun*, February 3, http.lasvegassun.com/news/2000/feb/ 03/station-casinos-grant-aids-in-opening-problem-gamb/, accessed October 2006.

Stutz, Howard. 2007a. "Debit-Slot Plan Gets No Votes: Bank Plastic Won't Be Connected with Slips for Ticket In–Ticket Out." *Las Vegas Review-Journal*, September 21, www.lvrj.com/business/9914897.html, accessed July 2007.

———. 2007b. "A Step Closer to Going Mobile." *Las Vegas Review Journal*, October 30, www.lvrj.com/business/10884801.html, accessed July 2007.

Suchman, Lucy. 2007a. "Feminist STS and the Sciences of the Artificial." In *The Handbook of Science and Technology Studies*, 3rd. ed., edited by E. Hacket, O. Amsterdamska, M. Lynch, and J. Wajcman, 139–64. Cambridge, MA: MIT Press.

———. 2007b. *Human-Machine Reconfigurations: Plans and Situated Actions*, 2nd exp. ed. New York: Cambridge University Press.

"Suicide Rates by State." 1997. *Associated Press*, August 28.

Taber, Julian I. 2001. *In the Shadow of Chance: The Pathological Gambler*. Reno: University of Nevada Press.

Taylor, Frederick W. 1967 [1911]. *The Principles of Scientific Management*. New York: W. W. Norton.

Taylor, T. L. 2006. *Play Between Worlds: Exploring Online Game Culture*. Cambridge, MA: MIT Press.

Terranova, Tiziana. 2000. "Free Labor: Producing Culture for the Digital Economy." *Social Text* 18 (8): 33–58.

Thomas, Anna C., G. B. Sullivan, and F.C.L. Allen. 2009. "A Theoretical Model of EGM Problem Gambling: More Than a Cognitive Escape." *International Journal of Mental Health and Addiction* 7 (8): 97–107.

Thomas, Anna C., S. Moore, M. Kyrios, G. Bates, and D. Meredyth. 2011. "Gambling Accessibility: A Scale to Measure Gambler Preferences." *Journal of Gambling Studies* 27 (1): 129–43.

Thompson, E. P. 1967. "Time, Work-Discipline, and Industrial Capitalism." *Past & Present* 38 (1): 56–97.

Thompson, Gary. 1999. "Video Slots Taking Over Casino Floors." *Las Vegas Sun*, September 14.

Thompson, Isaiah. 2009. "Meet Your New Neighbor: How Slot Machines Are Secretly Designed to Seduce and Destroy You, and How the Government Is in on It." *Philadelphia City Paper*, January 7, citypaper.net/articles/2009/01/08/foxwoods-sugarhouse-pennsylvania-gaming-control-board, accessed February 2009.

Thrift, Nigel. 2006. "Re-Inventing Invention: New Tendencies in Capitalist Commodification." *Economy and Society* 35: 279–306.

Tilley, Alvin R. 2002. *The Measure of Man and Woman: Human Factors in Design*. New York: Wiley.

Tita, Bob. 2008. "Casino fined $800K for Marketing to Banned Gamblers." *Chicago Business*, May 19, http.chicagobusiness.com/cgi-bin/news.pl?id=29493&seenIt=1, accessed July 2009.

TNS Consultants. 2011. "World Count of Gaming Machines 2008: A Marketing Research Report." A report prepared for the Gaming Technologies Association in Australia.

Trevorrow, K., and S. Moore. 1998. "The Association between Loneliness, Social Isolation, and Women's Electronic Gaming Machine Gambling." *Journal of Gambling Studies* 14: 263–84.

Turdean, Cristina. 2012. "Betting on Computers: Digital Technologies and the Rise of the Casino (1950–2000)." PhD diss., Hagley Program, Department of History, University of Delaware.

Turkle, Sherry. 1984. *The Second Self: Computers and the Human Spirit*. New York: Simon and Schuster.

———. 1997. *Life on the Screen: Identity in the Age of the Internet*. New York: Touchstone.

———. 2011. *Alone Together: Why We Expect More from Technology and Less from Each Other*. New York: Basic Books.

Turner, Nigel. 1999. "Chequered Expectations: Predictors of Approval of Opening a Casino in the Niagara Community." *Journal of Gambling Studies* 15: 45–70.

———. 2011. "Volatility, House Edge and Prize Structure of Gambling Games." *Journal of Gambling Studies* 27: 607–23.

Turner, Nigel, and R. Horbay. 2004. "How Do Slot Machines and Other Electronic Gambling Machines Actually Work?" *Journal of Gambling Issues* 11, http.ghsouthern.org.au/infobase/JGI-Issue11-turner-horbay.pdf, accessed April 2007.

United Way of Southern Nevada and Nevada Community Foundation. 2003. *Southern Nevada Community Assessment*. September 2003. Las Vegas.

Valenzuela, Terence D., D. J. Roe, G. Nichol, L. L. Clark, D. W. Spaite, and R. G. Hardman. 2000. "Outcomes of Rapid Defibrillation by Security Officers after Cardiac Arrest in Casinos." *New England Journal of Medicine* 343: 1206–9.

Valverde, Mariana. 1998. *Diseases of the Will: Alcohol and the Dilemmas of Freedom*. Cambridge: Cambridge University Press.

Vander Bilt, J., H. H. Dodge, R. Pandav, H. J. Shaffer, and M. Ganguli. 2004. "Gambling Participation and Social Support among Older Adults: A Longitudinal Community Study." *Journal of Gambling Studies* 20 (4): 373–89.

Velotta, Richard N. 2009. "Manufacturer of Slot That Can Match Gambler's Desired Pace Is Licensed." *Las Vegas Sun*, September 25, http.lasvegassun.com/staff/richard-n-velotta/, accessed May 2010.

Venturi, Robert, S. Izenour, and D. S. Brown. 1972. *Learning from Las Vegas*. Cambridge, MA: MIT Press.

Verbeek, Peter-Paul. 2005a. "Artifacts and Attachment: A Post-Script Philosophy of Mediation." In *Inside the Politics of Technology: Agency and Normativity in the Co-Production of Technology and Society*, edited by H. Harbers, 125–46. Amsterdam: Amsterdam University Press.

———. 2005b. *What Things Do: Philosophical Reflections on Technology, Agency, and Design*. University Park: Pennsylvania State University Press.

Villano, Matt. 2009. "Daniel Lee: A Music Man of Slot Machines." *SFGate, San Francisco Chronicle*, December 3, articles.sfgate.com/2009-12-03/entertainment/17183069_1_slot-machines-igt-music, accessed May 2010.

Vinegar, Aron, and M. J. Golec, eds. 2008. *Relearning from Las Vegas*. Minneapolis: University of Minnesota Press.

Virillio, Paul. 1995. *The Art of the Motor*. Minneapolis, MN: University of Minnesota Press.

Volberg, Rachel. 1996. "Gambling and Problem Gambling in New York: A Ten-Year Replication Survey, 1986–1996." Report to the New York Council on Problem Gambling.

———. 2001. *When the Chips Are Down: Problem Gambling in America*. New York: The Century Foundation.

———. 2002. "Gambling and Problem Gambling in Nevada." Report to the Nevada Department of Human Resources. Gemini Research, Ltd.

———. 2004. "Fifteen Years of Problem Gambling Prevalence Research: What Do We Know? Where Do We Go?" *Journal of Gambling Issues* 10: 1–19.

Volberg, Rachel, and M. Wray. 2007. "Legal Gambling and Problem Gambling as Mechanisms of Social Domination? Some Considerations for Future Research." *American Behavioral Scientist* 51: 56–85.

Vrecko, Scott. 2007. "Capital Ventures into Biology: Biosocial Dynamics in the Industry and Science of Gambling." *Economy and Society* 37 (1): 50–67.

———. 2010. "Civilizing Technologies and the Control of Deviance." *Biosocieties* 5 (1): 36–51.

Wajcman, Judy. 2008. "Life in the Fast Lane? Towards a Sociology of Technology and Time." *The British Journal of Sociology* 59 (1): 59–77.

Wakefield, J. K. 1997. "Diagnosing DSM-IV—Part I: DSM-IV and the Concept of Disorder." *Behaviour Research and Therapy* 35: 633–49.

Walker, Michael. B. 1992. "Irrational Thinking among Slot Machine Players." *Journal of Gambling Studies* 8 (3): 245–61.

Wanner, Brigitte, R. Ladouceur, A. V. Auclair, and F. Vitaro. 2006. "Flow and Dissociation: Examination of Mean Levels, Cross-Links, and Links to Emotional Well-Being across Sports and Recreational and Pathological Gambling." *Journal of Gambling Studies* 22 (3): 289–304.

Ward, Matt. 2005. "The Gaming Crystal Ball." *Global Gaming Business* (September): 25–28.

Weatherly, J. N., and A. Brandt. 2004. "Participants' Sensitivity to Percentage Payback and Credit Value When Playing a Slot-Machine Simulation." *Behavior and Social Issues* 13: 33–50.

Weber, Max. 1946 [1922]. "Science as a Vocation." In *From Max Weber: Essays in Sociology*, edited and translated by H. H. Gerth and C. Wright Mills, 129–56. New York: Oxford University Press.

———. 1978 [1956]. *Economy and Society: An Outline of Interpretive Sociology.* Berkeley: University of California Press.

Weinert, Joe. 1999. "High Profits for Low Denominations." *International Gaming and Wagering Business*, G2E Edition.

Weingarten, Marc. 2006. "In Las Vegas, the Wagering is Going Mobile." *New York Times*, May 3: 4.

Welte, J. W., W. F. Wieczorek, G. M. Barnes, M. C. Tidwell, and J. H. Hoffman. 2004. "The Relationship of Ecological and Geographic Factors to Gambling Behavior and Pathology." *Journal of Gambling Studies* 20: 405–23.

Williams, Rosalind H. 1982. *Dream Worlds: Mass Consumption in Late Nineteenth-Century France.* Berkeley: University of California Press.

Williams, R. J., and R. T. Wood. 2004. "Final Report: The Demographic Sources of Ontario Gaming Revenue." Report prepared for the Ontario Problem Gambling Research Centre.

Wilson, John. 2003. "Slot Machine Volatility Index." *Slot Tech Magazine*, December: 10–17.

———. 2004a. "Virtual Reels? Physical Reels? Just the Real Truth." *Slot Tech Magazine* (January): 18–22.

———. 2004b. "PAR Excellence: Improve Your Edge." *Slot Tech Magazine* (February): 16–23.

———. 2004c. "PAR Excellence: Part 2." *Slot Tech Magazine* (March): 16–21.

———. 2004d. "PAR Excellence: Part 3." *Slot Tech Magazine* (April): 20–26.

———. 2004e. "PAR Excellence—Improving your Game, Part IV." *Slot Tech Magazine* (May): 21–24.

———. 2004f. "PAR Excellence—Part V: The End Is Here!" *Slot Tech Magazine* (June): 24–29.

———. 2007. "Visual Analytics Part 3: The Power of Mariposa." *Casino Enterprise Management*, May, http.casinoenterprisemanagement.com/articles/june -2007/visual-analytics-part-3-power-mariposa.

———. 2008. "The Slot Mathemagician Presents: Tapping the True Potential of Predictive Analytics." *Casino Enterprise Management*, http.casinoenterprise

management.com/articles/july-2007/slot-mathemagician-presents-mathe
matical-magic-behind-producing-progressive-payou.

———. 2009a. "The Vicious Cycle, Part II: Volatility." *Casino Enterprise Management*, April, http.casinoenterprisemanagement.com/articles/may-2009/vicious
-cycle-part-ii-volatility.

———. 2009b. "The Vicious Cycle, Part IV: The Balancing Act." *Casino Enterprise Management*, July, http.casinoenterprisemanagement.com/articles/july-2009/
vicious-cycle-part-iv-balancing-act.

———. 2010a. "Meaningful Hit Frequency, Pt. I: An Operator's Guide to Player Satisfaction." *Casino Enterprise Management*, January, http.casinoenterprise-
management.com/articles/january-2010/meaningful-hit-frequency-pt-i-opera
tor%E2%80%99s-guide-player-satisfaction.

———. 2010b. "Meaningful Hit Frequency, Pt. II: Significant and Insignificant Wins." *Casino Enterprise Management*, February, http.casinoenterpriseman-
agement.com/articles/february-2010/meaningful-hit-frequency-part-ii-signifi
cant-and-insignificant-wins.

Winner, Langdon. 1977. *Autonomous Technology: Technics Out-of-Control as a Theme in Political Thought*. Cambridge, MA: MIT Press.

———. 1986. "Do Artifacts Have Politics?" In *The Whale and the Reactor: A Search for Limits in an Age of High Technology*, edited by L. Winner, 19–39. Chicago: University of Chicago Press.

Winnicott, D. W. 1971. *Playing and Reality*. London: Tavistock Publications.

Wiser, Rob. 2006. "Running the Floor: Red Rock Casino Offers Cutting Edge Product." *Strictly Slots* (May): 36.

Witcher, Butch. 2000. "Top 10 To-Do List for Slot Operations." *Casino Journal* (July): 24–25.

"WMS Showcases Casino Evolved at 2007 Global Gaming Expo with Innovation, Technology, and Networked Capabilities." 2007. *Business Wire*, November 8, findarticles.com/p/articles/mi_m0EIN/is_2007_Nov_8, accessed December 2007.

Woo, G. 1998. "UNLV Las Vegas Metropolitan Poll." Cannon Center for Survey Research. Las Vegas: University of Las Vegas.

Wood, R.T.A., and M. D. Griffiths. 2007. "A Quantitative Investigation of Problem Gambling as an Escape-Based Coping Strategy." *Psychology and Psychotherapy: Theory, Research, and Practice* 80: 107–25.

Woolgar, Stephen. 1991. "Configuring the User: The Case of Usability Trials." In *A Sociology of Monsters: Essays on Power, Technology, and Domination*, edited by J. Law, 58–99. London: Routledge.

Woolley, Richard. 2008. "Economic Technologies: The Liberalizing and Governing of Poker Machine Gambling Consumption." *New Zealand Sociology* 23: 135–53.

———. 2009. "Commercialization and Culture in Australian Gambling." *Continuum* 23 (2): 183–96.

Woolley, Richard, and C. Livingstone. 2009. "Into the Zone: Innovation in the Australian Poker Machine Industry." In *Global Gambling: Cultural Perspectives on Gambling Organizations*, edited by S. Kingma, 38–63. New York: Routledge.

Wray, Matt, M. Miller, J. Gurvey, J. Carroll, and I. Kawachi. 2008. "Leaving Las Vegas: Does Exposure to Las Vegas Increase Risk for Suicide?" *Social Science and Medicine* 67: 1882–88.

Young, Martin, M. Stevens, and W. Tyler. 2006. *Northern Territory Gambling Prevalence Survey 2005*. School for Social and Policy Research, Charles Darwin University.

Zaloom, Caitlin. 2006. *Out of the Pits: Traders and Technology from Chicago to London*. Chicago: University of Chicago Press.

———. 2009. "How to Read the Future: The Yield Curve, Affect, and Financial Prediction." *Public Culture* 21: 2.

———. 2010. "The Derivative World." *The Hedgehog Review* (Summer).

Zangeneh, Masood, and T. Hason. 2006. "Suicide and Gambling." *International Journal of Mental Health and Addiction* 4 (3): 191–93.

Zangeneh, Masood, and E. Haydon. 2004. "Psycho-Structural Cybernetic Model, Feedback and Problem Gambling: A New Theoretical Approach." *International Journal of Mental Health and Addiction* 1 (2): 25–31.

Zelizer, Viviana. 1979. *Markets and Morals*. Princeton, NJ: Princeton University Press.

Žižek, Slavoj. 1998. "Risk Society and Its Discontents." *Historical Materialism* 2 (1): 143–64.

Zwick, Detlev. 2005. "Where the Action Is: Internet Stock Trading as Edgework." *Journal of Computer-Mediated Communication* 11 (1): 22–43.

Index